Cram101 Textbook Outlines to accompany:

Essential Cell Biology

Alberts, et al., 2nd Edition

An Academic Internet Publishers (AIPI) publication (c) 2007.

You have a discounted membership at www.Cram101.com with this book.

Get all of the practice tests for the chapters of this textbook, and access in-depth reference material for writing essays and papers. Here is an example from a Cram101 Biology text:

When you need problem solving help with math, stats, and other disciplines, www.Cram101.com will walk through the formulas and solutions step by step.

With Cram101.com online, you also have access to extensive reference material.

You will nail those essays and papers. Here is an example from a Cram101 Biology text:

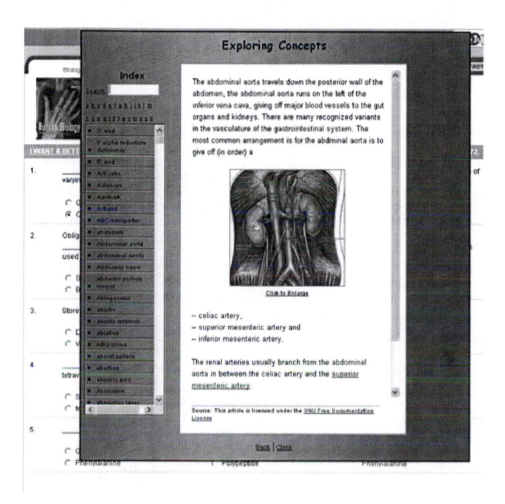

Visit **www.Cram101.com**, click Sign Up at the top of the screen, and enter DK73DW in the promo code box on the registration screen. Access to www.Cram101.com is normally $9.95, but because you have purchased this book, your access fee is only $4.95. Sign up and stop highlighting textbooks forever.

Learning System

Cram101 Textbook Outlines is a learning system. The notes in this book are the highlights of your textbook, you will never have to highlight a book again.

How to use this book. Take this book to class, it is your notebook for the lecture. The notes and highlights on the left hand side of the pages follow the outline and order of the textbook. All you have to do is follow along while your intructor presents the lecture. Circle the items emphasized in class and add other important information on the right side. With Cram101 Textbook Outlines you'll spend less time writing and more time listening. Learning becomes more efficient.

Cram101.com Online

Increase your studying efficiency by using Cram101.com's practice tests and online reference material. It is the perfect complement to Cram101 Textbook Outlines. Use self-teaching matching tests or simulate in-class testing with comprehensive multiple choice tests, or simply use Cram's true and false tests for quick review. Cram101.com even allows you to enter your in-class notes for an integrated studying format combining the textbook notes with your class notes.

Visit **www.Cram101.com**, click Sign Up at the top of the screen, and enter **DK73DW2602** in the promo code box on the registration screen. Access to www.Cram101.com is normally $9.95, but because you have purchased this book, your access fee is only $4.95. Sign up and stop highlighting textbooks forever.

Essential Cell Biology
Alberts, et al., 2nd

CONTENTS

Fungus	A fungus is a eukaryotic organism that digests its food externally and absorbs the nutrient molecules into its cells.
Colony	Colony refers to a cluster or assemblage of microorganisms growing on the surface of an agar culture medium. A colony also refers to several individual organisms of the same species living closely together, usually for mutual benefit, such as stronger defences, the ability to attack bigger prey,
Cell	The cell is the structural and functional unit of all living organisms, and is sometimes called the "building block of life."
Cell biology	The biological discipline involving the study of cells and their functions is called cell biology. This includes their physiological properties such as their structure and the organelles they contain, their environment and interactions, their life cycle, division and function (physiology) and eventual death.
Evolution	In biology, evolution is the process by which novel traits arise in populations and are passed on from generation to generation. Its action over large stretches of time explains the origin of new species and ultimately the vast diversity of the biological world.
Habitat	Habitat refers to a place where an organism lives; an environmental situation in which an organism lives.
Species	Group of similarly constructed organisms capable of interbreeding and producing fertile offspring is a species.
Egg	An egg is the zygote, resulting from fertilization of the ovum. It nourishes and protects the embryo.
Cilia	Numerous short, hairlike structures projecting from the cell surface that enable locomotion are cilia.
Nerve cell	A cell specialized to originate or transmit nerve impulses is referred to as nerve cell.
Cerebellum	The cerebellum is a region of the brain that plays an important role in the integration of sensory perception and motor output. The cerebellum integrates these two functions, using the constant feedback on body position to fine-tune motor movements.
Brain	The part of the central nervous system involved in regulating and controlling body activity and interpreting information from the senses transmitted through the nervous system is referred to as the brain.
Cell wall	Cell wall refers to a protective layer external to the plasma membrane in plant cells, bacteria, fungi, and some protists; protects the cell and helps maintain its shape.
Cellulose	A large polysaccharide composed of many glucose monomers linked into cable-like fibrils that provide structural support in plant cell walls is referred to as cellulose.
Stem	Stem refers to that part of a plant's shoot system that supports the leaves and reproductive structures.
Bacterium	Most bacterium are microscopic and unicellular, with a relatively simple cell structure lacking a cell nucleus, and organelles such as mitochondria and chloroplasts. They are the most abundant of all organisms. They are ubiquitous in soil, water, and as symbionts of other organisms.
Flagellum	A flagellum is a whip-like organelle that many unicellular organisms, and some multicellular ones, use to move about.
Neutrophil	Neutrophil refers to phagocytic white blood cell that can engulf bacteria and viruses in infected tissue; part of the body's nonspecific defense system.
Blood	Blood is a circulating tissue composed of fluid plasma and cells. The main function of blood is to supply nutrients (oxygen, glucose) and constitutional elements to tissues and to remove waste products.
Surface layer	The upper layer of water that is mixed by wind, waves, and currents is the surface layer .
Microorganism	A microorganism is an organism that is so small that it is microscopic (invisible to the naked eye).

They are often illustrated using single-celled, or unicellular organisms; however, some unicellular protists are visible to the naked eye, and some multicellular species are microscopic.

Macrophage	Macrophage is a cell found in tissues that are responsible for phagocytosis of pathogens, dead cells and cellular debris. They are part of the innate immune system. Their main role is the removal of pathogens and necrotic debris.
Tissue	Group of similar cells which perform a common function is called tissue.
Plasma membrane	Membrane surrounding the cytoplasm that consists of a phospholipid bilayer with embedded proteins is referred to as plasma membrane.
Oxygen	Oxygen is a chemical element in the periodic table. It has the symbol O and atomic number 8. Oxygen is the second most common element on Earth, composing around 46% of the mass of Earth's crust and 28% of the mass of Earth as a whole, and is the third most common element in the universe.
Sunlight	Sunlight in the broad sense is the total spectrum of electromagnetic radiation given off by the Sun.
Molecule	A molecule is the smallest particle of a pure chemical substance that still retains its chemical composition and properties.
Hormone	A hormone is a chemical messenger from one cell to another. All multicellular organisms produce hormones. The best known hormones are those produced by endocrine glands of vertebrate animals, but hormones are produced by nearly every organ system and tissue type in a human or animal body. Hormone molecules are secreted directly into the bloodstream, they move by circulation or diffusion to their target cells, which may be nearby cells in the same tissue or cells of a distant organ of the body.
Pigment	Pigment is any material resulting in color in plant or animal cells which is the result of selective absorption.
Starch	Biochemically, starch is a combination of two polymeric carbohydrates (polysaccharides) called amylose and amylopectin.
Muscle	Muscle is a contractile form of tissue. It is one of the four major tissue types, the other three being epithelium, connective tissue and nervous tissue. Muscle contraction is used to move parts of the body, as well as to move substances within the body.
Multicellular	Multicellular organisms are those organisms consisting of more than one cell, and having differentiated cells that perform specialized functions. Most life that can be seen with the naked eye is multicellular, as are all animals (i.e. members of the kingdom Animalia) and plants (i.e. members of the kingdom Plantae).
Sperm	Sperm refers to the male sex cell with three distinct parts at maturity: head, middle piece, and tail.
Microscope	A microscope is an instrument for viewing objects that are too small to be seen by the naked or unaided
Reproduction	Biological reproduction is the biological process by which new individual organisms are produced. Reproduction is a fundamental feature of all known life; each individual organism exists as the result of reproduction by an antecedent.
Molecular biology	Molecular biology overlaps with other areas of biology and chemistry, particularly genetics and biochemistry. Molecular biology chiefly concerns itself with understanding the interactions between the various systems of a cell, including the interrelationship of DNA, RNA and protein synthesis and learning how these interactions are regulated.
Biochemistry	Biochemistry studies how complex chemical reactions give rise to life. It is a hybrid branch of chemistry which specialises in the chemical processes in living organisms.
Metabolism	Metabolism is the biochemical modification of chemical compounds in living organisms and cells. This includes the biosynthesis of complex organic molecules (anabolism) and their breakdown (catabolism).
Biology	Biology is the branch of science dealing with the study of life. It is concerned with the

Go to **Cram101.com** for the Practice Tests for this Chapter.

characteristics, classification, and behaviors of organisms, how species come into existence, and the interactions they have with each other and with the environment.

Homeostasis	Homeostasis is the property of an open system, especially living organisms, to regulate its internal environment to maintain a stable, constant condition, by means of multiple dynamic equilibrium adjustments, controlled by interrelated regulation mechanisms.
Molecular motors	Molecular motors are biological "nanomachines" and are the essential agents of movement in living organisms.
Catalyst	A chemical that speeds up a reaction but is not used up in the reaction is a catalyst.
Transcription	Transcription is the process through which a DNA sequence is enzymatically copied by an RNA polymerase to produce a complementary RNA. Or, in other words, the transfer of genetic information from DNA into
Amino acid	An amino acid is any molecule that contains both amino and carboxylic acid functional groups. They are the basic structural building units of proteins. They form short polymer chains called peptides or polypeptides which in turn form structures called proteins.
Protein	A protein is a complex, high-molecular-weight organic compound that consists of amino acids joined by peptide bonds. They are essential to the structure and function of all living cells and viruses. Many are enzymes or subunits of enzymes.
Translation	Translation is the second process of protein biosynthesis. In translation, messenger RNA is decoded to produce a specific polypeptide according to the rules specified by the genetic code.
Virus	Obligate intracellular parasite of living cells consisting of an outer capsid and an inner core of nucleic acid is referred to as virus. The term virus usually refers to those particles that infect eukaryotes whilst the term bacteriophage or phage is used to describe those infecting prokaryotes.
Host	Host is an organism that harbors a parasite, mutual partner, or commensal partner; or a cell infected by a virus.
Daughter cell	A cell formed by cell division of a parent cell is a daughter cell.
Gene	Gene refers to a discrete unit of hereditary information consisting of a specific nucleotide sequence in DNA . Most of the genes of a eukaryote are located in its chromosomal DNA; a few are carried by the DNA of mitochondria and chloroplasts.
Sexual reproduction	The propagation of organisms involving the union of gametes from two parents is sexual reproduction.
Mutation	Mutation refers to a change in the nucleotide sequence of DNA; the ultimate source of genetic diversity.
Animal cell	An animal cell is a form of eukaryotic cell which make up many tissues in animals. The animal cell is distinct from other eukaryotes, most notably those of plants, as they lack cell walls and chloroplasts, and they have smaller vacuoles.
Genome	The genome of an organism is the whole hereditary information of an organism that is encoded in the DNA (or, for some viruses, RNA). This includes both the genes and the non-coding sequences. The genome of an organism is a complete DNA sequence of one set of chromosomes.
Skin	Skin is an organ of the integumentary system composed of a layer of tissues that protect underlying muscles and organs.
Eye	An eye is an organ that detects light. Different kinds of light-sensitive organs are found in a variety of creatures.
Light microscope	An optical instrument with lenses that refract visible light to magnify images and project them into a viewer's eye or onto photographic film is referred to as light microscope.

Visible light	That portion of the electromagnetic spectrum detected as various colors by the human eye, ranging in wavelength from about 380 nm to about 750 rim is called visible light.
Microscopy	Microscopy is any technique for producing visible images of structures or details too small to otherwise be seen by the human eye, using a microscope or other magnification tool.
Yeast	Yeast refers to common term for several families of unicellular fungi. Includes species used for brewing beer and making bread, as well as pathogenic species.
Salt	Salt is a term used for ionic compounds composed of positively charged cations and negatively charged anions, so that the product is neutral and without a net charge.
Lens	The lens or crystalline lens is a transparent, biconvex structure in the eye that, along with the cornea, helps to refract light to focus on the retina. Its function is thus similar to a man-made optical lens.
Cork	Cork is a tissue found in some plants, which consists of tightly packed dead cells. It allows improved insulation and prevents loss of water or nutrients on the inner bark of woody plants.
Cell theory	The theory that all living things are composed of cells and that all cells come from other cells is referred to as the cell theory.
Plant cell	A cell that is a structural and functional unit of a plant is a plant cell.
Hair cell	The hair cell is a sensory cell of both the auditory system and the vestibular system in all vertebrates. In mammals, the auditory hair cells are located within the organ of Corti on a thin basilar membrane in the cochlea of the inner ear.
Flower	A flower is the reproductive structure of a flowering plant. The flower structure contains the plant's reproductive organs, and its function is to produce seeds through sexual reproduction.
Natural selection	Natural selection is the process by which biological individuals that are endowed with favorable or deleterious traits end up reproducing more or less than other individuals that do not possess such traits.
Organelle	In cell biology, an organelle is one of several structures with specialized functions, suspended in the cytoplasm of a eukaryotic cell.
Fluorescence microscope	A Fluorescence Microscope is a light microscope used to study properties of organic or inorganic substances using the phenomena of fluorescence and phosphorescence instead of, or in addition to, reflection and absorption.
Staining	Staining is a biochemical technique of adding a class-specific (DNA, proteins, lipids, carbohydrates) dye to a substrate to qualify or quantify the presence of a specific compound. They are frequently used to highlight structures in tissues for viewing, often with the aid of different microscopes.
Fibroblast	A fibroblast is a cell that makes the structural fibers and ground substance of connective tissue.
Root	In vascular plants, the root is that organ of a plant body that typically lies below the surface of the soil. However, this is not always the case, since a root can also be aerial (that is, growing above the ground) or aerating (that is, growing up above the ground or especially above water).
Wavelength	The distance between crests of adjacent waves, such as those of the electromagnetic spectrum is wavelength.
Fluorescence	Fluorescence is a luminescence that is mostly found as an optical phenomenon in cold bodies, in which the molecular absorption of a photon triggers the emission of a lower-energy photon with a longer wavelength. The energy difference between the absorbed and emitted photons ends up as molecular vibrations or heat.
Embryo	Embryo refers to a developing stage of a multicellular organism. In humans, the stage in the development of offspring from the first division of the zygote until body structures begin to appear,

Go to **Cram101.com** for the Practice Tests for this Chapter.

about the ninth week of gestation.

Insect	An arthropod that usually has three body segments , three pairs of legs, and one or two pairs of wings is called an insect. They are the largest and (on land) most widely-distributed taxon within the phylum Arthropoda. They comprise the most diverse group of animals on the earth, with around 925,000 species described
Actin	Actin is a globular protein that polymerizes helically forming filaments, which like the other two components of the cellular cytoskeleton form a three-dimensional network inside an eukaryotic cell. They provide mechanical support for the cell, determine the cell shape, enable cell movements .
Electron microscope	The electron microscope is a microscope that can magnify very small details with high resolving power due to the use of electrons as the source of illumination, magnifying at levels up to 500,000 times.
Electron	The electron is a light fundamental subatomic particle that carries a negative electric charge. The electron is a spin-1/2 lepton, does not participate in strong interactions and has no substructure.
Stereocilia	Stereocilia are mechanosensing organelles of hair cells, which respond to fluid motion or fluid pressure changes in numerous types of animals for numerous functions. As acoustic sensors in mammals, they are lined up in the Organ of Corti in the cochlea of the inner ear.
Micrograph	A micrograph is a photograph or similar image taken through a microscope or similar device to show a magnified image of an item.
Inner ear	The Inner ear consists of the cochlea, where a wave is created by a difference in pressure between the scala vestibuli and the scala tympani. The cochlea has three fluid filled sections. The perilymph fluid in the canals differs from the endolymph fluid in the cochlear duct. The organ of Corti is the sensor of pressure variations.
Kidney	The kidney is a bean-shaped excretory organ in vertebrates. Part of the urinary system, the kidneys filter wastes (especially urea) from the blood and excrete them, along with water, as urine.
Fern	A fern is any one of a group of about 20,000 species of plants classified in the Division Pteridophyta, formerly known as Filicophyta. A fern is a vascular plant that differs from the more primitive lycophytes in having true leaves (megaphylls) and from the more advanced seed plants (gymnosperms and angiosperms) in lacking seeds.
Extracellular matrix	Extracellular matrix is any material part of a tissue that is not part of any cell. Extracellular matrix is the defining feature of connective tissue.
Histology	Histology is the study of tissue sectioned as a thin slice, using a microscope. It can be described as microscopic anatomy.
Anatomy	Anatomy is the branch of biology that deals with the structure and organization of living things. It can be divided into animal anatomy (zootomy) and plant anatomy (phytonomy).
Nucleus	In cell biology, the nucleus is found in all eukaryotic cells that contains most of the cell's genetic material. The nucleus has two primary functions: to control chemical reactions within the cytoplasm and to store information needed for cellular division.
Cytoplasm	Cytoplasm refers to everything inside a cell between the plasma membrane and the nucleus; consists of a semifluid medium and organelles.
Resin	Resin is a hydrocarbon secretion of many plants, particularly coniferous trees, valued for its chemical constituents and uses such as varnishes and adhesives.
Plasma	In physics and chemistry, a plasma is an ionized gas, and is usually considered to be a distinct phase of matter. "Ionized" in this case means that at least one electron has been dissociated from a significant fraction of the molecules.
Tissue culture	Process of growing tissue artificially in usually a liquid medium in laboratory glassware is referred

to as tissue culture.

Fiber	Fiber is a class of materials that are continuous filaments or are in discrete elongated pieces, similar to lengths of thread. They are of great importance in the biology of both plants and animals, for holding tissues together.
Bacteria	The domain that contains procaryotic cells with primarily diacyl glycerol diesters in their membranes and with bacterial rRNA. Bacteria also is a general term for organisms that are composed of procaryotic cells and are not multicellular.
Liver	The liver is an organ in vertebrates, including humans. It plays a major role in metabolism and has a number of functions in the body including drug detoxification, glycogen storage, and plasma protein synthesis. It also produces bile, which is important for digestion.
Ribosome	A ribosome is an organelle composed of rRNA and ribosomal proteins. It translates mRNA into a polypeptide chain (e.g., a protein). It can be thought of as a factory that builds a protein from a set of genetic instructions.
Syphilis	Syphilis refers to a sexually transmitted bacterial infection of the reproductive organs; if untreated, can damage the nervous and circulatory systems.
Genus	In biology, a genus is a taxonomic grouping. That is, in the classification of living organisms, a genus is considered to be distinct from other such genera. A genus has one or more species: if it has more than one species these are likely to be morphologically more similar than species belonging to different genera.
Matrix	In biology, matrix (plural: matrices) is the material between animal or plant cells, the material (or tissue) in which more specialized structures are embedded, and a specific part of the mitochondrion that is the site of oxidation of organic molecules.
Growth rate	A measure of the change in population size per individual per unit of time is called growth rate.
Population	Group of organisms of the same species occupying a certain area and sharing a common gene pool is referred to as population.
Antibiotic	Antibiotic refers to substance such as penicillin or streptomycin that is toxic to microorganisms. Usually a product of a particular microorvanism or plant.
Anaerobic	An anaerobic organism is any organism that does not require oxygen for growth.
Organic compound	An organic compound is any member of a large class of chemical compounds whose molecules contain carbon, with the exception of carbides, carbonates, carbon oxides and gases containing carbon.
Photosynthesis	Photosynthesis is a biochemical process in which plants, algae, and some bacteria harness the energy of light to produce food. Ultimately, nearly all living things depend on energy produced from photosynthesis for their nourishment, making it vital to life on Earth.
Biosynthesis	Biosynthesis is a phenomenon where chemical compounds are produced from simpler reagents. Biosynthesis, unlike chemical synthesis, takes place within living organisms and is generally catalysed by enzymes. The process is vital part of metabolism.
Atmosphere	Earth's atmosphere is a layer of gases surrounding the planet Earth and retained by the Earth's gravity. It contains roughly 78% nitrogen and 21% oxygen, with trace amounts of other gases.
Carbon	Carbon is a chemical element in the periodic table that has the symbol C and atomic number 6. An abundant nonmetallic, tetravalent element, carbon has several allotropic forms.
Chloroplast	A chloroplast is an organelle found in plant cells and eukaryotic algae which conduct photosynthesis. They are similar to mitochondria but are found only in plants. They are surrounded by a double membrane with an intermembrane space; they have their own DNA and are involved in energy metabolism;
Eubacteria	Bacteria are a major group of living organisms. The term "bacteria" has variously applied to all

Go to **Cram101.com** for the Practice Tests for this Chapter.

prokaryotes or to a major group of them, otherwise called the eubacteria, depending on ideas about their relationships.

Archaea	The Archaea are a major division of living organisms. Although there is still uncertainty in the exact phylogeny of the groups, Archaea, Eukaryotes and Bacteria are the fundamental classifications in what is called the three-domain system.
Domain	In biology, a domain is the top-level grouping of organisms in scientific classification.
Soil	Soil is material capable of supporting plant life. Soil forms through a variety of soil formation processes, and includes weathered rock "parent material" combined with dead and living organic matter and air.
Sediment	Sediment is any particulate matter that can be transported by fluid flow and which eventually is deposited as a layer of solid particles on the bed or bottom of a body of water or other liquid.
Stomach	The stomach is an organ in the alimentary canal used to digest food. It's primary function is not the absorption of nutrients from digested food; rather, the main job of the stomach is to break down large food molecules into smaller ones, so that they can be absorbed into the blood more easily.
Sulfur	Sulfur is the chemical element in the periodic table that has the symbol S and atomic number 16. It is an abundant, tasteless, odorless, multivalent non-metal. Sulfur, in its native form, is a yellow crystaline solid. In nature, it can be found as the pure element or as sulfide and sulfate minerals.
Sludge	Sludge refers to a general term for the precipitated solid matter produced during water and sewage treatment; solid particles composed of organic matter and microorganisms that are involved in aerobic sewage treatment .
Acid	An acid is a water-soluble, sour-tasting chemical compound that when dissolved in water, gives a solution with a pH of less than 7.
Filament	The stamen is the male organ of a flower. Each stamen generally has a stalk called the filament, and, on top of the filament, an anther. The filament is a long chain of proteins, such as those found in hair, muscle, or in flagella.
Doubling time	Doubling time refers to number of years it takes for a population to double in size. Also the amount of time it takes for a cell to divide, or for a population of cells (such as a tumor) to double in size. As cells divide more rapidly, the doubling time becomes shorter.
Nuclear envelope	The nuclear envelope refers to the double membrane of the nucleus that encloses genetic material in eukaryotic cells. It separates the contents of the nucleus (DNA in particular) from the cytosol.
Chromosome	A chromosome is, minimally, a very long, continuous piece of DNA, which contains many genes, regulatory elements and other intervening nucleotide sequences.
Polymer	Polymer is a generic term used to describe a very long molecule consisting of structural units and repeating units connected by covalent chemical bonds.
Mitochondrion	Mitochondrion refers to an organelle in eukaryotic cells where cellular respiration occurs. Enclosed by two concentric membranes, it is where most of the cell's ATP is made.
Mitochondria	Mitochondria are organelles found in most eukaryotic cells, including those of plants, animals, fungi, and protists. Mitochondria are sometimes described as "cellular power plants", because their primary function is to convert organic materials into energy in the form of ATP.
Inner membrane	The inner membrane is a membrane (phospholipid bilayer) of an organelle that is within the outer membrane. The inner membrane is present within the mitochondria and the chloroplast of cells.
Symbiotic relationship	Symbiotic relationship refers to an interspecific interaction in which one species, the symbiont, lives in or on another species, the host; a close association between organisms of two or more species.
Cellular	Cellular respiration is the process in which the chemical bonds of energy-rich molecules such as

respiration	glucose are converted into energy usable for life processes.
Carbon dioxide	Carbon dioxide is an atmospheric gas comprized of one carbon and two oxygen atoms. A very widely known chemical compound, it is frequently called by its formula CO_2. In its solid state, it is commonly known as dry ice.
Algae	The algae consist of several different groups of living organisms that capture light energy through photosynthesis, converting inorganic substances into simple sugars with the captured energy.
Cell membrane	A component of every biological cell, the selectively permeable cell membrane is a thin and structured bilayer of phospholipid and protein molecules that envelopes the cell. It separates a cell's interior from its surroundings and controls what moves in and out.
Symbiosis	Symbiosis is an interaction between two organisms living together in more or less intimate association or even the merging of two dissimilar organisms. The term host is usually used for the larger (macro) of the two members of a symbiosis.
Chemical energy	Chemical energy refers to energy stored in the chemical bonds of molecules; a form of potential energy.
Chlorophyll	Chlorophyll is a green photosynthetic pigment found in plants, algae, and cyanobacteria. In plant photosynthesis incoming light is absorbed by chlorophyll and other accessory pigments in the antenna complexes of photosystem I and photosystem II.
Sugar	A sugar is the simplest molecule that can be identified as a carbohydrate. These include monosaccharides and disaccharides, trisaccharides and the oligosaccharides. The term "glyco-" indicates the presence of a sugar in an otherwise non-carbohydrate substance.
Digestion	Digestion refers to the mechanical and chemical breakdown of food into molecules small enough for the body to absorb; the second main stage of food processing, following ingestion.
Secretion	Secretion is the process of segregating, elaborating, and releasing chemicals from a cell, or a secreted chemical substance or amount of substance.
Endoplasmic reticulum	The endoplasmic reticulum is an organelle found in all eukaryotic cells. It modifies proteins, makes macromolecules, and transfers substances throughout the cell.
Golgi apparatus	Golgi apparatus refers to an organelle in eukaryotic cells consisting of stacks of membranous sacs that modify, store, and ship products of the endoplasmic reticulum.
Moss	Moss is a small plant rarely taller than 2 inches (50 mm). They typically grow close together in clumps or mats in damp or shady locations. They do not have flowers and their simple leaves cover the thin wiry stems. At certain times they produces spore capsules which may appear as beak-like capsules borne aloft on thin stalks.
Leaf	In botany, a leaf is an above-ground plant organ specialized for photosynthesis. For this purpose, a leaf is typically flat (laminar) and thin, to expose the chloroplast containing cells (chlorenchyma tissue) to light over a broad area, and to allow light to penetrate fully into the tissues.
Mitochondrial DNA	Mitochondrial DNA is DNA not located in the nucleus of the cell but in the mitochondria, parts of the cell that generate fuel in the form of adenosine triphosphate, which drives the varied machinery of the cell. Unlike most of the cell, the function of which is defined by the nuclear DNA, the mitochondria have their own DNA and are assumed to have evolved separately.
Cytosol	The cytosol is the internal fluid of the cell, and a large part of cell metabolism occurs here. Proteins within the cytosol play an important role in signal transduction pathways, glycolysis; also, they act as intracellular receptors and form part of the ribosomes, enabling further protein synthesis
Intracellular digestion	Intracellular digestion refers to a form of digestion in which food is taken into cells by phagocytosis. It is found in sponges and most protozoa and coelenterates.
Excretion	Excretion is the biological process by which an organism chemically separates waste products from its

Go to **Cram101.com** for the Practice Tests for this Chapter.

body. The waste products are then usually expelled from the body by elimination.

Lysosome	Lysosome refers to a digestive organelle in eukaryotic cells; contains hydrolytic enzymes that digest the cell's food and wastes. They are found in both plant and animal cells, and are built in the Golgi apparatus.
Vesicle	In cell biology, a vesicle is a relatively small and enclosed compartment, separated from the cytosol by at least one lipid bilayer.
Budding	A means of asexual reproduction whereby a new individual developed from an outgrowth of a parent splits off and lives independently is referred to as budding.
Cellular component	The cellular component involves the movement of white blood cells from blood vessels into the inflamed tissue. The white blood cells, or leukocytes, take on an important role in inflammation; they extravasate (filter out) from the capillaries into tissue, and act as phagocytes, picking up bacteria and cellular debris. They may also aid by walling off an infection and preventing its spread.
Endocytosis	Endocytosis is a process where cells absorb material (molecules or other cells) from outside by engulfing it with their cell membranes.
Neurotransmitter	A neurotransmitter is a chemical that is used to relay, amplify and modulate electrical signals between a neuron and another cell.
Exocytosis	Exocytosis is the process by which a cell is able to release large biomolecules through its membrane. While in protozoa the exocytosis may serve the function of wasting unnecessary products, in multicellular organisms exocytosis serves signalling or regulatory function.
Chemical reaction	Chemical reaction refers to a process leading to chemical changes in matter; involves the making and/or breaking of chemical bonds.
Cytoskeleton	Cytoskeleton refers to a meshwork of fine fibers in the cytoplasm of a eukaryotic cell; includes microfilaments, intermediate filaments, and microtubules.
Microtubule	Microtubule is a protein structure found within cells, one of the components of the cytoskeleton. They have diameter of ~ 24 nm and varying length from several micrometers to possible millimeters in axons of nerve cells. They serve as structural components within cells and are involved in many cellular processes including mitosis, cytokinesis, and vesicular transport.
Rods	Rods, are photoreceptor cells in the retina of the eye that can function in less intense light than can the other type of photoreceptor, cone cells.
Predator	A predator is an animal or other organism that hunts and kills other organisms for food in an act called predation.
Protozoa	Protozoa are single-celled eukaryotes (organisms with nuclei) that show some characteristics usually associated with animals, most notably mobility and heterotrophy. They are often grouped in the kingdom Protista together with the plant-like algae.
Cell nucleus	The cell nucleus is found in all eukaryotic cells that contains most of the cell's genetic material. They have two primary functions: to control chemical reactions within the cytoplasm and to store information needed for cellular division.
Mitosis	Mitosis is the process by which a cell separates its duplicated genome into two identical halves. It is generally followed immediately by cytokinesis which divides the cytoplasm and cell membrane.
Nitrate	Nitrate refers to a salt of nitric acid; a compound containing the radical NO_3; biologically, the final form of nitrogen from the oxidation of organic nitrogen compounds.
Heredity	The transmission of characteristics from parent to offspring is heredity.
X-ray crystallography	Technique for determining the three-dimensional arrangement of atoms in a molecule based on the diffraction pattern of X-rays passing through a crystal of the molecule is x-ray crystallography.

Protein structure	A protein structure are amino acid chains, made up from 20 different L-α-amino acids, also referred to as residues, that fold into unique three-dimensional structures.
Sperm Whale	The Sperm Whale (Physeter macrocephalus) is the largest of all toothed whales and is believed to be the largest toothed animal to ever inhabit Earth.
Myoglobin	Myoglobin is a single-chain protein of 153 amino acids, containing a heme (iron-containing porphyrin) group in the center. With a molecular weight of 16,700 Daltons, it is the primary oxygen-carrying pigment of muscle tissues.
Hemoglobin	Hemoglobin is the iron-containing oxygen-transport metalloprotein in the red cells of the blood in mammals and other animals. Hemoglobin transports oxygen from the lungs to the rest of the body, such as to the muscles, where it releases the oxygen load.
Green fluorescent protein	Green fluorescent protein refers to fluorescent protein isolated from a jellyfish. Widely used as a marker in cell biology.
Actin filament	An actin filament is a helical protein filament formed by the polymerization of globular actin molecules. They provide mechanical support for the cell, determine the cell shape, enable cell movements; and participate in certain cell junctions.
Peroxisome	Enzyme-filled vesicle in which fatty acids and amino acids are metabolized to hydrogen peroxide that is broken down to harmless products is called peroxisome.
Nucleolus	The nucleolus is, strictly speaking, a "suborganelle" of the nucleus, which is an organelle. It is roughly spherical-shaped surrounded by a layer of condensed chromatin. No membrane separates the nucleolus from the nucleoplasm.
Golgi	Golgi discovered a method of staining nervous tissue which would stain a limited number of cells at random, in their entirety. This enabled him to view the paths of nerve cells in the brain for the first time. He called his discovery the black reaction. It is now known universally as the Golgi stain.
Bacillus	Bacillus is a genus of rod-shaped bacteria. The word "bacillus" is also used to describe any rod-shaped bacterium, and in this sense, they are found in many different groups of bacteria.
Archaean	The Archaean is a geologic eon that refers to the time before the Proterozoic, 2500 Mya (million years ago). Instead of being based on stratigraphy, this date is defined chronometrically.
Versatile	The anther can be attached to the filament in two ways, versatile is when it is attached at its center to the filament; pollen is then released through pores (poricidal dehiscence).
Model organism	A model organism is a species that is extensively studied to understand particular biological phenomena, with the expectation that discoveries made in the organism model will provide insight into the workings of other organisms.
Organ	Organ refers to a structure consisting of several tissues adapted as a group to perform specific functions.
Dinoflagellate	A unicellular photosynthetic alga with two flagella situated in perpendicular grooves in cellulose plates covering the cell is a dinoflagellate.
Heliozoan	Heliozoan refers to an aquatic animal-like protist; they are roughly spherical amoeboids with many stiff, microtubule-supported projections called axopods radiating outward from the cell surface.
Euglenoid	A protist characterized by one or more whiplike flagella that are used for locomotion and by a photorecepto is referred to as a euglenoid. They are one of the best-known groups of flagellates, commonly found in freshwater especially when it is rich in organic materials, with a few marine and endosymbiotic members.
Ciliate	Ciliate is one of the most important groups of protists, common almost everywhere there is water. They

Go to **Cram101.com** for the Practice Tests for this Chapter.

are a type of protozoan that moves by means of cilia.

Amoeba	Amoeba is a genus of protozoa that moves by means of temporary projections called pseudopods, and is well-known as a representative unicellular organism. Amoeba itself is found in freshwater, typically on decaying vegetation from streams, but is not especially common in nature.
Cancer	Cancer is a class of diseases or disorders characterized by uncontrolled division of cells and the ability of these cells to invade other tissues, either by direct growth into adjacent tissue through invasion or by implantation into distant sites by metastasis.
Escherichia coli	Escherichia coli is one of the main species of bacteria that live in the lower intestines of warm-blooded animals, including birds and mammals. They are necessary for the proper digestion of food and are part of the intestinal flora. Its presence in groundwater is a common indicator of fecal contamination.
Vertebrate	Vertebrate is a subphylum of chordates, specifically, those with backbones or spinal columns. They started to evolve about 530 million years ago during the Cambrian explosion, which is part of the Cambrian period.
Nucleotide	A nucleotide is a chemical compound that consists of a heterocyclic base, a sugar, and one or more phosphate groups. In the most common nucleotides the base is a derivative of purine or pyrimidine, and the sugar is pentose - deoxyribose or ribose. They are the structural units of RNA and DNA.
Saccharomyces cerevisiae	Saccharomyces cerevisiae is a species of budding yeast. It is perhaps the most important yeast thanks to its use since ancient times in baking and brewing. It is believed that it was originally isolated from the skins of grapes.
Cell division	Cell division is the process by which a cell (called the parent cell) divides into two cells (called daughter cells). Cell division is usually a small segment of a larger cell cycle. In meiosis, however, a cell is permanently transformed and cannot divide again.
Mutant	A mutant (also known to early geneticists as a "monster") is an individual, organism, or new genetic character arising or resulting from an instance of mutation, which is a sudden structural change within the DNA of a gene or chromosome of an organism resulting in the creation of a new character or trait not found in the parental type.
Flowering plants	The flowering plants (also called angiosperms) are a major group of land plants. They comprise one of the two groups in the seed plants: the flowering plants cover their seeds by including them in a true fruit.
Ecosystem	In general terms an ecosystem can be thought of as an assemblage of organisms (plant, animal and other living organisms living together with their environment, functioning as a loose unit. That is, a dynamic and complex whole, interacting as an "ecological unit".
Genetics	Genetics is the science of genes, heredity, and the variation of organisms.
Physiology	The study of the function of cells, tissues, and organs is referred to as physiology.
Crop	An organ, found in both earthworms and birds, in which ingested food is temporarily stored before being passed to the gizzard, where it is pulverized is the crop.
Homo sapiens	Homo sapiens are bipedal primates of the superfamily Hominoidea, together with the other apes—chimpanzees, gorillas, orangutans, and gibbons. They are the dominant sentient species on planet Earth.
Drosophila melanogaster	Species of small fly, commonly called a fruit fly, much used in genetic studies of development are called drosophila melanogaster.
Fruit	A fruit is the ripened ovary—together with seeds—of a flowering plant. In many species, the fruit incorporates the ripened ovary and surrounding tissues.

Cell cycle	An orderly sequence of events that extends from the time a eukaryotic cell divides to form two daughter cells to the time those daughter cells divide again is called cell cycle.
Petri dish	Petri dish refers to a shallow dish consisting of two round, overlapping halves that is used to grow microorganisms on solid culture medium; the top is larger than the bottom of the dish to prevent contamination of the culture.
Replica plating	Replica plating refers to a technique for isolating mutants from a population by plating cells from each colony growing on a nonselective agar medium onto plates with selective media or environmental conditions, such as the lack of a nutrient or the presence of an antibiotic or a phage; the location of mutants on the original plate can be determined from growth patterns on the replica plates.
Schizosaccha-omyces pombe	Schizosaccharomyces pombe, also called "fission yeast," is a species of yeast. It is used as a model organism in molecular and cell biology. It is a unicellular eukaryote, whose cells are rod-shaped. Cells typically measure 2 to 3 micrometres in diameter and 7 to 14 micrometres in length.
Elongation	Elongation refers to a phase of DNA replication, transcription, or translation that successively adds nucleotides or amino acids to a growing macromolecule.
Fission	A means of asexual reproduction whereby a parent separates into two or more genetically identical individuals of about equal size is referred to as fission.
Style	The style is a stalk connecting the stigma with the ovary below containing the transmitting tract, which facilitates the movement of the male gamete to the ovule.
Budding yeast	Budding yeast refers to common name often given to the baker's yeast Saccharomyces cerevisiae, a common experimental organism, which divides by budding off a smaller cell.
Drosophila	Drosophila is part of the phylum Arthropoda, a phylum of segmented animals with paired, jointed appendages and a hard exoskeleton made of chitin. They have an open circulatory system with a dorsal heart, with hemocoel occupying most of the body cavity, and a reduced coelom.
Zygote	Diploid cell formed by the union of sperm and egg is referred to as zygote.
Hermaphrodite	Hermaphrodite refers to an organism of a species whose members possess both male and female sexual organs during their lives. In many species, hermaphroditism is a normal part of the life-cycle. Generally, hermaphroditism occurs in the invertebrates, although it occurs in a fair number of fish, and to a lesser degree in other vertebrates.
Mammal	Homeothermic vertebrate characterized especially by the presence of hair and mammary glands is a mammal.
Immunology	Immunology refers to the branch of science that deals with the immune system and attempts to understand the many phenomena that are responsible for both acquired and innate immunity. It also includes the use of antibodyantigen reactions in other laboratory work .
Genetic engineering	Genetic engineering, genetic modification (GM), and the now-deprecated gene splicing are terms for the process of manipulating genes,usually outside the organism's normal reproductive process.
Homologous	Homologous refers to describes organs or molecules that are similar because of their common evolutionary origin. Specifically it describes similarities in protein or nucleic acid sequence.
Human genome	The human genome is the genome of Homo sapiens. It is made up of 23 chromosome pairs with a total of about 3 billion DNA base pairs.
Haploid	Haploid cells bear one copy of each chromosome.
Bony fish	Osteichthyes are the bony fish, a group paraphyletic to the land vertebrates, which are sometimes included. Most belong to the Actinopterygii.
Molecular evolution	Molecular evolution refers to changes in protein and DNA sequences over time. We use this information to estimate how recently species diverged from a common ancestor.

Go to **Cram101.com** for the Practice Tests for this Chapter.

Reptile	Member of a class of terrestrial vertebrates with internal fertilization, scaly skin, and an egg with a leathery shell is called reptile.
Oxidation	Oxidation refers to the loss of electrons from a substance involved in a redox reaction; always accompanies reduction.
Insertion	At DNA level, an insertion means the insertion of a few base pairs into a genetic sequence. This can often happen in microsatellite regions due to the DNA polymerase slipping.
Generation time	Generation time refers to the time between the birth of a parent and the birth of its offspring. The time interval between successive cell divisions.
Cancer cell	A cell that divides and reproduces abnormally and has the potential to spread throughout the body, crowding out normal cells and tissue is referred to as a cancer cell.
Polysaccharide	Polymer made from sugar monomers is a polysaccharide. They are relatively complex carbohydrates.
Nucleic acid	A nucleic acid is a complex, high-molecular-weight biochemical macromolecule composed of nucleotide chains that convey genetic information. The most common are deoxyribonucleic acid (DNA) and ribonucleic acid (RNA). They are found in all living cells and viruses.
Lipid	Lipid is one class of aliphatic hydrocarbon-containing organic compounds essential for the structure and function of living cells. They are characterized by being water-insoluble but soluble in nonpolar organic solvents.

Cell	The cell is the structural and functional unit of all living organisms, and is sometimes called the "building block of life."
Biology	Biology is the branch of science dealing with the study of life. It is concerned with the characteristics, classification, and behaviors of organisms, how species come into existence, and the interactions they have with each other and with the environment.
Molecule	A molecule is the smallest particle of a pure chemical substance that still retains its chemical composition and properties.
Chemical bond	Chemical bond refers to an attraction between two atoms resulting from a sharing of outer-shell electrons or the presence of opposite charges on the atoms. The bonded atoms gain complete outer electron shells.
Hydrogen	Hydrogen is a chemical element in the periodic table that has the symbol H and atomic number 1. At standard temperature and pressure it is a colorless, odorless, nonmetallic, univalent, tasteless, highly flammable diatomic gas.
Element	A chemical element, often called simply element, is a chemical substance that cannot be divided or changed into other chemical substances by any ordinary chemical technique. An element is a class of substances that contain the same number of protons in all its atoms.
Carbon	Carbon is a chemical element in the periodic table that has the symbol C and atomic number 6. An abundant nonmetallic, tetravalent element, carbon has several allotropic forms.
Atom	An atom is the smallest possible particle of a chemical element that retains its chemical properties.
Polar molecule	Molecule that displays an uneven distribution of electrons over its structure, for example, water is a polar molecule.
Polysaccharide	Polymer made from sugar monomers is a polysaccharide. They are relatively complex carbohydrates.
Cell membrane	A component of every biological cell, the selectively permeable cell membrane is a thin and structured bilayer of phospholipid and protein molecules that envelopes the cell. It separates a cell's interior from its surroundings and controls what moves in and out.
Covalent bond	A covalent bond is an intramolecular form of chemical bonding characterized by the sharing of one or more pairs of electrons between two elements, producing a mutual attraction that holds the resultant molecule together.
Hydrogen bond	A hydrogen bond is a type of attractive intermolecular force that exists between two partial electric charges of opposite polarity. Although stronger than most other intermolecular forces, the typical hydrogen bond is much weaker than both the ionic bond and the covalent bond.
Macromolecule	A macromolecule is a molecule of high relative molecular mass, the structure of which essentially comprises the multiple repetition of units derived, actually or conceptually, from molecules of low relative molecular mass.
Nucleotide	A nucleotide is a chemical compound that consists of a heterocyclic base, a sugar, and one or more phosphate groups. In the most common nucleotides the base is a derivative of purine or pyrimidine, and the sugar is pentose - deoxyribose or ribose. They are the structural units of RNA and DNA.
Fatty acid	A fatty acid is a carboxylic acid (or organic acid), often with a long aliphatic tail (long chains), either saturated or unsaturated.
Ionic bond	Ionic bond refers to an attraction between two ions with opposite electrical charges. The electrical attraction of the opposite charges holds the ions together.

Amino acid	An amino acid is any molecule that contains both amino and carboxylic acid functional groups. They are the basic structural building units of proteins. They form short polymer chains called peptides or polypeptides which in turn form structures called proteins.
Electron	The electron is a light fundamental subatomic particle that carries a negative electric charge. The electron is a spin-1/2 lepton, does not participate in strong interactions and has no substructure.
Protein	A protein is a complex, high-molecular-weight organic compound that consists of amino acids joined by peptide bonds. They are essential to the structure and function of all living cells and viruses. Many are enzymes or subunits of enzymes.
Nucleus	In cell biology, the nucleus is found in all eukaryotic cells that contains most of the cell's genetic material. The nucleus has two primary functions: to control chemical reactions within the cytoplasm and to store information needed for cellular division.
Sugar	A sugar is the simplest molecule that can be identified as a carbohydrate. These include monosaccharides and disaccharides, trisaccharides and the oligosaccharides. The term "glyco-" indicates the presence of a sugar in an otherwise non-carbohydrate substance.
Acid	An acid is a water-soluble, sour-tasting chemical compound that when dissolved in water, gives a solution with a pH of less than 7.
Atomic number	In chemistry and physics, the atomic number (Z) is the number of protons found in the nucleus of an atom. In an atom of neutral charge, the number of electrons also equals the atomic number.
Neutron	An electrically neutral particle , found in the nucleus of an atom is referred to as neutron.
Proton	Positive subatomic particle, located in the nucleus and having a weight of approximately one atomic mass unit is referred to as a proton.
Distribution	Distribution in pharmacology is a branch of pharmacokinetics describing reversible transfer of drug from one location to another within the body.
Subatomic particle	Subatomic particle refers to the particles of which atoms are made- electrons, protons, and neutrons.
Isotope	An isotope is a form of an element whose nuclei have the same atomic number - the number of protons in the nucleus - but different mass numbers because they contain different numbers of neutrons.
Radioactive decay	Radioactive decay is the set of various processes by which unstable atomic nuclei (nuclides) emit subatomic particles (radiation).
Molecular weight	The molecular mass of a substance, called molecular weight and abbreviated as MW, is the mass of one molecule of that substance, relative to the unified atomic mass unit u (equal to 1/12 the mass of one atom of carbon-12).
Hydrogen atom	A hydrogen atom is an atom of the element hydrogen. It is composed of a single negatively-charged electron, attending a positively-charged proton which is the nucleus of the hydrogen atom. The electron is bound to the proton by the Coulomb force.
Nitrogen	A colorless and tasteless and mostly inert diatomic non-metal gas that is an essential constituent of proteins is nitrogen.
Oxygen	Oxygen is a chemical element in the periodic table. It has the symbol O and atomic number 8. Oxygen is the second most common element on Earth, composing around 46% of the mass of Earth's crust and 28% of the mass of Earth as a whole, and is the third most common element in the universe.

Go to **Cram101.com** for the Practice Tests for this Chapter.

Crust	A crust is the outer layer of a planet, part of its lithosphere. Planetary crust is generally composed of a less dense material than that of its deeper layers. The crust of the Earth is composed mainly of basalt and granite.
Mole	The atomic weight of a substance, expressed in grams. One mole is defined as the mass of 6.0222 3 1023 atoms.
Glucose	Glucose, a simple monosaccharide sugar, is one of the most important carbohydrates and is used as a source of energy in animals and plants. Glucose is one of the main products of photosynthesis and starts respiration.
Sodium	Sodium is the chemical element in the periodic table that has the symbol Na (Natrium in Latin) and atomic number 11. Sodium is a soft, waxy, silvery reactive metal belonging to the alkali metals that is abundant in natural compounds (especially halite). It is highly reactive.
Relative abundance	Differences in the abundance of species within a community is relative abundance.
Electron shell	The electron shell is a group of atomic orbitals with the same value of the principal quantum number n. The electron shell determines the chemical properties of the atom.
Chemical reaction	Chemical reaction refers to a process leading to chemical changes in matter; involves the making and/or breaking of chemical bonds.
Rearrangement	A change in the usual order and arrangement of genetic material either within the chromosome complement or within a gene locus is rearrangement. Where the nature of the rearrangement has been determined, the type may be searched for directly under the following designations: reciprocal translocation, Robertsonian translocation, insertion, transposition, inversion, deletion, and duplication.
Tissue	Group of similar cells which perform a common function is called tissue.
Valence	The bonding capacity of an atom generally equal to the number of unpaired electrons in the atom's outermost shell is a valence.
Salt	Salt is a term used for ionic compounds composed of positively charged cations and negatively charged anions, so that the product is neutral and without a net charge.
Ion	Ion refers to an atom or molecule that has gained or lost one or more electrons, thus acquiring an electrical charge.
Cation	A positively charged ion which has fewer electrons than protons is a cation.
Anion	A negatively-charged ion, which has more electrons in its electron shell than it has protons in its nucleus, is known as an anion, for it is attracted to anodes; a positively-charged ion, which has fewer electrons than protons, is known as a cation, for it is attracted to cathodes.
Potassium	Potassium is a chemical element in the periodic table. It has the symbol K (L. kalium) and atomic number 19. Potassium is a soft silvery-white metallic alkali metal that occurs naturally bound to other elements in seawater and many minerals.
Magnesium	Magnesium is the chemical element in the periodic table that has the symbol Mg and atomic number 12 and an atomic mass of 24.31.
Calcium	Calcium is the chemical element in the periodic table that has the symbol Ca and atomic number 20. Calcium is a soft grey alkaline earth metal that is used as a reducing agent in the extraction of thorium, zirconium and uranium. Calcium is also the fifth most abundant element in the Earth's crust.

Go to **Cram101.com** for the Practice Tests for this Chapter.

Crystal	Crystal is a solid in which the constituent atoms, molecules, or ions are packed in a regularly ordered, repeating pattern extending in all three spatial dimensions.
Single covalent bond	A covalent bond in which two atoms share one pair of electrons is called single covalent bond.
Catalyst	A chemical that speeds up a reaction but is not used up in the reaction is a catalyst.
Enzyme	An enzyme is a protein that catalyzes, or speeds up, a chemical reaction. They are essential to sustain life because most chemical reactions in biological cells would occur too slowly, or would lead to different products, without them.
Single bond	The most common type of covalent bond is the single bond, sharing only one pair of electrons between two atoms. It usually consists of one sigma bond.
Double bond	Double bond refers to a type of covalent bond in which two atoms share two pairs of electrons; symbolized by a pair of lines between the bonded atoms. An example is in ethylene (between the carbon atoms). It usually consists of one sigma bond and one pi bond.
Ethylene	Ethylene functions as a hormone in plants. It stimulates Ethylene (or IUPAC name ethene) is the simplest alkene hydrocarbon, consisting of four hydrogen atoms and two carbon atoms connected by a double bond.
Benzene	Benzene is an organic chemical compound that is a colorless and flammable liquid with a pleasant, sweet smell. Benzene is a known carcinogen. It is a minor, or additive, component of gasoline. It is an important industrial solvent and precursor in the production of drugs, plastics, gasoline, synthetic rubber, and dyes.
Polar covalent bond	A polar covalent bond is a form of covalent bonding that happens when atoms of two different elements with different electronegativities bond resulting in an unequal sharing of electrons.
Nonpolar molecule	A molecule whose electric charge is evenly balanced from one end of the molecule to the other is called nonpolar molecule.
Surface tension	A measure of how difficult it is to stretch or break the surface of a liquid is referred to as surface tension.
Linkage	Linkage refers to the patterns of assortment of genes that are located on the same chromosome. Important because if the genes are located relatively far apart, crossing over is more likely to occur between them than if they are close together.
Alcohol	Alcohol is a general term, applied to any organic compound in which a hydroxyl group (-OH) is bound to a carbon atom, which in turn is bound to other hydrogen and/or carbon atoms. The general formula for a simple acyclic alcohol is $C_nH_{2n+1}OH$.
Hydrophobic	Hydrophobic refers to being electrically neutral and nonpolar, and thus prefering other neutral and nonpolar solvents or molecular environments. Hydrophobic is often used interchangeably with "oily" or "lipophilic."
Nonpolar	Lacking any asymmetric accumulation of positive and negative charge. Nonpolar molecules are generally insoluble in water.
Acetic acid	Acetic acid, also known as ethanoic acid, is an organic chemical compound best recognized for giving vinegar its sour taste and pungent smell.
Hydronium ion	A hydronium ion is the common name for the cation H_3O+ derived from protonation of water.
Silicon	Silicon is the chemical element in the periodic table that has the symbol Si and atomic number 14. It is the second most abundant element in the Earth's crust, making up 25.7% of it by weight.

Carboxyl	A carboxyl is the univalent radical -COOH; present in and characteristic of organic acids.
Carbonyl	A carbonyl group is a functional group composed of a carbon atom double-bonded to an oxygen atom. The term carbonyl can also refer to carbon monoxide as a ligand in an inorganic or organometallic complex.
Methyl	In chemistry, a methyl group is a hydrophobic alkyl functional group derived from methane (CH_4). It has the formula $-CH_3$ and is very often abbreviated -Me.
Nucleic acid	A nucleic acid is a complex, high-molecular-weight biochemical macromolecule composed of nucleotide chains that convey genetic information. The most common are deoxyribonucleic acid (DNA) and ribonucleic acid (RNA). They are found in all living cells and viruses.
Monomer	In chemistry, a monomer is a small molecule that may become chemically bonded to other monomers to form a polymer.
Tide	The periodic, rhythmic rise and fall of the sea surface caused by changes in gravitational forces external to the Earth is referred to as the tide.
Structural formula	A drawing that shows the number of atoms, types of bonds, and spacial arrangement of atoms within the molecule is called structural formula.
Chemical symbol	Shorthand used to represent one atom of an element, such as Al for aluminum or C for carbon is a chemical symbol.
Chemical formula	Symbols used to represent the kind and number of atoms in a compound are collectively called chemical formula.
Isomer	An isomer is a molecule with the same chemical formula and often with the same kinds of bonds between atoms, but in which the atoms are arranged differently. That is to say, they have different structural formula.
Monosaccharide	A monosaccharide is simplest form of a carbohydrate. They consist of one sugar and are usually colorless, water-soluble, crystalline solids. Some monosaccharides have a sweet taste. They are the building blocks of disaccharides like sucrose and polysaccharides.
Disaccharide	A disaccharide is a sugar (a carbohydrate) composed of two monosaccharides. The two monosaccharides are bonded via a condensation reaction.
Fructose	Fructose is a simple sugar (monosaccharide) found in many foods and one of the three most important blood sugars along with glucose and galactose.
Sucrose	A disaccharide composed of glucose and fructose is called sucrose.
Oligosaccharide	An oligosaccharide is a saccharide polymer containing a small number (typically three to six) of component sugars, also known as simple sugars. They are generally found either O- or N-linked to compatible amino acid side chains in proteins or to lipid moieties.
Polymer	Polymer is a generic term used to describe a very long molecule consisting of structural units and repeating units connected by covalent chemical bonds.
Condensation reaction	A condensation reaction is a chemical reaction in which two molecules or moieties react and become covalently bonded to one another by the concurrent loss of a small molecule, often water, methanol, or a type of hydrogen halide such as HCl.
Hydroxyl group	The term hydroxyl group is used to describe the functional group -OH when it is a substituent in an organic compound.
Hydrolysis	Hydrolysis is a chemical process in which a molecule is cleaved into two parts by the addition of a molecule of water.
Glycogen	Glycogen refers to a complex, extensively branched polysaccharide of many glucose monomers;

Go to **Cram101.com** for the Practice Tests for this Chapter.

serves as an energy-storage molecule in liver and muscle cells.

Starch	Biochemically, starch is a combination of two polymeric carbohydrates (polysaccharides) called amylose and amylopectin.
Plant cell	A cell that is a structural and functional unit of a plant is a plant cell.
Cellulose	A large polysaccharide composed of many glucose monomers linked into cable-like fibrils that provide structural support in plant cell walls is referred to as cellulose.
Mucus	Mucus is a slippery secretion of the lining of various membranes in the body (mucous membranes). Mucus aids in the protection of the lungs by trapping foreign particles that enter the nose during normal breathing. Additionally, it prevents tissues from drying out.
Plasma membrane	Membrane surrounding the cytoplasm that consists of a phospholipid bilayer with embedded proteins is referred to as plasma membrane.
Glycoprotein	A macromolecule consisting of one or more polypeptides linked to short chains of sugars is called glycoprotein.
Glycolipid	Glycolipid refers to lipid in plasma membranes that bears a carbohydrate chain attached to a hydrophobic tail.
Blood	Blood is a circulating tissue composed of fluid plasma and cells. The main function of blood is to supply nutrients (oxygen, glucose) and constitutional elements to tissues and to remove waste products.
Hydrocarbon chain	A hydrocarbon chain consists of a long series of carbon atoms joined to each other and also joined to two hydrogen atoms.
Carboxylic acid	An organic compound containing a carboxyl group is a carboxylic acid.
Hydrophilic	A hydrophilic molecule or portion of a molecule is one that is typically charge-polarized and capable of hydrogen bonding, enabling it to dissolve more readily in water than in oil or other hydrophobic solvents.
Hydrocarbon	A chemical compound composed only of the elements carbon and hydrogen is called hydrocarbon.
Unsaturated fatty acid	Fatty acid molecule that has one or more double bonds between the atoms of its carbon chain is called unsaturated fatty acid.
Saturated fatty acid	Saturated fatty acid refers to molecule that lacks double bonds between the carbons of its hydrocarbon chain. The chain bears the maximum number of hydrogens.
Side chain	In organic chemistry and biochemistry a side chain is a part of a molecule attached to a core structure. Often the side chain can vary for a given core. In biochemistry the peptide or protein side chains are the variable parts of amino acids extending from the peptide backbone.
Triacylglycerol	Triacylglycerol refers to molecule composed of three fatty acids esterified to glycerol. The main constituent of fat droplets in animal tissues and of vegetable oils.
Cytoplasm	Cytoplasm refers to everything inside a cell between the plasma membrane and the nucleus; consists of a semifluid medium and organelles.
Glycerol	Glycerol is a three-carbon substance that forms the backbone of fatty acids in fats. When the body uses stored fat as a source of energy, glycerol and fatty acids are released into the bloodstream. The glycerol component can be converted to glucose by the liver and provides energy for cellular metabolism.
Saturated fat	Saturated fat is fat that consists of triglycerides containing only fatty acids that have no double bonds between the carbon atoms of the fatty acid chain (hence, they are fully

saturated with hydrogen atoms).

Cholesterol	Cholesterol is a steroid, a lipid, and an alcohol, found in the cell membranes of all body tissues, and transported in the blood plasma of all animals. It is an important component of the membranes of cells, providing stability; it makes the membrane's fluidity stable over a bigger temperature interval.
Amphipathic	An amphipathic molecule contains both hydrophobic and hydrophilic groups. The hydrophobic group can be a long carbon chain, with the form: $CH_3(CH_2)_n$, with $4 < n < 16$.
Phospholipid	Phospholipid is a class of lipids formed from four components: fatty acids, a negatively-charged phosphate group, an alcohol and a backbone. Phospholipids with a glycerol backbone are known as glycerophospholipids or phosphoglycerides.
Organelle	In cell biology, an organelle is one of several structures with specialized functions, suspended in the cytoplasm of a eukaryotic cell.
Phosphate	A phosphate is a polyatomic ion or radical consisting of one phosphorus atom and four oxygen. In the ionic form, it carries a -3 formal charge, and is denoted PO_4^{3-}.
Lipid bilayer	A lipid bilayer is a membrane or zone of a membrane composed of lipid molecules (usually phospholipids). The lipid bilayer is a critical component of all biological membranes, including cell membranes, and is a prerequisite for cell-based organisms.
Amino group	An amino group is an ammonia-like functional group composed of a nitrogen and two hydrogen atoms covalently linked. $-NH_2$
Alanine	Alanine (Ala) also 2-aminopropanoic acid is a non-essential α-amino acid. It exists as two distinct enantiomers - L-alanine and D-alanine. L-alanine is one of the 20 amino acids most widely used in protein synthesis, second to leucine.
Carboxyl group	In an organic molecule, a functional group consisting of an oxygen atom doublebonded to a carbon atom that is also bonded to a hydroxyl group is referred to as a carboxyl group.
Polypeptide	Polypeptide refers to polymer of many amino acids linked by peptide bonds.
Peptide bond	A peptide bond is a chemical bond formed between two molecules when the carboxyl group of one molecule reacts with the amino group of the other molecule, releasing a molecule of water.
C-terminus	The C-terminus of a protein or polypeptide is the extremity of the amino acid chain terminated by a free carboxyl group (-COOH).
Polarity	In cell biology, polarity refers to cells not being point-symmetrical in their spatial organization. In horticulture, polarity refers to the condition in which cuttings grow shoots at the distil end and roots at the proximal end.
Bacteria	The domain that contains procaryotic cells with primarily diacyl glycerol diesters in their membranes and with bacterial rRNA. Bacteria also is a general term for organisms that are composed of procaryotic cells and are not multicellular.
Evolution	In biology, evolution is the process by which novel traits arise in populations and are passed on from generation to generation. Its action over large stretches of time explains the origin of new species and ultimately the vast diversity of the biological world.
Genetic code	The genetic code is a set of rules that maps DNA sequences to proteins in the living cell, and is employed in the process of protein synthesis. Nearly all living things use the same genetic code, called the standard genetic code, although a few organisms use minor variations of the standard code.
Metabolism	Metabolism is the biochemical modification of chemical compounds in living organisms and

Go to **Cram101.com** for the Practice Tests for this Chapter.

cells. This includes the biosynthesis of complex organic molecules (anabolism) and their breakdown (catabolism).

Glutamic acid

Glutamic acid is one of the 20 standard amino acids used by all organisms in their proteins. It is critical for proper cell function, but it is not an essential nutrient in humans because glutamic acid can be manufactured from other compounds.

Lysine

Lysine is one of the 20 amino acids normally found in proteins. With its 4-aminobutyl side-chain, it is classified as a basic amino acid, along with arginine and histidine.

Nucleoside

Molecule composed of a purine or pyrimidine base covalently linked to a ribose or deoxyribose sugar is a nucleoside.

Deoxyribose

Deoxyribose is an aldopentose, a monosaccharide containing five carbon atoms, and including an aldehyde functional group.

Residue

A residue refers to a portion of a larger molecule, a specific monomer of a polysaccharide, protein or nucleic acid.

Ribose

Ribose is an aldopentose — a monosaccharide containing five carbon atoms, and including an aldehyde functional group. It has chemical formula $C_5H_{10}O_5$.

N-terminus

The N-terminus refers to the extremity of a protein or polypeptide terminated by an amino acid with a free amine group ($-NH_2$).

Pyrimidine

Pyrimidine refers to one of two families of nitrogenous bases found in nucleotides. Cytosine , thymine , and uracil are pyrimidines.

Cytosine

Cytosine is one of the 5 main nucleobases used in storing and transporting genetic information within a cell in the nucleic acids DNA and RNA. It is a pyrimidine derivative, with a heterocyclic aromatic ring and two substituents attached. The nucleoside of cytosine is cytidine.

Thymine

Thymine, also known as 5-methyluracil, is a pyrimidine nucleobase. It is found in the nucleic acid DNA. In RNA thymine is replaced with uracil in most cases. In DNA, thymine(T) binds to adenine (A) via two hydrogen bonds to assist in stabilizing the nucleic acid structures.

Uracil

Uracil is one of the four RNA nucleobases, replacing thymine as found in DNA. Just like thymine, uracil can form a base pair with adenine via two hydrogen bonds, but it lacks the methyl group present in thymine. Uracil, in comparison to thymine, will more readily degenerate into cytosine.

Adenine

Adenine is one of the two purine nucleobases used in forming nucleotides of the nucleic acids DNA and RNA. In DNA, adenine (A) binds to thymine (T) via two hydrogen bonds to assist in stabilizing the nucleic acid structures. In RNA, adenine binds to uracil (U).

Guanine

Guanine is one of the five main nucleobases found in nucleic acids. Guanine is a purine derivative, and in Watson-Crick base pairing forms three hydrogen bonds with cytosine. Guanine "stacks" vertically with the other nucleobases via aromatic interactions.

Purine

Purine refers to one of two families of nitrogenous bases found in nucleotides. Adenine and guanine are purines.

Adenosine triphosphate

Adenosine triphosphate is the nucleotide known in biochemistry as the "molecular currency" of intracellular energy transfer; that is, able to store and transport chemical energy within cells.

Adenosine

Adenosine is a nucleoside comprized of adenine attached to a ribose (ribofuranose) moiety via a β-N_9-glycosidic bond. Adenosine plays an important role in biochemical processes, such as energy transfer - as adenosine triphosphate (ATP) and adenosine diphosphate (ADP) - as well as in signal transduction as cyclic adenosine monophosphate, cAMP.

Go to **Cram101.com** for the Practice Tests for this Chapter.

Phosphate group	The functional group -0PO$_3$H$_2$; the transfer of energy from one compound to another is often accomplished by the transfer of a phosphate group.
Animal cell	An animal cell is a form of eukaryotic cell which make up many tissues in animals. The animal cell is distinct from other eukaryotes, most notably those of plants, as they lack cell walls and chloroplasts, and they have smaller vacuoles.
Oxidation	Oxidation refers to the loss of electrons from a substance involved in a redox reaction; always accompanies reduction.
Deoxyribonuc-eic acid	Deoxyribonucleic acid is a nucleic acid that contains the genetic instructions specifying the biological development of all cellular forms of life. It is a long polymer of nucleotides and encodes the sequence of the amino acid residues in proteins using the genetic code, a triplet code of nucleotides.
Phosphodiester bond	A phosphodiester bond is a group of strong covalent bonds between the phosphorus atom in a phosphate group and two other molecules over two ester bonds. Phosphodiester bonds are central to all life on Earth, as they make up the backbone of the strands of DNA.
Phosphodiester linkage	Phosphodiester linkage refers to set of covalent chemical bonds formed when two hydroxyl groups are linked in ester linkage to the same phosphate group. This linkage joins adjacent nucleotides in RNA or DNA.
Polynucleotide	Polynucleotide refers to a polymer consisting of many nucleotide monomers; serves as a blueprint for proteins and, through the actions of proteins, for all cellular activities. The two types are DNA and RNA.
Versatile	The anther can be attached to the filament in two ways, versatile is when it is attached at its center to the filament; pollen is then released through pores (poricidal dehiscence).
Microtubule	Microtubule is a protein structure found within cells, one of the components of the cytoskeleton. They have diameter of ~ 24 nm and varying length from several micrometers to possible millimeters in axons of nerve cells. They serve as structural components within cells and are involved in many cellular processes including mitosis, cytokinesis, and vesicular transport.
Chromosome	A chromosome is, minimally, a very long, continuous piece of DNA, which contains many genes, regulatory elements and other intervening nucleotide sequences.
Histone	Histone refers to a small basic protein molecule associated with DNA and important in DNA packing in the eukaryotic chromosome.
Polymerization	Polymerization is a process of reacting monomer molecules together in a chemical reaction to form linear chains or a three-dimensional network of polymer chains.
Carbohydrate	Carbohydrate is a chemical compound that contains oxygen, hydrogen, and carbon atoms. They consist of monosaccharide sugars of varying chain lengths and that have the general chemical formula C$_n$(H$_2$O)$_n$ or are derivatives of such.
Collagen	Collagen is the main protein of connective tissue in animals and the most abundant protein in mammals, making up about 1/4 of the total. It is one of the long, fibrous structural proteins whose functions are quite different from those of globular proteins such as enzymes.
Albumin	Albumin refers generally to any protein with water solubility, which is moderately soluble in concentrated salt solutions, and experiences heat coagulation (protein denaturation).
Gelatin	Gelatin is a translucent brittle solid substance, colorless or slightly yellow, nearly tasteless and odorless, which is created by prolonged boiling of animal skin, connective tissue or bones. It has many uses in food, medicine, and manufacturing. Substances that contain or resemble gelatin are called gelatinous.

Go to **Cram101.com** for the Practice Tests for this Chapter.

Egg	An egg is the zygote, resulting from fertilization of the ovum. It nourishes and protects the embryo.
Heterogeneous	A heterogeneous compound, mixture, or other such object is one that consists of many different items, which are often not easily sorted or separated, though they are clearly distinct.
Serum	Serum is the same as blood plasma except that clotting factors (such as fibrin) have been removed. Blood plasma contains fibrinogen.
Peptide	Peptide is the family of molecules formed from the linking, in a defined order, of various amino acids. The link between one amino acid residue and the next is an amide bond, and is sometimes referred to as a peptide bond.
Osmotic pressure	Osmotic pressure is the pressure produced by a solution in a space that is enclosed by a differentially permeable membrane.
Dalton	A measure of mass for atoms and subatomic particles is a dalton.
Hemoglobin	Hemoglobin is the iron-containing oxygen-transport metalloprotein in the red cells of the blood in mammals and other animals. Hemoglobin transports oxygen from the lungs to the rest of the body, such as to the muscles, where it releases the oxygen load.
Iron	Iron is essential to all organisms, except for a few bacteria. It is mostly stably incorporated in the inside of metalloproteins, because in exposed or in free form it causes production of free radicals that are generally toxic to cells.
Ultracentrifuge	Ultracentrifuge refers to a machine that spins test tubes at the fastest speeds to separate liquids and particles of different densities.
Svedberg	Svedberg refers to the unit used in expressing the sedimentation coefficient; the greater a particle's Svedberg value, the faster it travels in a centrifuge.
Sediment	Sediment is any particulate matter that can be transported by fluid flow and which eventually is deposited as a layer of solid particles on the bed or bottom of a body of water or other liquid.
Gradient	Gradient refers to a difference in concentration, pressure, or electrical charge between two regions.
Biochemistry	Biochemistry studies how complex chemical reactions give rise to life. It is a hybrid branch of chemistry which specialises in the chemical processes in living organisms.
Convection	Convection is the transfer of heat by currents within a fluid. It may arise from temperature differences either within the fluid or between the fluid and its boundary, other sources of density variations (such as variable salinity), or from the application of an external motive force.
Centrifuge	Centrifuge refers to a device in which a sample can be spun around a central axis at high speed, creating a centrifugal force that mimics a very strong gravitational force. Used to separate mixtures of suspended materials.
Homogeneous	Homogeneous refers both to animals and plants, of having a resemblance in structure, due to descent from a common progenitor with subsequent modification.
Diffraction	Diffraction is the bending and spreading of waves when they meet an obstruction. It can occur with any type of wave, including sound waves, water waves, and electromagnetic waves such as light and radio waves.
X-Ray	X-Ray refers to diagnostic test in which an image is created using low doses of radiation.
Conformation	The three-dimensional shape of a molecule is its conformation. The conformation is

	particularly important in proteins.
Biological systems	Complex interactive networks that function both within individual cells and among groups of cells within an organism are called biological systems.
Substrate	A substrate is a molecule which is acted upon by an enzyme. Each enzyme recognizes only the specific substrate of the reaction it catalyzes. A surface in or on which an organism lives.
Double helix	Double helix refers to the form of native DNA, referring to its two adjacent polynucleotide strands wound into a spiral shape.
Helix	A helix is a twisted shape like a spring, screw or a spiral staircase. They are important in biology, as DNA and many proteins have spiral substructures, known a alpha helix.
Catalysis	Catalysis is the acceleration of the reaction rate of a chemical reaction by means of a substance, called a catalyst, that is itself not consumed by the overall reaction.
Globular protein	Globular protein refers to any protein with an approximately rounded shape. Such proteins are contrasted with highly elongated, fibrous proteins such as collagen.
Ribosome	A ribosome is an organelle composed of rRNA and ribosomal proteins. It translates mRNA into a polypeptide chain (e.g., a protein). It can be thought of as a factory that builds a protein from a set of genetic instructions.
Electron microscope	The electron microscope is a microscope that can magnify very small details with high resolving power due to the use of electrons as the source of illumination, magnifying at levels up to 500,000 times.
Micrograph	A micrograph is a photograph or similar image taken through a microscope or similar device to show a magnified image of an item.
Protein synthesis	The process whereby the tRNA utilizes the mRNA as a guide to arrange the amino acids in their proper sequence according to the genetic information in the chemical code of DNA is referred to as protein synthesis.
DNA replication	DNA replication is the process of copying a double-stranded DNA strand in a cell, prior to cell division. The two resulting double strands are identical (if the replication went well), and each of them consists of one original and one newly synthesized strand.
Specificity	A medical diagnostic test for a certain disease, specificity is the proportion of true negatives of all the negative samples tested.
Chemical energy	Chemical energy refers to energy stored in the chemical bonds of molecules; a form of potential energy.
Amine	An organic compound with one or more amino groups is called amine. They contain nitrogen as the key atom. Structurally amines resemble ammonia, wherein one or more hydrogen atoms are replaced by organic substituents such as alkyl and aryl groups.
Amide	An amide is either the organic functional group characterized by a carbonyl group linked to a nitrogen atom or a compound that contains this functional group, or a particular inorganic anion.
Esters	Esters are organic compounds in which an organic group replaces a hydrogen atom in an oxygen acid. An oxygen acid is an acid whose molecule has an -OH group from which the hydrogen (H) can dissociate as an H^+ ion.
Heat of vaporization	The energy that must be supplied to a compound to transform it from a liquid into a gas at its boiling temperature is called heat of vaporization.
Specific heat	The amount of energy required to raise the temperature of 1 gram of a substance by 1 °C is specific heat.

Go to **Cram101.com** for the Practice Tests for this Chapter.

Solvent	A solvent is a liquid that dissolves a solid, liquid, or gaseous solute, resulting in a solution. The most common solvent in everyday life is water.
Solute	Substance that is dissolved in a solvent, forming a solution is referred to as a solute.
Hydrogen ion	A single proton with a charge of + 1. The dissociation of a water molecule leads to the generation of a hydroxide ion and a hydrogen ion. The hydrogen ion is hydrated in aqueous solutions and is usually written as H_2O^+.
PH scale	A scale from 0 to 14 reflecting the concentration of hydrogen ions in solution is a pH scale. The lower numbers denote acidic conditions and the upper numbers denote basic, or alkaline, conditions.
Species	Group of similarly constructed organisms capable of interbreeding and producing fertile offspring is a species.
Ammonia	Ammonia is a compound of nitrogen and hydrogen with the formula NH_3. At standard temperature and pressure ammonia is a gas. It is toxic and corrosive to some materials, and has a characteristic pungent odor.
Hydroxide	Hydroxide is a polyatomic ion consisting of oxygen and hydrogen: OH− . It has a charge of −1. Hydroxide is one of the simplest of the polyatomic ions.
Aldehyde	An aldehyde is either a functional group consisting of a terminal carbonyl group or a compound containing a terminal carbonyl group.
Pentose	A pentose is a monosaccharide with five carbon atoms.
Ketone	A ketone is either the functional group characterized by a carbonyl group linked to two other carbon atoms or a compound that contains this functional group. A ketone can be generally represented by the formula: $R_1(CO)R_2$
Hexose	A hexose is a monosaccharide with six carbon atoms having the chemical formula $C_6H_{12}O_6$.
Mannose	Mannose is a sugar monomer of the hexose series of carbohydrates. Mannose enters the carbohydrate metabolism stream by phosphorylation and conversion to fructose-6-phosphate.
Galactose	Galactose is a type of sugar found in dairy products, in sugar beets and other gums and mucilages. It is also synthesized by the body, where it forms part of glycolipids and glycoproteins in several tissues.
Lactose	Lactose is a disaccharide that makes up around 2-8% of the solids in milk. Lactose is a disaccharide consisting of two subunits, a galactose and a glucose linked together.
Maltose	A disaccharide composed of two glucose molecules joined by a glycosidic bond is maltose.
Complex oligosaccharide	Complex oligosaccharide refers to a chain of sugars attached to a glycoprotein that is generated by trimming of the original oligosaccharide attached in the endoplasmic reticulum and subsequent addition of further sugars.
Ester linkage	Ester linkage refers to a condensation reaction in which the carboxyl group of a fatty acid reacts with the hydroxyl group of an alcohol. Lipids are formed in this way.
Skeleton	In biology, the skeleton or skeletal system is the biological system providing physical support in living organisms.
Lipid	Lipid is one class of aliphatic hydrocarbon-containing organic compounds essential for the structure and function of living cells. They are characterized by being water-insoluble but soluble in nonpolar organic solvents.
Steroid	A steroid is a lipid characterized by a carbon skeleton with four fused rings. Different steroids vary in the functional groups attached to these rings. Hundreds of distinct steroids

Go to **Cram101.com** for the Practice Tests for this Chapter.

have been identified in plants and animals. Their most important role in most living systems is as hormones.

Triglyceride	Triglyceride is a glyceride in which the glycerol is esterified with three fatty acids. They are the main constituent of vegetable oil and animal fats and play an important role in metabolism as energy sources. They contain a bit more than twice as much energy as carbohydrates and proteins.
Steroid hormone	A lipid made from cholesterol that activates the transcription of specific genes in target cells is referred to as steroid hormone.
Testosterone	Testosterone is a steroid hormone from the androgen group. Testosterone is secreted in the testes of men and the ovaries of women. It is the principal male sex hormone and the "original" anabolic steroid. In both males and females, it plays key roles in health and well-being.
Polar region	An area surrounding one of the two magnetic poles of a planet is a polar region.
Histidine	Histidine is one of the 20 most common natural amino acids present in proteins. In the nutritional sense, in humans, histidine is considered an essential amino acid, but mostly only in children.
Arginine	Arginine is an α-amino acid. The L-form is one of the 20 most common natural amino acids. In mammals, arginine is classified as a semiessential or conditionally essential amino acid, depending on the developmental stage and health status of the individual.
Asparagine	Asparagine is one of the 20 most common natural amino acids on Earth. It has carboxamide as the side chain's functional group. It is considered a non-essential amino acid.
Disulfide bond	A disulfide bond (SS-bond), also called a disulfide bridge, is a strong covalent bond between two sulfhydryl (-SH) groups. This bond is very important to the folding, structure, and function of proteins.
Glutamine	Glutamine is one of the 20 amino acids encoded by the standard genetic code. Its side chain is an amide; it is formed by replacing a side-chain hydroxyl of glutamic acid with an amine functional group.
Cysteine	Cysteine is a naturally occurring hydrophobic amino acid which has a thiol group and is found in most proteins, though only in small quantities.
Ribonucleic acid	Ribonucleic acid is a nucleic acid polymer consisting of covalently bound nucleotides. It's nucleotides contain ribose rings unlike DNA, which contains deoxyribose. It serves as the template for translation of genes into proteins, transferring amino acids to the ribosome to form proteins.
Coenzyme	Nonprotein organic molecule that aids the action of the enzyme to which it is loosely bound is referred to as coenzyme.
Coenzyme A	Small molecule used in the enzymatic transfer of acyl groups in the cell is coenzyme A.
Radius	The radius is the bone of the forearm that extends from the inside of the elbow to the thumb side of the wrist. The radius is situated on the lateral side of the ulna, which exceeds it in length and size.
Hydrophobic force	Force exerted by the hydrogen-bonded network of water molecules that brings two nonpolar surfaces together by excluding water between them is a hydrophobic force.
Sulfur	Sulfur is the chemical element in the periodic table that has the symbol S and atomic number 16. It is an abundant, tasteless, odorless, multivalent non-metal. Sulfur, in its native form, is a yellow crystaline solid. In nature, it can be found as the pure element or as sulfide and sulfate minerals.

Go to **Cram101.com** for the Practice Tests for this Chapter.

Cell biology	The biological discipline involving the study of cells and their functions is called cell biology. This includes their physiological properties such as their structure and the organelles they contain, their environment and interactions, their life cycle, division and function (physiology) and eventual death.
Chloroplast	A chloroplast is an organelle found in plant cells and eukaryotic algae which conduct photosynthesis. They are similar to mitochondria but are found only in plants. They are surrounded by a double membrane with an intermembrane space; they have their own DNA and are involved in energy metabolism;
Sunlight	Sunlight in the broad sense is the total spectrum of electromagnetic radiation given off by the Sun.
Electromagnetic energy	Electromagnetic energy is a form of energy present in any electric field or magnetic field, or in any volume containing electromagnetic radiation. The SI unit of electrical energy is the joule, while the unit used by electrical utility companies is the watt-hour (W·h) or the kilowatt-hour (kW·h).
Chlorophyll	Chlorophyll is a green photosynthetic pigment found in plants, algae, and cyanobacteria. In plant photosynthesis incoming light is absorbed by chlorophyll and other accessory pigments in the antenna complexes of photosystem I and photosystem II.
Leaf	In botany, a leaf is an above-ground plant organ specialized for photosynthesis. For this purpose, a leaf is typically flat (laminar) and thin, to expose the chloroplast containing cells (chlorenchyma tissue) to light over a broad area, and to allow light to penetrate fully into the tissues.

Go to **Cram101.com** for the Practice Tests for this Chapter.

Nucleotide	A nucleotide is a chemical compound that consists of a heterocyclic base, a sugar, and one or more phosphate groups. In the most common nucleotides the base is a derivative of purine or pyrimidine, and the sugar is pentose - deoxyribose or ribose. They are the structural units of RNA and DNA.
Amino acid	An amino acid is any molecule that contains both amino and carboxylic acid functional groups. They are the basic structural building units of proteins. They form short polymer chains called peptides or polypeptides which in turn form structures called proteins.
Molecule	A molecule is the smallest particle of a pure chemical substance that still retains its chemical composition and properties.
Lipid	Lipid is one class of aliphatic hydrocarbon-containing organic compounds essential for the structure and function of living cells. They are characterized by being water-insoluble but soluble in nonpolar organic solvents.
Sugar	A sugar is the simplest molecule that can be identified as a carbohydrate. These include monosaccharides and disaccharides, trisaccharides and the oligosaccharides. The term "glyco-" indicates the presence of a sugar in an otherwise non-carbohydrate substance.
Cell	The cell is the structural and functional unit of all living organisms, and is sometimes called the "building block of life."
Macromolecule	A macromolecule is a molecule of high relative molecular mass, the structure of which essentially comprises the multiple repetition of units derived, actually or conceptually, from molecules of low relative molecular mass.
Nucleic acid	A nucleic acid is a complex, high-molecular-weight biochemical macromolecule composed of nucleotide chains that convey genetic information. The most common are deoxyribonucleic acid (DNA) and ribonucleic acid (RNA). They are found in all living cells and viruses.
Protein	A protein is a complex, high-molecular-weight organic compound that consists of amino acids joined by peptide bonds. They are essential to the structure and function of all living cells and viruses. Many are enzymes or subunits of enzymes.
Chemical reaction	Chemical reaction refers to a process leading to chemical changes in matter; involves the making and/or breaking of chemical bonds.
Atom	An atom is the smallest possible particle of a chemical element that retains its chemical properties.
Enzyme	An enzyme is a protein that catalyzes, or speeds up, a chemical reaction. They are essential to sustain life because most chemical reactions in biological cells would occur too slowly, or would lead to different products, without them.
Substrate	A substrate is a molecule which is acted upon by an enzyme. Each enzyme recognizes only the specific substrate of the reaction it catalyzes. A surface in or on which an organism lives.
Catabolism	Catabolism is the part of metabolism that partitions molecules into smaller units. It is made up of degradative chemical reactions in the living cell. Large polymeric molecules are processed into their constituent monomeric units.
Activated carrier	Activated carrier is a small diffusible molecule in cells that stores easily exchangeable energy in the form of one or more energy-rich covalent bonds. Examples are ATP and NADPH.
Metabolic pathway	A metabolic pathway is a series of chemical reactions occurring within a cell, catalyzed by enzymes, to achieve in either the formation of a metabolic product to be used or stored by the cell, or the initiation of another metabolic pathway.
Electron carrier	Electron carrier refers to a molecule that conveys electrons within a cell; one of several membrane molecules that make up electron transport chains.

Biosynthesis	Biosynthesis is a phenomenon where chemical compounds are produced from simpler reagents. Biosynthesis, unlike chemical synthesis, takes place within living organisms and is generally catalysed by enzymes. The process is vital part of metabolism.
Free energy	The term thermodynamic free energy denotes the total amount of energy in a physical system which can be converted to do work.
Metabolism	Metabolism is the biochemical modification of chemical compounds in living organisms and cells. This includes the biosynthesis of complex organic molecules (anabolism) and their breakdown (catabolism).
Catalysis	Catalysis is the acceleration of the reaction rate of a chemical reaction by means of a substance, called a catalyst, that is itself not consumed by the overall reaction.
Diffusion	Diffusion refers to the spontaneous movement of particles of any kind from where they are more concentrated to where they are less concentrated.
Oxidation	Oxidation refers to the loss of electrons from a substance involved in a redox reaction; always accompanies reduction.
Sunlight	Sunlight in the broad sense is the total spectrum of electromagnetic radiation given off by the Sun.
Reactant	A reactant is any substance initially present in a chemical reaction. These reactants react with each other to form the products of a chemical reaction. In a chemical equation, the reactants are the elements or compounds on the left hand side of the reaction equation.
Electron	The electron is a light fundamental subatomic particle that carries a negative electric charge. The electron is a spin-1/2 lepton, does not participate in strong interactions and has no substructure.
Polymer	Polymer is a generic term used to describe a very long molecule consisting of structural units and repeating units connected by covalent chemical bonds.
Cell metabolism	Cell metabolism is the process (or really the sum of many ongoing individual processes) by which living cells process nutrient molecules and maintain a living state.
Biochemistry	Biochemistry studies how complex chemical reactions give rise to life. It is a hybrid branch of chemistry which specialises in the chemical processes in living organisms.
Chemical bond	Chemical bond refers to an attraction between two atoms resulting from a sharing of outer-shell electrons or the presence of opposite charges on the atoms. The bonded atoms gain complete outer electron shells.
Second law of thermodynamics	The second law of thermodynamics, in a concise form, states that the total entropy of any thermodynamically isolated system tends to increase over time, approaching a maximum value.
Isolated system	An Isolated system, is a physical system that does not interact with its surroundings. It obeys a number of conservation laws: its total energy and mass stay constant. They cannot enter or exit, but can only move around inside.
Entropy	Entropy is a measure of the amount of energy in a physical system that cannot be used to do work. In simpler terms, it is also a measure of the disorder and randomness present in a system.
Pollen grain	Pollen grain in seed plants, the sperm-producing microgametophyte.
Microtubule	Microtubule is a protein structure found within cells, one of the components of the cytoskeleton. They have diameter of ~ 24 nm and varying length from several micrometers to possible millimeters in axons of nerve cells. They serve as structural components within cells and are involved in many cellular processes including mitosis, cytokinesis, and

	vesicular transport.
Parasite	A parasite is an organism that spends a significant portion of its life in or on the living tissue of a host organism and which causes harm to the host without immediately killing it. They also commonly show highly specialized adaptations allowing them to exploit host resources.
Sperm	Sperm refers to the male sex cell with three distinct parts at maturity: head, middle piece, and tail.
Virus	Obligate intracellular parasite of living cells consisting of an outer capsid and an inner core of nucleic acid is referred to as virus. The term virus usually refers to those particles that infect eukaryotes whilst the term bacteriophage or phage is used to describe those infecting prokaryotes.
Bacteria	The domain that contains procaryotic cells with primarily diacyl glycerol diesters in their membranes and with bacterial rRNA. Bacteria also is a general term for organisms that are composed of procaryotic cells and are not multicellular.
Thermodynamics	Thermodynamics is a branch of physics that studies the effects of changes in temperature, pressure, and volume on physical systems at the macroscopic scale by analyzing the collective motion of their particles using statistics.
Potential energy	Stored energy as a result of location or spatial arrangement is referred to as potential energy.
Photosynthesis	Photosynthesis is a biochemical process in which plants, algae, and some bacteria harness the energy of light to produce food. Ultimately, nearly all living things depend on energy produced from photosynthesis for their nourishment, making it vital to life on Earth.
Kinetic energy	Kinetic energy refers to energy that is actually doing work; the energy of a mass of matter that is moving. Moving matter performs work by transferring its motion to other matter, such as leg muscles pushing bicycle pedals.
Bond energy	Strength of the chemical linkage between two atoms, measured by the energy in kilocalories or kilojoules needed to break it is called bond energy.
Hydrogen	Hydrogen is a chemical element in the periodic table that has the symbol H and atomic number 1. At standard temperature and pressure it is a colorless, odorless, nonmetallic, univalent, tasteless, highly flammable diatomic gas.
Oxygen	Oxygen is a chemical element in the periodic table. It has the symbol O and atomic number 8. Oxygen is the second most common element on Earth, composing around 46% of the mass of Earth's crust and 28% of the mass of Earth as a whole, and is the third most common element in the universe.
Molecular motors	Molecular motors are biological "nanomachines" and are the essential agents of movement in living organisms.
Microorganism	A microorganism is an organism that is so small that it is microscopic (invisible to the naked eye). They are often illustrated using single-celled, or unicellular organisms; however, some unicellular protists are visible to the naked eye, and some multicellular species are microscopic.
Electromagnetic energy	Electromagnetic energy is a form of energy present in any electric field or magnetic field, or in any volume containing electromagnetic radiation. The SI unit of electrical energy is the joule, while the unit used by electrical utility companies is the watt-hour (W·h) or the kilowatt-hour (kW·h).
Carbon dioxide	Carbon dioxide is an atmospheric gas comprized of one carbon and two oxygen atoms. A very

	widely known chemical compound, it is frequently called by its formula CO_2. In its solid state, it is commonly known as dry ice.
Nitrogen	A colorless and tasteless and mostly inert diatomic non-metal gas that is an essential constituent of proteins is nitrogen.
Ammonia	Ammonia is a compound of nitrogen and hydrogen with the formula NH_3. At standard temperature and pressure ammonia is a gas. It is toxic and corrosive to some materials, and has a characteristic pungent odor.
Element	A chemical element, often called simply element, is a chemical substance that cannot be divided or changed into other chemical substances by any ordinary chemical technique. An element is a class of substances that contain the same number of protons in all its atoms.
Nitrate	Nitrate refers to a salt of nitric acid; a compound containing the radical NO_3; biologically, the final form of nitrogen from the oxidation of organic nitrogen compounds.
Carbon	Carbon is a chemical element in the periodic table that has the symbol C and atomic number 6. An abundant nonmetallic, tetravalent element, carbon has several allotropic forms.
Soil	Soil is material capable of supporting plant life. Soil forms through a variety of soil formation processes, and includes weathered rock "parent material" combined with dead and living organic matter and air.
Salt	Salt is a term used for ionic compounds composed of positively charged cations and negatively charged anions, so that the product is neutral and without a net charge.
Chemical group	A set of covalently linked atoms, such as a hydroxyl group or an amino group, the chemical behavior of which is well characterized is referred to as a chemical group.
Light-independent reaction	In photosynthesis, light-independent reaction, also somewhat misleadingly called the dark reaction, are chemical reactions that convert carbon dioxide and other compounds into glucose.
Chemical energy	Chemical energy refers to energy stored in the chemical bonds of molecules; a form of potential energy.
Plant cell	A cell that is a structural and functional unit of a plant is a plant cell.
Cellular respiration	Cellular respiration is the process in which the chemical bonds of energy-rich molecules such as glucose are converted into energy usable for life processes.
Hydrogen atom	A hydrogen atom is an atom of the element hydrogen. It is composed of a single negatively-charged electron, attending a positively-charged proton which is the nucleus of the hydrogen atom. The electron is bound to the proton by the Coulomb force.
Atmosphere	Earth's atmosphere is a layer of gases surrounding the planet Earth and retained by the Earth's gravity. It contains roughly 78% nitrogen and 21% oxygen, with trace amounts of other gases.
Respiration	Respiration is the process by which an organism obtains energy by reacting oxygen with glucose to give water, carbon dioxide and ATP (energy). Respiration takes place on a cellular level in the mitochondria of the cells and provide the cells with energy.
Biosphere	The biosphere is that part of a planet's outer shell — including air, land, surface rocks and water — within which life occurs, and which biotic processes in turn alter or transform.
Algae	The algae consist of several different groups of living organisms that capture light energy through photosynthesis, converting inorganic substances into simple sugars with the captured energy.
Fossil fuel	Fossil fuel refers to an energy deposit formed from the remains of extinct organisms.

Catalyst	A chemical that speeds up a reaction but is not used up in the reaction is a catalyst.
Polar covalent bond	A polar covalent bond is a form of covalent bonding that happens when atoms of two different elements with different electronegativities bond resulting in an unequal sharing of electrons.
Covalent bond	A covalent bond is an intramolecular form of chemical bonding characterized by the sharing of one or more pairs of electrons between two elements, producing a mutual attraction that holds the resultant molecule together.
Sulfur	Sulfur is the chemical element in the periodic table that has the symbol S and atomic number 16. It is an abundant, tasteless, odorless, multivalent non-metal. Sulfur, in its native form, is a yellow crystaline solid. In nature, it can be found as the pure element or as sulfide and sulfate minerals.
Nucleus	In cell biology, the nucleus is found in all eukaryotic cells that contains most of the cell's genetic material. The nucleus has two primary functions: to control chemical reactions within the cytoplasm and to store information needed for cellular division.
Activation energy	The activation energy is the threshold energy, or the energy that must be overcome in order for a chemical reaction to occur. Activation energy may otherwise be denoted as the minimum energy necessary for a specific chemical reaction to occur.
Acetic acid	Acetic acid, also known as ethanoic acid, is an organic chemical compound best recognized for giving vinegar its sour taste and pungent smell.
Ethanol	Ethanol is a flammable, colorless chemical compound, one of the alcohols that is most often found in alcoholic beverages. In common parlance, it is often referred to simply as alcohol. Its chemical formula is C_2H_5OH, also written as C_2H_6O.
Ion	Ion refers to an atom or molecule that has gained or lost one or more electrons, thus acquiring an electrical charge.
Active site	The active site of an enzyme is the binding site where catalysis occurs. The structure and chemical properties of the active site allow the recognition and binding of the substrate.
Standard free-energy change	Free-energy change of two reacting molecules at standard temperature and pressure when all components are present at a concentration of 1 mole per liter is called standard free-energy change.
Coupled reaction	Coupled reaction refers to a pair of reactions, one cxergonic and one endergonic, that are linked together such that the energy produced by the exergonic reaction provides the energy needed to drive the endergonic reaction.
Fructose	Fructose is a simple sugar (monosaccharide) found in many foods and one of the three most important blood sugars along with glucose and galactose.
Calorie	Calorie refers to the amount of energy that raises the temperature of 1 g of water by 1°C.
Glucose	Glucose, a simple monosaccharide sugar, is one of the most important carbohydrates and is used as a source of energy in animals and plants. Glucose is one of the main products of photosynthesis and starts respiration.
Sucrose	A disaccharide composed of glucose and fructose is called sucrose.
Mole	The atomic weight of a substance, expressed in grams. One mole is defined as the mass of 6.0222 3 1023 atoms.
Hydrolysis	Hydrolysis is a chemical process in which a molecule is cleaved into two parts by the addition of a molecule of water.
Phosphate	A phosphate is a polyatomic ion or radical consisting of one phosphorus atom and four oxygen.

	In the ionic form, it carries a -3 formal charge, and is denoted PO_4^{3-}.
Acetyl	The acetyl radical contains a methyl group single-bonded to a carbonyl. The carbon of the carbonyl has an lone electron available, with which it forms a chemical bond to the remainder of the molecule.
Chemical equilibrium	The condition in which the 'forward' reaction of reactants to products proceeds at the same rate as the 'backward' reaction from products to reactants, so that no net change in chemical composition occurs is referred to as chemical equilibrium.
Siphon	The tube-like extension through which water flows in and out of the mantle cavity in bivalves and cephalopods, and in tunicates is called siphon.
Root	In vascular plants, the root is that organ of a plant body that typically lies below the surface of the soil. However, this is not always the case, since a root can also be aerial (that is, growing above the ground) or aerating (that is, growing up above the ground or especially above water).
Ribosome	A ribosome is an organelle composed of rRNA and ribosomal proteins. It translates mRNA into a polypeptide chain (e.g., a protein). It can be thought of as a factory that builds a protein from a set of genetic instructions.
Cytoplasm	Cytoplasm refers to everything inside a cell between the plasma membrane and the nucleus; consists of a semifluid medium and organelles.
Cytosol	The cytosol is the internal fluid of the cell, and a large part of cell metabolism occurs here. Proteins within the cytosol play an important role in signal transduction pathways, glycolysis; also, they act as intracellular receptors and form part of the ribosomes, enabling further protein synthesis
Enzyme-substrate complex	A temporary molecule formed when an enzyme attaches itself to a substrate molecule is an enzyme-substrate complex.
Bicarbonate ion	The bicarbonate ion consists of one central carbon atom surrounded by three identical oxygen atoms in a trigonal planar arrangement, with a hydrogen atom attached to one of the oxygens.
Tissue	Group of similar cells which perform a common function is called tissue.
Lungs	Lungs are the essential organs of respiration in air-breathing vertebrates. Their principal function is to transport oxygen from the atmosphere into the bloodstream, and to excrete carbon dioxide from the bloodstream into the atmosphere.
Carbonic anhydrase	Carbonic anhydrase is a family of zinc-containing enzymes that catalyze the rapid interconversion of carbon dioxide and water into carbonic acid, protons, and bicarbonate ions.
Spectrophoto-eter	An instrument that measures the proportions of light of different wavelengths absorbed and transmitted by a pigment solution is a spectrophotometer.
Inhibitor	An inhibitor is a type of effector (biology) that decreases or prevents the rate of a chemical reaction. They are often called negative catalysts.
Toxin	Toxin refers to a microbial product or component that can injure another cell or organism at low concentrations. Often the term refers to a poisonous protein, but toxins may be lipids and other substances.
Enzyme activity	Enzyme activity is the catalytic effect exerted by an enzyme.
Competitive inhibition	The formation of a temporary enzyme-inhibitor complex that interferes with the normal formation of enzyme-substrate complexes, resulting in a decreased turnover is referred to as

Go to **Cram101.com** for the Practice Tests for this Chapter.

competitive inhibition.

Competitive inhibitor	A substance that reduces the activity of an enzyme by binding to the enzyme's active site in place of the substrate is referred to as a competitive inhibitor; It's structure mimics that of the enzyme's substrate.
Ethylene	Ethylene functions as a hormone in plants. It stimulates Ethylene (or IUPAC name ethene) is the simplest alkene hydrocarbon, consisting of four hydrogen atoms and two carbon atoms connected by a double bond.
Acid	An acid is a water-soluble, sour-tasting chemical compound that when dissolved in water, gives a solution with a pH of less than 7.
Shoot	In botany, the shoot is one of two primary sections of a plant; the other is the root. The shoot refers to what is generally the upper portion of a plant, and consists of stems, leaves, flowers, and fruits. It is derived from the embryonic epicotyl, the portion of the embryo above the point of attachment to the seed leaves (cotyledons).
Alcohol dehydrogenase	Alcohol dehydrogenase is a group of dehydrogenase enzymes that occur in many organisms and facilitate the conversion between alcohols and aldehydes or ketones. In humans and many other animals, they serve to break down alcohols which could otherwise be toxic; in yeast and many bacteria they catalyze the opposite reaction as part of fermentation.
Pollutant	Pollutant refers to any natural or artificial substance that enters the ecosystem in such quantities that it does harm to the ecosystem; any introduced substance that makes a resource unfit for a specific purpose.
Genetic engineering	Genetic engineering, genetic modification (GM), and the now-deprecated gene splicing are terms for the process of manipulating genes, usually outside the organism's normal reproductive process.
Bacterium	Most bacterium are microscopic and unicellular, with a relatively simple cell structure lacking a cell nucleus, and organelles such as mitochondria and chloroplasts. They are the most abundant of all organisms. They are ubiquitous in soil, water, and as symbionts of other organisms.
Gene	Gene refers to a discrete unit of hereditary information consisting of a specific nucleotide sequence in DNA . Most of the genes of a eukaryote are located in its chromosomal DNA; a few are carried by the DNA of mitochondria and chloroplasts.
Adenosine	Adenosine is a nucleoside comprized of adenine attached to a ribose (ribofuranose) moiety via a β-N_9-glycosidic bond. Adenosine plays an important role in biochemical processes, such as energy transfer - as adenosine triphosphate (ATP) and adenosine diphosphate (ADP) - as well as in signal transduction as cyclic adenosine monophosphate, cAMP.
Versatile	The anther can be attached to the filament in two ways, versatile is when it is attached at its center to the filament; pollen is then released through pores (poricidal dehiscence).
Phosphorylation	Phosphorylation refers to reaction in which a phosphate group becomes covalently coupled to another molecule.
Hydrolysis reaction	Hydrolysis is a chemical process in which a molecule is cleaved into two parts by the addition of a molecule of water. This is distinct from a hydrolysis reaction, in which water molecules are added to a substance, but no cleavage occurs.
Linkage	Linkage refers to the patterns of assortment of genes that are located on the same chromosome. Important because if the genes are located relatively far apart, crossing over is more likely to occur between them than if they are close together.
Phospholipid	Phospholipid is a class of lipids formed from four components: fatty acids, a negatively-

Go to **Cram101.com** for the Practice Tests for this Chapter.

charged phosphate group, an alcohol and a backbone. Phospholipids with a glycerol backbone are known as glycerophospholipids or phosphoglycerides.

Adenine	Adenine is one of the two purine nucleobases used in forming nucleotides of the nucleic acids DNA and RNA. In DNA, adenine (A) binds to thymine (T) via two hydrogen bonds to assist in stabilizing the nucleic acid structures. In RNA, adenine binds to uracil (U).
Glutamine	Glutamine is one of the 20 amino acids encoded by the standard genetic code. Its side chain is an amide; it is formed by replacing a side-chain hydroxyl of glutamic acid with an amine functional group.
Proton	Positive subatomic particle, located in the nucleus and having a weight of approximately one atomic mass unit is referred to as a proton.
Phosphate group	The functional group $-OPO_3H_2$; the transfer of energy from one compound to another is often accomplished by the transfer of a phosphate group.
Carboxyl	A carboxyl is the univalent radical -COOH; present in and characteristic of organic acids.
Methyl	In chemistry, a methyl group is a hydrophobic alkyl functional group derived from methane (CH_4). It has the formula $-CH_3$ and is very often abbreviated -Me.
Carboxyl group	In an organic molecule, a functional group consisting of an oxygen atom doublebonded to a carbon atom that is also bonded to a hydroxyl group is referred to as a carboxyl group.
Coenzyme A	Small molecule used in the enzymatic transfer of acyl groups in the cell is coenzyme A.
Biotin	Biotin is a low-molecular-weight compound used as a coenzyme. Useful technically as a covalent label for proteins, allowing them to be detected by the egg protein avidin, which binds extremely tightly to biotin.
Thioester bond	Thioester bond refers to high-energy bond formed by a condensation reaction between an acid group and a thiol group; seen, for example, in acetyl coa and in many enzyme-substrate complexes.
Acetate	Acetate is the anion of a salt or ester of acetic acid.
Ribose	Ribose is an aldopentose — a monosaccharide containing five carbon atoms, and including an aldehyde functional group. It has chemical formula $C_5H_{10}O_5$.
Pyruvate carboxylase	Pyruvate carboxylase is an enzyme of the ligase class that catalyzes the irreversible carboxylation of pyruvate to form oxaloacetate.
Group transfer	The exchange of atoms between molecules is a group transfer.
Pyruvate	Pyruvate is the ionized form of pyruvic acid. It is an important chemical compound in biochemistry. It is the output of the breakdown of glucose known as glycolysis, and (in aerobic respiration) the main input for the citric acid cycle via acetyl-CoA.
Polysaccharide	Polymer made from sugar monomers is a polysaccharide. They are relatively complex carbohydrates.
Condensation reaction	A condensation reaction is a chemical reaction in which two molecules or moieties react and become covalently bonded to one another by the concurrent loss of a small molecule, often water, methanol, or a type of hydrogen halide such as HCl.
Monomer	In chemistry, a monomer is a small molecule that may become chemically bonded to other monomers to form a polymer.
Nucleoside	Molecule composed of a purine or pyrimidine base covalently linked to a ribose or deoxyribose sugar is a nucleoside.
Polynucleotide	Polynucleotide refers to a polymer consisting of many nucleotide monomers; serves as a

	blueprint for proteins and, through the actions of proteins, for all cellular activities. The two types are DNA and RNA.
Cellular metabolism	The sum of all chemical changes that take place in a cell through which energy and basic components are provided for essential processes, including the synthesis of new molecules and the breakdown and removal of others is called cellular metabolism.
Reproduction	Biological reproduction is the biological process by which new individual organisms are produced. Reproduction is a fundamental feature of all known life; each individual organism exists as the result of reproduction by an antecedent.
Animal cell	An animal cell is a form of eukaryotic cell which make up many tissues in animals. The animal cell is distinct from other eukaryotes, most notably those of plants, as they lack cell walls and chloroplasts, and they have smaller vacuoles.
Dissociation	Dissociation is a general process in which complexes, molecules, or salts separate or split into smaller molecules, ions, or radicals, usually in a reversible manner.
Transformation	Transformation is the genetic alteration of a cell resulting from the introduction, uptake and expression of foreign genetic material (DNA or RNA).
Carbon skeleton	The chain of carbon atoms that forms the structural backbone of an organic molecule is called carbon skeleton.
Metabolite	The term metabolite is usually restricted to small molecules. They are the intermediates and products of metabolism. A primary metabolite is directly involved in the normal growth, development, and reproduction. A secondary metabolite is not directly involved in those processes, but usually has important ecological function.
Mutation	Mutation refers to a change in the nucleotide sequence of DNA; the ultimate source of genetic diversity.
Rearrangement	A change in the usual order and arrangement of genetic material either within the chromosome complement or within a gene locus is rearrangement. Where the nature of the rearrangement has been determined, the type may be searched for directly under the following designations: reciprocal translocation, Robertsonian translocation, insertion, transposition, inversion, deletion, and duplication.

Protein structure	A protein structure are amino acid chains, made up from 20 different L-α-amino acids, also referred to as residues, that fold into unique three-dimensional structures.
Microscope	A microscope is an instrument for viewing objects that are too small to be seen by the naked or unaided eye.
Protein	A protein is a complex, high-molecular-weight organic compound that consists of amino acids joined by peptide bonds. They are essential to the structure and function of all living cells and viruses. Many are enzymes or subunits of enzymes.
Cell	The cell is the structural and functional unit of all living organisms, and is sometimes called the "building block of life."
Acid	An acid is a water-soluble, sour-tasting chemical compound that when dissolved in water, gives a solution with a pH of less than 7.
Chemical reaction	Chemical reaction refers to a process leading to chemical changes in matter; involves the making and/or breaking of chemical bonds.
Molecule	A molecule is the smallest particle of a pure chemical substance that still retains its chemical composition and properties.
Enzyme	An enzyme is a protein that catalyzes, or speeds up, a chemical reaction. They are essential to sustain life because most chemical reactions in biological cells would occur too slowly, or would lead to different products, without them.
Plasma membrane	Membrane surrounding the cytoplasm that consists of a phospholipid bilayer with embedded proteins is referred to as plasma membrane.
Helix	A helix is a twisted shape like a spring, screw or a spiral staircase. They are important in biology, as DNA and many proteins have spiral substructures, known a alpha helix.
Elastic fiber	Elastic fiber is a bundles of proteins (elastin) found in connective tissue and produced by fibroblasts and smooth muscle cells in arteries.
Polypeptide	Polypeptide refers to polymer of many amino acids linked by peptide bonds.
Filament	The stamen is the male organ of a flower. Each stamen generally has a stalk called the filament, and, on top of the filament, an anther. The filament is a long chain of proteins, such as those found in hair, muscle, or in flagella.
Hormone	A hormone is a chemical messenger from one cell to another. All multicellular organisms produce hormones. The best known hormones are those produced by endocrine glands of vertebrate animals, but hormones are produced by nearly every organ system and tissue type in a human or animal body. Hormone molecules are secreted directly into the bloodstream, they move by circulation or diffusion to their target cells, which may be nearby cells in the same tissue or cells of a distant organ of the body.
Toxin	Toxin refers to a microbial product or component that can injure another cell or organism at low concentrations. Often the term refers to a poisonous protein, but toxins may be lipids and other substances.
Muscle	Muscle is a contractile form of tissue. It is one of the four major tissue types, the other three being epithelium, connective tissue and nervous tissue. Muscle contraction is used to move parts of the body, as well as to move substances within the body.
Embryo	Embryo refers to a developing stage of a multicellular organism. In humans, the stage in the development of offspring from the first division of the zygote until body structures begin to appear, about the ninth week of gestation.
Nerve	A nerve is an enclosed, cable-like bundle of nerve fibers or axons, which includes the glia

that ensheath the axons in myelin.

Allosteric enzyme	Allosteric enzyme refers to an enzyme whose activity is altered by the binding of a small effector or modulator molecule at a regulatory site separate from the catalytic site; effector binding causes a conformational change in the enzyme and its catalytic site, which leads to enzyme activation or inhibition.
Motor protein	Protein that uses energy derived from nucleoside triphosphate hydrolysis to propel itself along a protein filament or another polymeric molecule is called motor protein.
Tissue	Group of similar cells which perform a common function is called tissue.
Structural protein	A protein that is important for holding cells and organisms together, such as the proteins that make up the cell membrane, muscles, tendons, and blood is a structural protein.
Microtubule	Microtubule is a protein structure found within cells, one of the components of the cytoskeleton. They have diameter of ~ 24 nm and varying length from several micrometers to possible millimeters in axons of nerve cells. They serve as structural components within cells and are involved in many cellular processes including mitosis, cytokinesis, and vesicular transport.
Epithelial	Functions of epithelial cells include secretion, absorption, protection, transcellular transport, sensation detection, and selective permeability.
Tubulin	The protein subunit of microtubules is referred to as tubulin.
Actin	Actin is a globular protein that polymerizes helically forming filaments, which like the other two components of the cellular cytoskeleton form a three-dimensional network inside an eukaryotic cell. They provide mechanical support for the cell, determine the cell shape, enable cell movements .
Fiber	Fiber is a class of materials that are continuous filaments or are in discrete elongated pieces, similar to lengths of thread. They are of great importance in the biology of both plants and animals, for holding tissues together.
Ion	Ion refers to an atom or molecule that has gained or lost one or more electrons, thus acquiring an electrical charge.
Transport protein	A transport protein is a protein involved in facilitated diffusion. Changes in the conformation move the binding site to the opposite side of the protein.
Cell membrane	A component of every biological cell, the selectively permeable cell membrane is a thin and structured bilayer of phospholipid and protein molecules that envelopes the cell. It separates a cell's interior from its surroundings and controls what moves in and out.
Receptor protein	Protein located in the plasma membrane or within the cell that binds to a substance that alters some metabolic aspect of the cell is referred to as receptor protein. It will only link up with a substance that has a certain shape that allows it to bind to the receptor.
Gene regulatory protein	General name for any protein that binds to a specific DNA sequence to alter the expression of a gene is referred to as gene regulatory protein.
Gene	Gene refers to a discrete unit of hereditary information consisting of a specific nucleotide sequence in DNA . Most of the genes of a eukaryote are located in its chromosomal DNA; a few are carried by the DNA of mitochondria and chloroplasts.
Green fluorescent protein	Green fluorescent protein refers to fluorescent protein isolated from a jellyfish. Widely used as a marker in cell biology.
Jellyfish	Jellyfish are marine invertebrates belonging to the Scyphozoa class, and in turn the phylum

Cnidaria. The body of an adult jellyfish is composed of a bell-shaped, jellylike substance enclosing its internal structure, from which the creature's tentacles suspend.

Mussel

A mussel is a bivalve mollusk that can be found in lakes, rivers, creeks, intertidal areas, and throughout the ocean. The saltwater mussels (family Mytilidae) and freshwater mussels (family Unionidae) are not thought to be closely related and are grouped in different subclasses, despite considerable similarities in appearance.

Blood

Blood is a circulating tissue composed of fluid plasma and cells. The main function of blood is to supply nutrients (oxygen, glucose) and constitutional elements to tissues and to remove waste products.

Peptide bond

A peptide bond is a chemical bond formed between two molecules when the carboxyl group of one molecule reacts with the amino group of the other molecule, releasing a molecule of water.

Amino acid

An amino acid is any molecule that contains both amino and carboxylic acid functional groups. They are the basic structural building units of proteins. They form short polymer chains called peptides or polypeptides which in turn form structures called proteins.

Glycine

Glycine (Gly, G) is a nonpolar amino acid. It is the simplest of the 20 standard (proteinogenic) amino acids: its side chain is a hydrogen atom. Because there is a second hydrogen atom at the α carbon, glycine is not optically active.

Carboxyl group

In an organic molecule, a functional group consisting of an oxygen atom doublebonded to a carbon atom that is also bonded to a hydroxyl group is referred to as a carboxyl group.

Amino group

An amino group is an ammonia-like functional group composed of a nitrogen and two hydrogen atoms covalently linked. $-NH_2$

Nitrogen

A colorless and tasteless and mostly inert diatomic non-metal gas that is an essential constituent of proteins is nitrogen.

Electron

The electron is a light fundamental subatomic particle that carries a negative electric charge. The electron is a spin-1/2 lepton, does not participate in strong interactions and has no substructure.

Carbon

Carbon is a chemical element in the periodic table that has the symbol C and atomic number 6. An abundant nonmetallic, tetravalent element, carbon has several allotropic forms.

Atom

An atom is the smallest possible particle of a chemical element that retains its chemical properties.

Condensation reaction

A condensation reaction is a chemical reaction in which two molecules or moieties react and become covalently bonded to one another by the concurrent loss of a small molecule, often water, methanol, or a type of hydrogen halide such as HCl.

Insulin

Insulin is a polypeptide hormone that regulates carbohydrate metabolism. Apart from being the primary effector in carbohydrate homeostasis, it also has a substantial effect on small vessel muscle tone, controls storage and release of fat (triglycerides) and cellular uptake of both amino acids and some electrolytes.

Side chain

In organic chemistry and biochemistry a side chain is a part of a molecule attached to a core structure. Often the side chain can vary for a given core. In biochemistry the peptide or protein side chains are the variable parts of amino acids extending from the peptide backbone.

Polypeptide backbone

Polypeptide backbone refers to the chain of repeating carbon and nitrogen atoms, linked by peptide bonds, in a polypeptide or protein. The side chains of the amino acids project from this backbone.

Hydrophobic

Hydrophobic refers to being electrically neutral and nonpolar, and thus prefering other

Go to **Cram101.com** for the Practice Tests for this Chapter.

	neutral and nonpolar solvents or molecular environments. Hydrophobic is often used interchangeably with "oily" or "lipophilic."
Nonpolar	Lacking any asymmetric accumulation of positive and negative charge. Nonpolar molecules are generally insoluble in water.
Covalent bond	A covalent bond is an intramolecular form of chemical bonding characterized by the sharing of one or more pairs of electrons between two elements, producing a mutual attraction that holds the resultant molecule together.
Carboxyl	A carboxyl is the univalent radical -COOH; present in and characteristic of organic acids.
Distribution	Distribution in pharmacology is a branch of pharmacokinetics describing reversible transfer of drug from one location to another within the body.
Phenylalanine	Phenylalanine is an essential amino acid. The genetic disorder phenylketonuria is an inability to metabolize phenylalanine.
Tryptophan	Tryptophan is a sleep-promoting amino acid and a precursor for serotonin (a neurotransmitter) and melatonin (a neurohormone). Tryptophan has been implicated as a possible cause of schizophrenia in people who cannot metabolize it properly.
Cytosol	The cytosol is the internal fluid of the cell, and a large part of cell metabolism occurs here. Proteins within the cytosol play an important role in signal transduction pathways, glycolysis; also, they act as intracellular receptors and form part of the ribosomes, enabling further protein synthesis
Leucine	Leucine is one of the 20 most common amino acids and coded for by DNA. It is isomeric with isoleucine. Nutritionally, in humans, leucine is an essential amino acid.
Valine	Nutritionally, valine is also an essential amino acid. It is named after the plant valerian. In sickle-cell disease, it substitutes for the hydrophilic amino acid glutamic acid in hemoglobin.
Polar molecule	Molecule that displays an uneven distribution of electrons over its structure, for example, water is a polar molecule.
Hydrogen bond	A hydrogen bond is a type of attractive intermolecular force that exists between two partial electric charges of opposite polarity. Although stronger than most other intermolecular forces, the typical hydrogen bond is much weaker than both the ionic bond and the covalent bond.
Histidine	Histidine is one of the 20 most common natural amino acids present in proteins. In the nutritional sense, in humans, histidine is considered an essential amino acid, but mostly only in children.
Glutamine	Glutamine is one of the 20 amino acids encoded by the standard genetic code. Its side chain is an amide; it is formed by replacing a side-chain hydroxyl of glutamic acid with an amine functional group.
Arginine	Arginine is an α-amino acid. The L-form is one of the 20 most common natural amino acids. In mammals, arginine is classified as a semiessential or conditionally essential amino acid, depending on the developmental stage and health status of the individual.
Hydrophobic force	Force exerted by the hydrogen-bonded network of water molecules that brings two nonpolar surfaces together by excluding water between them is a hydrophobic force.
Conformation	The three-dimensional shape of a molecule is its conformation. The conformation is particularly important in proteins.
Free energy	The term thermodynamic free energy denotes the total amount of energy in a physical system

Go to **Cram101.com** for the Practice Tests for this Chapter.

which can be converted to do work.

Protein folding	Protein folding is the process by which a protein structure assumes its functional shape or conformation.
Solvent	A solvent is a liquid that dissolves a solid, liquid, or gaseous solute, resulting in a solution. The most common solvent in everyday life is water.
Lysozyme	Lysozyme is an enzyme (EC 3.2.1.17), commonly referred to as the "body's own antibiotic" since it kills bacteria. It is abundantly present in a number of secretions, such as tears (except bovine tears).
Biochemistry	Biochemistry studies how complex chemical reactions give rise to life. It is a hybrid branch of chemistry which specialises in the chemical processes in living organisms.
Prion	Prion is an infectious particle consisting of protein only and no nucleic acid which is believed to be linked to several diseases of the central nervous system.
Brain	The part of the central nervous system involved in regulating and controlling body activity and interpreting information from the senses transmitted through the nervous system is referred to as the brain.
Chaperone	Protein that helps other proteins avoid misfolding pathways that produce inactive or aggregated polypeptides is called a chaperone.
Cytoplasm	Cytoplasm refers to everything inside a cell between the plasma membrane and the nucleus; consists of a semifluid medium and organelles.
Macromolecule	A macromolecule is a molecule of high relative molecular mass, the structure of which essentially comprises the multiple repetition of units derived, actually or conceptually, from molecules of low relative molecular mass.
Genome	The genome of an organism is the whole hereditary information of an organism that is encoded in the DNA (or, for some viruses, RNA). This includes both the genes and the non-coding sequences. The genome of an organism is a complete DNA sequence of one set of chromosomes.
Urea	Urea is an organic compound of carbon, nitrogen, oxygen and hydrogen, CON_2H_4 or $(NH_2)_2CO$. Urea is essentially a waste product: it has no physiological function. It is dissolved in blood and excreted by the kidney.
DNA sequence	A DNA sequence is a succession of letters representing the primary structure of a real or hypothetical DNA molecule or strand, The possible letters are A, C, G, and T, representing the four nucleotide subunits of a DNA strand (adenine, cytosine, guanine, thymine).
Peptide	Peptide is the family of molecules formed from the linking, in a defined order, of various amino acids. The link between one amino acid residue and the next is an amide bond, and is sometimes referred to as a peptide bond.
X-Ray	X-Ray refers to diagnostic test in which an image is created using low doses of radiation.
Heterodimer	Protein complex composed of two different polypeptide chains is called heterodimer.
Electron microscope	The electron microscope is a microscope that can magnify very small details with high resolving power due to the use of electrons as the source of illumination, magnifying at levels up to 500,000 times.
Radiation	The emission of electromagnetic waves by all objects warmer than absolute zero is referred to as radiation.
Antibody	An antibody is a protein used by the immune system to identify and neutralize foreign objects like bacteria and viruses. Each antibody recognizes a specific antigen unique to its target.

Matrix	In biology, matrix (plural: matrices) is the material between animal or plant cells, the material (or tissue) in which more specialized structures are embedded, and a specific part of the mitochondrion that is the site of oxidation of organic molecules.
Electrophoresis	Electrophoresis is the movement of an electrically charged substance under the influence of an electric field. This movement is due to the Lorentz force, which may be related to fundamental electrical properties of the body under study and the ambient electrical conditions.
Polymer	Polymer is a generic term used to describe a very long molecule consisting of structural units and repeating units connected by covalent chemical bonds.
Protease	Protease refers to an enzyme that breaks peptide bonds between amino acids of proteins.
Residue	A residue refers to a portion of a larger molecule, a specific monomer of a polysaccharide, protein or nucleic acid.
Trypsin	The enzyme trypsin is produced in the pancreas in the form of trypsinogen, and is then transported to the small intestine, where begins the digestion of proteins to polypeptides and amino acids.
Lysine	Lysine is one of the 20 amino acids normally found in proteins. With its 4-aminobutyl side-chain, it is classified as a basic amino acid, along with arginine and histidine.
Mass spectrometry	Mass spectrometry is an analytical technique used to measure the mass-to-charge ratio (m/q) of ions. It is most generally used to find the composition of a physical sample by generating a mass spectrum representing the masses of sample components.
Cleavage	Cleavage refers to cytokinesis in animal cells and in some protists, characterized by pinching in of the plasma membrane.
Recombinant DNA	Recombinant DNA is an artificial DNA sequence resulting from the combining of two other DNA sequences in a plasmid.
Bacteria	The domain that contains procaryotic cells with primarily diacyl glycerol diesters in their membranes and with bacterial rRNA. Bacteria also is a general term for organisms that are composed of procaryotic cells and are not multicellular.
X-ray crystallography	Technique for determining the three-dimensional arrangement of atoms in a molecule based on the diffraction pattern of X-rays passing through a crystal of the molecule is x-ray crystallography.
Crystal	Crystal is a solid in which the constituent atoms, molecules, or ions are packed in a regularly ordered, repeating pattern extending in all three spatial dimensions.
Mass spectrometer	A mass spectrometer produces a mass spectrum of a sample to find its composition. This is normally achieved by ionizing the sample and separating ions of differing masses and recording their relative abundance by measuring intensities of ion flux.
Digestion	Digestion refers to the mechanical and chemical breakdown of food into molecules small enough for the body to absorb; the second main stage of food processing, following ingestion.
Diffraction pattern	Characteristic pattern which arises when the propagation of waves (eg electromagnetic waves) is affected by objects in their path (eg crystals in the path of X-ray radiation) a diffraction pattern.
Ligand	Any molecule that binds to a specific receptor site on a protein or other molecule is called a ligand.
Dalton	A measure of mass for atoms and subatomic particles is a dalton.
Hydrogen	Hydrogen is a chemical element in the periodic table that has the symbol H and atomic number

Go to **Cram101.com** for the Practice Tests for this Chapter.

1. At standard temperature and pressure it is a colorless, odorless, nonmetallic, univalent, tasteless, highly flammable diatomic gas.

Ribosome	A ribosome is an organelle composed of rRNA and ribosomal proteins. It translates mRNA into a polypeptide chain (e.g., a protein). It can be thought of as a factory that builds a protein from a set of genetic instructions.
Ribulose bisphosphate	Five-carbon compound that combines with and fixes carbon dioxide during the Calvin cycle and is later regenerated by the same cycle is ribulose bisphosphate.
Photosynthesis	Photosynthesis is a biochemical process in which plants, algae, and some bacteria harness the energy of light to produce food. Ultimately, nearly all living things depend on energy produced from photosynthesis for their nourishment, making it vital to life on Earth.
Fixation	Fixation in population genetics occurs when the frequency of a gene reaches 1.Fixation in biochemistry, histology, cell biology and pathology refers to the technique of preserving a specimen for microscopic study, making it intact and stable, but dead.
Cellulase	Cellulase refers to an enzyme that catalyzes the breakdown of the carbohydrate cellulose into its component glucose molecules; almost entirely restricted to microorganisms.
Domain	In biology, a domain is the top-level grouping of organisms in scientific classification.
N-terminus	The N-terminus refers to the extremity of a protein or polypeptide terminated by an amino acid with a free amine group ($-NH_2$).
Receptor	A receptor is a protein on the cell membrane or within the cytoplasm or cell nucleus that binds to a specific molecule (a ligand), such as a neurotransmitter, hormone, or other substance, and initiates the cellular response to the ligand. Receptor, in immunology, the region of an antibody which shows recognition of an antigen.
Coiled-coil	Especially stable rodlike structure in proteins which is formed by two of these a helices coiled around each other is a coiled-coil.
Hydrophilic	A hydrophilic molecule or portion of a molecule is one that is typically charge-polarized and capable of hydrogen bonding, enabling it to dissolve more readily in water than in oil or other hydrophobic solvents.
Lipid	Lipid is one class of aliphatic hydrocarbon-containing organic compounds essential for the structure and function of living cells. They are characterized by being water-insoluble but soluble in nonpolar organic solvents.
Antiparallel	Antiparallel refers to describes the relative orientation of the two strands in a DNA double helix; the polarity of one strand is oriented in the opposite direction to that of the other.
C-terminus	The C-terminus of a protein or polypeptide is the extremity of the amino acid chain terminated by a free carboxyl group (-COOH).
Climate	Weather condition of an area including especially prevailing temperature and average daily/yearly rainfall over a long period of time is called climate.
Insect	An arthropod that usually has three body segments , three pairs of legs, and one or two pairs of wings is called an insect. They are the largest and (on land) most widely-distributed taxon within the phylum Arthropoda. They comprise the most diverse group of animals on the earth, with around 925,000 species described
Lipid bilayer	A lipid bilayer is a membrane or zone of a membrane composed of lipid molecules (usually phospholipids). The lipid bilayer is a critical component of all biological membranes, including cell membranes, and is a prerequisite for cell-based organisms.
Phospholipid	Phospholipid is a class of lipids formed from four components: fatty acids, a negatively-

Go to **Cram101.com** for the Practice Tests for this Chapter.

charged phosphate group, an alcohol and a backbone. Phospholipids with a glycerol backbone are known as glycerophospholipids or phosphoglycerides.

Hydrocarbon	A chemical compound composed only of the elements carbon and hydrogen is called hydrocarbon.
Primary structure	The primary structure of an unbranched biopolymer, such as a molecule of DNA, RNA or protein, is the specific nucleotide or peptide sequence from the beginning to the end of the molecule.
Secondary structure	Secondary structure refers to the second level of protein structure; the regular patterns of coils or folds of a polypeptide chain.
Element	A chemical element, often called simply element, is a chemical substance that cannot be divided or changed into other chemical substances by any ordinary chemical technique. An element is a class of substances that contain the same number of protons in all its atoms.
Evolution	In biology, evolution is the process by which novel traits arise in populations and are passed on from generation to generation. Its action over large stretches of time explains the origin of new species and ultimately the vast diversity of the biological world.
Hydroxyl group	The term hydroxyl group is used to describe the functional group -OH when it is a substituent in an organic compound.
Cytochrome	Cytochrome refers to colored, heme-containing protein that transfers electrons during cellular respiration and photosynthesis.
Dehydrogenase	An enzyme that catalyzes a chemical reaction during which one or more hydrogen atoms are removed from a molecule is dehydrogenase.
Immunoglobulin	Immunoglobulin refers to a globular plasma protein that functions as an antibody.
Light chain	Light chain refers to one of the smaller polypeptides of a multisubunit protein such as myosin or immunoglobulin.
Natural selection	Natural selection is the process by which biological individuals that are endowed with favorable or deleterious traits end up reproducing more or less than other individuals that do not possess such traits.
Mutation	Mutation refers to a change in the nucleotide sequence of DNA; the ultimate source of genetic diversity.
Drosophila	Drosophila is part of the phylum Arthropoda, a phylum of segmented animals with paired, jointed appendages and a hard exoskeleton made of chitin. They have an open circulatory system with a dorsal heart, with hemocoel occupying most of the body cavity, and a reduced coelom.
Yeast	Yeast refers to common term for several families of unicellular fungi. Includes species used for brewing beer and making bread, as well as pathogenic species.
Serine protease	Type of protease that has a reactive serine in the active center of the enzyme is called serine protease.
Chymotrypsin	Chymotrypsin is a digestive enzyme that can perform proteolysis. It facilitates the cleavage of peptide bonds by a hydrolysis reaction, a process which albeit thermodynamically favorable, occurs extremely slowly in the absence of a catalyst.
Active site	The active site of an enzyme is the binding site where catalysis occurs. The structure and chemical properties of the active site allow the recognition and binding of the substrate.
Hydrolysis	Hydrolysis is a chemical process in which a molecule is cleaved into two parts by the addition of a molecule of water.
Substrate	A substrate is a molecule which is acted upon by an enzyme. Each enzyme recognizes only the

specific substrate of the reaction it catalyzes. A surface in or on which an organism lives.

Serine	Serine, organic compound, one of the 20 amino acids commonly found in animal proteins. Only the L-stereoisomer appears in mammalian protein. It is not essential to the human diet, since it can be synthesized in the body from other metabolites, including glycine.
Protein subunit	A protein subunit is a single protein molecule that assembles (or "coassembles") with other protein molecules to form a multimeric or oligomeric protein. Many naturally-occurring proteins and enzymes are multimeric.
Dimer	A dimer refers to a molecule composed of two similar subunits or monomers linked together. It is a special case of a polymer.
Neuraminidase	Neuraminidase is an antigenic glycoprotein enzyme found on the surface of the Influenza virus.
Tetramer	A tetramer is a protein with four subunits. There are homo-tetramers (all subunits are identical) such as glutathione S-transferase, dimers of hetero-dimers such as haemoglobin (a dimer of an alpha/beta dimer), and hetero-tetramers, where each subunit is different.
Helical	A helix is a twisted shape like a spring, screw or a spiral staircase. Helices are important in biology, as DNA is helical and many proteins have helical substructures, known as alpha helices.
Hemoglobin	Hemoglobin is the iron-containing oxygen-transport metalloprotein in the red cells of the blood in mammals and other animals. Hemoglobin transports oxygen from the lungs to the rest of the body, such as to the muscles, where it releases the oxygen load.
Oxygen	Oxygen is a chemical element in the periodic table. It has the symbol O and atomic number 8. Oxygen is the second most common element on Earth, composing around 46% of the mass of Earth's crust and 28% of the mass of Earth as a whole, and is the third most common element in the universe.
Globular protein	Globular protein refers to any protein with an approximately rounded shape. Such proteins are contrasted with highly elongated, fibrous proteins such as collagen.
Keratin	Keratin is a family of fibrous structural proteins; tough and insoluble, they form the hard but nonmineralized structures found in reptiles, birds and mammals.
Collagen	Collagen is the main protein of connective tissue in animals and the most abundant protein in mammals, making up about 1/4 of the total. It is one of the long, fibrous structural proteins whose functions are quite different from those of globular proteins such as enzymes.
Capsid	Capsid refers to protein coat of a virus, formed by the self-assembly of one or more protein subunits into a geometrically regular structure.
Viral	Viral phenomena are objects or patterns able to replicate themselves or convert other objects into copies of themselves when these objects are exposed to them.
Virus	Obligate intracellular parasite of living cells consisting of an outer capsid and an inner core of nucleic acid is referred to as virus. The term virus usually refers to those particles that infect eukaryotes whilst the term bacteriophage or phage is used to describe those infecting prokaryotes.
Elastin	Elastin, is a protein in connective tissue that is elastic and allows many tissues in the body to resume their shape after stretching or contracting. Elastin helps skin to return to its original position when it is poked or pinched.
Lungs	Lungs are the essential organs of respiration in air-breathing vertebrates. Their principal function is to transport oxygen from the atmosphere into the bloodstream, and to excrete carbon dioxide from the bloodstream into the atmosphere.

Go to **Cram101.com** for the Practice Tests for this Chapter.

Skin	Skin is an organ of the integumentary system composed of a layer of tissues that protect underlying muscles and organs.
Extracellular matrix	Extracellular matrix is any material part of a tissue that is not part of any cell. Extracellular matrix is the defining feature of connective tissue.
Collagen fibril	Collagen fibril refers to extracellular structure formed by self-assembly of secreted fibrillar collagen subunits. An abundant constituent of the extracellular matrix in many animal tissues.
Reducing agent	A substance that can donate electrons to another substance. The reducing agent becomes oxidized, and its partner becomes reduced.
Disulfide bond	A disulfide bond (SS-bond), also called a disulfide bridge, is a strong covalent bond between two sulfhydryl (-SH) groups. This bond is very important to the folding, structure, and function of proteins.
Cysteine	Cysteine is a naturally occurring hydrophobic amino acid which has a thiol group and is found in most proteins, though only in small quantities.
Chemical group	A set of covalently linked atoms, such as a hydroxyl group or an amino group, the chemical behavior of which is well characterized is referred to as a chemical group.
Hexokinase	A hexokinase is an enzyme that phosphorylates a six-carbon sugar, a hexose, to a hexose phosphate. In most tissues and organisms, glucose is the most important substrate of hexokinases, and glucose 6-phosphate the most important product.
Glucose	Glucose, a simple monosaccharide sugar, is one of the most important carbohydrates and is used as a source of energy in animals and plants. Glucose is one of the main products of photosynthesis and starts respiration.
Versatile	The anther can be attached to the filament in two ways, versatile is when it is attached at its center to the filament; pollen is then released through pores (poricidal dehiscence).
Microorganism	A microorganism is an organism that is so small that it is microscopic (invisible to the naked eye). They are often illustrated using single-celled, or unicellular organisms; however, some unicellular protists are visible to the naked eye, and some multicellular species are microscopic.
Antigen-binding site	Antigen-binding site refers to a region of the antibody molecule responsible for its recognition and binding function.
Protein domain	Protein domain refers to portion of a protein that has a tertiary structure of its own. Larger proteins are generally composed of several domains, each connected to the next by short flexible regions of polypeptide chain.
Single bond	The most common type of covalent bond is the single bond, sharing only one pair of electrons between two atoms. It usually consists of one sigma bond.
Isomer	An isomer is a molecule with the same chemical formula and often with the same kinds of bonds between atoms, but in which the atoms are arranged differently. That is to say, they have different structural formula.
Bacterium	Most bacterium are microscopic and unicellular, with a relatively simple cell structure lacking a cell nucleus, and organelles such as mitochondria and chloroplasts. They are the most abundant of all organisms. They are ubiquitous in soil, water, and as symbionts of other organisms.
Antigen	An antigen is a substance that stimulates an immune response, especially the production of antibodies. They are usually proteins or polysaccharides, but can be any type of molecule, including small molecules (haptens) coupled to a protein (carrier).

Go to **Cram101.com** for the Practice Tests for this Chapter.

Heavy chain	The larger of the two types of polypeptide in an immunoglobulin molecule is referred to as heavy chain.
Polysaccharide	Polymer made from sugar monomers is a polysaccharide. They are relatively complex carbohydrates.
Cell wall	Cell wall refers to a protective layer external to the plasma membrane in plant cells, bacteria, fungi, and some protists; protects the cell and helps maintain its shape.
Activation energy	The activation energy is the threshold energy, or the energy that must be overcome in order for a chemical reaction to occur. Activation energy may otherwise be denoted as the minimum energy necessary for a specific chemical reaction to occur.
Catalysis	Catalysis is the acceleration of the reaction rate of a chemical reaction by means of a substance, called a catalyst, that is itself not consumed by the overall reaction.
Sugar	A sugar is the simplest molecule that can be identified as a carbohydrate. These include monosaccharides and disaccharides, trisaccharides and the oligosaccharides. The term "glyco-" indicates the presence of a sugar in an otherwise non-carbohydrate substance.
Enzyme-substrate complex	A temporary molecule formed when an enzyme attaches itself to a substrate molecule is an enzyme-substrate complex.
Nucleic acid	A nucleic acid is a complex, high-molecular-weight biochemical macromolecule composed of nucleotide chains that convey genetic information. The most common are deoxyribonucleic acid (DNA) and ribonucleic acid (RNA). They are found in all living cells and viruses.
Nucleotide	A nucleotide is a chemical compound that consists of a heterocyclic base, a sugar, and one or more phosphate groups. In the most common nucleotides the base is a derivative of purine or pyrimidine, and the sugar is pentose - deoxyribose or ribose. They are the structural units of RNA and DNA.
Rearrangement	A change in the usual order and arrangement of genetic material either within the chromosome complement or within a gene locus is rearrangement. Where the nature of the rearrangement has been determined, the type may be searched for directly under the following designations: reciprocal translocation, Robertsonian translocation, insertion, transposition, inversion, deletion, and duplication.
Phosphate group	The functional group $-OPO_3H_2$; the transfer of energy from one compound to another is often accomplished by the transfer of a phosphate group.
Polymerization	Polymerization is a process of reacting monomer molecules together in a chemical reaction to form linear chains or a three-dimensional network of polymer chains.
Protein kinase	Enzyme that transfers the terminal phosphate group of ATP to a specific amino acid of a target protein is protein kinase.
Membrane transport protein	Membrane transport protein refers to membrane protein that mediates the passage of ions or molecules across a membrane. Examples are ion channels and carrier proteins.
Potassium	Potassium is a chemical element in the periodic table. It has the symbol K (L. kalium) and atomic number 19. Potassium is a soft silvery-white metallic alkali metal that occurs naturally bound to other elements in seawater and many minerals.
Sodium	Sodium is the chemical element in the periodic table that has the symbol Na (Natrium in Latin) and atomic number 11. Sodium is a soft, waxy, silvery reactive metal belonging to the alkali metals that is abundant in natural compounds (especially halite). It is highly reactive.

Myosin	Myosin is a large family of motor proteins found in eukaryotic tissues. They are responsible for actin-based motility.
ATPase	ATPase is a class of enzymes that catalyze the decomposition of adenosine triphosphate into adenosine diphosphate and a free phosphate ion. This dephosphorylation reaction releases energy, which the enzyme harnesses to drive other chemical reactions that would not otherwise occur. This process is widely used in all known forms of life.
Thrombin	Thrombin refers to an enzyme that converts fibrinogen to fibrin threads during blood clotting.
Pepsin	Pepsin is a digestive protease released by the chief cells in the stomach that functions to degrade food proteins into peptides. It was the first animal enzyme to be discovered.
Aspartic Acid	Aspartic acid is one of the 20 natural proteinogenic amino acids which are the building blocks of proteins. As its name indicates, it is the carboxylic acid analog of asparagine. It is non-essential in mammals, and might serve as an excitatory neurotransmitter in the brain.
Glutamic acid	Glutamic acid is one of the 20 standard amino acids used by all organisms in their proteins. It is critical for proper cell function, but it is not an essential nutrient in humans because glutamic acid can be manufactured from other compounds.
Transition state	The transition state of a chemical reaction is a particular configuration along the reaction coordinate. It is defined as the state corresponding to the highest energy along this reaction coordinate. At this point, assuming a perfectly irreversible reaction, colliding reactant molecules will always go on to form products.
Chemical bond	Chemical bond refers to an attraction between two atoms resulting from a sharing of outer-shell electrons or the presence of opposite charges on the atoms. The bonded atoms gain complete outer electron shells.
Sugar bond	The sugar bond is formed between the side chain of an amino acid having an OH group and an acidic amino group.
Reactant	A reactant is any substance initially present in a chemical reaction. These reactants react with each other to form the products of a chemical reaction. In a chemical equation, the reactants are the elements or compounds on the left hand side of the reaction equation.
Oligosaccharide	An oligosaccharide is a saccharide polymer containing a small number (typically three to six) of component sugars, also known as simple sugars. They are generally found either O- or N-linked to compatible amino acid side chains in proteins or to lipid moieties.
Disaccharide	A disaccharide is a sugar (a carbohydrate) composed of two monosaccharides. The two monosaccharides are bonded via a condensation reaction.
Proton	Positive subatomic particle, located in the nucleus and having a weight of approximately one atomic mass unit is referred to as a proton.
Retinal	Retinal is fundamental in the transduction of light into visual signals in the photoreceptor level of the retina.
Heme	A or heme is a metal-containing cofactor that consists of an iron atom contained in the center of a large heterocyclic organic ring called a porphyrin. Although porphyrins do not necessarily contain iron, a substantial fraction of porphyrin-containing metalloproteins do in fact have heme as their prosthetic subunit. It is made a matter of common knowledge, because of its vitality as a part of hemoglobin, vital in the human body's red blood cells.
Rhodopsin	Rhodopsin is expressed in vertebrate photoreceptor cells. It is a pigment of the retina that is responsible for both the formation of the photoreceptor cells and the first events in the perception of light. Rhodopsins belong to the class of G-protein coupled receptors. It is the

Go to **Cram101.com** for the Practice Tests for this Chapter.

chemical that allows night-vision, and is extremely sensitive to light.

Eye	An eye is an organ that detects light. Different kinds of light-sensitive organs are found in a variety of creatures.
Iron	Iron is essential to all organisms, except for a few bacteria. It is mostly stably incorporated in the inside of metalloproteins, because in exposed or in free form it causes production of free radicals that are generally toxic to cells.
Rod cell	Rod cell refers to photoreceptor cells in the retina of the eye that can function in less intense light than can the other type of photoreceptor, cone cells. Since they are more light-sensitive, they are responsible for night vision. There are about 100 million of them in the human retina.
Pigment	Pigment is any material resulting in color in plant or animal cells which is the result of selective absorption.
Retina	The retina is a thin layer of cells at the back of the eyeball of vertebrates and some cephalopods; it is the part of the eye which converts light into nervous signals.
Carboxypeptidase	An enzyme found within the small intestine that splits off one amino acid at a time, beginning at the end of the polypeptide that has a free carboxyl group is called carboxypeptidase.
Zinc	Zinc is a chemical element in the periodic table that has the symbol Zn and atomic number 30.
Hydrolysis reaction	Hydrolysis is a chemical process in which a molecule is cleaved into two parts by the addition of a molecule of water. This is distinct from a hydrolysis reaction, in which water molecules are added to a substance, but no cleavage occurs.
Biotin	Biotin is a low-molecular-weight compound used as a coenzyme. Useful technically as a covalent label for proteins, allowing them to be detected by the egg protein avidin, which binds extremely tightly to biotin.
Vitamin	A Vitamin is an organic molecule required by a living organism in minute amounts for proper health. An organism deprived of all sources of a particular vitamin will eventually suffer from disease symptoms specific to that vitamin.
Enzyme activity	Enzyme activity is the catalytic effect exerted by an enzyme.
Regulatory site	Regulatory site refers to site on an enzyme, other than the active site, that binds a molecule that affects enzyme activity.
Feedback inhibition	A post-translational control mechanism in which the end product of a biochemical pathway inhibits the activity of the first enzyme of this pathway is referred to as feedback inhibition.
Negative regulation	Process resulting in the transcription of a specific gene or operon normally being repressed is negative regulation.
Positive regulation	Process resulting in a specific gene or operon being transcribed, usually as the result of interaction of proteins with DNA is called positive regulation.
Inhibitor	An inhibitor is a type of effector (biology) that decreases or prevents the rate of a chemical reaction. They are often called negative catalysts.
Phosphorylation	Phosphorylation refers to reaction in which a phosphate group becomes covalently coupled to another molecule.
Population	Group of organisms of the same species occupying a certain area and sharing a common gene pool is referred to as population.

Go to **Cram101.com** for the Practice Tests for this Chapter.

Allosteric regulation	Allosteric regulation refers to the process by which enzyme action is enhanced or inhibited by small organic molecules that act as regulators by binding to the enzyme and altering its active site.
Cytosine	Cytosine is one of the 5 main nucleobases used in storing and transporting genetic information within a cell in the nucleic acids DNA and RNA. It is a pyrimidine derivative, with a heterocyclic aromatic ring and two substituents attached. The nucleoside of cytosine is cytidine.
Glycolysis	Glycolysis refers to the multistep chemical breakdown of a molecule of glucose into two molecules of pyruvic acid; the first stage of cellular respiration in all organisms; occurs in the cytoplasmic fluid.
Catabolism	Catabolism is the part of metabolism that partitions molecules into smaller units. It is made up of degradative chemical reactions in the living cell. Large polymeric molecules are processed into their constituent monomeric units.
Positive feedback	Mechanism of homeostatic response in which the output intensifies and increases the likelihood of response, instead of countering it and canceling it is called positive feedback.
Protein phosphatase	Protein phosphatase refers to an enzyme that removes phosphate groups from proteins, often functioning to reverse the effect of a protein kinase.
Phosphatase	A phosphatase is an enzyme that hydrolyses phosphoric acid monoesters into a phosphate ion and a molecule with a free hydroxyl group.
Stimulus	Stimulus in a nervous system, a factor that triggers sensory transduction.
Guanosine triphosphate	Guanosine triphosphate is also known as guanosine-5'-triphosphate. It is a purine nucleotide that is incorporated into the growing RNA chain during RNA synthesis, and used as a source of energy for protein synthesis.
Guanine	Guanine is one of the five main nucleobases found in nucleic acids. Guanine is a purine derivative, and in Watson-Crick base pairing forms three hydrogen bonds with cytosine. Guanine "stacks" vertically with the other nucleobases via aromatic interactions.
Chromosome	A chromosome is, minimally, a very long, continuous piece of DNA, which contains many genes, regulatory elements and other intervening nucleotide sequences.
Protein synthesis	The process whereby the tRNA utilizes the mRNA as a guide to arrange the amino acids in their proper sequence according to the genetic information in the chemical code of DNA is referred to as protein synthesis.
Elongation	Elongation refers to a phase of DNA replication, transcription, or translation that successively adds nucleotides or amino acids to a growing macromolecule.
Hydrogen atom	A hydrogen atom is an atom of the element hydrogen. It is composed of a single negatively-charged electron, attending a positively-charged proton which is the nucleus of the hydrogen atom. The electron is bound to the proton by the Coulomb force.
Phosphate	A phosphate is a polyatomic ion or radical consisting of one phosphorus atom and four oxygen. In the ionic form, it carries a -3 formal charge, and is denoted PO_4^{3-}.
DNA replication	DNA replication is the process of copying a double-stranded DNA strand in a cell, prior to cell division. The two resulting double strands are identical (if the replication went well), and each of them consists of one original and one newly synthesized strand.
Budding	A means of asexual reproduction whereby a new individual developed from an outgrowth of a parent splits off and lives independently is referred to as budding.

Go to **Cram101.com** for the Practice Tests for this Chapter.

Vesicle	In cell biology, a vesicle is a relatively small and enclosed compartment, separated from the cytosol by at least one lipid bilayer.
Nucleoside	Molecule composed of a purine or pyrimidine base covalently linked to a ribose or deoxyribose sugar is a nucleoside.
Lock-and-key	The lock-and-key structure in biochemistry is a theory on why enzymes catalyse reactions. This theory states that all enzymes and substrates have specified structures and chemical properties. The substrate fits into the enzyme's active site, and they react. The substrate is broken down, and then the enzyme can act on the next substrate.
Carbon dioxide	Carbon dioxide is an atmospheric gas comprized of one carbon and two oxygen atoms. A very widely known chemical compound, it is frequently called by its formula CO_2. In its solid state, it is commonly known as dry ice.
Ethanol	Ethanol is a flammable, colorless chemical compound, one of the alcohols that is most often found in alcoholic beverages. In common parlance, it is often referred to simply as alcohol. Its chemical formula is C_2H_5OH, also written as C_2H_6O.
Sucrose	A disaccharide composed of glucose and fructose is called sucrose.
Molecular weight	The molecular mass of a substance, called molecular weight and abbreviated as MW, is the mass of one molecule of that substance, relative to the unified atomic mass unit u (equal to 1/12 the mass of one atom of carbon-12).
Ultracentrifuge	Ultracentrifuge refers to a machine that spins test tubes at the fastest speeds to separate liquids and particles of different densities.
Svedberg	Svedberg refers to the unit used in expressing the sedimentation coefficient; the greater a particle's Svedberg value, the faster it travels in a centrifuge.
Chromatography	Biochemical technique in which a mixture of substances is separated by charge, size, or some other property by allowing it to partition between a mobile phase and a stationary phase is called chromatography.
Sperm Whale	The Sperm Whale (Physeter macrocephalus) is the largest of all toothed whales and is believed to be the largest toothed animal to ever inhabit Earth.
Myoglobin	Myoglobin is a single-chain protein of 153 amino acids, containing a heme (iron-containing porphyrin) group in the center. With a molecular weight of 16,700 Daltons, it is the primary oxygen-carrying pigment of muscle tissues.
Diffraction	Diffraction is the bending and spreading of waves when they meet an obstruction. It can occur with any type of wave, including sound waves, water waves, and electromagnetic waves such as light and radio waves.
Clone	A group of genetically identical cells or organisms derived by asexual reproduction from a single parent is called a clone.
Allosteric protein	Allosteric protein refers to protein that changes from one conformation to another when it binds another molecule or when it is covalently modified.
Metabolic pathway	A metabolic pathway is a series of chemical reactions occurring within a cell, catalyzed by enzymes, to achieve in either the formation of a metabolic product to be used or stored by the cell, or the initiation of another metabolic pathway.
Metabolite	The term metabolite is usually restricted to small molecules. They are the intermediates and products of metabolism. A primary metabolite is directly involved in the normal growth, development, and reproduction. A secondary metabolite is not directly involved in those processes, but usually has important ecological function.

Organelle	In cell biology, an organelle is one of several structures with specialized functions, suspended in the cytoplasm of a eukaryotic cell.
Centrifuge	Centrifuge refers to a device in which a sample can be spun around a central axis at high speed, creating a centrifugal force that mimics a very strong gravitational force. Used to separate mixtures of suspended materials.
Sediment	Sediment is any particulate matter that can be transported by fluid flow and which eventually is deposited as a layer of solid particles on the bed or bottom of a body of water or other liquid.
Gradient	Gradient refers to a difference in concentration, pressure, or electrical charge between two regions.
Salt	Salt is a term used for ionic compounds composed of positively charged cations and negatively charged anions, so that the product is neutral and without a net charge.
Cellular component	The cellular component involves the movement of white blood cells from blood vessels into the inflamed tissue. The white blood cells, or leukocytes, take on an important role in inflammation; they extravasate (filter out) from the capillaries into tissue, and act as phagocytes, picking up bacteria and cellular debris. They may also aid by walling off an infection and preventing its spread.
Gel electrophoresis	Gel electrophoresis is a group of techniques used by scientists to separate molecules based on physical characteristics such as size, shape, or isoelectric point.
Isoelectric point	The isoelectric point is the pH at which a molecule carries no net electrical charge. In order to have a sharp isoelectric point, a molecule must be amphoteric, meaning it must have both acidic and basic functional groups. Proteins and amino acids are common molecules that meet this requirement.
Buffer	A chemical substance that resists changes in pH by accepting H^+ ions from or donating H^+ ions to solutions is called a buffer.
Specificity	A medical diagnostic test for a certain disease, specificity is the proportion of true negatives of all the negative samples tested.
B cell	A B cell is a lymphocyte that is produced in bone marrow and plays a large role in the humoral immune response.
Vertebrate	Vertebrate is a subphylum of chordates, specifically, those with backbones or spinal columns. They started to evolve about 530 million years ago during the Cambrian explosion, which is part of the Cambrian period.
Monoclonal antibodies	Monoclonal antibodies are antibodies that are identical because they were produced by one type of immune cell, all clones of a single parent cell.
Tumor	An abnormal mass of cells that forms within otherwise normal tissue is a tumor. This growth can be either malignant or benign
Hybrid	Hybrid refers to the offspring of parents of two different species or of two different varieties of one species; the offspring of two parents that differ in one or more inherited traits; an individual that is heterozygous for one or more pair of genes.
Plant cell	A cell that is a structural and functional unit of a plant is a plant cell.
Light microscope	An optical instrument with lenses that refract visible light to magnify images and project them into a viewer's eye or onto photographic film is referred to as light microscope.
Fluorescence	Fluorescence is a luminescence that is mostly found as an optical phenomenon in cold bodies, in which the molecular absorption of a photon triggers the emission of a lower-energy photon

Go to **Cram101.com** for the Practice Tests for this Chapter.

with a longer wavelength. The energy difference between the absorbed and emitted photons ends up as molecular vibrations or heat.

Mutant

A mutant (also known to early geneticists as a "monster") is an individual, organism, or new genetic character arising or resulting from an instance of mutation, which is a sudden structural change within the DNA of a gene or chromosome of an organism resulting in the creation of a new character or trait not found in the parental type.

Chromosome	A chromosome is, minimally, a very long, continuous piece of DNA, which contains many genes, regulatory elements and other intervening nucleotide sequences.
Cell	The cell is the structural and functional unit of all living organisms, and is sometimes called the "building block of life."
Genetics	Genetics is the science of genes, heredity, and the variation of organisms.
Gene	Gene refers to a discrete unit of hereditary information consisting of a specific nucleotide sequence in DNA . Most of the genes of a eukaryote are located in its chromosomal DNA; a few are carried by the DNA of mitochondria and chloroplasts.
Daughter cell	A cell formed by cell division of a parent cell is a daughter cell.
Multicellular	Multicellular organisms are those organisms consisting of more than one cell, and having differentiated cells that perform specialized functions. Most life that can be seen with the naked eye is multicellular, as are all animals (i.e. members of the kingdom Animalia) and plants (i.e. members of the kingdom Plantae).
Protein	A protein is a complex, high-molecular-weight organic compound that consists of amino acids joined by peptide bonds. They are essential to the structure and function of all living cells and viruses. Many are enzymes or subunits of enzymes.
Chemical reaction	Chemical reaction refers to a process leading to chemical changes in matter; involves the making and/or breaking of chemical bonds.
Gene expression	Gene expression is the process by which a gene's information is converted into the structures and functions of a cell. Gene expression is a multi-step process that begins with transcription, post transcriptional modification and translation, followed by folding, post-translational modification and targeting.
Macromolecule	A macromolecule is a molecule of high relative molecular mass, the structure of which essentially comprises the multiple repetition of units derived, actually or conceptually, from molecules of low relative molecular mass.
Nucleotide	A nucleotide is a chemical compound that consists of a heterocyclic base, a sugar, and one or more phosphate groups. In the most common nucleotides the base is a derivative of purine or pyrimidine, and the sugar is pentose - deoxyribose or ribose. They are the structural units of RNA and DNA.
Molecule	A molecule is the smallest particle of a pure chemical substance that still retains its chemical composition and properties.
Heredity	The transmission of characteristics from parent to offspring is heredity.
Enzyme	An enzyme is a protein that catalyzes, or speeds up, a chemical reaction. They are essential to sustain life because most chemical reactions in biological cells would occur too slowly, or would lead to different products, without them.
Deoxyribonuc-eic acid	Deoxyribonucleic acid is a nucleic acid that contains the genetic instructions specifying the biological development of all cellular forms of life. It is a long polymer of nucleotides and encodes the sequence of the amino acid residues in proteins using the genetic code, a triplet code of nucleotides.
Light microscope	An optical instrument with lenses that refract visible light to magnify images and project them into a viewer's eye or onto photographic film is referred to as light microscope.
Plant cell	A cell that is a structural and functional unit of a plant is a plant cell.
Conformation	The three-dimensional shape of a molecule is its conformation. The conformation is particularly important in proteins.

Polymer	Polymer is a generic term used to describe a very long molecule consisting of structural units and repeating units connected by covalent chemical bonds.
Diffraction	Diffraction is the bending and spreading of waves when they meet an obstruction. It can occur with any type of wave, including sound waves, water waves, and electromagnetic waves such as light and radio waves.
Helix	A helix is a twisted shape like a spring, screw or a spiral staircase. They are important in biology, as DNA and many proteins have spiral substructures, known a alpha helix.
X-Ray	X-Ray refers to diagnostic test in which an image is created using low doses of radiation.
Phosphate group	The functional group $-OPO_3H_2$; the transfer of energy from one compound to another is often accomplished by the transfer of a phosphate group.
Sugar	A sugar is the simplest molecule that can be identified as a carbohydrate. These include monosaccharides and disaccharides, trisaccharides and the oligosaccharides. The term "glyco-" indicates the presence of a sugar in an otherwise non-carbohydrate substance.
Polynucleotide	Polynucleotide refers to a polymer consisting of many nucleotide monomers; serves as a blueprint for proteins and, through the actions of proteins, for all cellular activities. The two types are DNA and RNA.
Phosphate	A phosphate is a polyatomic ion or radical consisting of one phosphorus atom and four oxygen. In the ionic form, it carries a -3 formal charge, and is denoted PO_4^{3-}.
Cytosine	Cytosine is one of the 5 main nucleobases used in storing and transporting genetic information within a cell in the nucleic acids DNA and RNA. It is a pyrimidine derivative, with a heterocyclic aromatic ring and two substituents attached. The nucleoside of cytosine is cytidine.
Adenine	Adenine is one of the two purine nucleobases used in forming nucleotides of the nucleic acids DNA and RNA. In DNA, adenine (A) binds to thymine (T) via two hydrogen bonds to assist in stabilizing the nucleic acid structures. In RNA, adenine binds to uracil (U).
Guanine	Guanine is one of the five main nucleobases found in nucleic acids. Guanine is a purine derivative, and in Watson-Crick base pairing forms three hydrogen bonds with cytosine. Guanine "stacks" vertically with the other nucleobases via aromatic interactions.
Thymine	Thymine, also known as 5-methyluracil, is a pyrimidine nucleobase. It is found in the nucleic acid DNA. In RNA thymine is replaced with uracil in most cases. In DNA, thymine(T) binds to adenine (A) via two hydrogen bonds to assist in stabilizing the nucleic acid structures.
Polarity	In cell biology, polarity refers to cells not being point-symmetrical in their spatial organization. In horticulture, polarity refers to the condition in which cuttings grow shoots at the distil end and roots at the proximal end.
Hydrogen bond	A hydrogen bond is a type of attractive intermolecular force that exists between two partial electric charges of opposite polarity. Although stronger than most other intermolecular forces, the typical hydrogen bond is much weaker than both the ionic bond and the covalent bond.
Antiparallel	Antiparallel refers to describes the relative orientation of the two strands in a DNA double helix; the polarity of one strand is oriented in the opposite direction to that of the other.
Antibiotic	Antibiotic refers to substance such as penicillin or streptomycin that is toxic to microorganisms. Usually a product of a particular microorvanism or plant.
Immune system	The immune system is the system of specialized cells and organs that protect an organism from outside biological influences. When the immune system is functioning properly, it protects the body against bacteria and viral infections, destroying cancer cells and foreign

substances.

Bacteria	The domain that contains procaryotic cells with primarily diacyl glycerol diesters in their membranes and with bacterial rRNA. Bacteria also is a general term for organisms that are composed of procaryotic cells and are not multicellular.
Transforming principle	Griffith's experiment was conducted in 1928 by Frederick Griffith which was one of the first experiments suggesting that bacteria are capable of transferring genetic information, otherwise known as the transforming principle, which was later discovered to be DNA.
Heritable	Heritable refers to able to be inherited; in biology usually refers to genetically determined traits.
Climate	Weather condition of an area including especially prevailing temperature and average daily/yearly rainfall over a long period of time is called climate.
Transformation	Transformation is the genetic alteration of a cell resulting from the introduction, uptake and expression of foreign genetic material (DNA or RNA).
Mutagen	A chemical or physical agent that interacts with DNA and causes a mutation is referred to as mutagen.
Bacterium	Most bacterium are microscopic and unicellular, with a relatively simple cell structure lacking a cell nucleus, and organelles such as mitochondria and chloroplasts. They are the most abundant of all organisms. They are ubiquitous in soil, water, and as symbionts of other organisms.
Virus	Obligate intracellular parasite of living cells consisting of an outer capsid and an inner core of nucleic acid is referred to as virus. The term virus usually refers to those particles that infect eukaryotes whilst the term bacteriophage or phage is used to describe those infecting prokaryotes.
Streptococcus	Streptococcus is a genus of spherical, Gram-positive bacteria of the phylum Firmicutes. These bacteria grow in chains or pairs, with cell division occurring only along one axis.
Polysaccharide	Polymer made from sugar monomers is a polysaccharide. They are relatively complex carbohydrates.
Capsule	A sticky layer that surrounds the bacterial cell wall, protects the cell surface, and sometimes helps glue the cell to surfaces is called the capsule. In botany, a capsule is a type of dry fruit as in the poppy, iris, foxglove, etc. as well as another term for the sporangium of mosses and hornworts.
Viral	Viral phenomena are objects or patterns able to replicate themselves or convert other objects into copies of themselves when these objects are exposed to them.
Radioactive	A term used to describe the property of releasing energy or particles from an unstable atom is called radioactive.
Centrifuge	Centrifuge refers to a device in which a sample can be spun around a central axis at high speed, creating a centrifugal force that mimics a very strong gravitational force. Used to separate mixtures of suspended materials.
Host	Host is an organism that harbors a parasite, mutual partner, or commensal partner; or a cell infected by a virus.
Phosphorus	Phosphorus is the chemical element in the periodic table that has the symbol P and atomic number 15.
Isotope	An isotope is a form of an element whose nuclei have the same atomic number - the number of protons in the nucleus - but different mass numbers because they contain different numbers of

	neutrons.
Sulfur	Sulfur is the chemical element in the periodic table that has the symbol S and atomic number 16. It is an abundant, tasteless, odorless, multivalent non-metal. Sulfur, in its native form, is a yellow crystaline solid. In nature, it can be found as the pure element or as sulfide and sulfate minerals.
Complementary base pair	A pair of bases in which the identity of one base defines the identity of its partner base is a complementary base pair. In DNA, adenine is complementary to thymine and guanine is complementary to cytosine; in RNA, adenine is complementary to uracil, and guanine to cytosine.
Double helix	Double helix refers to the form of native DNA, referring to its two adjacent polynucleotide strands wound into a spiral shape.
Base pair	Two nucleotides on opposite complementary DNA or RNA strands that are connected via hydrogen bonds are called a base pair.
Phosphodiester bond	A phosphodiester bond is a group of strong covalent bonds between the phosphorus atom in a phosphate group and two other molecules over two ester bonds. Phosphodiester bonds are central to all life on Earth, as they make up the backbone of the strands of DNA.
Biology	Biology is the branch of science dealing with the study of life. It is concerned with the characteristics, classification, and behaviors of organisms, how species come into existence, and the interactions they have with each other and with the environment.
Amino acid	An amino acid is any molecule that contains both amino and carboxylic acid functional groups. They are the basic structural building units of proteins. They form short polymer chains called peptides or polypeptides which in turn form structures called proteins.
Minor groove	Minor groove refers to area in double-stranded DNA between the antiparallel sugar phosphate backbones, which includes the hydrogen-bonded nucleotide bases.
Genetic code	The genetic code is a set of rules that maps DNA sequences to proteins in the living cell, and is employed in the process of protein synthesis. Nearly all living things use the same genetic code, called the standard genetic code, although a few organisms use minor variations of the standard code.
Major groove	Area of open space present in turns of the alpha-helix in the common staircase model of double-stranded DNA is the major groove.
Amino group	An amino group is an ammonia-like functional group composed of a nitrogen and two hydrogen atoms covalently linked. $-NH_2$
Hydrophilic	A hydrophilic molecule or portion of a molecule is one that is typically charge-polarized and capable of hydrogen bonding, enabling it to dissolve more readily in water than in oil or other hydrophobic solvents.
Complementary sequence	Complementary sequence refers to a nucleic acid base sequence that can form a doublestranded structure by matching base pairs with another sequence; the complementary sequence to 5' GTAC 3' is 3' CATG 5'.
Hemoglobin	Hemoglobin is the iron-containing oxygen-transport metalloprotein in the red cells of the blood in mammals and other animals. Hemoglobin transports oxygen from the lungs to the rest of the body, such as to the muscles, where it releases the oxygen load.
DNA sequence	A DNA sequence is a succession of letters representing the primary structure of a real or hypothetical DNA molecule or strand, The possible letters are A, C, G, and T, representing the four nucleotide subunits of a DNA strand (adenine, cytosine, guanine, thymine).
Human genome	The human genome is the genome of Homo sapiens. It is made up of 23 chromosome pairs with a

Go to **Cram101.com** for the Practice Tests for this Chapter.

total of about 3 billion DNA base pairs.

Genome	The genome of an organism is the whole hereditary information of an organism that is encoded in the DNA (or, for some viruses, RNA). This includes both the genes and the non-coding sequences. The genome of an organism is a complete DNA sequence of one set of chromosomes.
Cell nucleus	The cell nucleus is found in all eukaryotic cells that contains most of the cell's genetic material. They have two primary functions: to control chemical reactions within the cytoplasm and to store information needed for cellular division.
Cell division	Cell division is the process by which a cell (called the parent cell) divides into two cells (called daughter cells). Cell division is usually a small segment of a larger cell cycle. In meiosis, however, a cell is permanently transformed and cannot divide again.
Nucleus	In cell biology, the nucleus is found in all eukaryotic cells that contains most of the cell's genetic material. The nucleus has two primary functions: to control chemical reactions within the cytoplasm and to store information needed for cellular division.
Circular DNA	Circular DNA is found in bacteria and other archaea. While the individual strands of a linear double helix represent two distinct and separable molecules, this need not be true for circular DNA. If the strands twist an odd number of times around one another in completing the DNA loop, then they are covalently joined into a single molecule.
Mitosis	Mitosis is the process by which a cell separates its duplicated genome into two identical halves. It is generally followed immediately by cytokinesis which divides the cytoplasm and cell membrane.
DNA replication	DNA replication is the process of copying a double-stranded DNA strand in a cell, prior to cell division. The two resulting double strands are identical (if the replication went well), and each of them consists of one original and one newly synthesized strand.
DNA repair	Collective name for those biochemical processes that correct accidental changes in the DNA is referred to as dna repair.
Chromatin	Chromatin refers to the combination of DNA and proteins that constitute chromosomes; often used to refer to the diffuse, very extended form taken by the chromosomes when a eukaryotic cell is not dividing.
Staining	Staining is a biochemical technique of adding a class-specific (DNA, proteins, lipids, carbohydrates) dye to a substrate to qualify or quantify the presence of a specific compound. They are frequently used to highlight structures in tissues for viewing, often with the aid of different microscopes.
Homologous chromosome	Homologous chromosome refers to similarly constructed chromosomes with the same shape and that contain genes for the same traits.
Sex chromosome	The X or Y chromosome in human beings that determines the sex of an individual. Females have two X chromosomes in diploid cells; males have an X and aY chromosome. The sex chromosome comprises the 23rd chromosome pair in a karyotype.
X chromosome	The X chromosome is the female sex chromosome that carries genes involved in sex determination. Females have two X chromosomes, while males have one X and one Y chromosome.
Y chromosome	Male sex chromosome that carries genes involved in sex determination is referred to as the Y chromosome. It contains the genes that cause testis development, thus determining maleness.
Germ cell	A germ cell is a kind of cell that is part of the germline, and is involved in the reproduction of organisms. There are different kinds, which include gametogonia, gametocytes, and gametes.
Homologs	Genes or regulatory DNA sequences that are similar in different species because of descent

Go to **Cram101.com** for the Practice Tests for this Chapter.

from a common ancestral sequence are homologs.

Blood	Blood is a circulating tissue composed of fluid plasma and cells. The main function of blood is to supply nutrients (oxygen, glucose) and constitutional elements to tissues and to remove waste products.
Sperm	Sperm refers to the male sex cell with three distinct parts at maturity: head, middle piece, and tail.
Egg	An egg is the zygote, resulting from fertilization of the ovum. It nourishes and protects the embryo.
Karyotype	A karyotype is the complete set of all chromosomes of a cell of any living organism. The chromosomes are arranged and displayed (often on a photo) in a standard format: in pairs, ordered by size.
Cancer	Cancer is a class of diseases or disorders characterized by uncontrolled division of cells and the ability of these cells to invade other tissues, either by direct growth into adjacent tissue through invasion or by implantation into distant sites by metastasis.
Evolution	In biology, evolution is the process by which novel traits arise in populations and are passed on from generation to generation. Its action over large stretches of time explains the origin of new species and ultimately the vast diversity of the biological world.
Species	Group of similarly constructed organisms capable of interbreeding and producing fertile offspring is a species.
Ataxia	Ataxia is unsteady and clumsy motion of the limbs or trunk due to a failure of the gross coordination of muscle movements. Ataxia often occurs when parts of the nervous system that control movement are damaged.
Mammal	Homeothermic vertebrate characterized especially by the presence of hair and mammary glands is a mammal.
Yeast	Yeast refers to common term for several families of unicellular fungi. Includes species used for brewing beer and making bread, as well as pathogenic species.
Amoeba	Amoeba is a genus of protozoa that moves by means of temporary projections called pseudopods, and is well-known as a representative unicellular organism. Amoeba itself is found in freshwater, typically on decaying vegetation from streams, but is not especially common in nature.
Genome size	Genome size refers to the total amount of DNA contained within one copy of a genome. It is typically measured in terms of mass (in picograms, or trillionths [10
Interphase	The period in the eukaryotic cell cycle when the cell is not actually dividing is referred to as interphase. During interphase, the cell obtains nutrients, and duplicates its chromosomes.
Nuclear envelope	The nuclear envelope refers to the double membrane of the nucleus that encloses genetic material in eukaryotic cells. It separates the contents of the nucleus (DNA in particular) from the cytosol.
Segregation	The separation of homologous chromosomes during mitosis and meiosis. Known as Mendel's theory of Segregation.
Cell cycle	An orderly sequence of events that extends from the time a eukaryotic cell divides to form two daughter cells to the time those daughter cells divide again is called cell cycle.
M phase	Mitosis and cytokinesis together is defined as the mitotic M phase of the cell cycle, the division of the mother cell into two daughter cells, each the genetic equivalent of the parent cell.

Go to **Cram101.com** for the Practice Tests for this Chapter.

Mitotic spindle	Mitotic spindle refers to a spindle-shaped structure formed of microtubules and associated proteins that is involved in the movement of chromosomes during mitosis and meiosis.
Microtubule	Microtubule is a protein structure found within cells, one of the components of the cytoskeleton. They have diameter of ~ 24 nm and varying length from several micrometers to possible millimeters in axons of nerve cells. They serve as structural components within cells and are involved in many cellular processes including mitosis, cytokinesis, and vesicular transport.
Centromere	The centromere is a region of a eukaryotic chromosome where the kinetochore is assembled; the site where spindle fibers of the mitotic spindle attach to the chromosome during mitosis. It is also the site of the primary constriction visible in microscopy images of chromosomes. Finally, it is the site at which a chromatid and its identical sister attach together during the process of cell reproduction.
Telomere	A telomere is a region of highly repetitive DNA at the end of a chromosome that functions as a disposable buffer.
Duplicated chromosome	Duplicated chromosome refers to a eukaryotic chromosome following DNA replication; consists of two sister chromatids joined at the centromeres.
Replication origin	Location on a DNA molecule at which DNA replication is initiated is referred to as the replication origin.
Duplication	Duplication refers to repetition of part of a chromosome resulting from fusion with a fragment from a homologous chromosome; can result from an error in meiosis or from mutagenesis.
Nucleolus	The nucleolus is, strictly speaking, a "suborganelle" of the nucleus, which is an organelle. It is roughly spherical-shaped surrounded by a layer of condensed chromatin. No membrane separates the nucleolus from the nucleoplasm.
Micrograph	A micrograph is a photograph or similar image taken through a microscope or similar device to show a magnified image of an item.
Fibroblast	A fibroblast is a cell that makes the structural fibers and ground substance of connective tissue.
Electron	The electron is a light fundamental subatomic particle that carries a negative electric charge. The electron is a spin-1/2 lepton, does not participate in strong interactions and has no substructure.
Nuclear pore	Opening in the nuclear envelope which permits the passage of proteins into the nucleus and ribosomal subunits out of the nucleus is a nuclear pore.
Heterochromatin	Heterochromatin is tightly packed form of DNA. It's major characteristic is that it is not transcribed.
Endoplasmic reticulum	The endoplasmic reticulum is an organelle found in all eukaryotic cells. It modifies proteins, makes macromolecules, and transfers substances throughout the cell.
Inner nuclear membrane	Inner nuclear membrane refers to the innermost of the two nuclear membranes. It contains binding sites for chromatin and the nuclear lamina on its internal face.
Nuclear lamina	Nuclear lamina refers to fibrous meshwork of proteins on the inner surface of the inner nuclear membrane. It is made up of a network of intermediate filaments formed from nuclear lamins.
Filament	The stamen is the male organ of a flower. Each stamen generally has a stalk called the filament, and, on top of the filament, an anther. The filament is a long chain of proteins, such as those found in hair, muscle, or in flagella.

Ribosomal RNA	The most prominent examples of non-coding Ribosomal RNA are non-coding RNA that are involved in the process of translation and gene expression.
Electron microscope	The electron microscope is a microscope that can magnify very small details with high resolving power due to the use of electrons as the source of illumination, magnifying at levels up to 500,000 times.
Nucleosome	Nucleosome refers to the beadlike unit of DNA packing in a eukaryotic cell; consists of DNA wound around a protein core made up of eight histone molecules.
Histone	Histone refers to a small basic protein molecule associated with DNA and important in DNA packing in the eukaryotic chromosome.
Dissociation	Dissociation is a general process in which complexes, molecules, or salts separate or split into smaller molecules, ions, or radicals, usually in a reversible manner.
Nucleosome core particle	A nucleosome core particle is the central part of a nucleosome. It consists of about 147 bp of double stranded DNA and four pairs of histones known as the histone octamer.
Digestion	Digestion refers to the mechanical and chemical breakdown of food into molecules small enough for the body to absorb; the second main stage of food processing, following ingestion.
Nuclease	Enzyme that cleaves phosphodiester bonds in nucleic acids is referred to as nuclease.
Linker DNA	Linker DNA is a synthetic DNA that carries the recognition site for a restriction enzyme and that can bind 2 DNA fragments.
Sugar-phosphate backbone	Sugar-phosphate backbone refers to the alternating chain of sugar and phosphate to which DNA and RNA nitrogenous bases are attached.
Core histones	Proteins that form the core of the nucleosome: H2A, H2B, H3, and H4 are referred to as core histones.
Arginine	Arginine is an α-amino acid. The L-form is one of the 20 most common natural amino acids. In mammals, arginine is classified as a semiessential or conditionally essential amino acid, depending on the developmental stage and health status of the individual.
Lysine	Lysine is one of the 20 amino acids normally found in proteins. With its 4-aminobutyl side-chain, it is classified as a basic amino acid, along with arginine and histidine.
Salt	Salt is a term used for ionic compounds composed of positively charged cations and negatively charged anions, so that the product is neutral and without a net charge.
Highly conserved	Highly conserved refers to genes or proteins whose sequences are very similar in different species.
Fiber	Fiber is a class of materials that are continuous filaments or are in discrete elongated pieces, similar to lengths of thread. They are of great importance in the biology of both plants and animals, for holding tissues together.
Chromatid	Chromatid refers to one of two component parts of a chromosome formed by replication and attached at the centromere.
Population	Group of organisms of the same species occupying a certain area and sharing a common gene pool is referred to as population.
Biosynthesis	Biosynthesis is a phenomenon where chemical compounds are produced from simpler reagents. Biosynthesis, unlike chemical synthesis, takes place within living organisms and is generally catalysed by enzymes. The process is vital part of metabolism.
Pigment	Pigment is any material resulting in color in plant or animal cells which is the result of selective absorption.

Go to **Cram101.com** for the Practice Tests for this Chapter.

Colony	Colony refers to a cluster or assemblage of microorganisms growing on the surface of an agar culture medium. A colony also refers to several individual organisms of the same species living closely together, usually for mutual benefit, such as stronger defences, the ability to attack bigger prey, etc.
Position effect	Differences in gene expression that depend on the position of the gene on the chromosome and probably reflect differences in the state of the chromatin along the chromosome is referred to as position effect.
Drosophila	Drosophila is part of the phylum Arthropoda, a phylum of segmented animals with paired, jointed appendages and a hard exoskeleton made of chitin. They have an open circulatory system with a dorsal heart, with hemocoel occupying most of the body cavity, and a reduced coelom.
Fruit	A fruit is the ripened ovary—together with seeds—of a flowering plant. In many species, the fruit incorporates the ripened ovary and surrounding tissues.
Mutation	Mutation refers to a change in the nucleotide sequence of DNA; the ultimate source of genetic diversity.
Eye	An eye is an organ that detects light. Different kinds of light-sensitive organs are found in a variety of creatures.
Mutant	A mutant (also known to early geneticists as a "monster") is an individual, organism, or new genetic character arising or resulting from an instance of mutation, which is a sudden structural change within the DNA of a gene or chromosome of an organism resulting in the creation of a new character or trait not found in the parental type.
Embryo	Embryo refers to a developing stage of a multicellular organism. In humans, the stage in the development of offspring from the first division of the zygote until body structures begin to appear, about the ninth week of gestation.
X-inactivation	X-inactivation is inactivation of one copy of the X chromosome in the somatic cells of female mammals. X-inactivation leads to clumped chromatin termed Barr bodies, which are generally considered inert.
Tissue	Group of similar cells which perform a common function is called tissue.
Organ	Organ refers to a structure consisting of several tissues adapted as a group to perform specific functions.
Clone	A group of genetically identical cells or organisms derived by asexual reproduction from a single parent is called a clone.
Hydrolysis	Hydrolysis is a chemical process in which a molecule is cleaved into two parts by the addition of a molecule of water.
Photoreceptor	A photoreceptor is a specialized type of neuron that is capable of phototransduction. More specifically, the photoreceptor sends signals to other neurons by a change in its membrane potential when it absorbs photons.
Color vision	Ability to detect the color of an object, dependent on three kinds of cone cells is called color vision.
Cone cell	The cone cell is a photoreceptor in the retina of the eye which functions only in relatively bright light. There are about 6 million in the human eye, concentrated at the fovea. They gradually become more sparse towards the outside of the retina. They are less sensitive to light than the rod cells, but allow the perception of color and detail.
Retina	The retina is a thin layer of cells at the back of the eyeball of vertebrates and some cephalopods; it is the part of the eye which converts light into nervous signals.

Linkage	Linkage refers to the patterns of assortment of genes that are located on the same chromosome. Important because if the genes are located relatively far apart, crossing over is more likely to occur between them than if they are close together.

126

Go to **Cram101.com** for the Practice Tests for this Chapter.

DNA replication	DNA replication is the process of copying a double-stranded DNA strand in a cell, prior to cell division. The two resulting double strands are identical (if the replication went well), and each of them consists of one original and one newly synthesized strand.
Daughter cell	A cell formed by cell division of a parent cell is a daughter cell.
Recombination	Genetic recombination is the transmission-genetic process by which the combinations of alleles observed at different loci in two parental individuals become shuffled in offspring individuals.
Duplication	Duplication refers to repetition of part of a chromosome resulting from fusion with a fragment from a homologous chromosome; can result from an error in meiosis or from mutagenesis.
Cell	The cell is the structural and functional unit of all living organisms, and is sometimes called the "building block of life."
Radiation	The emission of electromagnetic waves by all objects warmer than absolute zero is referred to as radiation.
Molecule	A molecule is the smallest particle of a pure chemical substance that still retains its chemical composition and properties.
Mutation	Mutation refers to a change in the nucleotide sequence of DNA; the ultimate source of genetic diversity.
Antibiotic	Antibiotic refers to substance such as penicillin or streptomycin that is toxic to microorganisms. Usually a product of a particular microorvanism or plant.
Bacteria	The domain that contains procaryotic cells with primarily diacyl glycerol diesters in their membranes and with bacterial rRNA. Bacteria also is a general term for organisms that are composed of procaryotic cells and are not multicellular.
Homologous Recombination	Homologous Recombination is the process by which two chromosomes, paired up during prophase I of meiosis, exchange some distal portion of their DNA.
Replication origin	Location on a DNA molecule at which DNA replication is initiated is referred to as the replication origin.
Replication fork	Y-shaped region of a replicating DNA molecule at which the two daughter strands are formed and separate is called the replication fork.
DNA polymerase	A DNA polymerase is an enzyme that assists in DNA replication. Such enzymes catalyze the polymerization of deoxyribonucleotides alongside a DNA strand, which they "read" and use as a template. The newly polymerized molecule is complementary to the template strand and identical to the template's partner strand.
DNA sequence	A DNA sequence is a succession of letters representing the primary structure of a real or hypothetical DNA molecule or strand, The possible letters are A, C, G, and T, representing the four nucleotide subunits of a DNA strand (adenine, cytosine, guanine, thymine).
Human genome	The human genome is the genome of Homo sapiens. It is made up of 23 chromosome pairs with a total of about 3 billion DNA base pairs.
Telomerase	An enzyme critical to the successful replication of telomeres at chromosome ends is called telomerase.
Retrovirus	A retrovirus is a virus which has a genome consisting of two RNA molecules, which may or may not be identical. It relies on the enzyme reverse transcriptase to perform the reverse transcription of its genome from RNA into DNA, which can then be integrated into the host's genome with an integrase enzyme.

Go to **Cram101.com** for the Practice Tests for this Chapter.

DNA repair	Collective name for those biochemical processes that correct accidental changes in the DNA is referred to as dna repair.
Chromosome	A chromosome is, minimally, a very long, continuous piece of DNA, which contains many genes, regulatory elements and other intervening nucleotide sequences.
Element	A chemical element, often called simply element, is a chemical substance that cannot be divided or changed into other chemical substances by any ordinary chemical technique. An element is a class of substances that contain the same number of protons in all its atoms.
Protein	A protein is a complex, high-molecular-weight organic compound that consists of amino acids joined by peptide bonds. They are essential to the structure and function of all living cells and viruses. Many are enzymes or subunits of enzymes.
Species	Group of similarly constructed organisms capable of interbreeding and producing fertile offspring is a species.
Primer	A primer is a nucleic acid strand, or a related molecule that serves as a starting point for DNA replication. In most natural DNA replication, the ultimate primer for DNA synthesis is a short strand of RNA.
Virus	Obligate intracellular parasite of living cells consisting of an outer capsid and an inner core of nucleic acid is referred to as virus. The term virus usually refers to those particles that infect eukaryotes whilst the term bacteriophage or phage is used to describe those infecting prokaryotes.
Gene	Gene refers to a discrete unit of hereditary information consisting of a specific nucleotide sequence in DNA . Most of the genes of a eukaryote are located in its chromosomal DNA; a few are carried by the DNA of mitochondria and chloroplasts.
Evolution	In biology, evolution is the process by which novel traits arise in populations and are passed on from generation to generation. Its action over large stretches of time explains the origin of new species and ultimately the vast diversity of the biological world.
Cell division	Cell division is the process by which a cell (called the parent cell) divides into two cells (called daughter cells). Cell division is usually a small segment of a larger cell cycle. In meiosis, however, a cell is permanently transformed and cannot divide again.
Genome	The genome of an organism is the whole hereditary information of an organism that is encoded in the DNA (or, for some viruses, RNA). This includes both the genes and the non-coding sequences. The genome of an organism is a complete DNA sequence of one set of chromosomes.
Animal cell	An animal cell is a form of eukaryotic cell which make up many tissues in animals. The animal cell is distinct from other eukaryotes, most notably those of plants, as they lack cell walls and chloroplasts, and they have smaller vacuoles.
Nucleotide	A nucleotide is a chemical compound that consists of a heterocyclic base, a sugar, and one or more phosphate groups. In the most common nucleotides the base is a derivative of purine or pyrimidine, and the sugar is pentose - deoxyribose or ribose. They are the structural units of RNA and DNA.
Base pair	Two nucleotides on opposite complementary DNA or RNA strands that are connected via hydrogen bonds are called a base pair.
Template strand	The strand of the DNA double helix from which RNA is transcribed is called a template strand.
Complementary DNA	Complementary DNA is DNA synthesized from a mature mRNA template. It is often used to clone eukaryotic genes in prokaryotes.
Double helix	Double helix refers to the form of native DNA, referring to its two adjacent polynucleotide strands wound into a spiral shape.

Go to **Cram101.com** for the Practice Tests for this Chapter.

Helix	A helix is a twisted shape like a spring, screw or a spiral staircase. They are important in biology, as DNA and many proteins have spiral substructures, known a alpha helix.
Hydrogen bond	A hydrogen bond is a type of attractive intermolecular force that exists between two partial electric charges of opposite polarity. Although stronger than most other intermolecular forces, the typical hydrogen bond is much weaker than both the ionic bond and the covalent bond.
Style	The style is a stalk connecting the stigma with the ovary below containing the transmitting tract, which facilitates the movement of the male gamete to the ovule.
Simple cell	A neuron in the striate cortex that is maximally sensitive to the position and orientation of edges in the receptive field is called a simple cell.
Yeast	Yeast refers to common term for several families of unicellular fungi. Includes species used for brewing beer and making bread, as well as pathogenic species.
Helical	A helix is a twisted shape like a spring, screw or a spiral staircase. Helices are important in biology, as DNA is helical and many proteins have helical substructures, known as alpha helices.
Cation	A positively charged ion which has fewer electrons than protons is a cation.
Rearrangement	A change in the usual order and arrangement of genetic material either within the chromosome complement or within a gene locus is rearrangement. Where the nature of the rearrangement has been determined, the type may be searched for directly under the following designations: reciprocal translocation, Robertsonian translocation, insertion, transposition, inversion, deletion, and duplication.
Multicellular	Multicellular organisms are those organisms consisting of more than one cell, and having differentiated cells that perform specialized functions. Most life that can be seen with the naked eye is multicellular, as are all animals (i.e. members of the kingdom Animalia) and plants (i.e. members of the kingdom Plantae).
Cancer	Cancer is a class of diseases or disorders characterized by uncontrolled division of cells and the ability of these cells to invade other tissues, either by direct growth into adjacent tissue through invasion or by implantation into distant sites by metastasis.
S phase	Stage of the cell cycle during which chromosome replication occurs is called S phase.
Plasmid	Plasmid is a circular double-stranded DNA molecule that is separate from the chromosomal DNA. They usually occur in bacteria and often contain genes that confer a selective advantage to the bacterium harboring them, e.g., the ability to make the bacterium antibiotic resistant.
Origin of replication	DNA sequence at which helicase unwinds the DNA double helix and DNA polymerase binds to initiate DNA replication is called the origin of replication.
Complementary sequence	Complementary sequence refers to a nucleic acid base sequence that can form a doublestranded structure by matching base pairs with another sequence; the complementary sequence to 5' GTAC 3' is 3' CATG 5'.
Genomic dna	DNA constituting the genome of a cell or an organism. Often used in contrast to cdna. Genomic DNA clones represent DNA cloned directly from chromosomal DNA, and a collection of such clones from a given genome is a genomic DNA library.
Fluorescence	Fluorescence is a luminescence that is mostly found as an optical phenomenon in cold bodies, in which the molecular absorption of a photon triggers the emission of a lower-energy photon with a longer wavelength. The energy difference between the absorbed and emitted photons ends up as molecular vibrations or heat.
DNA microarray	A DNA microarray is a collection of microscopic DNA spots attached to a solid surface, such

as glass, plastic or silicon chip forming an array.

Population	Group of organisms of the same species occupying a certain area and sharing a common gene pool is referred to as population.
Electron microscope	The electron microscope is a microscope that can magnify very small details with high resolving power due to the use of electrons as the source of illumination, magnifying at levels up to 500,000 times.
Chromatin	Chromatin refers to the combination of DNA and proteins that constitute chromosomes; often used to refer to the diffuse, very extended form taken by the chromosomes when a eukaryotic cell is not dividing.
Enzyme	An enzyme is a protein that catalyzes, or speeds up, a chemical reaction. They are essential to sustain life because most chemical reactions in biological cells would occur too slowly, or would lead to different products, without them.
Condensation reaction	A condensation reaction is a chemical reaction in which two molecules or moieties react and become covalently bonded to one another by the concurrent loss of a small molecule, often water, methanol, or a type of hydrogen halide such as HCl.
Polymerization	Polymerization is a process of reacting monomer molecules together in a chemical reaction to form linear chains or a three-dimensional network of polymer chains.
Nucleoside	Molecule composed of a purine or pyrimidine base covalently linked to a ribose or deoxyribose sugar is a nucleoside.
Hydrolysis	Hydrolysis is a chemical process in which a molecule is cleaved into two parts by the addition of a molecule of water.
Monomer	In chemistry, a monomer is a small molecule that may become chemically bonded to other monomers to form a polymer.
Phosphate	A phosphate is a polyatomic ion or radical consisting of one phosphorus atom and four oxygen. In the ionic form, it carries a -3 formal charge, and is denoted PO_4^{3-}.
Micrograph	A micrograph is a photograph or similar image taken through a microscope or similar device to show a magnified image of an item.
Electron	The electron is a light fundamental subatomic particle that carries a negative electric charge. The electron is a spin-1/2 lepton, does not participate in strong interactions and has no substructure.
Embryo	Embryo refers to a developing stage of a multicellular organism. In humans, the stage in the development of offspring from the first division of the zygote until body structures begin to appear, about the ninth week of gestation.
Nucleosome	Nucleosome refers to the beadlike unit of DNA packing in a eukaryotic cell; consists of DNA wound around a protein core made up of eight histone molecules.
Polynucleotide	Polynucleotide refers to a polymer consisting of many nucleotide monomers; serves as a blueprint for proteins and, through the actions of proteins, for all cellular activities. The two types are DNA and RNA.
Free energy	The term thermodynamic free energy denotes the total amount of energy in a physical system which can be converted to do work.
Polarity	In cell biology, polarity refers to cells not being point-symmetrical in their spatial organization. In horticulture, polarity refers to the condition in which cuttings grow shoots at the distil end and roots at the proximal end.
Lagging strand	In DNA replication, the lagging strand is the DNA strand at the opposite side of the

Go to **Cram101.com** for the Practice Tests for this Chapter.

	replication fork from the leading strand. It goes from 5' to 3' (these numbers indicate the position of the molecule in respect to the carbon atoms it contains).
Polymerase	DNA or RNA enzymes that catalyze the synthesis of nucleic acids on preexisting nucleic acid templates, assembling RNA from ribonucleotides or DNA from deoxyribonucleotides is referred to as polymerase.
Proofreading	The correction of an error in DNA replication just after an incorrectly paired base is added to the growing polynucleotide chain is called proofreading.
Exonuclease	Enzyme that cleaves nucleotides one at a time off the end of a DNA or RNA molecule is referred to as exonuclease.
X-ray crystallography	Technique for determining the three-dimensional arrangement of atoms in a molecule based on the diffraction pattern of X-rays passing through a crystal of the molecule is x-ray crystallography.
Crystallography	Crystallography is the experimental science of determining the arrangement of atoms in solids.
Mutant	A mutant (also known to early geneticists as a "monster") is an individual, organism, or new genetic character arising or resulting from an instance of mutation, which is a sudden structural change within the DNA of a gene or chromosome of an organism resulting in the creation of a new character or trait not found in the parental type.
Domain	In biology, a domain is the top-level grouping of organisms in scientific classification.
Primase	Primase refers to the enzyme that builds a short RNA primer at the start of a replicated DNA segment.
Elongation	Elongation refers to a phase of DNA replication, transcription, or translation that successively adds nucleotides or amino acids to a growing macromolecule.
Nuclease	Enzyme that cleaves phosphodiester bonds in nucleic acids is referred to as nuclease.
Ligase	In biochemistry, a ligase is an enzyme that can catalyse the joining of two molecules by forming a new chemical bond, with accompanying hydrolysis of adenosine triphosphate or other similar molecules.
Single-strand binding protein	Single-strand binding protein, binds single stranded regions of DNA to prevent premature reannealing.
Helicase	Helicase refers to a class of enzymes vital to all living organisms. Its function is to temporarily separate the two strands of a DNA double helix so that DNA or RNA synthesis can take place.
Okazaki fragment	An Okazaki fragment is a relatively short fragment of DNA created on the lagging strand during DNA replication.
Bacterium	Most bacterium are microscopic and unicellular, with a relatively simple cell structure lacking a cell nucleus, and organelles such as mitochondria and chloroplasts. They are the most abundant of all organisms. They are ubiquitous in soil, water, and as symbionts of other organisms.
DNA ligase	DNA ligase is a particular type of ligase that can link together DNA strands that have double-strand breaks.
Leading strand	One of the two newly synthesized strands of DNA found at a replication fork. The leading strand is made by continuous synthesis in the 5'-to-3' direction.
DNA helicase	An enzyme that catalyzes the unwinding of the DNA double helix during DNA replication is referred to as DNA helicase.

Circular DNA	Circular DNA is found in bacteria and other archaea. While the individual strands of a linear double helix represent two distinct and separable molecules, this need not be true for circular DNA. If the strands twist an odd number of times around one another in completing the DNA loop, then they are covalently joined into a single molecule.
Telomere	A telomere is a region of highly repetitive DNA at the end of a chromosome that functions as a disposable buffer.
Cell biology	The biological discipline involving the study of cells and their functions is called cell biology. This includes their physiological properties such as their structure and the organelles they contain, their environment and interactions, their life cycle, division and function (physiology) and eventual death.
Amino acid	An amino acid is any molecule that contains both amino and carboxylic acid functional groups. They are the basic structural building units of proteins. They form short polymer chains called peptides or polypeptides which in turn form structures called proteins.
Glutamic acid	Glutamic acid is one of the 20 standard amino acids used by all organisms in their proteins. It is critical for proper cell function, but it is not an essential nutrient in humans because glutamic acid can be manufactured from other compounds.
Valine	Nutritionally, valine is also an essential amino acid. It is named after the plant valerian. In sickle-cell disease, it substitutes for the hydrophilic amino acid glutamic acid in hemoglobin.
Sickle-cell anemia	Sickle-cell anemia refers to a disease caused by a point mutation. This malfunction produces sickle-shaped red blood cells. Sickle-cell anemia is the name of a specific form of sickle cell disease in which there is homozygosity for the mutation that causes Hgb S.
Heterozygous	Heterozygous means that the organism carries a different version of that gene on each of the two corresponding chromosomes.
Malaria	Malaria refers to potentially fatal human disease caused by the protozoan parasite Plasmodium, which is transmitted by the bite of an infected mosquito.
Blood	Blood is a circulating tissue composed of fluid plasma and cells. The main function of blood is to supply nutrients (oxygen, glucose) and constitutional elements to tissues and to remove waste products.
Homozygous	When an organism is referred to as being homozygous for a specific gene, it means that it carries two identical copies of that gene for a given trait on the two corresponding chromosomes.
Parasite	A parasite is an organism that spends a significant portion of its life in or on the living tissue of a host organism and which causes harm to the host without immediately killing it. They also commonly show highly specialized adaptations allowing them to exploit host resources.
Colon	The colon is the part of the intestine from the cecum to the rectum. Its primary purpose is to extract water from feces.
Organ	Organ refers to a structure consisting of several tissues adapted as a group to perform specific functions.
Germ cell	A germ cell is a kind of cell that is part of the germline, and is involved in the reproduction of organisms. There are different kinds, which include gametogonia, gametocytes, and gametes.
Somatic cell	A somatic cell is generally taken to mean any cell forming the body of an organism.
Clone	A group of genetically identical cells or organisms derived by asexual reproduction from a

single parent is called a clone.

Depurination	DNA alteration in which the hydrolysis of a purine base, either A or G, from the deoxyribose-phosphate backbone occurs is referred to as depurination.
Deamination	The removal of an amin group from normal DNA is referred to as deamination.
Cytosine	Cytosine is one of the 5 main nucleobases used in storing and transporting genetic information within a cell in the nucleic acids DNA and RNA. It is a pyrimidine derivative, with a heterocyclic aromatic ring and two substituents attached. The nucleoside of cytosine is cytidine.
Adenine	Adenine is one of the two purine nucleobases used in forming nucleotides of the nucleic acids DNA and RNA. In DNA, adenine (A) binds to thymine (T) via two hydrogen bonds to assist in stabilizing the nucleic acid structures. In RNA, adenine binds to uracil (U).
Guanine	Guanine is one of the five main nucleobases found in nucleic acids. Guanine is a purine derivative, and in Watson-Crick base pairing forms three hydrogen bonds with cytosine. Guanine "stacks" vertically with the other nucleobases via aromatic interactions.
Uracil	Uracil is one of the four RNA nucleobases, replacing thymine as found in DNA. Just like thymine, uracil can form a base pair with adenine via two hydrogen bonds, but it lacks the methyl group present in thymine. Uracil, in comparison to thymine, will more readily degenerate into cytosine.
Amino group	An amino group is an ammonia-like functional group composed of a nitrogen and two hydrogen atoms covalently linked. $-NH_2$
Metabolism	Metabolism is the biochemical modification of chemical compounds in living organisms and cells. This includes the biosynthesis of complex organic molecules (anabolism) and their breakdown (catabolism).
Ultraviolet radiation	Ultraviolet radiation refers to radiation similar to light but with wavelengths slightly shorter than violet light and with more energy. The greater energy causes it to severely burn and otherwise damage biological tissues.
Thymine dimer	Thymine dimer refers to a pair of abnormally chemically bonded adjacent thymine bases in DNA, resulting from damage by ultra-violet irradiation. The cellular processes that repair this lesion often make errors that create mutations. There are enzymes which can repair the damage.
Pyrimidine	Pyrimidine refers to one of two families of nitrogenous bases found in nucleotides. Cytosine , thymine , and uracil are pyrimidines.
Sunlight	Sunlight in the broad sense is the total spectrum of electromagnetic radiation given off by the Sun.
Deletion	Deletion refers to the loss of one or more nucleotides from a gene by mutation; the loss of a fragment of a chromosome.
Linkage	Linkage refers to the patterns of assortment of genes that are located on the same chromosome. Important because if the genes are located relatively far apart, crossing over is more likely to occur between them than if they are close together.
Thymine	Thymine, also known as 5-methyluracil, is a pyrimidine nucleobase. It is found in the nucleic acid DNA. In RNA thymine is replaced with uracil in most cases. In DNA, thymine(T) binds to adenine (A) via two hydrogen bonds to assist in stabilizing the nucleic acid structures.
Skin	Skin is an organ of the integumentary system composed of a layer of tissues that protect underlying muscles and organs.

Go to **Cram101.com** for the Practice Tests for this Chapter.

Covalent bond	A covalent bond is an intramolecular form of chemical bonding characterized by the sharing of one or more pairs of electrons between two elements, producing a mutual attraction that holds the resultant molecule together.
Sugar-phosphate backbone	Sugar-phosphate backbone refers to the alternating chain of sugar and phosphate to which DNA and RNA nitrogenous bases are attached.
Ligation	Ligation refers to enzymatically catalyzed formation of a phosphodiester bond that links two DNA molecules.
Sugar	A sugar is the simplest molecule that can be identified as a carbohydrate. These include monosaccharides and disaccharides, trisaccharides and the oligosaccharides. The term "glyco-" indicates the presence of a sugar in an otherwise non-carbohydrate substance.
Phosphodiester bond	A phosphodiester bond is a group of strong covalent bonds between the phosphorus atom in a phosphate group and two other molecules over two ester bonds. Phosphodiester bonds are central to all life on Earth, as they make up the backbone of the strands of DNA.
Homologous	Homologous refers to describes organs or molecules that are similar because of their common evolutionary origin. Specifically it describes similarities in protein or nucleic acid sequence.
Crossing-over	Exchange of corresponding segments of genetic material between nonsister chromatids of homologous chromosomes during synapsis of meiosis I is called crossing-over.
Highly conserved	Highly conserved refers to genes or proteins whose sequences are very similar in different species.
Reassortment	Reassortment is the exchange of DNA between viruses inside a host cell. Two or more viruses of different strains (but usually the same species) infect a single cell and pool their genetic material creating numerous genetically diverse progeny viruses.
Site-specific recombination	Site-specific recombination refers to type of recombination that does not require extensive similarity in the two DNA sequences undergoing recombination. Can occur between two different DNA molecules or within a single DNA molecule.
Host	Host is an organism that harbors a parasite, mutual partner, or commensal partner; or a cell infected by a virus.
Nucleic acid	A nucleic acid is a complex, high-molecular-weight biochemical macromolecule composed of nucleotide chains that convey genetic information. The most common are deoxyribonucleic acid (DNA) and ribonucleic acid (RNA). They are found in all living cells and viruses.
Viral	Viral phenomena are objects or patterns able to replicate themselves or convert other objects into copies of themselves when these objects are exposed to them.
Human evolution	Human evolution is the process of change and development, or evolution, by which human beings emerged as a distinct species.
Fossil	A preserved remnant or impression of an organism that lived in the past is referred to as fossil.
Homology	Homology is used in reference to protein or DNA sequences, meaning that the given sequences share a common ancestor. Sequence homology may also indicate common function.
Holliday junction	Holliday junction refers to x-shaped structure observed in DNA undergoing recombination, in which the two DNA molecules are held together at the site of crossing-over, also called a cross-strand exchange.
Crossing over	An essential element of meiosis occurring during prophase when nonsister chromatids exchange portions of DNA strands is called crossing over.

Go to **Cram101.com** for the Practice Tests for this Chapter.

Transposon	DNA segment that carries the genes required for transposition and moves about the chromosome; if it contains genes other than those required for transposition, it may be called a composite transposon. Often the name is reserved only for transposable elements that also contain genes unrelated to transposition.
Tetracycline	Tetracycline is an antibiotic produced by the streptomyces bacterium, indicated for use against many bacterial infections. It is commonly used to treat acne.
Antibiotic resistance	The ability of a mutated pathogen to resist the effects of an antibiotic that normally kills it is an antibiotic resistance.
Transposition	Transposition is a method in genetics where a transposon is inserted into the studied gene to help identify the function or silence the selected gene.
Retrotransposon	Type of transposable element that moves by being first transcribed into an RNA copy that is then reconverted to DNA by reverse transcriptase and inserted elsewhere in the chromosomes is referred to as retrotransposon.
Reverse transcriptase	Reverse transcriptase is an enzyme that is able to transcribe RNA into DNA. That is, reverse transcriptase is able to copy genetic information from RNA to DNA, which is the reverse of the more typical direction
Blood clotting	A complex process by which platelets, the protein fibrin, and red blood cells block an irregular surface in or on the body, such as a damaged blood vessel, sealing the wound is referred to as blood clotting.
Translocation	A chromosomal mutation in which a portion of one chromosome breaks off and becomes attached to another chromosome is referred to as translocation.
Hemophilia	Hemophilia is the name of any of several hereditary genetic illnesses that impair the body's ability to control bleeding. Genetic deficiencies cause lowered plasma clotting factor activity so as to compromise blood-clotting; when a blood vessel is injured, a scab will not form and the vessel can continue to bleed excessively for a very long period of time.
Insertion	At DNA level, an insertion means the insertion of a few base pairs into a genetic sequence. This can often happen in microsatellite regions due to the DNA polymerase slipping.
RNA polymerase	The enzyme RNA polymerase is a nucleotidyltransferase that polymerises ribonucleotides in accordance with the information present in DNA. RNA polymerase enzymes are essential and are found in all organisms.
Primate	A primate is any member of the biological group that contains all lemurs, monkeys, apes, and humans.
Mammal	Homeothermic vertebrate characterized especially by the presence of hair and mammary glands is a mammal.
Oxygen	Oxygen is a chemical element in the periodic table. It has the symbol O and atomic number 8. Oxygen is the second most common element on Earth, composing around 46% of the mass of Earth's crust and 28% of the mass of Earth as a whole, and is the third most common element in the universe.
Transposable element	Transposable element refers to segment of DNA that can move from one position in a genome to another. Also called a transposon.
Reproduction	Biological reproduction is the biological process by which new individual organisms are produced. Reproduction is a fundamental feature of all known life; each individual organism exists as the result of reproduction by an antecedent.
Herpes simplex virus	The herpes simplex virus is a virus that manifests itself in two common viral infections, each marked by painful, watery blisters in the skin or mucous membranes (such as the mouth or

Go to **Cram101.com** for the Practice Tests for this Chapter.

lips) or on the genitals. The disease is contagious, particularly during an outbreak, and is incurable.

Cold sore	Cold sore refers to a lesion caused by the herpes simplex virus; usually occurs on the border of the lips or nares. Also known as a fever blister or herpes labialis.
Plant cell	A cell that is a structural and functional unit of a plant is a plant cell.
Polypeptide	Polypeptide refers to polymer of many amino acids linked by peptide bonds.
Complex viruses	Complex viruses refers to viruses with capsids having a complex symmetry that is neither icosahedral nor helical.
Biosynthesis	Biosynthesis is a phenomenon where chemical compounds are produced from simpler reagents. Biosynthesis, unlike chemical synthesis, takes place within living organisms and is generally catalysed by enzymes. The process is vital part of metabolism.
Ribosome	A ribosome is an organelle composed of rRNA and ribosomal proteins. It translates mRNA into a polypeptide chain (e.g., a protein). It can be thought of as a factory that builds a protein from a set of genetic instructions.
DNA transcription	DNA transcription is the process through which a DNA sequence is enzymatically copied by an RNA polymerase to produce a complementary RNA. In the case of protein-encoding DNA, transcription is the beginning of the process that ultimately leads to the translation of the genetic code into a functional peptide or protein.
Translation	Translation is the second process of protein biosynthesis. In translation, messenger RNA is decoded to produce a specific polypeptide according to the rules specified by the genetic code.
Lysis	Lysis refers to the death of a cell by bursting, often by viral or osmotic mechanisms that compromise the integrity of the cellular membrane.
Hybrid	Hybrid refers to the offspring of parents of two different species or of two different varieties of one species; the offspring of two parents that differ in one or more inherited traits; an individual that is heterozygous for one or more pair of genes.
Immunodeficiency	Immunodeficiency is a state in which the immune system's ability to fight infectious disease is compromized or entirely absent. Most cases of immunodeficiency are either congenital or acquired.
Provirus	A provirus is a retrovirus that has integrated itself into the DNA of a host cell. To do this, the RNA of the retrovirus is transcribed into DNA by reverse transcriptase, then inserted into the host genome by an integrase.
Bacteriophage	Bacteriophage refers to a virus that infects bacteria; also called a phage.
Adenovirus	The adenovirus genome is linear, non-segmented double stranded DNA which is around 30-38kbp. This allows the virus to theoretically carry between 30-40 genes. They infect both humans and animals.
Influenza	Influenza or flu refers to an acute viral infection of the respiratory tract, occurring in isolated cases, epidemics, and pandemics. Influenza is caused by three strains of influenza virus, labeled types A, B, and C, based on the antigens of their protein coats.
Capsid	Capsid refers to protein coat of a virus, formed by the self-assembly of one or more protein subunits into a geometrically regular structure.
Reverse transcription	Reverse transcription is the process by which reverse transcriptase synthesizes DNA strands complementary to an RNA template. The product of reverse transcription is a cDNA molecule.
Integrase	Integrase is an enzyme produced by a virus that enables genetic material that is helpful to

the virus, proviral DNA, to be integrated into the DNA of the infected cell. It is a key component in the pre-integration complex (PIC).

Chemical reaction	Chemical reaction refers to a process leading to chemical changes in matter; involves the making and/or breaking of chemical bonds.
Genetic recombination	Genetic recombination refers to the production, by crossing over and/or independent assortment of chromosomes during meiosis, of offspring with allele combinations different from those in the parents.
Ribonucleic acid	Ribonucleic acid is a nucleic acid polymer consisting of covalently bound nucleotides. It's nucleotides contain ribose rings unlike DNA, which contains deoxyribose. It serves as the template for translation of genes into proteins, transferring amino acids to the ribosome to form proteins.
Isotope	An isotope is a form of an element whose nuclei have the same atomic number - the number of protons in the nucleus - but different mass numbers because they contain different numbers of neutrons.
Bacterial chromosome	The single, circular DNA molecule found in bacteria is a bacterial chromosome.
Oxidation	Oxidation refers to the loss of electrons from a substance involved in a redox reaction; always accompanies reduction.
Glucose	Glucose, a simple monosaccharide sugar, is one of the most important carbohydrates and is used as a source of energy in animals and plants. Glucose is one of the main products of photosynthesis and starts respiration.
Centromere	The centromere is a region of a eukaryotic chromosome where the kinetochore is assembled; the site where spindle fibers of the mitotic spindle attach to the chromosome during mitosis. It is also the site of the primary constriction visible in microscopy images of chromosomes. Finally, it is the site at which a chromatid and its identical sister attach together during the process of cell reproduction.
Protein synthesis	The process whereby the tRNA utilizes the mRNA as a guide to arrange the amino acids in their proper sequence according to the genetic information in the chemical code of DNA is referred to as protein synthesis.
Messenger RNA	Messenger RNA is RNA that encodes and carries information from DNA to sites of protein synthesis.
Peptide bond	A peptide bond is a chemical bond formed between two molecules when the carboxyl group of one molecule reacts with the amino group of the other molecule, releasing a molecule of water.

Deoxyribonuc-eic acid	Deoxyribonucleic acid is a nucleic acid that contains the genetic instructions specifying the biological development of all cellular forms of life. It is a long polymer of nucleotides and encodes the sequence of the amino acid residues in proteins using the genetic code, a triplet code of nucleotides.
Nucleotide	A nucleotide is a chemical compound that consists of a heterocyclic base, a sugar, and one or more phosphate groups. In the most common nucleotides the base is a derivative of purine or pyrimidine, and the sugar is pentose - deoxyribose or ribose. They are the structural units of RNA and DNA.
Protein	A protein is a complex, high-molecular-weight organic compound that consists of amino acids joined by peptide bonds. They are essential to the structure and function of all living cells and viruses. Many are enzymes or subunits of enzymes.
Genome	The genome of an organism is the whole hereditary information of an organism that is encoded in the DNA (or, for some viruses, RNA). This includes both the genes and the non-coding sequences. The genome of an organism is a complete DNA sequence of one set of chromosomes.
Cell	The cell is the structural and functional unit of all living organisms, and is sometimes called the "building block of life."
DNA code	A sequence of three nucleotides of a DNA molecule is a DNA code.
Gene	Gene refers to a discrete unit of hereditary information consisting of a specific nucleotide sequence in DNA . Most of the genes of a eukaryote are located in its chromosomal DNA; a few are carried by the DNA of mitochondria and chloroplasts.
Amino acid	An amino acid is any molecule that contains both amino and carboxylic acid functional groups. They are the basic structural building units of proteins. They form short polymer chains called peptides or polypeptides which in turn form structures called proteins.
Protein synthesis	The process whereby the tRNA utilizes the mRNA as a guide to arrange the amino acids in their proper sequence according to the genetic information in the chemical code of DNA is referred to as protein synthesis.
Ribonucleic acid	Ribonucleic acid is a nucleic acid polymer consisting of covalently bound nucleotides. It's nucleotides contain ribose rings unlike DNA, which contains deoxyribose. It serves as the template for translation of genes into proteins, transferring amino acids to the ribosome to form proteins.
Nucleic acid	A nucleic acid is a complex, high-molecular-weight biochemical macromolecule composed of nucleotide chains that convey genetic information. The most common are deoxyribonucleic acid (DNA) and ribonucleic acid (RNA). They are found in all living cells and viruses.
Chromosome	A chromosome is, minimally, a very long, continuous piece of DNA, which contains many genes, regulatory elements and other intervening nucleotide sequences.
Molecule	A molecule is the smallest particle of a pure chemical substance that still retains its chemical composition and properties.
Molecular biology	Molecular biology overlaps with other areas of biology and chemistry, particularly genetics and biochemistry. Molecular biology chiefly concerns itself with understanding the interactions between the various systems of a cell, including the interrelationship of DNA, RNA and protein synthesis and learning how these interactions are regulated.
Central dogma	The central dogma of molecular biology deals with the detailed residue-by-residue transfer of sequential information. It states that such information cannot be transferred from protein to either protein or nucleic acid.
Bacteria	The domain that contains procaryotic cells with primarily diacyl glycerol diesters in their

membranes and with bacterial rRNA. Bacteria also is a general term for organisms that are composed of procaryotic cells and are not multicellular.

RNA splicing	RNA splicing refers to the removal of introns and joining of exons in eukaryotic RNA, forming an mRNA molecule with a continuous coding sequence; occurs before mRNA leaves the nucleus.
Translation	Translation is the second process of protein biosynthesis. In translation, messenger RNA is decoded to produce a specific polypeptide according to the rules specified by the genetic code.
Amplification	In molecular biology, amplification (polymerase chain reaction or PCR) is the method for creating multiple copies of DNA (or RNA) without using a living organism, such as E. coli or yeast.
Transcription	Transcription is the process through which a DNA sequence is enzymatically copied by an RNA polymerase to produce a complementary RNA. Or, in other words, the transfer of genetic information from DNA into RNA.
DNA sequence	A DNA sequence is a succession of letters representing the primary structure of a real or hypothetical DNA molecule or strand, The possible letters are A, C, G, and T, representing the four nucleotide subunits of a DNA strand (adenine, cytosine, guanine, thymine).
Polymer	Polymer is a generic term used to describe a very long molecule consisting of structural units and repeating units connected by covalent chemical bonds.
Phosphodiester bond	A phosphodiester bond is a group of strong covalent bonds between the phosphorus atom in a phosphate group and two other molecules over two ester bonds. Phosphodiester bonds are central to all life on Earth, as they make up the backbone of the strands of DNA.
Deoxyribose	Deoxyribose is an aldopentose, a monosaccharide containing five carbon atoms, and including an aldehyde functional group.
Adenine	Adenine is one of the two purine nucleobases used in forming nucleotides of the nucleic acids DNA and RNA. In DNA, adenine (A) binds to thymine (T) via two hydrogen bonds to assist in stabilizing the nucleic acid structures. In RNA, adenine binds to uracil (U).
Guanine	Guanine is one of the five main nucleobases found in nucleic acids. Guanine is a purine derivative, and in Watson-Crick base pairing forms three hydrogen bonds with cytosine. Guanine "stacks" vertically with the other nucleobases via aromatic interactions.
Ribose	Ribose is an aldopentose — a monosaccharide containing five carbon atoms, and including an aldehyde functional group. It has chemical formula $C_5H_{10}O_5$.
Sugar	A sugar is the simplest molecule that can be identified as a carbohydrate. These include monosaccharides and disaccharides, trisaccharides and the oligosaccharides. The term "glyco-" indicates the presence of a sugar in an otherwise non-carbohydrate substance.
Thymine	Thymine, also known as 5-methyluracil, is a pyrimidine nucleobase. It is found in the nucleic acid DNA. In RNA thymine is replaced with uracil in most cases. In DNA, thymine(T) binds to adenine (A) via two hydrogen bonds to assist in stabilizing the nucleic acid structures.
Uracil	Uracil is one of the four RNA nucleobases, replacing thymine as found in DNA. Just like thymine, uracil can form a base pair with adenine via two hydrogen bonds, but it lacks the methyl group present in thymine. Uracil, in comparison to thymine, will more readily degenerate into cytosine.
Cytosine	Cytosine is one of the 5 main nucleobases used in storing and transporting genetic information within a cell in the nucleic acids DNA and RNA. It is a pyrimidine derivative, with a heterocyclic aromatic ring and two substituents attached. The nucleoside of cytosine is cytidine.

153

Linkage	Linkage refers to the patterns of assortment of genes that are located on the same chromosome. Important because if the genes are located relatively far apart, crossing over is more likely to occur between them than if they are close together.
Polypeptide	Polypeptide refers to polymer of many amino acids linked by peptide bonds.
DNA replication	DNA replication is the process of copying a double-stranded DNA strand in a cell, prior to cell division. The two resulting double strands are identical (if the replication went well), and each of them consists of one original and one newly synthesized strand.
Double helix	Double helix refers to the form of native DNA, referring to its two adjacent polynucleotide strands wound into a spiral shape.
Base pair	Two nucleotides on opposite complementary DNA or RNA strands that are connected via hydrogen bonds are called a base pair.
Methyl	In chemistry, a methyl group is a hydrophobic alkyl functional group derived from methane (CH_4). It has the formula $-CH_3$ and is very often abbreviated -Me.
Complementary sequence	Complementary sequence refers to a nucleic acid base sequence that can form a doublestranded structure by matching base pairs with another sequence; the complementary sequence to 5' GTAC 3' is 3' CATG 5'.
Template strand	The strand of the DNA double helix from which RNA is transcribed is called a template strand.
RNA polymerase	The enzyme RNA polymerase is a nucleotidyltransferase that polymerises ribonucleotides in accordance with the information present in DNA. RNA polymerase enzymes are essential and are found in all organisms.
Enzyme	An enzyme is a protein that catalyzes, or speeds up, a chemical reaction. They are essential to sustain life because most chemical reactions in biological cells would occur too slowly, or would lead to different products, without them.
Helix	A helix is a twisted shape like a spring, screw or a spiral staircase. They are important in biology, as DNA and many proteins have spiral substructures, known a alpha helix.
Polymerization	Polymerization is a process of reacting monomer molecules together in a chemical reaction to form linear chains or a three-dimensional network of polymer chains.
Polymerase	DNA or RNA enzymes that catalyze the synthesis of nucleic acids on preexisting nucleic acid templates, assembling RNA from ribonucleotides or DNA from deoxyribonucleotides is referred to as polymerase.
DNA polymerase	A DNA polymerase is an enzyme that assists in DNA replication. Such enzymes catalyze the polymerization of deoxyribonucleotides alongside a DNA strand, which they "read" and use as a template. The newly polymerized molecule is complementary to the template strand and identical to the template's partner strand.
Ribosomal RNA	The most prominent examples of non-coding Ribosomal RNA are non-coding RNA that are involved in the process of translation and gene expression.
Ribosome	A ribosome is an organelle composed of rRNA and ribosomal proteins. It translates mRNA into a polypeptide chain (e.g., a protein). It can be thought of as a factory that builds a protein from a set of genetic instructions.
Electron	The electron is a light fundamental subatomic particle that carries a negative electric charge. The electron is a spin-1/2 lepton, does not participate in strong interactions and has no substructure.
Transfer RNA	Transfer RNA is a small RNA chain (74-93 nucleotides) that transfers a specific amino acid to a growing polypeptide chain at the ribosomal site of protein synthesis during translation. It

Go to **Cram101.com** for the Practice Tests for this Chapter.

has sites for amino-acid attachment and codon (a particular sequence of 3 bases) recognition.

Micrograph	A micrograph is a photograph or similar image taken through a microscope or similar device to show a magnified image of an item.
Acid	An acid is a water-soluble, sour-tasting chemical compound that when dissolved in water, gives a solution with a pH of less than 7.
Promoter	In genetics, a promoter is a DNA sequence that enables a gene to be transcribed. The promoter is recognized by RNA polymerase, which then initiates transcription.
Sigma factor	Subunit of RNA polymerase that facilitates binding to promoter sites on DNA is referred to as sigma factor.
Terminator	Terminator refers to a special sequence of nucleotides in DNA that marks the end of a gene; it signals RNA polymerase to release the newly made RNA molecule, which then departs from the gene.
Elongation	Elongation refers to a phase of DNA replication, transcription, or translation that successively adds nucleotides or amino acids to a growing macromolecule.
Primer	A primer is a nucleic acid strand, or a related molecule that serves as a starting point for DNA replication. In most natural DNA replication, the ultimate primer for DNA synthesis is a short strand of RNA.
Nucleus	In cell biology, the nucleus is found in all eukaryotic cells that contains most of the cell's genetic material. The nucleus has two primary functions: to control chemical reactions within the cytoplasm and to store information needed for cellular division.
Cytoplasm	Cytoplasm refers to everything inside a cell between the plasma membrane and the nucleus; consists of a semifluid medium and organelles.
RNA processing	RNA processing refers to modification of RNA before it leaves the nucleus, a process unique to eukaryotes.
Histology	Histology is the study of tissue sectioned as a thin slice, using a microscope. It can be described as microscopic anatomy.
Primary transcript	Primary transcript is an RNA molecule that has not yet undergone any modification after its synthesis.
Cleavage	Cleavage refers to cytokinesis in animal cells and in some protists, characterized by pinching in of the plasma membrane.
Polyadenylation	Polyadenylation is the covalent linkage of a polyadenylyl moiety to a messenger RNA (mRNA) molecule. It is part of the route to producing mature messenger RNA for translation, in the larger process of protein synthesis to produce proteins.
Intron	An intron is a section of DNA within a gene that does not encode part of the protein that the gene produces, and is spliced out of the mRNA that is transcribed from the gene before it is translated.
Exon	An exon is the region of DNA within a gene that is not spliced out from the transcribed RNA and is retained in the final messenger RNA (mRNA) molecule.
Splicing	In genetics, splicing is a modification of genetic information after transcription, in which introns are removed and exons are joined. Splicing is an essential process in eukaryotic pre-mRNA processing that must precede translation.
Hemoglobin	Hemoglobin is the iron-containing oxygen-transport metalloprotein in the red cells of the blood in mammals and other animals. Hemoglobin transports oxygen from the lungs to the rest of the body, such as to the muscles, where it releases the oxygen load.

Hemophilia	Hemophilia is the name of any of several hereditary genetic illnesses that impair the body's ability to control bleeding. Genetic deficiencies cause lowered plasma clotting factor activity so as to compromise blood-clotting; when a blood vessel is injured, a scab will not form and the vessel can continue to bleed excessively for a very long period of time.
Mutation	Mutation refers to a change in the nucleotide sequence of DNA; the ultimate source of genetic diversity.
Spliceosome	A spliceosome is a complex of RNA and many protein subunits, that remove the non-coding introns from unprocessed mRNA.
Consensus sequence	A consensus sequence is a way of representing the results of a multiple sequence alignment, where related sequences are compared to each other, and similar functional sequence motifs are found. The consensus sequence shows which residues are conserved, and which residues are variable.
Rearrangement	A change in the usual order and arrangement of genetic material either within the chromosome complement or within a gene locus is rearrangement. Where the nature of the rearrangement has been determined, the type may be searched for directly under the following designations: reciprocal translocation, Robertsonian translocation, insertion, transposition, inversion, deletion, and duplication.
Cell nucleus	The cell nucleus is found in all eukaryotic cells that contains most of the cell's genetic material. They have two primary functions: to control chemical reactions within the cytoplasm and to store information needed for cellular division.
Coiled-coil	Especially stable rodlike structure in proteins which is formed by two of these a helices coiled around each other is a coiled-coil.
Tropomyosin	Protein that blocks muscle contraction until calcium ions are present is referred to as tropomyosin.
Smooth muscle	Smooth muscle is a type of non-striated muscle, found within the "walls" of hollow organs; such as blood vessels, the bladder, the uterus, and the gastrointestinal tract. Smooth muscle is used to move matter within the body, via contraction; it generally operates "involuntarily", without nerve stimulation.
Muscle	Muscle is a contractile form of tissue. It is one of the four major tissue types, the other three being epithelium, connective tissue and nervous tissue. Muscle contraction is used to move parts of the body, as well as to move substances within the body.
Fibroblast	A fibroblast is a cell that makes the structural fibers and ground substance of connective tissue.
Nuclear transport	Gated transport mechanisms by which proteins or RNA are moved across the nuclear membrane is referred to as nuclear transport.
Receptor	A receptor is a protein on the cell membrane or within the cytoplasm or cell nucleus that binds to a specific molecule (a ligand), such as a neurotransmitter, hormone, or other substance, and initiates the cellular response to the ligand. Receptor, in immunology, the region of an antibody which shows recognition of an antigen.
Cytosol	The cytosol is the internal fluid of the cell, and a large part of cell metabolism occurs here. Proteins within the cytosol play an important role in signal transduction pathways, glycolysis; also, they act as intracellular receptors and form part of the ribosomes, enabling further protein synthesis
Gene expression	Gene expression is the process by which a gene's information is converted into the structures and functions of a cell. Gene expression is a multi-step process that begins with transcription, post transcriptional modification and translation, followed by folding, post-

translational modification and targeting.

Evolution	In biology, evolution is the process by which novel traits arise in populations and are passed on from generation to generation. Its action over large stretches of time explains the origin of new species and ultimately the vast diversity of the biological world.
Yeast	Yeast refers to common term for several families of unicellular fungi. Includes species used for brewing beer and making bread, as well as pathogenic species.
Genetic code	The genetic code is a set of rules that maps DNA sequences to proteins in the living cell, and is employed in the process of protein synthesis. Nearly all living things use the same genetic code, called the standard genetic code, although a few organisms use minor variations of the standard code.
Codon	Codon refers to a three-nucleotide sequence in mRNA that specifies a particular amino acid or polypeptide termination signal; the basic unit of the genetic code.
Reading frame	In biology, a reading frame is a contiguous and non-overlapping set of three-nucleotide codons in DNA or RNA. There are 3 possible reading frames in a strand. A reading frame that contains a start codon and a stop codon is called an open reading frame.
Stop codon	In mRNA, one of three triplets that signal gene translation to stop is called stop codon.
Colon	The colon is the part of the intestine from the cecum to the rectum. Its primary purpose is to extract water from feces.
Polynucleotide	Polynucleotide refers to a polymer consisting of many nucleotide monomers; serves as a blueprint for proteins and, through the actions of proteins, for all cellular activities. The two types are DNA and RNA.
Hydrogen bond	A hydrogen bond is a type of attractive intermolecular force that exists between two partial electric charges of opposite polarity. Although stronger than most other intermolecular forces, the typical hydrogen bond is much weaker than both the ionic bond and the covalent bond.
Anticodon	An anticodon is a unit made up of three nucleotides which play an important role in various DNA cycles, including RNA translation. Each tRNA contains a specific anticodon triplet sequence that can base-pair to one or more codons for an amino acid.
D loop	D loop refers to the first structure formed during DNA replication of chloroplast and mitochondrial chromosomes where the area of replication is different on the two strands.
Clover	Clover (Trifolium) is a genus of about 300 species of plants in the pea family Fabaceae. They are found chiefly in northern temperate regions, but also, like many other north temperate genera, on the mountains in the tropics.
Leaf	In botany, a leaf is an above-ground plant organ specialized for photosynthesis. For this purpose, a leaf is typically flat (laminar) and thin, to expose the chloroplast containing cells (chlorenchyma tissue) to light over a broad area, and to allow light to penetrate fully into the tissues.
Pseudouridine	Pseudouridine is the C-glycoside isomer of the nucleoside uridine, and it is the most prevalent of the over one hundred different modified nucleosides found in RNA
Diffraction	Diffraction is the bending and spreading of waves when they meet an obstruction. It can occur with any type of wave, including sound waves, water waves, and electromagnetic waves such as light and radio waves.
X-Ray	X-Ray refers to diagnostic test in which an image is created using low doses of radiation.
Sequencing	Determining the order of nucleotides in a DNA or RNA molecule or the order of amino acids in

Go to **Cram101.com** for the Practice Tests for this Chapter.

a protein is sequencing.

Cell-free system	Fractionated cell homogenate that retains a particular biological function of the intact cell, and in which biochemical reactions and cell processes can be more easily studied is a cell-free system.
Centrifuge	Centrifuge refers to a device in which a sample can be spun around a central axis at high speed, creating a centrifugal force that mimics a very strong gravitational force. Used to separate mixtures of suspended materials.
Cellular component	The cellular component involves the movement of white blood cells from blood vessels into the inflamed tissue. The white blood cells, or leukocytes, take on an important role in inflammation; they extravasate (filter out) from the capillaries into tissue, and act as phagocytes, picking up bacteria and cellular debris. They may also aid by walling off an infection and preventing its spread.
Radioactive	A term used to describe the property of releasing energy or particles from an unstable atom is called radioactive.
Sediment	Sediment is any particulate matter that can be transported by fluid flow and which eventually is deposited as a layer of solid particles on the bed or bottom of a body of water or other liquid.
Peptide	Peptide is the family of molecules formed from the linking, in a defined order, of various amino acids. The link between one amino acid residue and the next is an amide bond, and is sometimes referred to as a peptide bond.
Phosphorylase	Phosphorylase is a family of allosteric enzymes that catalyze the production of glucose-1-phosphate from a polyglucose such as glycogen, starch or maltodextrin.
Homogeneous	Homogeneous refers both to animals and plants, of having a resemblance in structure, due to descent from a common progenitor with subsequent modification.
Phenylalanine	Phenylalanine is an essential amino acid. The genetic disorder phenylketonuria is an inability to metabolize phenylalanine.
Proline	Proline is one of the twenty proteinogenic units which are used in living organisms as the building blocks of proteins. The other nineteen units are all primary amino acids, but due to the (3-carbon) cyclic sidechain binding back to the nitrogen of the backbone, proline lacks a primary amine group ($-NH_2$).
Lysine	Lysine is one of the 20 amino acids normally found in proteins. With its 4-aminobutyl side-chain, it is classified as a basic amino acid, along with arginine and histidine.
Cysteine	Cysteine is a naturally occurring hydrophobic amino acid which has a thiol group and is found in most proteins, though only in small quantities.
Residue	A residue refers to a portion of a larger molecule, a specific monomer of a polysaccharide, protein or nucleic acid.
Valine	Nutritionally, valine is also an essential amino acid. It is named after the plant valerian. In sickle-cell disease, it substitutes for the hydrophilic amino acid glutamic acid in hemoglobin.
Alanine	Alanine (Ala) also 2-aminopropanoic acid is a non-essential α-amino acid. It exists as two distinct enantiomers - L-alanine and D-alanine. L-alanine is one of the 20 amino acids most widely used in protein synthesis, second to leucine.
Species	Group of similarly constructed organisms capable of interbreeding and producing fertile offspring is a species.

Glycine	Glycine (Gly, G) is a nonpolar amino acid. It is the simplest of the 20 standard (proteinogenic) amino acids: its side chain is a hydrogen atom. Because there is a second hydrogen atom at the α carbon, glycine is not optically active.
Charged tRNA	A tRNA molecule to which the corresponding amino acid has been attached by an aminoacyl-tRNA synthetase is referred to as charged tRNA.
Hydrolysis	Hydrolysis is a chemical process in which a molecule is cleaved into two parts by the addition of a molecule of water.
Dalton	A measure of mass for atoms and subatomic particles is a dalton.
Endoplasmic reticulum	The endoplasmic reticulum is an organelle found in all eukaryotic cells. It modifies proteins, makes macromolecules, and transfers substances throughout the cell.
Peptide bond	A peptide bond is a chemical bond formed between two molecules when the carboxyl group of one molecule reacts with the amino group of the other molecule, releasing a molecule of water.
Amino group	An amino group is an ammonia-like functional group composed of a nitrogen and two hydrogen atoms covalently linked. $-NH_2$
Carboxyl	A carboxyl is the univalent radical -COOH; present in and characteristic of organic acids.
Ribozyme	An enzymatic RNA molecule that catalyzes chemical reactions is called ribozyme.
Biology	Biology is the branch of science dealing with the study of life. It is concerned with the characteristics, classification, and behaviors of organisms, how species come into existence, and the interactions they have with each other and with the environment.
Conformation	The three-dimensional shape of a molecule is its conformation. The conformation is particularly important in proteins.
X-ray crystallography	Technique for determining the three-dimensional arrangement of atoms in a molecule based on the diffraction pattern of X-rays passing through a crystal of the molecule is x-ray crystallography.
N-terminal end	The N-terminal end refers to the extremity of a protein or polypeptide terminated by an amino acid with a free amine group (NH_2).
C-terminus	The C-terminus of a protein or polypeptide is the extremity of the amino acid chain terminated by a free carboxyl group (-COOH).
Protein subunit	A protein subunit is a single protein molecule that assembles (or "coassembles") with other protein molecules to form a multimeric or oligomeric protein. Many naturally-occurring proteins and enzymes are multimeric.
Ultracentrifuge	Ultracentrifuge refers to a machine that spins test tubes at the fastest speeds to separate liquids and particles of different densities.
Start codon	Start codon refers to on mRNA, the specific threenucleotide sequence to which an initiator tRNA molecule binds, starting translation of genetic information.
Initiator tRNA	Initiator trna refers to special tRNA that intiates translation. It always carries the amino acid methionine.
Methionine	Methionine and cysteine are the only sulfur-containing proteinogenic amino acids. The methionine derivative S-adenosyl methionine (SAM) serves as a methyl donor.
Initiation factor	Initiation factor refers to protein that promotes the proper association of ribosomes with messenger RNA and is required for the initiation of protein synthesis.
Peptidyl transferase	Peptidyl transferase is an enzyme found in ribosomes which helps form peptide links between adjacent amino acids during the translation process of protein biosynthesis.

Chaperone	Protein that helps other proteins avoid misfolding pathways that produce inactive or aggregated polypeptides is called a chaperone.
Polyribosome	String of ribosomes simultaneously translating regions of the same mRNA strand during protein synthesis is referred to as a polyribosome.
Polysome	Polysome refers to a complex consisting of a threadlike molecule of messenger RNA and several ribosomes. The ribosomes move along the mRNA, synthesizing polypeptide chains as they proceed.
Antibiotic	Antibiotic refers to substance such as penicillin or streptomycin that is toxic to microorganisms. Usually a product of a particular microorvanism or plant.
Inhibitor	An inhibitor is a type of effector (biology) that decreases or prevents the rate of a chemical reaction. They are often called negative catalysts.
Population	Group of organisms of the same species occupying a certain area and sharing a common gene pool is referred to as population.
Proteolysis	Degradation of a protein by cellular enzymes called proteases or by intramolecular digestion at one or more of its peptide bonds is referred to as proteolysis.
Protease	Protease refers to an enzyme that breaks peptide bonds between amino acids of proteins.
Active site	The active site of an enzyme is the binding site where catalysis occurs. The structure and chemical properties of the active site allow the recognition and binding of the substrate.
Proteasome	Large protein complex in the cytosol with proteolytic activity that is responsible for degrading proteins that have been marked for destruction by ubiquitylation or by some other means is referred to as a proteasome.
Ubiquitin	Ubiquitin is a small protein that occurs in all eukaryotic cells. Its main function is to mark other proteins for destruction, known as proteolysis. Several ubiquitin molecules attach to the condemned protein, and it then moves to a proteasome, a barrel-shaped structure where the proteolysis occurs.
Digestion	Digestion refers to the mechanical and chemical breakdown of food into molecules small enough for the body to absorb; the second main stage of food processing, following ingestion.
Electron microscope	The electron microscope is a microscope that can magnify very small details with high resolving power due to the use of electrons as the source of illumination, magnifying at levels up to 500,000 times.
Chemical reaction	Chemical reaction refers to a process leading to chemical changes in matter; involves the making and/or breaking of chemical bonds.
Catalyst	A chemical that speeds up a reaction but is not used up in the reaction is a catalyst.
Catalysis	Catalysis is the acceleration of the reaction rate of a chemical reaction by means of a substance, called a catalyst, that is itself not consumed by the overall reaction.
Origin of life	Research into the origin of life is a limited field of research despite its profound impact on biology and human understanding of the natural world. Progress in this field is generally slow and sporadic, though it still draws the attention of many due to the gravity of the question being investigated.
Autocatalysis	A single chemical reaction is said to have undergone autocatalysis, if the reaction product is itself the catalyst for that reaction.
Versatile	The anther can be attached to the filament in two ways, versatile is when it is attached at its center to the filament; pollen is then released through pores (poricidal dehiscence).

Go to **Cram101.com** for the Practice Tests for this Chapter.

Substrate	A substrate is a molecule which is acted upon by an enzyme. Each enzyme recognizes only the specific substrate of the reaction it catalyzes. A surface in or on which an organism lives.
In vitro	In vitro is an experimental technique where the experiment is performed in a test tube, or generally outside a living organism or cell.
Carbohydrate	Carbohydrate is a chemical compound that contains oxygen, hydrogen, and carbon atoms. They consist of monosaccharide sugars of varying chain lengths and that have the general chemical formula $C_n(H_2O)_n$ or are derivatives of such.
Glucose	Glucose, a simple monosaccharide sugar, is one of the most important carbohydrates and is used as a source of energy in animals and plants. Glucose is one of the main products of photosynthesis and starts respiration.
Mole	The atomic weight of a substance, expressed in grams. One mole is defined as the mass of 6.0222 3 1023 atoms.
Initiation codon	Initiation codon refers to nucleotide triplet that marks the precise spot in the nucleotide sequence of an mRNA where the code for a particular polypeptide begins.
Control group	Control group refers to a group in an experiment in which there are no manipulated variables. It serves as the basis for comparison in a controlled experiment.
Covalent bond	A covalent bond is an intramolecular form of chemical bonding characterized by the sharing of one or more pairs of electrons between two elements, producing a mutual attraction that holds the resultant molecule together.
Translocation	A chromosomal mutation in which a portion of one chromosome breaks off and becomes attached to another chromosome is referred to as translocation.
Triplet code	The normal version of the genetic code in which a sequence of three nucleotides codes for the synthesis of a specific amino acid is a triplet code.
Tryptophan	Tryptophan is a sleep-promoting amino acid and a precursor for serotonin (a neurotransmitter) and melatonin (a neurohormone). Tryptophan has been implicated as a possible cause of schizophrenia in people who cannot metabolize it properly.
Molecular weight	The molecular mass of a substance, called molecular weight and abbreviated as MW, is the mass of one molecule of that substance, relative to the unified atomic mass unit u (equal to 1/12 the mass of one atom of carbon-12).
Insertion	At DNA level, an insertion means the insertion of a few base pairs into a genetic sequence. This can often happen in microsatellite regions due to the DNA polymerase slipping.
Deletion	Deletion refers to the loss of one or more nucleotides from a gene by mutation; the loss of a fragment of a chromosome.
Multicellular	Multicellular organisms are those organisms consisting of more than one cell, and having differentiated cells that perform specialized functions. Most life that can be seen with the naked eye is multicellular, as are all animals (i.e. members of the kingdom Animalia) and plants (i.e. members of the kingdom Plantae).
Gene regulatory protein	General name for any protein that binds to a specific DNA sequence to alter the expression of a gene is referred to as gene regulatory protein.
Fruit	A fruit is the ripened ovary—together with seeds—of a flowering plant. In many species, the fruit incorporates the ripened ovary and surrounding tissues.
Embryo	Embryo refers to a developing stage of a multicellular organism. In humans, the stage in the development of offspring from the first division of the zygote until body structures begin to appear, about the ninth week of gestation.

Gene expression	Gene expression is the process by which a gene's information is converted into the structures and functions of a cell. Gene expression is a multi-step process that begins with transcription, post transcriptional modification and translation, followed by folding, post-translational modification and targeting.
Molecule	A molecule is the smallest particle of a pure chemical substance that still retains its chemical composition and properties.
Protein	A protein is a complex, high-molecular-weight organic compound that consists of amino acids joined by peptide bonds. They are essential to the structure and function of all living cells and viruses. Many are enzymes or subunits of enzymes.
Cell	The cell is the structural and functional unit of all living organisms, and is sometimes called the "building block of life."
Bacterium	Most bacterium are microscopic and unicellular, with a relatively simple cell structure lacking a cell nucleus, and organelles such as mitochondria and chloroplasts. They are the most abundant of all organisms. They are ubiquitous in soil, water, and as symbionts of other organisms.
Enzyme	An enzyme is a protein that catalyzes, or speeds up, a chemical reaction. They are essential to sustain life because most chemical reactions in biological cells would occur too slowly, or would lead to different products, without them.
Gene	Gene refers to a discrete unit of hereditary information consisting of a specific nucleotide sequence in DNA . Most of the genes of a eukaryote are located in its chromosomal DNA; a few are carried by the DNA of mitochondria and chloroplasts.
Multicellular	Multicellular organisms are those organisms consisting of more than one cell, and having differentiated cells that perform specialized functions. Most life that can be seen with the naked eye is multicellular, as are all animals (i.e. members of the kingdom Animalia) and plants (i.e. members of the kingdom Plantae).
Egg	An egg is the zygote, resulting from fertilization of the ovum. It nourishes and protects the embryo.
Lymphocyte	A lymphocyte is a type of white blood cell involved in the human body's immune system. There are two broad categories, namely T cells and B cells.
Neuron	The neuron is a major class of cells in the nervous system. In vertebrates, they are found in the brain, the spinal cord and in the nerves and ganglia of the peripheral nervous system, and their primary role is to process and transmit neural information.
Cell differentiation	Cell differentiation is a concept from developmental biology describing the process by which cells acquire a "type". The morphology of a cell may change dramatically during differentiation, but the genetic material remains the same, with few exceptions.
Immune system	The immune system is the system of specialized cells and organs that protect an organism from outside biological influences. When the immune system is functioning properly, it protects the body against bacteria and viral infections, destroying cancer cells and foreign substances.
Hemoglobin	Hemoglobin is the iron-containing oxygen-transport metalloprotein in the red cells of the blood in mammals and other animals. Hemoglobin transports oxygen from the lungs to the rest of the body, such as to the muscles, where it releases the oxygen load.
Pancreas	The pancreas is a retroperitoneal organ that serves two functions: exocrine - it produces pancreatic juice containing digestive enzymes, and endocrine - it produces several important hormones, namely insulin.

Glucagon	A peptide hormone secreted by islet cells in the pancreas that raises the level of glucose in the blood is referred to as glucagon. Glucagon is a 29 amino acid polypeptide acting as an important hormone in carbohydrate metabolism.
Hormone	A hormone is a chemical messenger from one cell to another. All multicellular organisms produce hormones. The best known hormones are those produced by endocrine glands of vertebrate animals, but hormones are produced by nearly every organ system and tissue type in a human or animal body. Hormone molecules are secreted directly into the bloodstream, they move by circulation or diffusion to their target cells, which may be nearby cells in the same tissue or cells of a distant organ of the body.
Insulin	Insulin is a polypeptide hormone that regulates carbohydrate metabolism. Apart from being the primary effector in carbohydrate homeostasis, it also has a substantial effect on small vessel muscle tone, controls storage and release of fat (triglycerides) and cellular uptake of both amino acids and some electrolytes.
Blood	Blood is a circulating tissue composed of fluid plasma and cells. The main function of blood is to supply nutrients (oxygen, glucose) and constitutional elements to tissues and to remove waste products.
Bacteria	The domain that contains procaryotic cells with primarily diacyl glycerol diesters in their membranes and with bacterial rRNA. Bacteria also is a general term for organisms that are composed of procaryotic cells and are not multicellular.
Retina	The retina is a thin layer of cells at the back of the eyeball of vertebrates and some cephalopods; it is the part of the eye which converts light into nervous signals.
Immune response	The body's defensive reaction to invasion by bacteria, viral agents, or other foreign substances is called the immune response.
Genome	The genome of an organism is the whole hereditary information of an organism that is encoded in the DNA (or, for some viruses, RNA). This includes both the genes and the non-coding sequences. The genome of an organism is a complete DNA sequence of one set of chromosomes.
Muscle	Muscle is a contractile form of tissue. It is one of the four major tissue types, the other three being epithelium, connective tissue and nervous tissue. Muscle contraction is used to move parts of the body, as well as to move substances within the body.
Nerve	A nerve is an enclosed, cable-like bundle of nerve fibers or axons, which includes the glia that ensheath the axons in myelin.
Differentiated cell	Differentiated cell refers to a mature cell specialized for a specific function and do not maintain the ability to generate other kinds of cells, or revert back to a less specialized cell; in plants, a differentiated cell normally does not divide.
Chromosome	A chromosome is, minimally, a very long, continuous piece of DNA, which contains many genes, regulatory elements and other intervening nucleotide sequences.
Nucleus	In cell biology, the nucleus is found in all eukaryotic cells that contains most of the cell's genetic material. The nucleus has two primary functions: to control chemical reactions within the cytoplasm and to store information needed for cellular division.
Skin	Skin is an organ of the integumentary system composed of a layer of tissues that protect underlying muscles and organs.
Nuclear transplantation	A technique in which the nucleus of one cell is placed into another cell that already has a nucleus or in which the nucleus has been previously destroyed is a nuclear transplantation.
DNA sequence	A DNA sequence is a succession of letters representing the primary structure of a real or hypothetical DNA molecule or strand, The possible letters are A, C, G, and T, representing

Go to **Cram101.com** for the Practice Tests for this Chapter.

the four nucleotide subunits of a DNA strand (adenine, cytosine, guanine, thymine).

Cell nucleus	The cell nucleus is found in all eukaryotic cells that contains most of the cell's genetic material. They have two primary functions: to control chemical reactions within the cytoplasm and to store information needed for cellular division.
Mammal	Homeothermic vertebrate characterized especially by the presence of hair and mammary glands is a mammal.
Gel electrophoresis	Gel electrophoresis is a group of techniques used by scientists to separate molecules based on physical characteristics such as size, shape, or isoelectric point.
Tadpole	A tadpole is a larval frog, toad, salamander, newt, or caecilian. In this stage it breathes by means of external or internal gills, is at first lacking legs, and has a finlike tail with which it swims as most fish do, by lateral undulation.
Embryo	Embryo refers to a developing stage of a multicellular organism. In humans, the stage in the development of offspring from the first division of the zygote until body structures begin to appear, about the ninth week of gestation.
Clone	A group of genetically identical cells or organisms derived by asexual reproduction from a single parent is called a clone.
Glucocorticoid	Glucocorticoid is a class of steroid hormones characterized by the ability to bind with the cortisol receptor and trigger similar effects. They are distinguished from mineralocorticoids and sex steroids by the specific receptors, target cells, and effects.
Liver	The liver is an organ in vertebrates, including humans. It plays a major role in metabolism and has a number of functions in the body including drug detoxification, glycogen storage, and plasma protein synthesis. It also produces bile, which is important for digestion.
Amino acid	An amino acid is any molecule that contains both amino and carboxylic acid functional groups. They are the basic structural building units of proteins. They form short polymer chains called peptides or polypeptides which in turn form structures called proteins.
Tyrosine	Tyrosine is one of the 20 amino acids that are used by cells to synthesize proteins. It plays a key role in signal transduction, since it can be tagged (phosphorylated) with a phosphate group by protein kinases to alter the functionality and activity of certain enzymes.
Glucose	Glucose, a simple monosaccharide sugar, is one of the most important carbohydrates and is used as a source of energy in animals and plants. Glucose is one of the main products of photosynthesis and starts respiration.
Transcription	Transcription is the process through which a DNA sequence is enzymatically copied by an RNA polymerase to produce a complementary RNA. Or, in other words, the transfer of genetic information from DNA into RNA.
Promoter region	A location on DNA to which RNA polymerase will bind and initiate transcription of the associated gene is called a promoter region.
RNA polymerase	The enzyme RNA polymerase is a nucleotidyltransferase that polymerises ribonucleotides in accordance with the information present in DNA. RNA polymerase enzymes are essential and are found in all organisms.
Initiation site	Initiation site refers to the site where DNA replication begins on a chromosome.
Nucleotide	A nucleotide is a chemical compound that consists of a heterocyclic base, a sugar, and one or more phosphate groups. In the most common nucleotides the base is a derivative of purine or pyrimidine, and the sugar is pentose - deoxyribose or ribose. They are the structural units of RNA and DNA.

Upstream	Upstream refers to movement opposite the direction RNA follows when moving along a gene.
Promoter	In genetics, a promoter is a DNA sequence that enables a gene to be transcribed. The promoter is recognized by RNA polymerase, which then initiates transcription.
Gene regulatory protein	General name for any protein that binds to a specific DNA sequence to alter the expression of a gene is referred to as gene regulatory protein.
Double helix	Double helix refers to the form of native DNA, referring to its two adjacent polynucleotide strands wound into a spiral shape.
Major groove	Area of open space present in turns of the alpha-helix in the common staircase model of double-stranded DNA is the major groove.
Base pair	Two nucleotides on opposite complementary DNA or RNA strands that are connected via hydrogen bonds are called a base pair.
Helix	A helix is a twisted shape like a spring, screw or a spiral staircase. They are important in biology, as DNA and many proteins have spiral substructures, known a alpha helix.
Hydrophobic interaction	The tendency for hydrophobic molecules to cluster together when immersed in water is called hydrophobic interaction.
Hydrogen bond	A hydrogen bond is a type of attractive intermolecular force that exists between two partial electric charges of opposite polarity. Although stronger than most other intermolecular forces, the typical hydrogen bond is much weaker than both the ionic bond and the covalent bond.
Ionic bond	Ionic bond refers to an attraction between two ions with opposite electrical charges. The electrical attraction of the opposite charges holds the ions together.
Biology	Biology is the branch of science dealing with the study of life. It is concerned with the characteristics, classification, and behaviors of organisms, how species come into existence, and the interactions they have with each other and with the environment.
Asparagine	Asparagine is one of the 20 most common natural amino acids on Earth. It has carboxamide as the side chain's functional group. It is considered a non-essential amino acid.
Sugar	A sugar is the simplest molecule that can be identified as a carbohydrate. These include monosaccharides and disaccharides, trisaccharides and the oligosaccharides. The term "glyco-" indicates the presence of a sugar in an otherwise non-carbohydrate substance.
Structural motif	In an unbranched, chain-like biological molecule, such as a protein or a strand of RNA, a structural motif is a three-dimensional structural element or fold within the chain, which appears also in a variety of other molecules.
Homeodomain	A conserved DNA-binding region of transcription factors encoded by the homeobox of homeotic genes is called homeodomain.
Adenine	Adenine is one of the two purine nucleobases used in forming nucleotides of the nucleic acids DNA and RNA. In DNA, adenine (A) binds to thymine (T) via two hydrogen bonds to assist in stabilizing the nucleic acid structures. In RNA, adenine binds to uracil (U).
Zinc finger	Zinc finger refers to DNA-binding structural motif present in many gene regulatory proteins. Composed of a loop of polypeptide chain held in a hairpin bend bound to a zinc atom.
Zinc	Zinc is a chemical element in the periodic table that has the symbol Zn and atomic number 30.
Leucine zipper	The leucine zipper is a type of structural motif found in parallel coiled coils. It is a common dimerization domain found in some DNA regulatory proteins. The main feature of the leucine zipper domain is the predominance of leucine at the d position of the heptad repeat.

Go to **Cram101.com** for the Practice Tests for this Chapter.

Dimer	A dimer refers to a molecule composed of two similar subunits or monomers linked together. It is a special case of a polymer.
Gene regulation	Gene regulation is the cellular control of the amount and timing of appearance (induction) of the functional product of a gene. Although a functional gene product may be an RNA or a protein, the majority of the known mechanisms regulate the expression of protein coding genes.
Specificity	A medical diagnostic test for a certain disease, specificity is the proportion of true negatives of all the negative samples tested.
Virus	Obligate intracellular parasite of living cells consisting of an outer capsid and an inner core of nucleic acid is referred to as virus. The term virus usually refers to those particles that infect eukaryotes whilst the term bacteriophage or phage is used to describe those infecting prokaryotes.
Circular DNA	Circular DNA is found in bacteria and other archaea. While the individual strands of a linear double helix represent two distinct and separable molecules, this need not be true for circular DNA. If the strands twist an odd number of times around one another in completing the DNA loop, then they are covalently joined into a single molecule.
Operator	An operator is a segment of DNA that regulates the activity of the structural genes of an operon it is linked to, by interacting with a specific repressor or activator. It is a regulatory sequence for shutting a gene down or turning it "on".
Operon	An operon is a group of key nucleotide sequences including an operator, a common promoter, and one or more structural genes that are controlled as a unit to produce messenger RNA (mRNA).
Allosteric protein	Allosteric protein refers to protein that changes from one conformation to another when it binds another molecule or when it is covalently modified.
Tryptophan	Tryptophan is a sleep-promoting amino acid and a precursor for serotonin (a neurotransmitter) and melatonin (a neurohormone). Tryptophan has been implicated as a possible cause of schizophrenia in people who cannot metabolize it properly.
Repressor	A repressor is a DNA-binding protein that regulates the expression of one or more genes by decreasing the rate of transcription.
Polymerase	DNA or RNA enzymes that catalyze the synthesis of nucleic acids on preexisting nucleic acid templates, assembling RNA from ribonucleotides or DNA from deoxyribonucleotides is referred to as polymerase.
Activator	An activator, is a DNA-binding protein that regulates one or more genes by increasing the rate of transcription.
Metabolite	The term metabolite is usually restricted to small molecules. They are the intermediates and products of metabolism. A primary metabolite is directly involved in the normal growth, development, and reproduction. A secondary metabolite is not directly involved in those processes, but usually has important ecological function.
Lac operon	The lac operon is an operon required for the transport and metabolism of lactose in Escherichia coli and some other enteric bacteria. It consists of three adjacent structural genes, a promoter, a terminator, and an operator.
Lactose	Lactose is a disaccharide that makes up around 2-8% of the solids in milk. Lactose is a disaccharide consisting of two subunits, a galactose and a glucose linked together.
Galactose	Galactose is a type of sugar found in dairy products, in sugar beets and other gums and mucilages. It is also synthesized by the body, where it forms part of glycolipids and

glycoproteins in several tissues.

Carbon	Carbon is a chemical element in the periodic table that has the symbol C and atomic number 6. An abundant nonmetallic, tetravalent element, carbon has several allotropic forms.
Disaccharide	A disaccharide is a sugar (a carbohydrate) composed of two monosaccharides. The two monosaccharides are bonded via a condensation reaction.
Biochemistry	Biochemistry studies how complex chemical reactions give rise to life. It is a hybrid branch of chemistry which specialises in the chemical processes in living organisms.
Genetics	Genetics is the science of genes, heredity, and the variation of organisms.
Bacteriophage	Bacteriophage refers to a virus that infects bacteria; also called a phage.
RRNA gene	rRNA gene is a component of the ribosomes, the protein synthetic factories in the cell. They make up at least 80% of the RNA molecules found in a typical eukaryotic cell.
Spliceosome	A spliceosome is a complex of RNA and many protein subunits, that remove the non-coding introns from unprocessed mRNA.
Bacterial chromosome	The single, circular DNA molecule found in bacteria is a bacterial chromosome.
Viral	Viral phenomena are objects or patterns able to replicate themselves or convert other objects into copies of themselves when these objects are exposed to them.
Prophage	A prophage is a phage chromosome inserted as part of the linear structure of the DNA chromosome of a bacterium.
Regulatory sequence	Regulatory sequence refers to dNA sequence to which a gene regulatory protein binds to control the rate of assembly of the transcirptional complex at the promoter.
Nucleosome	Nucleosome refers to the beadlike unit of DNA packing in a eukaryotic cell; consists of DNA wound around a protein core made up of eight histone molecules.
Chromatin	Chromatin refers to the combination of DNA and proteins that constitute chromosomes; often used to refer to the diffuse, very extended form taken by the chromosomes when a eukaryotic cell is not dividing.
TATA box	A TATA box is a DNA sequence found in the promoter region of most genes. It is the binding site of either transcription factors or histones and is involved in the process of transcription by RNA polymerase.
Transcription initiation complex	Transcription initiation complex refers to the completed assembly of transcription factors and RNA polymerase bound to the promoter.
Transcription factor	In molecular biology, a transcription factor is a protein that binds DNA at a specific promoter or enhancer region or site, where it regulates transcription.
Phosphorylation	Phosphorylation refers to reaction in which a phosphate group becomes covalently coupled to another molecule.
Phosphate group	The functional group -OPO_3H_2; the transfer of energy from one compound to another is often accomplished by the transfer of a phosphate group.
Protein kinase	Enzyme that transfers the terminal phosphate group of ATP to a specific amino acid of a target protein is protein kinase.
Elongation	Elongation refers to a phase of DNA replication, transcription, or translation that successively adds nucleotides or amino acids to a growing macromolecule.

Go to **Cram101.com** for the Practice Tests for this Chapter.

Highly conserved	Highly conserved refers to genes or proteins whose sequences are very similar in different species.
Evolution	In biology, evolution is the process by which novel traits arise in populations and are passed on from generation to generation. Its action over large stretches of time explains the origin of new species and ultimately the vast diversity of the biological world.
Yeast	Yeast refers to common term for several families of unicellular fungi. Includes species used for brewing beer and making bread, as well as pathogenic species.
Polyadenylation	Polyadenylation is the covalent linkage of a polyadenylyl moiety to a messenger RNA (mRNA) molecule. It is part of the route to producing mature messenger RNA for translation, in the larger process of protein synthesis to produce proteins.
Polypeptide	Polypeptide refers to polymer of many amino acids linked by peptide bonds.
Splicing	In genetics, splicing is a modification of genetic information after transcription, in which introns are removed and exons are joined. Splicing is an essential process in eukaryotic pre-mRNA processing that must precede translation.
Domain	In biology, a domain is the top-level grouping of organisms in scientific classification.
Phosphatase	A phosphatase is an enzyme that hydrolyses phosphoric acid monoesters into a phosphate ion and a molecule with a free hydroxyl group.
Phosphate	A phosphate is a polyatomic ion or radical consisting of one phosphorus atom and four oxygen. In the ionic form, it carries a -3 formal charge, and is denoted PO_4^{3-}.
In vitro	In vitro is an experimental technique where the experiment is performed in a test tube, or generally outside a living organism or cell.
Enhancer	An enhancer is a short region of DNA that can be bound with proteins to enhance transcription levels of genes in a gene-cluster.
Histone	Histone refers to a small basic protein molecule associated with DNA and important in DNA packing in the eukaryotic chromosome.
Acetyl	The acetyl radical contains a methyl group single-bonded to a carbonyl. The carbon of the carbonyl has an lone electron available, with which it forms a chemical bond to the remainder of the molecule.
Histone acetylation	The attachment of acetyl groups to certain amino acids of histone proteins is referred to as histone acetylation.
Holoenzyme	Holoenzyme may refer either to the complete and operative form of an enzyme with multiple protein subunits or to the combination of an apoenzyme with its cofactor.
Combinatorial control	Combinatorial control describes the control of a step in a cellular process, such as the initiation of DNA transcription, by a combination of proteins rather than by any individual
Fertilization	Fertilization is fusion of gametes to form a new organism. In animals, the process involves a sperm fusing with an ovum, which eventually leads to the development of an embryo.
Drosophila	Drosophila is part of the phylum Arthropoda, a phylum of segmented animals with paired, jointed appendages and a hard exoskeleton made of chitin. They have an open circulatory system with a dorsal heart, with hemocoel occupying most of the body cavity, and a reduced coelom.
Mutation	Mutation refers to a change in the nucleotide sequence of DNA; the ultimate source of genetic diversity.
Larva	A free-living, sexually immature form in some animal life cycles that may differ from the

	adult in morphology, nutrition, and habitat is called larva.
Cytoplasm	Cytoplasm refers to everything inside a cell between the plasma membrane and the nucleus; consists of a semifluid medium and organelles.
Cellularization	The formation of cells around each nucleus in a multinucleate cytoplasm, transforming it into a multicellular structure is referred to as cellularization.
Plasma membrane	Membrane surrounding the cytoplasm that consists of a phospholipid bilayer with embedded proteins is referred to as plasma membrane.
Duplication	Duplication refers to repetition of part of a chromosome resulting from fusion with a fragment from a homologous chromosome; can result from an error in meiosis or from mutagenesis.
Anteroposterior	Anteroposterior describes the axis running from the head to the tail of the animal body.
DNA construct	A DNA construct is an artificially constructed segment of nucleic acid that is going to be "transplanted" into a target tissue or cell.
Gradient	Gradient refers to a difference in concentration, pressure, or electrical charge between two regions.
Enzyme activity	Enzyme activity is the catalytic effect exerted by an enzyme.
Positional information	Information supplied to or possessed by cells according to their position in a multicellular organism. A cell's internal record of its positional information is called its positional value.
Gene control region	DNA sequences required to initiate transcription of a given gene and control the rate of initiation is referred to as gene control region.
Regulatory site	Regulatory site refers to site on an enzyme, other than the active site, that binds a molecule that affects enzyme activity.
Skeletal muscle	Skeletal muscle is a type of striated muscle, attached to the skeleton. They are used to facilitate movement, by applying force to bones and joints; via contraction. They generally contract voluntarily (via nerve stimulation), although they can contract involuntarily.
Myoblast	Myoblast is a type of stem cell that exists in muscles. Skeletal muscle cells are called muscle fibers and are made when myoblasts fuse together; muscle fibers therefore have multiple nuclei.
Glucocorticoid receptor	The glucocorticoid receptor (GR) is a ligand-activated intracytoplasmatic transcription factor that interacts with high affinity to cortisol and other glucocorticoids.
Fibroblast	A fibroblast is a cell that makes the structural fibers and ground substance of connective tissue.
Antibody	An antibody is a protein used by the immune system to identify and neutralize foreign objects like bacteria and viruses. Each antibody recognizes a specific antigen unique to its target.
Connective tissue	Connective tissue is any type of biological tissue with an extensive extracellular matrix and often serves to support, bind together, and protect organs.
Smooth muscle	Smooth muscle is a type of non-striated muscle, found within the "walls" of hollow organs; such as blood vessels, the bladder, the uterus, and the gastrointestinal tract. Smooth muscle is used to move matter within the body, via contraction; it generally operates "involuntarily", without nerve stimulation.
Daughter cell	A cell formed by cell division of a parent cell is a daughter cell.
DNA replication	DNA replication is the process of copying a double-stranded DNA strand in a cell, prior to

cell division. The two resulting double strands are identical (if the replication went well), and each of them consists of one original and one newly synthesized strand.

Organ	Organ refers to a structure consisting of several tissues adapted as a group to perform specific functions.
Eye	An eye is an organ that detects light. Different kinds of light-sensitive organs are found in a variety of creatures.
Vertebrate	Vertebrate is a subphylum of chordates, specifically, those with backbones or spinal columns. They started to evolve about 530 million years ago during the Cambrian explosion, which is part of the Cambrian period.
Fruit	A fruit is the ripened ovary—together with seeds—of a flowering plant. In many species, the fruit incorporates the ripened ovary and surrounding tissues.
Protein structure	A protein structure are amino acid chains; made up from 20 different L-α-amino acids, also referred to as residues, that fold into unique three-dimensional structures.
Positive feedback	Mechanism of homeostatic response in which the output intensifies and increases the likelihood of response, instead of countering it and canceling it is called positive feedback.
Ribosomal RNA	The most prominent examples of non-coding Ribosomal RNA are non-coding RNA that are involved in the process of translation and gene expression.
Dimerization domain	Dimerization domain refers to region of a polypeptide that facilitates interactions with other molecules of the same polypeptide or with other polypeptides. Certain motifs such as the leucine zipper often serve as dimerization domains.
DNA-binding domain	A part of the three-dimensional structure of a transcription factor that binds to DNA is a DNA-binding domain.
Cleavage	Cleavage refers to cytokinesis in animal cells and in some protists, characterized by pinching in of the plasma membrane.
Biosynthesis	Biosynthesis is a phenomenon where chemical compounds are produced from simpler reagents. Biosynthesis, unlike chemical synthesis, takes place within living organisms and is generally catalysed by enzymes. The process is vital part of metabolism.
Arginine	Arginine is an α-amino acid. The L-form is one of the 20 most common natural amino acids. In mammals, arginine is classified as a semiessential or conditionally essential amino acid, depending on the developmental stage and health status of the individual.
Conformation	The three-dimensional shape of a molecule is its conformation. The conformation is particularly important in proteins.
Biotin	Biotin is a low-molecular-weight compound used as a coenzyme. Useful technically as a covalent label for proteins, allowing them to be detected by the egg protein avidin, which binds extremely tightly to biotin.

Nucleotide	A nucleotide is a chemical compound that consists of a heterocyclic base, a sugar, and one or more phosphate groups. In the most common nucleotides the base is a derivative of purine or pyrimidine, and the sugar is pentose - deoxyribose or ribose. They are the structural units of RNA and DNA.
Genome	The genome of an organism is the whole hereditary information of an organism that is encoded in the DNA (or, for some viruses, RNA). This includes both the genes and the non-coding sequences. The genome of an organism is a complete DNA sequence of one set of chromosomes.
Evolution	In biology, evolution is the process by which novel traits arise in populations and are passed on from generation to generation. Its action over large stretches of time explains the origin of new species and ultimately the vast diversity of the biological world.
Bacteria	The domain that contains procaryotic cells with primarily diacyl glycerol diesters in their membranes and with bacterial rRNA. Bacteria also is a general term for organisms that are composed of procaryotic cells and are not multicellular.
Cell	The cell is the structural and functional unit of all living organisms, and is sometimes called the "building block of life."
Species	Group of similarly constructed organisms capable of interbreeding and producing fertile offspring is a species.
Sequencing	Determining the order of nucleotides in a DNA or RNA molecule or the order of amino acids in a protein is sequencing.
Gene	Gene refers to a discrete unit of hereditary information consisting of a specific nucleotide sequence in DNA . Most of the genes of a eukaryote are located in its chromosomal DNA; a few are carried by the DNA of mitochondria and chloroplasts.
Cell division	Cell division is the process by which a cell (called the parent cell) divides into two cells (called daughter cells). Cell division is usually a small segment of a larger cell cycle. In meiosis, however, a cell is permanently transformed and cannot divide again.
Pedigree	A record of one's ancestors, offspring, siblings, and their offspring that may be used to determine the pattern of certain genes or disease inheritance within a family is a pedigree.
Transposable element	Transposable element refers to segment of DNA that can move from one position in a genome to another. Also called a transposon.
Exon shuffling	The exchange of exons among different genes during evolution, producing mosaic proteins with two or more distinct functions is an exon shuffling.
Somatic cell	A somatic cell is generally taken to mean any cell forming the body of an organism.
DNA sequence	A DNA sequence is a succession of letters representing the primary structure of a real or hypothetical DNA molecule or strand, The possible letters are A, C, G, and T, representing the four nucleotide subunits of a DNA strand (adenine, cytosine, guanine, thymine).
Human genome	The human genome is the genome of Homo sapiens. It is made up of 23 chromosome pairs with a total of about 3 billion DNA base pairs.
Gene family	Set of closely related genes with slightly different functions that most likely arose from a succession of gene duplication events is a gene family.
Duplication	Duplication refers to repetition of part of a chromosome resulting from fusion with a fragment from a homologous chromosome; can result from an error in meiosis or from mutagenesis.
Junk DNA	In molecular biology, junk DNA is a collective label for the portions of the DNA sequence of a chromosome or a genome for which no function has yet been identified.

Exon	An exon is the region of DNA within a gene that is not spliced out from the transcribed RNA and is retained in the final messenger RNA (mRNA) molecule.
Origin of life	Research into the origin of life is a limited field of research despite its profound impact on biology and human understanding of the natural world. Progress in this field is generally slow and sporadic, though it still draws the attention of many due to the gravity of the question being investigated.
Cell lineage	The ancestry of a cell is called cell lineage. A pedigree of cells related through asexual division.
Germ cell	A germ cell is a kind of cell that is part of the germline, and is involved in the reproduction of organisms. There are different kinds, which include gametogonia, gametocytes, and gametes.
Zygote	Diploid cell formed by the union of sperm and egg is referred to as zygote.
Gamete	A gamete is a specialized germ cell that unites with another gamete during fertilization in organisms that reproduce sexually. They are haploid cells; that is, they contain one complete set of chromosomes. When they unite they form a zygote—a cell having two complete sets of chromosomes and therefore diploid.
Mutation	Mutation refers to a change in the nucleotide sequence of DNA; the ultimate source of genetic diversity.
Cancer	Cancer is a class of diseases or disorders characterized by uncontrolled division of cells and the ability of these cells to invade other tissues, either by direct growth into adjacent tissue through invasion or by implantation into distant sites by metastasis.
Sexual reproduction	The propagation of organisms involving the union of gametes from two parents is sexual reproduction.
Chromosome	A chromosome is, minimally, a very long, continuous piece of DNA, which contains many genes, regulatory elements and other intervening nucleotide sequences.
Deletion	Deletion refers to the loss of one or more nucleotides from a gene by mutation; the loss of a fragment of a chromosome.
Hybrid	Hybrid refers to the offspring of parents of two different species or of two different varieties of one species; the offspring of two parents that differ in one or more inherited traits; an individual that is heterozygous for one or more pair of genes.
Intron	An intron is a section of DNA within a gene that does not encode part of the protein that the gene produces, and is spliced out of the mRNA that is transcribed from the gene before it is translated.
Rearrangement	A change in the usual order and arrangement of genetic material either within the chromosome complement or within a gene locus is rearrangement. Where the nature of the rearrangement has been determined, the type may be searched for directly under the following designations: reciprocal translocation, Robertsonian translocation, insertion, transposition, inversion, deletion, and duplication.
Point mutation	A point mutation, or substitution, is a type of mutation that causes the replacement of a single base nucleotide with another nucleotide.
Mutant	A mutant (also known to early geneticists as a "monster") is an individual, organism, or new genetic character arising or resulting from an instance of mutation, which is a sudden structural change within the DNA of a gene or chromosome of an organism resulting in the creation of a new character or trait not found in the parental type.
Essential	An essential nutrient is a nutrient required for normal body functioning that can not be

Go to **Cram101.com** for the Practice Tests for this Chapter.

nutrient	synthesized by the body. Categories of essential nutrient include vitamins, dietary minerals, essential fatty acids and essential amino acids.
Antibiotic	Antibiotic refers to substance such as penicillin or streptomycin that is toxic to microorganisms. Usually a product of a particular microorvanism or plant.
Neutral mutation	Neutral mutation refers to a mutation that changes the nucleotide sequence of a gene but has little or no effect on the function of the organism.
Amino acid	An amino acid is any molecule that contains both amino and carboxylic acid functional groups. They are the basic structural building units of proteins. They form short polymer chains called peptides or polypeptides which in turn form structures called proteins.
Protein	A protein is a complex, high-molecular-weight organic compound that consists of amino acids joined by peptide bonds. They are essential to the structure and function of all living cells and viruses. Many are enzymes or subunits of enzymes.
Recombination	Genetic recombination is the transmission-genetic process by which the combinations of alleles observed at different loci in two parental individuals become shuffled in offspring individuals.
Homologous	Homologous refers to describes organs or molecules that are similar because of their common evolutionary origin. Specifically it describes similarities in protein or nucleic acid sequence.
Cell membrane	A component of every biological cell, the selectively permeable cell membrane is a thin and structured bilayer of phospholipid and protein molecules that envelopes the cell. It separates a cell's interior from its surroundings and controls what moves in and out.
Archaea	The Archaea are a major division of living organisms. Although there is still uncertainty in the exact phylogeny of the groups, Archaea, Eukaryotes and Bacteria are the fundamental classifications in what is called the three-domain system.
Unequal crossing-over	A defect in DNA caused by erroneous recombination in which one homologous chromosome ends up with a duplication while the other homolog sustains a deletion is called unequal crossing-over.
Transposon	DNA segment that carries the genes required for transposition and moves about the chromosome; if it contains genes other than those required for transposition, it may be called a composite transposon. Often the name is reserved only for transposable elements that also contain genes unrelated to transposition.
Crossing-over	Exchange of corresponding segments of genetic material between nonsister chromatids of homologous chromosomes during synapsis of meiosis I is called crossing-over.
Multicellular	Multicellular organisms are those organisms consisting of more than one cell, and having differentiated cells that perform specialized functions. Most life that can be seen with the naked eye is multicellular, as are all animals (i.e. members of the kingdom Animalia) and plants (i.e. members of the kingdom Plantae).
Hemoglobin	Hemoglobin is the iron-containing oxygen-transport metalloprotein in the red cells of the blood in mammals and other animals. Hemoglobin transports oxygen from the lungs to the rest of the body, such as to the muscles, where it releases the oxygen load.
Diffusion	Diffusion refers to the spontaneous movement of particles of any kind from where they are more concentrated to where they are less concentrated.
Tissue	Group of similar cells which perform a common function is called tissue.
Oxygen	Oxygen is a chemical element in the periodic table. It has the symbol O and atomic number 8. Oxygen is the second most common element on Earth, composing around 46% of the mass of

	Earth's crust and 28% of the mass of Earth as a whole, and is the third most common element in the universe.
Polypeptide	Polypeptide refers to polymer of many amino acids linked by peptide bonds.
Molecule	A molecule is the smallest particle of a pure chemical substance that still retains its chemical composition and properties.
Insect	An arthropod that usually has three body segments , three pairs of legs, and one or two pairs of wings is called an insect. They are the largest and (on land) most widely-distributed taxon within the phylum Arthropoda. They comprise the most diverse group of animals on the earth, with around 925,000 species described
Vertebrate	Vertebrate is a subphylum of chordates, specifically, those with backbones or spinal columns. They started to evolve about 530 million years ago during the Cambrian explosion, which is part of the Cambrian period.
Gene mutation	Mutation (point or larger change) that results from changes within the structure of a gene is gene mutation.
Primate	A primate is any member of the biological group that contains all lemurs, monkeys, apes, and humans.
Pseudogene	A pseudogene is a nucleotide sequences that is similar to a normal gene, but does not produce a functional final product.
Mammal	Homeothermic vertebrate characterized especially by the presence of hair and mammary glands is a mammal.
Dimer	A dimer refers to a molecule composed of two similar subunits or monomers linked together. It is a special case of a polymer.
Genus	In biology, a genus is a taxonomic grouping. That is, in the classification of living organisms, a genus is considered to be distinct from other such genera. A genus has one or more species: if it has more than one species these are likely to be morphologically more similar than species belonging to different genera.
Protein domain	Protein domain refers to portion of a protein that has a tertiary structure of its own. Larger proteins are generally composed of several domains, each connected to the next by short flexible regions of polypeptide chain.
Homologous chromosome	Homologous chromosome refers to similarly constructed chromosomes with the same shape and that contain genes for the same traits.
Domain	In biology, a domain is the top-level grouping of organisms in scientific classification.
Spontaneous mutation	Spontaneous mutation is a mutation occurring in the absence of mutagens, usually due to errors in the normal functioning of cellular enzymes.
Insertion	At DNA level, an insertion means the insertion of a few base pairs into a genetic sequence. This can often happen in microsatellite regions due to the DNA polymerase slipping.
Homologous Recombination	Homologous Recombination is the process by which two chromosomes, paired up during prophase I of meiosis, exchange some distal portion of their DNA.
Transcription	Transcription is the process through which a DNA sequence is enzymatically copied by an RNA polymerase to produce a complementary RNA. Or, in other words, the transfer of genetic information from DNA into RNA.
Chymotrypsin	Chymotrypsin is a digestive enzyme that can perform proteolysis. It facilitates the cleavage of peptide bonds by a hydrolysis reaction, a process which albeit thermodynamically favorable, occurs extremely slowly in the absence of a catalyst.

Splicing	In genetics, splicing is a modification of genetic information after transcription, in which introns are removed and exons are joined. Splicing is an essential process in eukaryotic pre-mRNA processing that must precede translation.
Transposition	Transposition is a method in genetics where a transposon is inserted into the studied gene to help identify the function or silence the selected gene.
Element	A chemical element, often called simply element, is a chemical substance that cannot be divided or changed into other chemical substances by any ordinary chemical technique. An element is a class of substances that contain the same number of protons in all its atoms.
Host	Host is an organism that harbors a parasite, mutual partner, or commensal partner; or a cell infected by a virus.
Transposase	Transposase refers to an enzyme that functions to insert a transposon into a new site in DNA.
Drosophila melanogaster	Species of small fly, commonly called a fruit fly, much used in genetic studies of development are called drosophila melanogaster.
Antennae	Antennae are paired appendages connected to the front-most segments of arthropods. In crustaceans, they are biramous and present on the first two segments of the head, with the smaller pair known as antennules. In insects, olfactory receptors on the antennae bind to odor molecules, including pheromones.
Fruit	A fruit is the ripened ovary—together with seeds—of a flowering plant. In many species, the fruit incorporates the ripened ovary and surrounding tissues.
Plasmid	Plasmid is a circular double-stranded DNA molecule that is separate from the chromosomal DNA. They usually occur in bacteria and often contain genes that confer a selective advantage to the bacterium harboring them, e.g., the ability to make the bacterium antibiotic resistant.
Micrograph	A micrograph is a photograph or similar image taken through a microscope or similar device to show a magnified image of an item.
Sex pilus	Sex pilus refers to a thin protein appendage required for bacterial mating or conjugation. The cell with sex pili donates DNA to recipient cells.
Electron	The electron is a light fundamental subatomic particle that carries a negative electric charge. The electron is a spin-1/2 lepton, does not participate in strong interactions and has no substructure.
Pilus	A hairlike projection that is made of protein, located on the surface of certain bacteria, and is typically used to attach a bacterium to another cell is a pilus.
Virus	Obligate intracellular parasite of living cells consisting of an outer capsid and an inner core of nucleic acid is referred to as virus. The term virus usually refers to those particles that infect eukaryotes whilst the term bacteriophage or phage is used to describe those infecting prokaryotes.
Homologous genes	Genes in different species with enough sequence similarity to be evolutionarily related are referred to as homologous genes.
Homologs	Genes or regulatory DNA sequences that are similar in different species because of descent from a common ancestral sequence are homologs.
Yeast	Yeast refers to common term for several families of unicellular fungi. Includes species used for brewing beer and making bread, as well as pathogenic species.
Homo sapiens	Homo sapiens are bipedal primates of the superfamily Hominoidea, together with the other apes—chimpanzees, gorillas, orangutans, and gibbons. They are the dominant sentient species on planet Earth.

Go to **Cram101.com** for the Practice Tests for this Chapter.

Bacterium	Most bacterium are microscopic and unicellular, with a relatively simple cell structure lacking a cell nucleus, and organelles such as mitochondria and chloroplasts. They are the most abundant of all organisms. They are ubiquitous in soil, water, and as symbionts of other organisms.
Protist	A protist is a heterogeneous group of living things, comprising those eukaryotes that are neither animals, plants, nor fungi. They are a paraphyletic grade, rather than a natural group, and do not have much in common besides a relatively simple organization
Fungus	A fungus is a eukaryotic organism that digests its food externally and absorbs the nutrient molecules into its cells.
Natural selection	Natural selection is the process by which biological individuals that are endowed with favorable or deleterious traits end up reproducing more or less than other individuals that do not possess such traits.
Organ	Organ refers to a structure consisting of several tissues adapted as a group to perform specific functions.
Highly conserved	Highly conserved refers to genes or proteins whose sequences are very similar in different species.
Gene regulation	Gene regulation is the cellular control of the amount and timing of appearance (induction) of the functional product of a gene. Although a functional gene product may be an RNA or a protein, the majority of the known mechanisms regulate the expression of protein coding genes.
Genetic diversity	Genetic diversity is a characteristic of ecosystems and gene pools that describes an attribute which is commonly held to be advantageous for survival -- that there are many different versions of otherwise similar organisms.
Population	Group of organisms of the same species occupying a certain area and sharing a common gene pool is referred to as population.
Phylogenetic tree	A phylogenetic tree is a diagram showing the evolutionary interrelationships among various species or other entities that are believed to have a common ancestor.
Fusion	Fusion refers to the combination of two atoms into a single atom as a result of a collision, usually accompanied by the release of energy.
Retrotransposon	Type of transposable element that moves by being first transcribed into an RNA copy that is then reconverted to DNA by reverse transcriptase and inserted elsewhere in the chromosomes is referred to as retrotransposon.
Leptin	Leptin is a 16 kDa protein hormone that plays a key role in metabolism and regulation of adipose tissue. It is released by fat cells in amounts mirroring overall body fat stores. Thus, circulating leptin levels give the brain a reading of energy storage for the purposes of regulating appetite and metabolism.
Hormone	A hormone is a chemical messenger from one cell to another. All multicellular organisms produce hormones. The best known hormones are those produced by endocrine glands of vertebrate animals, but hormones are produced by nearly every organ system and tissue type in a human or animal body. Hormone molecules are secreted directly into the bloodstream, they move by circulation or diffusion to their target cells, which may be nearby cells in the same tissue or cells of a distant organ of the body.
Colon	The colon is the part of the intestine from the cecum to the rectum. Its primary purpose is to extract water from feces.
Acid	An acid is a water-soluble, sour-tasting chemical compound that when dissolved in water,

Go to **Cram101.com** for the Practice Tests for this Chapter.

gives a solution with a pH of less than 7.

Synteny	Synteny is the preserved order of genes between related organisms. Since the order of genes has a neutral effect in eukaryotes, an organism will have no ill effects from having genes re-arranged.
Staining	Staining is a biochemical technique of adding a class-specific (DNA, proteins, lipids, carbohydrates) dye to a substrate to qualify or quantify the presence of a specific compound. They are frequently used to highlight structures in tissues for viewing, often with the aid of different microscopes.
Structural gene	A structural gene is a gene that codes for any RNA or protein product other than a regulatory element.
Gene function	Gene function refers to generally, to govern the synthesis of a polypeptide; in Mendelian terms, a gene's specific contribution to phenotype.
Nucleotide substitution	Nucleotide substitution refers to a mutation that replaces one nucleotide in a DNA molecule with another; for example, a change from an adenine to a guanine.
Genetic drift	Genetic drift is the term used in population genetics to refer to the statistical drift over time of allele frequencies in a population due to random sampling effects in the formation of successive generations.
Ribosomal RNA	The most prominent examples of non-coding Ribosomal RNA are non-coding RNA that are involved in the process of translation and gene expression.
Conserved synteny	Conserved synteny refers to the occurrence of genomic collinearity between homologous genes in different organisms.
Noncoding DNA	In genetics, noncoding DNA describes DNA which does not contain instructions for making proteins (or other cell products such as RNAs).
Genome size	Genome size refers to the total amount of DNA contained within one copy of a genome. It is typically measured in terms of mass (in picograms, or trillionths [10
Microbe	A microbe is an organism that is so small that it is microscopic (invisible to the naked eye). Microorganisms are often illustrated using single-celled, or unicellular organisms; however, some unicellular protists are visible to the naked eye, and some multicellular species are microscopic.
Bacillus	Bacillus is a genus of rod-shaped bacteria. The word "bacillus" is also used to describe any rod-shaped bacterium, and in this sense, they are found in many different groups of bacteria.
Aquifex	Aquifex is a genus of bacteria. The two species generally classified in Aquifex are A. pyrophilus and A. aeolicus. Both are very thermophilic, growing best in water at 85° to 95°C. They are true bacteria as opposed to the other inhabitants of extreme environments, the Archaea.
Eye	An eye is an organ that detects light. Different kinds of light-sensitive organs are found in a variety of creatures.
Escherichia coli	Escherichia coli is one of the main species of bacteria that live in the lower intestines of warm-blooded animals, including birds and mammals. They are necessary for the proper digestion of food and are part of the intestinal flora. Its presence in groundwater is a common indicator of fecal contamination.
Sex chromosome	The X or Y chromosome in human beings that determines the sex of an individual. Females have two X chromosomes in diploid cells; males have an X and a Y chromosome. The sex chromosome comprises the 23rd chromosome pair in a karyotype.

Go to **Cram101.com** for the Practice Tests for this Chapter.

Autosome	An autosome is a non-sex chromosome. It is an ordinary paired chromosome that is the same in both sexes of a species.
Biology	Biology is the branch of science dealing with the study of life. It is concerned with the characteristics, classification, and behaviors of organisms, how species come into existence, and the interactions they have with each other and with the environment.
DNA-only transposon	DNA-only transposon refers to a type of transposable element that exists as DNA throughout its life cycle. Many types move by cut-and-paste transposition.
Heterochromatin	Heterochromatin is tightly packed form of DNA. It's major characteristic is that it is not transcribed.
Regulatory sequence	Regulatory sequence refers to dNA sequence to which a gene regulatory protein binds to control the rate of assembly of the transcirptional complex at the promoter.
Fossil	A preserved remnant or impression of an organism that lived in the past is referred to as fossil.
Drosophila	Drosophila is part of the phylum Arthropoda, a phylum of segmented animals with paired, jointed appendages and a hard exoskeleton made of chitin. They have an open circulatory system with a dorsal heart, with hemocoel occupying most of the body cavity, and a reduced coelom.
Identical twins	Identical twins occur when a single egg is fertilized to form one zygote (monozygotic) but the zygote then divides into two separate embryos. The two embryos develop into foetuses sharing the same womb. Monozygotic twins are genetically identical unless there has been a mutation in development, and they are almost always the same gender.
Single-nucleotide polymorphism	A Single-Nucleotide Polymorphism is a DNA sequence variation, occurring when a single nucleotide: adenine (A), thymine (T), cytosine (C) or guanine (G) - in the genome is altered.
Polymorphism	The presence in a population of more than one allele of a gene at a frequency greater than that of newly arising mutations is referred to as polymorphism.
Open reading frame	An open reading frame is any sequence of DNA or RNA that can be translated into a protein. In a gene, they are located between the start-code sequence (initiation codon) and the stop-code sequence (termination codon). They are usually encountered when sifting through pieces of DNA while trying to locate a gene.
Stop codon	In mRNA, one of three triplets that signal gene translation to stop is called stop codon.
Codon	Codon refers to a three-nucleotide sequence in mRNA that specifies a particular amino acid or polypeptide termination signal; the basic unit of the genetic code.
Protein synthesis	The process whereby the tRNA utilizes the mRNA as a guide to arrange the amino acids in their proper sequence according to the genetic information in the chemical code of DNA is referred to as protein synthesis.
Initiation codon	Initiation codon refers to nucleotide triplet that marks the precise spot in the nucleotide sequence of an mRNA where the code for a particular polypeptide begins.
Homology	Homology is used in reference to protein or DNA sequences, meaning that the given sequences share a common ancestor. Sequence homology may also indicate common function.
Venter	In insects the venter is the inferior portion of the abdomen, separated from the tergum by lateral sutures, and divided into segments.
Stem	Stem refers to that part of a plant's shoot system that supports the leaves and reproductive structures.

Expressed sequence tag	An expressed sequence tag or EST is a short sub-sequence of a transcribed protein-coding or non-protein coding DNA sequence. It was originally intended as a way to identify gene transcripts, but has since been instrumental in gene discovery and sequence determination.
Reading frame	In biology, a reading frame is a contiguous and non-overlapping set of three-nucleotide codons in DNA or RNA. There are 3 possible reading frames in a strand. A reading frame that contains a start codon and a stop codon is called an open reading frame.
Methionine	Methionine and cysteine are the only sulfur-containing proteinogenic amino acids. The methionine derivative S-adenosyl methionine (SAM) serves as a methyl donor.
Trait	In biology, a trait or character is a genetically inherited feature of an organism: Eye color is a character; brown eyes and blue eyes is a trait.
Genetic marker	A genetic marker is a specific piece of DNA with a known position on the genome. It is a genetic technique to follow a certain disease or gene. It is known that pieces of DNA that lie near each other, tend to be inherited to the next organism together.
Centromere	The centromere is a region of a eukaryotic chromosome where the kinetochore is assembled; the site where spindle fibers of the mitotic spindle attach to the chromosome during mitosis. It is also the site of the primary constriction visible in microscopy images of chromosomes. Finally, it is the site at which a chromatid and its identical sister attach together during the process of cell reproduction.
Regulatory gene	A gene that codes for a protein, such as a repressor, that controls the transcription of another gene or group of genes is referred to as a regulatory gene.
Embryonic stage	The embryonic stage lasts from the third through the eighth week following conception. During this stage the major organ systems undergo rapid differentiation.
Alternative splicing	Production of different mature mrnas from the same primary transcript by joining different combinations of exons is an alternative splicing.
Nerve cell	A cell specialized to originate or transmit nerve impulses is referred to as nerve cell.
Receptor	A receptor is a protein on the cell membrane or within the cytoplasm or cell nucleus that binds to a specific molecule (a ligand), such as a neurotransmitter, hormone, or other substance, and initiates the cellular response to the ligand. Receptor, in immunology, the region of an antibody which shows recognition of an antigen.
DNA code	A sequence of three nucleotides of a DNA molecule is a DNA code.
Genetic code	The genetic code is a set of rules that maps DNA sequences to proteins in the living cell, and is employed in the process of protein synthesis. Nearly all living things use the same genetic code, called the standard genetic code, although a few organisms use minor variations of the standard code.
Interferon	Interferon is a natural protein produced by the cells of the immune systems of most animals in response to challenges by foreign agents such as viruses, bacteria, parasites and tumor cells. They belong to the large class of glycoproteins known as cytokines.
Histone	Histone refers to a small basic protein molecule associated with DNA and important in DNA packing in the eukaryotic chromosome.
Root nodule	A swelling on a plant root consisting of plant cells that contains nitrogen-fixing bacteria is a root nodule.
Nitrogen	A colorless and tasteless and mostly inert diatomic non-metal gas that is an essential constituent of proteins is nitrogen.
Legume	Legume refers to a member of a family of plants characterized by root swellings in which

	nitrogen-fixing bacteria are housed; includes soybeans, lupines, alfalfa, and clover.
Blood	Blood is a circulating tissue composed of fluid plasma and cells. The main function of blood is to supply nutrients (oxygen, glucose) and constitutional elements to tissues and to remove waste products.
DNA replication	DNA replication is the process of copying a double-stranded DNA strand in a cell, prior to cell division. The two resulting double strands are identical (if the replication went well), and each of them consists of one original and one newly synthesized strand.

Cell biology	The biological discipline involving the study of cells and their functions is called cell biology. This includes their physiological properties such as their structure and the organelles they contain, their environment and interactions, their life cycle, division and function (physiology) and eventual death.
Gene	Gene refers to a discrete unit of hereditary information consisting of a specific nucleotide sequence in DNA . Most of the genes of a eukaryote are located in its chromosomal DNA; a few are carried by the DNA of mitochondria and chloroplasts.
Cell	The cell is the structural and functional unit of all living organisms, and is sometimes called the "building block of life."
Protein	A protein is a complex, high-molecular-weight organic compound that consists of amino acids joined by peptide bonds. They are essential to the structure and function of all living cells and viruses. Many are enzymes or subunits of enzymes.
Genetic engineering	Genetic engineering, genetic modification (GM), and the now-deprecated gene splicing are terms for the process of manipulating genes,usually outside the organism's normal reproductive process.
Selective breeding	Selective breeding refers to the mating of those members of a strain of animals or plants that manifest a particular characteristic, which may or may not be done deliberately, to affect the genetic makeup of future generations of that strain.
Trait	In biology, a trait or character is a genetically inherited feature of an organism: Eye color is a character; brown eyes and blue eyes is a trait.
Nucleotide	A nucleotide is a chemical compound that consists of a heterocyclic base, a sugar, and one or more phosphate groups. In the most common nucleotides the base is a derivative of purine or pyrimidine, and the sugar is pentose - deoxyribose or ribose. They are the structural units of RNA and DNA.
Genome	The genome of an organism is the whole hereditary information of an organism that is encoded in the DNA (or, for some viruses, RNA). This includes both the genes and the non-coding sequences. The genome of an organism is a complete DNA sequence of one set of chromosomes.
Polymerase chain reaction	Polymerase chain reaction is a molecular biology technique for enzymatically replicating DNA without using a living organism, such as E. coli or yeast. The technique allows a small amount of the DNA molecule to be amplified many times, in an exponential manner.
Recombinant DNA molecule	A recombinant DNA molecule is a new type of DNA sequence that's been constructed in the test tube from two or more distinct DNA sequences.
In situ hybridization	In situ hybridization refers to the use of a DNA or RNA probe to detect the presence of the complementary DNA sequence in cloned bacterial or cultured eukaryotic cells.
Restriction nuclease	Restriction nuclease refers to one of a large number of nucleases that can cleave a DNA molecule at any site where a specific short sequence of nucleotides occurs. Extensively used in recombinant DNA technology.
Gel electrophoresis	Gel electrophoresis is a group of techniques used by scientists to separate molecules based on physical characteristics such as size, shape, or isoelectric point.
DNA hybridization	A process by which the DNA from two species are mixed and heated so that interspecific double helixes are formed is called DNA hybridization.
Transgenic plant	A transgenic plant is a plant that has been genetically engineered, a breeding approach that uses recombinant DNA techniques to create plants with new characteristics. A transgenic plant is produced by adding one or more genes to a plant's genome, by a process called transformation.

Go to **Cram101.com** for the Practice Tests for this Chapter.

Recombinant DNA	Recombinant DNA is an artificial DNA sequence resulting from the combining of two other DNA sequences in a plasmid.
Hybridization	In molecular biology hybridization is the process of joining two complementary strands of
Nucleic acid	A nucleic acid is a complex, high-molecular-weight biochemical macromolecule composed of nucleotide chains that convey genetic information. The most common are deoxyribonucleic acid (DNA) and ribonucleic acid (RNA). They are found in all living cells and viruses.
DNA sequence	A DNA sequence is a succession of letters representing the primary structure of a real or hypothetical DNA molecule or strand, The possible letters are A, C, G, and T, representing the four nucleotide subunits of a DNA strand (adenine, cytosine, guanine, thymine).
Population	Group of organisms of the same species occupying a certain area and sharing a common gene pool is referred to as population.
DNA ligase	DNA ligase is a particular type of ligase that can link together DNA strands that have double-strand breaks.
Chromosome	A chromosome is, minimally, a very long, continuous piece of DNA, which contains many genes, regulatory elements and other intervening nucleotide sequences.
Molecule	A molecule is the smallest particle of a pure chemical substance that still retains its chemical composition and properties.
Cloning	Cloning is the process of creating an identical copy of an original.
Plasmid	Plasmid is a circular double-stranded DNA molecule that is separate from the chromosomal DNA. They usually occur in bacteria and often contain genes that confer a selective advantage to the bacterium harboring them, e.g., the ability to make the bacterium antibiotic resistant.
Vector	A vector is an organism that does not cause disease itself but which spreads infection by conveying pathogens from one host to another.
Tissue	Group of similar cells which perform a common function is called tissue.
Mutant	A mutant (also known to early geneticists as a "monster") is an individual, organism, or new genetic character arising or resulting from an instance of mutation, which is a sudden structural change within the DNA of a gene or chromosome of an organism resulting in the creation of a new character or trait not found in the parental type.
Clone	A group of genetically identical cells or organisms derived by asexual reproduction from a single parent is called a clone.
Acid	An acid is a water-soluble, sour-tasting chemical compound that when dissolved in water, gives a solution with a pH of less than 7.
Species	Group of similarly constructed organisms capable of interbreeding and producing fertile offspring is a species.
Heritable	Heritable refers to able to be inherited; in biology usually refers to genetically determined traits.
Mutation	Mutation refers to a change in the nucleotide sequence of DNA; the ultimate source of genetic diversity.
Insulin	Insulin is a polypeptide hormone that regulates carbohydrate metabolism. Apart from being the primary effector in carbohydrate homeostasis, it also has a substantial effect on small vessel muscle tone, controls storage and release of fat (triglycerides) and cellular uptake of both amino acids and some electrolytes.
Cancer	Cancer is a class of diseases or disorders characterized by uncontrolled division of cells

Go to **Cram101.com** for the Practice Tests for this Chapter.

and the ability of these cells to invade other tissues, either by direct growth into adjacent tissue through invasion or by implantation into distant sites by metastasis.

Protease	Protease refers to an enzyme that breaks peptide bonds between amino acids of proteins.
Blood	Blood is a circulating tissue composed of fluid plasma and cells. The main function of blood is to supply nutrients (oxygen, glucose) and constitutional elements to tissues and to remove waste products.
Macromolecule	A macromolecule is a molecule of high relative molecular mass, the structure of which essentially comprises the multiple repetition of units derived, actually or conceptually, from molecules of low relative molecular mass.
Pure culture	A population of cells that are identical because they arise from a single cell are called the pure culture.
Antibody	An antibody is a protein used by the immune system to identify and neutralize foreign objects like bacteria and viruses. Each antibody recognizes a specific antigen unique to its target.
Downstream	Downstream refers to a relative position in DNA or RNA. Relative to the position on the strand, downstream is the region towards the 3' end of the strand.
In vitro	In vitro is an experimental technique where the experiment is performed in a test tube, or generally outside a living organism or cell.
In vivo	In vivo is used to indicate the presence of a whole/living organism, in distinction to a partial or dead organism, or a computer model. Animal testing and clinical trials are forms of in vivo research.
Biochemistry	Biochemistry studies how complex chemical reactions give rise to life. It is a hybrid branch of chemistry which specialises in the chemical processes in living organisms.
Connective tissue	Connective tissue is any type of biological tissue with an extensive extracellular matrix and often serves to support, bind together, and protect organs.
Skeletal muscle	Skeletal muscle is a type of striated muscle, attached to the skeleton. They are used to facilitate movement, by applying force to bones and joints; via contraction. They generally contract voluntarily (via nerve stimulation), although they can contract involuntarily.
Muscle fiber	Cell with myofibrils containing actin and myosin filaments arranged within sarcomeres is a muscle fiber.
Nerve cell	A cell specialized to originate or transmit nerve impulses is referred to as nerve cell.
Epithelial	Functions of epithelial cells include secretion, absorption, protection, transcellular transport, sensation detection, and selective permeability.
Epithelium	Epithelium is a tissue composed of a layer of cells. Epithelium can be found lining internal (e.g. endothelium, which lines the inside of blood vessels) or external (e.g. skin) free surfaces of the body. Functions include secretion, absorption and protection.
Fibroblast	A fibroblast is a cell that makes the structural fibers and ground substance of connective tissue.
Collagen	Collagen is the main protein of connective tissue in animals and the most abundant protein in mammals, making up about 1/4 of the total. It is one of the long, fibrous structural proteins whose functions are quite different from those of globular proteins such as enzymes.
Synapse	A junction, or relay point, between two neurons, or between a neuron and an effector cell. Electrical and chemical signals are relayed from one cell to another at a synapse.
Axon	An axon is a long slender projection of a nerve cell, or neuron, which conducts electrical

Go to **Cram101.com** for the Practice Tests for this Chapter.

impulses away from the neuron's cell body or soma. They are in effect the primary transmission lines of the nervous system, and as bundles they help make up nerves.

Cell division	Cell division is the process by which a cell (called the parent cell) divides into two cells (called daughter cells). Cell division is usually a small segment of a larger cell cycle. In meiosis, however, a cell is permanently transformed and cannot divide again.
Vertebrate	Vertebrate is a subphylum of chordates, specifically, those with backbones or spinal columns. They started to evolve about 530 million years ago during the Cambrian explosion, which is part of the Cambrian period.
Somatic cell	A somatic cell is generally taken to mean any cell forming the body of an organism.
Telomerase	An enzyme critical to the successful replication of telomeres at chromosome ends is called telomerase.
Enzyme	An enzyme is a protein that catalyzes, or speeds up, a chemical reaction. They are essential to sustain life because most chemical reactions in biological cells would occur too slowly, or would lead to different products, without them.
Cell line	Cell line refers to population of cells of plant or animal origin capable of dividing indefinitely in culture.
Fluorescence	Fluorescence is a luminescence that is mostly found as an optical phenomenon in cold bodies, in which the molecular absorption of a photon triggers the emission of a lower-energy photon with a longer wavelength. The energy difference between the absorbed and emitted photons ends up as molecular vibrations or heat.
Micrograph	A micrograph is a photograph or similar image taken through a microscope or similar device to show a magnified image of an item.
Myoblast	Myoblast is a type of stem cell that exists in muscles. Skeletal muscle cells are called muscle fibers and are made when myoblasts fuse together; muscle fibers therefore have multiple nuclei.
Muscle	Muscle is a contractile form of tissue. It is one of the four major tissue types, the other three being epithelium, connective tissue and nervous tissue. Muscle contraction is used to move parts of the body, as well as to move substances within the body.
Oligodendrocyte	Oligodendrocyte refers to type of glial cell in the vertebrate central nervous system that forms a myelin sheath around axons.
Glial cell	A glial cell is a non-neuronal cell that provides support and nutrition, maintains homeostasis, form myelin, and participates in signal transmission in the nervous system.
Neuron	The neuron is a major class of cells in the nervous system. In vertebrates, they are found in the brain, the spinal cord and in the nerves and ganglia of the peripheral nervous system, and their primary role is to process and transmit neural information.
Brain	The part of the central nervous system involved in regulating and controlling body activity and interpreting information from the senses transmitted through the nervous system is referred to as the brain.
Homogeneous	Homogeneous refers both to animals and plants, of having a resemblance in structure, due to descent from a common progenitor with subsequent modification.
Stem	Stem refers to that part of a plant's shoot system that supports the leaves and reproductive structures.
Model organism	A model organism is a species that is extensively studied to understand particular biological phenomena, with the expectation that discoveries made in the organism model will provide

Go to **Cram101.com** for the Practice Tests for this Chapter.

insight into the workings of other organisms.

Drosophila	Drosophila is part of the phylum Arthropoda, a phylum of segmented animals with paired, jointed appendages and a hard exoskeleton made of chitin. They have an open circulatory system with a dorsal heart, with hemocoel occupying most of the body cavity, and a reduced coelom.
Phosphodiester bond	A phosphodiester bond is a group of strong covalent bonds between the phosphorus atom in a phosphate group and two other molecules over two ester bonds. Phosphodiester bonds are central to all life on Earth, as they make up the backbone of the strands of DNA.
Hydrolysis	Hydrolysis is a chemical process in which a molecule is cleaved into two parts by the addition of a molecule of water.
Nuclease	Enzyme that cleaves phosphodiester bonds in nucleic acids is referred to as nuclease.
Bacteria	The domain that contains procaryotic cells with primarily diacyl glycerol diesters in their membranes and with bacterial rRNA. Bacteria also is a general term for organisms that are composed of procaryotic cells and are not multicellular.
Bacterium	Most bacterium are microscopic and unicellular, with a relatively simple cell structure lacking a cell nucleus, and organelles such as mitochondria and chloroplasts. They are the most abundant of all organisms. They are ubiquitous in soil, water, and as symbionts of other organisms.
Host	Host is an organism that harbors a parasite, mutual partner, or commensal partner; or a cell infected by a virus.
Cleavage	Cleavage refers to cytokinesis in animal cells and in some protists, characterized by pinching in of the plasma membrane.
Electrode	An electrode is a conductor used to make contact with a nonmetallic part of a circuit (e.g. a semiconductor, an electrolyte or a vacuum).
Matrix	In biology, matrix (plural: matrices) is the material between animal or plant cells, the material (or tissue) in which more specialized structures are embedded, and a specific part of the mitochondrion that is the site of oxidation of organic molecules.
Radioisotope	Radioisotope refers to a radioactive isotope of an element. Examples are carbon-14 and hydrogen-3, or tritium.
Staining	Staining is a biochemical technique of adding a class-specific (DNA, proteins, lipids, carbohydrates) dye to a substrate to qualify or quantify the presence of a specific compound. They are frequently used to highlight structures in tissues for viewing, often with the aid of different microscopes.
Double helix	Double helix refers to the form of native DNA, referring to its two adjacent polynucleotide strands wound into a spiral shape.
Escherichia coli	Escherichia coli is one of the main species of bacteria that live in the lower intestines of warm-blooded animals, including birds and mammals. They are necessary for the proper digestion of food and are part of the intestinal flora. Its presence in groundwater is a common indicator of fecal contamination.
Restriction enzyme	Restriction enzyme refers to a bacterial enzyme that cuts up foreign DNA, thus protecting bacteria against intruding DNA from phages and other organisms. They are used in DNA technology to cut DNA molecules in reproducible ways.
Phosphorus	Phosphorus is the chemical element in the periodic table that has the symbol P and atomic number 15.

Go to **Cram101.com** for the Practice Tests for this Chapter.

Atom	An atom is the smallest possible particle of a chemical element that retains its chemical properties.
Dideoxy method	The standard method of DNA sequencing that uses chain-terminating (dideoxy) nucleotides is the dideoxy method.
Sequencing	Determining the order of nucleotides in a DNA or RNA molecule or the order of amino acids in a protein is sequencing.
Yeast	Yeast refers to common term for several families of unicellular fungi. Includes species used for brewing beer and making bread, as well as pathogenic species.
DNA sequencing	The process of determining the chemical composition of a DNA molecule is called DNA sequencing.
Centromere	The centromere is a region of a eukaryotic chromosome where the kinetochore is assembled; the site where spindle fibers of the mitotic spindle attach to the chromosome during mitosis. It is also the site of the primary constriction visible in microscopy images of chromosomes. Finally, it is the site at which a chromatid and its identical sister attach together during the process of cell reproduction.
Reagent	When purchasing or preparing chemicals, reagent describes chemical substances of sufficient purity for use in chemical analysis, chemical reactions or physical testing.
Hydroxyl group	The term hydroxyl group is used to describe the functional group -OH when it is a substituent in an organic compound.
Nucleoside	Molecule composed of a purine or pyrimidine base covalently linked to a ribose or deoxyribose sugar is a nucleoside.
DNA polymerase	A DNA polymerase is an enzyme that assists in DNA replication. Such enzymes catalyze the polymerization of deoxyribonucleotides alongside a DNA strand, which they "read" and use as a template. The newly polymerized molecule is complementary to the template strand and identical to the template's partner strand.
Polymerase	DNA or RNA enzymes that catalyze the synthesis of nucleic acids on preexisting nucleic acid templates, assembling RNA from ribonucleotides or DNA from deoxyribonucleotides is referred to as polymerase.
Primer	A primer is a nucleic acid strand, or a related molecule that serves as a starting point for DNA replication. In most natural DNA replication, the ultimate primer for DNA synthesis is a short strand of RNA.
Oligonucleotide	Oligonucleotide refers to a short single-stranded DNA molecule, typically with twenty or fewer base pairs. Oligonucleotides are often used as probes for detecting complementary DNA or RNA because they bind readily to their complements.
Electrophoresis	Electrophoresis is the movement of an electrically charged substance under the influence of an electric field. This movement is due to the Lorentz force, which may be related to fundamental electrical properties of the body under study and the ambient electrical conditions.
Radioactive	A term used to describe the property of releasing energy or particles from an unstable atom is called radioactive.
Bacterial chromosome	The single, circular DNA molecule found in bacteria is a bacterial chromosome.
Intron	An intron is a section of DNA within a gene that does not encode part of the protein that the gene produces, and is spliced out of the mRNA that is transcribed from the gene before it is translated.

Go to **Cram101.com** for the Practice Tests for this Chapter.

Multicellular	Multicellular organisms are those organisms consisting of more than one cell, and having differentiated cells that perform specialized functions. Most life that can be seen with the naked eye is multicellular, as are all animals (i.e. members of the kingdom Animalia) and plants (i.e. members of the kingdom Plantae).
Exon	An exon is the region of DNA within a gene that is not spliced out from the transcribed RNA and is retained in the final messenger RNA (mRNA) molecule.
Evolution	In biology, evolution is the process by which novel traits arise in populations and are passed on from generation to generation. Its action over large stretches of time explains the origin of new species and ultimately the vast diversity of the biological world.
Human genome	The human genome is the genome of Homo sapiens. It is made up of 23 chromosome pairs with a total of about 3 billion DNA base pairs.
Shotgun sequencing	Shotgun sequencing is a method used in genetics for sequencing long DNA strands. Since the chain termination method of DNA sequencing can only be used for fairly short strands, it is necessary to divide longer sequences up and then assemble the results to give the overall sequence.
Fragmentation	Fragmentation is a form of asexual reproduction where an organism is split into fragments. The splitting may or may not be intentional. Each of these fragments develops into a mature, fully grown new organism, and if the organism is split any further the process is repeated.
Repetitive DNA	Repetitive DNA refers to nucleotide sequences that are present in many copies in the DNA of a genome. The repeated sequences may be long or short and may be located next to each other or dispersed in the DNA.
Highly repetitive	DNA Short DNA sequences present in millions of copies in the genome, next to each other. In a In a reassociation experiment, denatured highly repetitive DNA reanneals very quickly.
Physiology	The study of the function of cells, tissues, and organs is referred to as physiology.
Restriction endonuclease	Restriction endonuclease refers to any one of several enzymes, produced by bacteria, that break foreign DNA molecules at very specific sites. Some produce 'sticky ends.' Extensively used in recombinant DNA technology.
Base pair	Two nucleotides on opposite complementary DNA or RNA strands that are connected via hydrogen bonds are called a base pair.
Covalent bond	A covalent bond is an intramolecular form of chemical bonding characterized by the sharing of one or more pairs of electrons between two elements, producing a mutual attraction that holds the resultant molecule together.
Hydrogen bond	A hydrogen bond is a type of attractive intermolecular force that exists between two partial electric charges of opposite polarity. Although stronger than most other intermolecular forces, the typical hydrogen bond is much weaker than both the ionic bond and the covalent bond.
Renaturation	Renaturation is the reassociation of single strands of nucleic acids into double-stranded helical forms.
Denaturation	Denaturation is a structural change in biomolecules such as nucleic acids and proteins, such that they are no longer in their native state, and their shape which allows for optimal activity.
DNA probe	DNA probe refers to a sequence of nucleotides that is complementary to the nucleotide sequence in a gene under study; used to locate a given gene within a DNA library.
Sickle-cell anemia	Sickle-cell anemia refers to a disease caused by a point mutation. This malfunction produces sickle-shaped red blood cells. Sickle-cell anemia is the name of a specific form of sickle

	cell disease in which there is homozygosity for the mutation that causes Hgb S.
Fetus	Fetus refers to a developing human from the ninth week of gestation until birth; has all the major structures of an adult.
Glutamic acid	Glutamic acid is one of the 20 standard amino acids used by all organisms in their proteins. It is critical for proper cell function, but it is not an essential nutrient in humans because glutamic acid can be manufactured from other compounds.
Amino acid	An amino acid is any molecule that contains both amino and carboxylic acid functional groups. They are the basic structural building units of proteins. They form short polymer chains called peptides or polypeptides which in turn form structures called proteins.
Valine	Nutritionally, valine is also an essential amino acid. It is named after the plant valerian. In sickle-cell disease, it substitutes for the hydrophilic amino acid glutamic acid in hemoglobin.
Restriction fragment	A DNA fragment resulting from cleavage of a DNA strand by a restriction enzyme. A restriction fragment can be analyzed using techniques such as gel electrophoresis.
Isotope	An isotope is a form of an element whose nuclei have the same atomic number - the number of protons in the nucleus - but different mass numbers because they contain different numbers of neutrons.
Blotting	Biochemical technique in which macromolecules separated on an agarose or polyacrylamide gel are transferred to a nylon membrane or sheet of paper, thereby immobilizing them for further analysis is called blotting.
Nitrocellulose	Nitrocellulose is a highly flammable compound formed by nitrating cellulose (e.g. through exposure to nitric acid or powerful nitrating agent). This compound, when used as a propellant or low order explosive, was known as guncotton.
Sponge	An invertebrates that consist of a complex aggregation of cells, including collar cells, and has a skeleton of fibers and/or spicules is a sponge. They are primitive, sessile, mostly marine, waterdwelling filter feeders that pump water through their matrix to filter out particulates of food matter.
Buffer	A chemical substance that resists changes in pH by accepting H^+ ions from or donating H^+ ions to solutions is called a buffer.
Denature	Denature is a structural change in biomolecules such as nucleic acids and proteins, such that they are no longer in their native state, and their shape which allows for optimal activity.
Autoradiograph	An autoradiograph is an image produced on a photographic film by the radiation from a radioactive substance. In this technique, a compound (such as a metabolite or DNA) is radiolabeled by a substance that emits either beta radiation or gamma rays.
Northern blotting	Northern blotting refers to technique used in molecular biology research to study gene expression in which RNA fragments separated by electrophoresis are immobilized on a paper sheet. A specific RNA is then detected by hybridization with a labeled nucleic acid probe.
Adaptation	A biological adaptation is an anatomical structure, physiological process or behavioral trait of an organism that has evolved over a period of time by the process of natural selection such that it increases the expected long-term reproductive success of the organism.
Complementary DNA	Complementary DNA is DNA synthesized from a mature mRNA template. It is often used to clone eukaryotic genes in prokaryotes.
Gene expression	Gene expression is the process by which a gene's information is converted into the structures and functions of a cell. Gene expression is a multi-step process that begins with transcription, post transcriptional modification and translation, followed by folding, post-

223

	translational modification and targeting.
Hormone	A hormone is a chemical messenger from one cell to another. All multicellular organisms produce hormones. The best known hormones are those produced by endocrine glands of vertebrate animals, but hormones are produced by nearly every organ system and tissue type in a human or animal body. Hormone molecules are secreted directly into the bloodstream, they move by circulation or diffusion to their target cells, which may be nearby cells in the same tissue or cells of a distant organ of the body.
Toxin	Toxin refers to a microbial product or component that can injure another cell or organism at low concentrations. Often the term refers to a poisonous protein, but toxins may be lipids and other substances.
Microscope	A microscope is an instrument for viewing objects that are too small to be seen by the naked or unaided eye.
Cancer cell	A cell that divides and reproduces abnormally and has the potential to spread throughout the body, crowding out normal cells and tissue is referred to as a cancer cell.
Cyclin	Cyclin refers to protein that periodically rises and falls in concentration in step with the eucaryotic cell cycle. They activate crucial protein kinases and thereby help control progression from one stage of the cell cycle to the next.
Mitosis	Mitosis is the process by which a cell separates its duplicated genome into two identical halves. It is generally followed immediately by cytokinesis which divides the cytoplasm and cell membrane.
Ligase	In biochemistry, a ligase is an enzyme that can catalyse the joining of two molecules by forming a new chemical bond, with accompanying hydrolysis of adenosine triphosphate or other similar molecules.
Blunt end	A sticky end and blunt end are the two possible configurations resulting from the breaking of double-stranded DNA.
Cell membrane	A component of every biological cell, the selectively permeable cell membrane is a thin and structured bilayer of phospholipid and protein molecules that envelopes the cell. It separates a cell's interior from its surroundings and controls what moves in and out.
Recombination	Genetic recombination is the transmission-genetic process by which the combinations of alleles observed at different loci in two parental individuals become shuffled in offspring individuals.
Transformation	Transformation is the genetic alteration of a cell resulting from the introduction, uptake and expression of foreign genetic material (DNA or RNA).
Antibiotic resistance	The ability of a mutated pathogen to resist the effects of an antibiotic that normally kills it is an antibiotic resistance.
Hemophilia	Hemophilia is the name of any of several hereditary genetic illnesses that impair the body's ability to control bleeding. Genetic deficiencies cause lowered plasma clotting factor activity so as to compromise blood-clotting; when a blood vessel is injured, a scab will not form and the vessel can continue to bleed excessively for a very long period of time.
Homologous Recombination	Homologous Recombination is the process by which two chromosomes, paired up during prophase I of meiosis, exchange some distal portion of their DNA.
Electron	The electron is a light fundamental subatomic particle that carries a negative electric charge. The electron is a spin-1/2 lepton, does not participate in strong interactions and has no substructure.
Cloning vector	Cloning vector refers to DNA molecule into which another DNA fragment of appropriate size can

	be integrated without loss of the vector's capacity for replication.
Virus	Obligate intracellular parasite of living cells consisting of an outer capsid and an inner core of nucleic acid is referred to as virus. The term virus usually refers to those particles that infect eukaryotes whilst the term bacteriophage or phage is used to describe those infecting prokaryotes.
Genomic dna	DNA constituting the genome of a cell or an organism. Often used in contrast to cdna. Genomic DNA clones represent DNA cloned directly from chromosomal DNA, and a collection of such clones from a given genome is a genomic DNA library.
Insertion	At DNA level, an insertion means the insertion of a few base pairs into a genetic sequence. This can often happen in microsatellite regions due to the DNA polymerase slipping.
Bacterial artificial chromosome	A bacterial artificial chromosome is a DNA construct, based on a fertility plasmid, used for transforming and cloning in bacteria, usually E. coli.
DNA library	A readily accessible, easily duplicable complete set of all the DNA of a particular organism, normally cloned into bacterial plasmids is a DNA library.
Genomic library	Genomic library refers to a set of DNA segments from an organism's genome. Each segment is usually carried by a plasmid or phage.
Bacterial colony	A bacterial colony is defined as a cluster of microorganisms growing on the surface of or within a solid medium, usually cultured from a single cell.
Petri dish	Petri dish refers to a shallow dish consisting of two round, overlapping halves that is used to grow microorganisms on solid culture medium; the top is larger than the bottom of the dish to prevent contamination of the culture.
Blood clotting	A complex process by which platelets, the protein fibrin, and red blood cells block an irregular surface in or on the body, such as a damaged blood vessel, sealing the wound is referred to as blood clotting.
Mass spectrometry	Mass spectrometry is an analytical technique used to measure the mass-to-charge ratio (m/q) of ions. It is most generally used to find the composition of a physical sample by generating a mass spectrum representing the masses of sample components.
Genetic code	The genetic code is a set of rules that maps DNA sequences to proteins in the living cell, and is employed in the process of protein synthesis. Nearly all living things use the same genetic code, called the standard genetic code, although a few organisms use minor variations of the standard code.
DNA clone	A section of DNA that has been inserted into a vector molecule, such as a plasmid or a phage chromosome, and then replicated to form many identical copies is called a DNA clone.
CDNA library	A cDNA library refers to a complete, or nearly complete, set of all the mRNAs contained within a cell or organism. Because working with mRNA is difficult, researchers use an enzyme called reverse transcriptase which will produce a DNA copy of each mRNA strand.
Hybrid	Hybrid refers to the offspring of parents of two different species or of two different varieties of one species; the offspring of two parents that differ in one or more inherited traits; an individual that is heterozygous for one or more pair of genes.
CDNA clone	A double-stranded DNA molecule that is carried in a vector and was synthesized in vitro from an mRNA sequence by using reverse transcriptase and DNA polymerase is a cDNA clone.
Transcription	Transcription is the process through which a DNA sequence is enzymatically copied by an RNA polymerase to produce a complementary RNA. Or, in other words, the transfer of genetic information from DNA into RNA.

Pathogen	A pathogen or infectious agent is a biological agent that causes disease or illness to its host.The term is most often used for agents that disrupt the normal physiology of a multicellular animal or plant.
Amplification	In molecular biology, amplification (polymerase chain reaction or PCR) is the method for creating multiple copies of DNA (or RNA) without using a living organism, such as E. coli or yeast.
Complementary sequence	Complementary sequence refers to a nucleic acid base sequence that can form a doublestranded structure by matching base pairs with another sequence; the complementary sequence to 5' GTAC 3' is 3' CATG 5'.
DNA fingerprint	The multilocus pattern produced by the detection of genotype at a group of unlinked, highly polymorphic loci is referred to as DNA fingerprint.
Identical twins	Identical twins occur when a single egg is fertilized to form one zygote (monozygotic) but the zygote then divides into two separate embryos. The two embryos develop into foetuses sharing the same womb. Monozygotic twins are genetically identical unless there has been a mutation in development, and they are almost always the same gender.
Viral	Viral phenomena are objects or patterns able to replicate themselves or convert other objects into copies of themselves when these objects are exposed to them.
Immunodeficiency	Immunodeficiency is a state in which the immune system's ability to fight infectious disease is compromized or entirely absent. Most cases of immunodeficiency are either congenital or acquired.
Microsatellite	A microsatellite is a short block of DNA sequence (a Tandemly Repetitive DNA sequence), often less than 150 base pairs long, that is repeated many times within the genome of an organism. Many repeats tend to be concentrated at the same locus.
Tandem repeat	A nucleotide sequence of DNA that is serially repeated many times is a tandem repeat.
Relative abundance	Differences in the abundance of species within a community is relative abundance.
Hemoglobin	Hemoglobin is the iron-containing oxygen-transport metalloprotein in the red cells of the blood in mammals and other animals. Hemoglobin transports oxygen from the lungs to the rest of the body, such as to the muscles, where it releases the oxygen load.
Promoter	In genetics, a promoter is a DNA sequence that enables a gene to be transcribed. The promoter is recognized by RNA polymerase, which then initiates transcription.
Insect	An arthropod that usually has three body segments , three pairs of legs, and one or two pairs of wings is called an insect. They are the largest and (on land) most widely-distributed taxon within the phylum Arthropoda. They comprise the most diverse group of animals on the earth, with around 925,000 species described
Expression vector	An expression vector is a relatively small DNA molecule that is used to introduce and express a specific gene into a target cell. Once the expression vector is inside the cell, the protein that is encoded by the gene is produced by the cellular transcription and translation machinery.
Chromatography	Biochemical technique in which a mixture of substances is separated by charge, size, or some other property by allowing it to partition between a mobile phase and a stationary phase is called chromatography.
Lysate	Lysate refers to population of phage particles released from the host bacteria at the end of the lytic cycle.
Cation	A positively charged ion which has fewer electrons than protons is a cation.

Go to **Cram101.com** for the Practice Tests for this Chapter.

Lysis	Lysis refers to the death of a cell by bursting, often by viral or osmotic mechanisms that compromise the integrity of the cellular membrane.
Growth factor	Growth factor is a protein that acts as a signaling molecule between cells (like cytokines and hormones) that attaches to specific receptors on the surface of a target cell and promotes differentiation and maturation of these cells.
Protein kinase	Enzyme that transfers the terminal phosphate group of ATP to a specific amino acid of a target protein is protein kinase.
Motor protein	Protein that uses energy derived from nucleoside triphosphate hydrolysis to propel itself along a protein filament or another polymeric molecule is called motor protein.
Regulatory sequence	Regulatory sequence refers to dNA sequence to which a gene regulatory protein binds to control the rate of assembly of the transcirptional complex at the promoter.
Specificity	A medical diagnostic test for a certain disease, specificity is the proportion of true negatives of all the negative samples tested.
Green fluorescent protein	Green fluorescent protein refers to fluorescent protein isolated from a jellyfish. Widely used as a marker in cell biology.
Fusion protein	A fusion protein is a protein created through genetic engineering from two or more proteins/peptides. This is achieved by creating a fusion gene: removing the stop codon from the DNA sequence of the first protein, then appending the DNA sequence of the second protein in frame. That DNA sequence will then be expressed by a cell as a single protein.
Distribution	Distribution in pharmacology is a branch of pharmacokinetics describing reversible transfer of drug from one location to another within the body.
Microscopy	Microscopy is any technique for producing visible images of structures or details too small to otherwise be seen by the human eye, using a microscope or other magnification tool.
Fruit	A fruit is the ripened ovary—together with seeds—of a flowering plant. In many species, the fruit incorporates the ripened ovary and surrounding tissues.
Eye	An eye is an organ that detects light. Different kinds of light-sensitive organs are found in a variety of creatures.
Phenotype	The phenotype of an individual organism is either its total physical appearance and constitution or a specific manifestation of a trait, such as size or eye color, that varies between individuals. It is determined to some extent by genotype.
Genotype	The genotype is the specific genetic makeup (the specific genome) of an individual, usually in the form of DNA. It codes for the phenotype of that individual.
Gene cloning	Gene cloning refers to the production of multiple copies of a gene. Isolating a gene and producing many identical copies of it so that it can be studied in detail.
Pheromone	Chemical signal that works at a distance and alters the behavior of another member of the same species is called a pheromone.
Daughter cell	A cell formed by cell division of a parent cell is a daughter cell.
Segregation	The separation of homologous chromosomes during mitosis and meiosis. Known as Mendel's theory of Segregation.
Translation	Translation is the second process of protein biosynthesis. In translation, messenger RNA is decoded to produce a specific polypeptide according to the rules specified by the genetic code.

Go to **Cram101.com** for the Practice Tests for this Chapter.

Site-directed mutagenesis	Introduction of a base change into a PCR protocol, so that the change is perpetuated is referred to as site-directed mutagenesis.
Protein folding	Protein folding is the process by which a protein structure assumes its functional shape or conformation.
Polypeptide	Polypeptide refers to polymer of many amino acids linked by peptide bonds.
Catalysis	Catalysis is the acceleration of the reaction rate of a chemical reaction by means of a substance, called a catalyst, that is itself not consumed by the overall reaction.
Ligand	Any molecule that binds to a specific receptor site on a protein or other molecule is called a ligand.
Transgenic organism	A transgenic organism is an organism whose genome has been subject to artificial modification. A transgenic organism may result when foreign DNA is inserted into the nucleus of a fertilized embryo.
Pancreas	The pancreas is a retroperitoneal organ that serves two functions: exocrine - it produces pancreatic juice containing digestive enzymes, and endocrine - it produces several important hormones, namely insulin.
Liver	The liver is an organ in vertebrates, including humans. It plays a major role in metabolism and has a number of functions in the body including drug detoxification, glycogen storage, and plasma protein synthesis. It also produces bile, which is important for digestion.
Skin	Skin is an organ of the integumentary system composed of a layer of tissues that protect underlying muscles and organs.
Transgenic	Referring to an animal or a plant that expresses DNA derived from another species is called transgenic.
Deletion	Deletion refers to the loss of one or more nucleotides from a gene by mutation; the loss of a fragment of a chromosome.
Knockout	A gene knockout is a genetically engineered organism that carries one or more genes in its chromosomes that has been made inoperative. So far such organisms have been engineered chiefly for research purposes.
RNA interference	RNA interference is a mechanism in molecular biology where the presence of certain fragments of double-stranded RNA interferes with the expression of a particular gene which shares a homologous sequence with the dsRNA.
Embryo	Embryo refers to a developing stage of a multicellular organism. In humans, the stage in the development of offspring from the first division of the zygote until body structures begin to appear, about the ninth week of gestation.
Gene function	Gene function refers to generally, to govern the synthesis of a polypeptide; in Mendelian terms, a gene's specific contribution to phenotype.
Intestine	The intestine is the portion of the alimentary canal extending from the stomach to the anus and, in humans and mammals, consists of two segments, the small intestine and the large intestine. The intestine is the part of the body responsible for extracting nutrition from food.
Complement	Complement is a group of proteins of the complement system, found in blood serum which act in concert with antibodies to achieve the destruction of non-self particles such as foreign blood cells or bacteria.
Callus	Callus refers to a lump of undifferentiated plant somatic tissue growing in culture.
Shoot	In botany, the shoot is one of two primary sections of a plant; the other is the root. The

shoot refers to what is generally the upper portion of a plant, and consists of stems, leaves, flowers, and fruits. It is derived from the embryonic epicotyl, the portion of the embryo above the point of attachment to the seed leaves (cotyledons).

Plant cell	A cell that is a structural and functional unit of a plant is a plant cell.
DNA helicase	An enzyme that catalyzes the unwinding of the DNA double helix during DNA replication is referred to as DNA helicase.
Transgene	Any piece of foreign DNA that researchers have inserted into the genome of an organism to modify the genome is a transgene.
Receptor	A receptor is a protein on the cell membrane or within the cytoplasm or cell nucleus that binds to a specific molecule (a ligand), such as a neurotransmitter, hormone, or other substance, and initiates the cellular response to the ligand. Receptor, in immunology, the region of an antibody which shows recognition of an antigen.
Leaf	In botany, a leaf is an above-ground plant organ specialized for photosynthesis. For this purpose, a leaf is typically flat (laminar) and thin, to expose the chloroplast containing cells (chlorenchyma tissue) to light over a broad area, and to allow light to penetrate fully into the tissues.
DNA repair	Collective name for those biochemical processes that correct accidental changes in the DNA is referred to as dna repair.
Helicase	Helicase refers to a class of enzymes vital to all living organisms. Its function is to temporarily separate the two strands of a DNA double helix so that DNA or RNA synthesis can take place.
Root	In vascular plants, the root is that organ of a plant body that typically lies below the surface of the soil. However, this is not always the case, since a root can also be aerial (that is, growing above the ground) or aerating (that is, growing up above the ground or especially above water).
Morphogenesis	Morphogenesis is one of three fundamental aspects of developmental biology along with the control of cell growth and cellular differentiation. Morphogenesis is concerned with the shapes of tissues, organs and entire organisms and the positions of the various specialized cell types.
Vitamin	A Vitamin is an organic molecule required by a living organism in minute amounts for proper health. An organism deprived of all sources of a particular vitamin will eventually suffer from disease symptoms specific to that vitamin.
Element	A chemical element, often called simply element, is a chemical substance that cannot be divided or changed into other chemical substances by any ordinary chemical technique. An element is a class of substances that contain the same number of protons in all its atoms.
Archaea	The Archaea are a major division of living organisms. Although there is still uncertainty in the exact phylogeny of the groups, Archaea, Eukaryotes and Bacteria are the fundamental classifications in what is called the three-domain system.
DNA markers	DNA markers refers to a purified fragment of DNA labeled with a radioactive isotope or fluorescent dye and used to identify complementary sequences by means of hybridization.
Genetic marker	A genetic marker is a specific piece of DNA with a known position on the genome. It is a genetic technique to follow a certain disease or gene. It is known that pieces of DNA that lie near each other, tend to be inherited to the next organism together.
Variable number tandem repeat	Short nucleotide sequences ranging from 14 to 100 nucleotides long that is repeated, in variable 'repeat numbers,' in the genomes of higher eukaryotes is referred to as a variable

number tandem repeat.

Hybridization probe	A hybridization probe is a short piece of DNA (on the order of 100-500 bases) that is denatured (by heating) into single strands and then radioactively labeled, usually with phosphorus.
Polymorphism	The presence in a population of more than one allele of a gene at a frequency greater than that of newly arising mutations is referred to as polymorphism.
Ecological niche	Ecological niche refers to a population's role in its community; the sum total of a species' use of the biotic and abiotic resources of its habitat.

Go to **Cram101.com** for the Practice Tests for this Chapter.

Molecule	A molecule is the smallest particle of a pure chemical substance that still retains its chemical composition and properties.
Cell	The cell is the structural and functional unit of all living organisms, and is sometimes called the "building block of life."
Light microscope	An optical instrument with lenses that refract visible light to magnify images and project them into a viewer's eye or onto photographic film is referred to as light microscope.
Plasma membrane	Membrane surrounding the cytoplasm that consists of a phospholipid bilayer with embedded proteins is referred to as plasma membrane.
Lipid	Lipid is one class of aliphatic hydrocarbon-containing organic compounds essential for the structure and function of living cells. They are characterized by being water-insoluble but soluble in nonpolar organic solvents.
Atom	An atom is the smallest possible particle of a chemical element that retains its chemical properties.
Selective channels	Selective passageways across a cell membrane formed by specialized membrane transport proteins are called selective channels.
Protein	A protein is a complex, high-molecular-weight organic compound that consists of amino acids joined by peptide bonds. They are essential to the structure and function of all living cells and viruses. Many are enzymes or subunits of enzymes.
Lipid bilayer	A lipid bilayer is a membrane or zone of a membrane composed of lipid molecules (usually phospholipids). The lipid bilayer is a critical component of all biological membranes, including cell membranes, and is a prerequisite for cell-based organisms.
Bacteria	The domain that contains procaryotic cells with primarily diacyl glycerol diesters in their membranes and with bacterial rRNA. Bacteria also is a general term for organisms that are composed of procaryotic cells and are not multicellular.
Membrane protein	A membrane protein is a protein molecule that is attached to, or associated with the membrane of a cell or an organelle. Membrane proteins can be classified into two groups, based on their attachment to the membrane.
Cell membrane	A component of every biological cell, the selectively permeable cell membrane is a thin and structured bilayer of phospholipid and protein molecules that envelopes the cell. It separates a cell's interior from its surroundings and controls what moves in and out.
Peroxisome	Enzyme-filled vesicle in which fatty acids and amino acids are metabolized to hydrogen peroxide that is broken down to harmless products is called peroxisome.
Nucleus	In cell biology, the nucleus is found in all eukaryotic cells that contains most of the cell's genetic material. The nucleus has two primary functions: to control chemical reactions within the cytoplasm and to store information needed for cellular division.
Golgi	Golgi discovered a method of staining nervous tissue which would stain a limited number of cells at random, in their entirety. This enabled him to view the paths of nerve cells in the brain for the first time. He called his discovery the black reaction. It is now known universally as the Golgi stain.
Animal cell	An animal cell is a form of eukaryotic cell which make up many tissues in animals. The animal cell is distinct from other eukaryotes, most notably those of plants, as they lack cell walls and chloroplasts, and they have smaller vacuoles.
Organelle	In cell biology, an organelle is one of several structures with specialized functions, suspended in the cytoplasm of a eukaryotic cell.

Go to **Cram101.com** for the Practice Tests for this Chapter.

Mitochondrion	Mitochondrion refers to an organelle in eukaryotic cells where cellular respiration occurs. Enclosed by two concentric membranes, it is where most of the cell's ATP is made.
Motility	Motility is the ability to move spontaneously and independently. The term can apply to single cells, or to multicellular organisms.
Vesicle	In cell biology, a vesicle is a relatively small and enclosed compartment, separated from the cytosol by at least one lipid bilayer.
Micrograph	A micrograph is a photograph or similar image taken through a microscope or similar device to show a magnified image of an item.
Electron	The electron is a light fundamental subatomic particle that carries a negative electric charge. The electron is a spin-1/2 lepton, does not participate in strong interactions and has no substructure.
Blood	Blood is a circulating tissue composed of fluid plasma and cells. The main function of blood is to supply nutrients (oxygen, glucose) and constitutional elements to tissues and to remove waste products.
Phosphate group	The functional group $-OPO_3H_2$; the transfer of energy from one compound to another is often accomplished by the transfer of a phosphate group.
Phospholipid	Phospholipid is a class of lipids formed from four components: fatty acids, a negatively-charged phosphate group, an alcohol and a backbone. Phospholipids with a glycerol backbone are known as glycerophospholipids or phosphoglycerides.
Hydrophilic	A hydrophilic molecule or portion of a molecule is one that is typically charge-polarized and capable of hydrogen bonding, enabling it to dissolve more readily in water than in oil or other hydrophobic solvents.
Hydrocarbon	A chemical compound composed only of the elements carbon and hydrogen is called hydrocarbon.
Hydrophobic	Hydrophobic refers to being electrically neutral and nonpolar, and thus prefering other neutral and nonpolar solvents or molecular environments. Hydrophobic is often used interchangeably with "oily" or "lipophilic."
Hydrocarbon chain	A hydrocarbon chain consists of a long series of carbon atoms joined to each other and also joined to two hydrogen atoms.
Amphipathic	An amphipathic molecule contains both hydrophobic and hydrophilic groups. The hydrophobic group can be a long carbon chain, with the form: $CH_3(CH_2)_n$, with $4 < n < 16$.
Phosphate	A phosphate is a polyatomic ion or radical consisting of one phosphorus atom and four oxygen. In the ionic form, it carries a -3 formal charge, and is denoted PO_4^{3-}.
Choline	Choline is a nutrient, essential for cardiovascular and brain function, and for cellular membrane composition and repair.
Fatty acid	A fatty acid is a carboxylic acid (or organic acid), often with a long aliphatic tail (long chains), either saturated or unsaturated.
Glycerol	Glycerol is a three-carbon substance that forms the backbone of fatty acids in fats. When the body uses stored fat as a source of energy, glycerol and fatty acids are released into the bloodstream. The glycerol component can be converted to glucose by the liver and provides energy for cellular metabolism.
Double bond	Double bond refers to a type of covalent bond in which two atoms share two pairs of electrons; symbolized by a pair of lines between the bonded atoms. An example is in ethylene (between the carbon atoms). It usually consists of one sigma bond and one pi bond.

Go to **Cram101.com** for the Practice Tests for this Chapter.

Carbon	Carbon is a chemical element in the periodic table that has the symbol C and atomic number 6. An abundant nonmetallic, tetravalent element, carbon has several allotropic forms.
Acid	An acid is a water-soluble, sour-tasting chemical compound that when dissolved in water, gives a solution with a pH of less than 7.
Cholesterol	Cholesterol is a steroid, a lipid, and an alcohol, found in the cell membranes of all body tissues, and transported in the blood plasma of all animals. It is an important component of the membranes of cells, providing stability; it makes the membrane's fluidity stable over a bigger temperature interval.
Galactose	Galactose is a type of sugar found in dairy products, in sugar beets and other gums and mucilages. It is also synthesized by the body, where it forms part of glycolipids and glycoproteins in several tissues.
Serine	Serine, organic compound, one of the 20 amino acids commonly found in animal proteins. Only the L-stereoisomer appears in mammalian protein. It is not essential to the human diet, since it can be synthesized in the body from other metabolites, including glycine.
Sugar	A sugar is the simplest molecule that can be identified as a carbohydrate. These include monosaccharides and disaccharides, trisaccharides and the oligosaccharides. The term "glyco-" indicates the presence of a sugar in an otherwise non-carbohydrate substance.
Acetone	In chemistry, acetone (also known as propanone, dimethyl ketone, 2-propanone, propan-2-one and â-ketopropane) is the simplest representative of the ketones.
Nonpolar	Lacking any asymmetric accumulation of positive and negative charge. Nonpolar molecules are generally insoluble in water.
Triacylglycerol	Triacylglycerol refers to molecule composed of three fatty acids esterified to glycerol. The main constituent of fat droplets in animal tissues and of vegetable oils.
Rearrangement	A change in the usual order and arrangement of genetic material either within the chromosome complement or within a gene locus is rearrangement. Where the nature of the rearrangement has been determined, the type may be searched for directly under the following designations: reciprocal translocation, Robertsonian translocation, insertion, transposition, inversion, deletion, and duplication.
Liposome	A liposome is a spherical vesicle with a membrane composed of a phospholipid bilayer used to deliver drugs or genetic material into a cell.
Solvent	A solvent is a liquid that dissolves a solid, liquid, or gaseous solute, resulting in a solution. The most common solvent in everyday life is water.
Diffusion	Diffusion refers to the spontaneous movement of particles of any kind from where they are more concentrated to where they are less concentrated.
Single bond	The most common type of covalent bond is the single bond, sharing only one pair of electrons between two atoms. It usually consists of one sigma bond.
Hydrogen atom	A hydrogen atom is an atom of the element hydrogen. It is composed of a single negatively-charged electron, attending a positively-charged proton which is the nucleus of the hydrogen atom. The electron is bound to the proton by the Coulomb force.
Yeast	Yeast refers to common term for several families of unicellular fungi. Includes species used for brewing beer and making bread, as well as pathogenic species.
Hydrogen	Hydrogen is a chemical element in the periodic table that has the symbol H and atomic number 1. At standard temperature and pressure it is a colorless, odorless, nonmetallic, univalent, tasteless, highly flammable diatomic gas.

Go to **Cram101.com** for the Practice Tests for this Chapter.

Unsaturated hydrocarbon	Unsaturated hydrocarbon refers to a compound containing only carbon and hydrogen atoms. One or more pairs of carbon atoms are connected by double bonds.
Sterol	A sterol, or steroid alcohols are a subgroup of steroids with a hydroxyl group in the 3-position of the A-ring. They are amphipathic lipids synthetized from Acetyl coenzyme A.
Steroid	A steroid is a lipid characterized by a carbon skeleton with four fused rings. Different steroids vary in the functional groups attached to these rings. Hundreds of distinct steroids have been identified in plants and animals. Their most important role in most living systems is as hormones.
Daughter cell	A cell formed by cell division of a parent cell is a daughter cell.
Glycolipid	Glycolipid refers to lipid in plasma membranes that bears a carbohydrate chain attached to a hydrophobic tail.
Cytosol	The cytosol is the internal fluid of the cell, and a large part of cell metabolism occurs here. Proteins within the cytosol play an important role in signal transduction pathways, glycolysis; also, they act as intracellular receptors and form part of the ribosomes, enabling further protein synthesis
Endoplasmic reticulum	The endoplasmic reticulum is an organelle found in all eukaryotic cells. It modifies proteins, makes macromolecules, and transfers substances throughout the cell.
Substrate	A substrate is a molecule which is acted upon by an enzyme. Each enzyme recognizes only the specific substrate of the reaction it catalyzes. A surface in or on which an organism lives.
Enzyme	An enzyme is a protein that catalyzes, or speeds up, a chemical reaction. They are essential to sustain life because most chemical reactions in biological cells would occur too slowly, or would lead to different products, without them.
Distribution	Distribution in pharmacology is a branch of pharmacokinetics describing reversible transfer of drug from one location to another within the body.
Budding	A means of asexual reproduction whereby a new individual developed from an outgrowth of a parent splits off and lives independently is referred to as budding.
Fusion	Fusion refers to the combination of two atoms into a single atom as a result of a collision, usually accompanied by the release of energy.
Vesicular transport	Transport of proteins from one cellular compartment to another by means of membrane-bounded intermediaries such as vesicles or organelle fragments is called vesicular transport.
Extracellular fluid	In some animals, including mammals, the extracellular fluid can be divided into 2 major subcompartments, interstitial fluid and blood plasma. The extracellular fluid can be further divided into 2 minor subcompartments, transcellular fluid and lymph.
Carbohydrate	Carbohydrate is a chemical compound that contains oxygen, hydrogen, and carbon atoms. They consist of monosaccharide sugars of varying chain lengths and that have the general chemical formula $C_n(H_2O)_n$ or are derivatives of such.
Metabolite	The term metabolite is usually restricted to small molecules. They are the intermediates and products of metabolism. A primary metabolite is directly involved in the normal growth, development, and reproduction. A secondary metabolite is not directly involved in those processes, but usually has important ecological function.
Ion	Ion refers to an atom or molecule that has gained or lost one or more electrons, thus acquiring an electrical charge.
Macromolecule	A macromolecule is a molecule of high relative molecular mass, the structure of which essentially comprises the multiple repetition of units derived, actually or conceptually,

from molecules of low relative molecular mass.

Peripheral membrane protein	Peripheral membrane protein is a protein that adhere only loosely to the biological membrane with which they are associated.
Transmembrane protein	Membrane protein that extends through the lipid bilayer, with part of its mass on either side of the membrane is referred to as a transmembrane protein.
Helix	A helix is a twisted shape like a spring, screw or a spiral staircase. They are important in biology, as DNA and many proteins have spiral substructures, known a alpha helix.
Side chain	In organic chemistry and biochemistry a side chain is a part of a molecule attached to a core structure. Often the side chain can vary for a given core. In biochemistry the peptide or protein side chains are the variable parts of amino acids extending from the peptide backbone.
Amino acid	An amino acid is any molecule that contains both amino and carboxylic acid functional groups. They are the basic structural building units of proteins. They form short polymer chains called peptides or polypeptides which in turn form structures called proteins.
Peptide	Peptide is the family of molecules formed from the linking, in a defined order, of various amino acids. The link between one amino acid residue and the next is an amide bond, and is sometimes referred to as a peptide bond.
Polypeptide backbone	Polypeptide backbone refers to the chain of repeating carbon and nitrogen atoms, linked by peptide bonds, in a polypeptide or protein. The side chains of the amino acids project from this backbone.
Hydrogen bond	A hydrogen bond is a type of attractive intermolecular force that exists between two partial electric charges of opposite polarity. Although stronger than most other intermolecular forces, the typical hydrogen bond is much weaker than both the ionic bond and the covalent bond.
Transmembrane receptor	A transmembrane receptor is an integral membrane protein, which resides and operates typically within a cell's plasma membrane, but also in the membranes of some subcellular compartments and organelles. Binding to a signalling molecule or sometimes to a pair of such molecules on one side of the membrane, they initiate a response on the other side.
Polypeptide	Polypeptide refers to polymer of many amino acids linked by peptide bonds.
Peptide bond	A peptide bond is a chemical bond formed between two molecules when the carboxyl group of one molecule reacts with the amino group of the other molecule, releasing a molecule of water.
Signal molecule	Extracellular or intracellular molecule that cues the response of a cell to the behavior of other cells or objects in the environment is called signal molecule.
Receptor	A receptor is a protein on the cell membrane or within the cytoplasm or cell nucleus that binds to a specific molecule (a ligand), such as a neurotransmitter, hormone, or other substance, and initiates the cellular response to the ligand. Receptor, in immunology, the region of an antibody which shows recognition of an antigen.
Outer membrane	The outer membrane refers to the outside membrane of an organelle which surrounds the rest of the organelle components. Both the chloroplast and the mitochondria have an outer membrane.
Mitochondria	Mitochondria are organelles found in most eukaryotic cells, including those of plants, animals, fungi, and protists. Mitochondria are sometimes described as "cellular power plants", because their primary function is to convert organic materials into energy in the form of ATP.
Antibiotic	Antibiotic refers to substance such as penicillin or streptomycin that is toxic to

Go to **Cram101.com** for the Practice Tests for this Chapter.

microorganisms. Usually a product of a particular microorvanism or plant.

Porin	A porin is a transmembrane protein that is large enough to facilitate passive diffusion. They are prevalent in the outer membrane of the mitochondria and Gram-negative bacteria.
Toxin	Toxin refers to a microbial product or component that can injure another cell or organism at low concentrations. Often the term refers to a poisonous protein, but toxins may be lipids and other substances.
Cone	Cone refers to a reproductive structure of gymnosperms that produces pollen in males or eggs in females.
Trimer	In biochemistry, a trimer is a macromolecular compound formed by three non-covalently bound macromolecules.
Sodium	Sodium is the chemical element in the periodic table that has the symbol Na (Natrium in Latin) and atomic number 11. Sodium is a soft, waxy, silvery reactive metal belonging to the alkali metals that is abundant in natural compounds (especially halite). It is highly reactive.
Reaction center	A photosynthetic reaction center is a protein which is the site of the light reactions of photosynthesis. The reaction center contains pigments such as chlorophyll and phaeophytin. These absorb light, promoting an electron to a higher energy level within the pigment.
Sunlight	Sunlight in the broad sense is the total spectrum of electromagnetic radiation given off by the Sun.
Bacteriorhod-psin	Bacteriorhodopsin is the photosynthetic pigment used by archaea, most notably halobacteria. It acts as a proton pump, i.e. it captures light energy and uses it to move protons across the membrane out of the cell.
Salt marsh	Salt marsh refers to a grassy area that extends along the shores of estuaries and sheltered coasts in temperate and subpolar regions.
Transport protein	A transport protein is a protein involved in facilitated diffusion. Changes in the conformation move the binding site to the opposite side of the protein.
Bacterium	Most bacterium are microscopic and unicellular, with a relatively simple cell structure lacking a cell nucleus, and organelles such as mitochondria and chloroplasts. They are the most abundant of all organisms. They are ubiquitous in soil, water, and as symbionts of other organisms.
Proton	Positive subatomic particle, located in the nucleus and having a weight of approximately one atomic mass unit is referred to as a proton.
Retinal	Retinal is fundamental in the transduction of light into visual signals in the photoreceptor level of the retina.
Monomer	In chemistry, a monomer is a small molecule that may become chemically bonded to other monomers to form a polymer.
Eye	An eye is an organ that detects light. Different kinds of light-sensitive organs are found in a variety of creatures.
Concentration gradient	Gradual change in chemical concentration from one point to another is called concentration gradient.
Retina	The retina is a thin layer of cells at the back of the eyeball of vertebrates and some cephalopods; it is the part of the eye which converts light into nervous signals.
Diffraction	Diffraction is the bending and spreading of waves when they meet an obstruction. It can occur with any type of wave, including sound waves, water waves, and electromagnetic waves such as

light and radio waves.

Crystal	Crystal is a solid in which the constituent atoms, molecules, or ions are packed in a regularly ordered, repeating pattern extending in all three spatial dimensions.
X-Ray	X-Ray refers to diagnostic test in which an image is created using low doses of radiation.
Cytochrome	Cytochrome refers to colored, heme-containing protein that transfers electrons during cellular respiration and photosynthesis.
Electron carrier	Electron carrier refers to a molecule that conveys electrons within a cell; one of several membrane molecules that make up electron transport chains.
Protein subunit	A protein subunit is a single protein molecule that assembles (or "coassembles") with other protein molecules to form a multimeric or oligomeric protein. Many naturally-occurring proteins and enzymes are multimeric.
Chlorophyll	Chlorophyll is a green photosynthetic pigment found in plants, algae, and cyanobacteria. In plant photosynthesis incoming light is absorbed by chlorophyll and other accessory pigments in the antenna complexes of photosystem I and photosystem II.
Cell cortex	Cell cortex refers to specialized layer of cytoplasm on the inner face of the plasma membrane. It functions as a mechanical support of the plasma membrane. In animal cells it is an actin-rich layer responsible for movements of the cell surface.
Spectrin	Spectrin is a cytoskeletal protein that lines the intracellular side of the plasma membrane of many cell types in pentagonal or hexagonal arrangements, forming a scaffolding and playing an important role in maintenance of plasma membrane integrity and cytoskeletal structure
Cortex	In anatomy and zoology the cortex is the outermost or superficial layer of an organ or the outer portion of the stem or root of a plant.
Blood vessel	A blood vessel is a part of the circulatory system and function to transport blood throughout the body. The most important types, arteries and veins, are so termed because they carry blood away from or towards the heart, respectively.
Oligosaccharide	An oligosaccharide is a saccharide polymer containing a small number (typically three to six) of component sugars, also known as simple sugars. They are generally found either O- or N-linked to compatible amino acid side chains in proteins or to lipid moieties.
Glycoprotein	A macromolecule consisting of one or more polypeptides linked to short chains of sugars is called glycoprotein.
Actin	Actin is a globular protein that polymerizes helically forming filaments, which like the other two components of the cellular cytoskeleton form a three-dimensional network inside an eukaryotic cell. They provide mechanical support for the cell, determine the cell shape, enable cell movements .
Dimer	A dimer refers to a molecule composed of two similar subunits or monomers linked together. It is a special case of a polymer.
Polysaccharide	Polymer made from sugar monomers is a polysaccharide. They are relatively complex carbohydrates.
Proteoglycan	Molecule consisting of one or more glycosaminoglycan chains attached to a core protein is referred to as proteoglycan.
Lectin	Lectin is a protein of non-immune origin that specifically interacts with sugar molecules (carbohydrates) without modifying them.
Linkage	Linkage refers to the patterns of assortment of genes that are located on the same chromosome. Important because if the genes are located relatively far apart, crossing over is

more likely to occur between them than if they are close together.

Multicellular	Multicellular organisms are those organisms consisting of more than one cell, and having differentiated cells that perform specialized functions. Most life that can be seen with the naked eye is multicellular, as are all animals (i.e. members of the kingdom Animalia) and plants (i.e. members of the kingdom Plantae).
Neutrophil	Neutrophil refers to phagocytic white blood cell that can engulf bacteria and viruses in infected tissue; part of the body's nonspecific defense system.
Endothelial cell	The endothelial cell controls the passage of materials — and the transit of white blood cells — into and out of the bloodstream. In some organs, there are highly differentiated cells to perform specialized 'filtering' functions.
Fluorescein	Fluorescein is a fluorophore commonly used in microscopy, in a type of dye laser as the gain medium, and in forensics and serology to detect latent blood stains. Fluorescein has an absorption maximum at 490 nm and emission maximum of 514 nm (in water).
Microscope	A microscope is an instrument for viewing objects that are too small to be seen by the naked or unaided eye.
Hybrid	Hybrid refers to the offspring of parents of two different species or of two different varieties of one species; the offspring of two parents that differ in one or more inherited traits; an individual that is heterozygous for one or more pair of genes.
Plasma	In physics and chemistry, a plasma is an ionized gas, and is usually considered to be a distinct phase of matter. "Ionized" in this case means that at least one electron has been dissociated from a significant fraction of the molecules.
Domain	In biology, a domain is the top-level grouping of organisms in scientific classification.
Epithelial	Functions of epithelial cells include secretion, absorption, protection, transcellular transport, sensation detection, and selective permeability.
Extracellular matrix	Extracellular matrix is any material part of a tissue that is not part of any cell. Extracellular matrix is the defining feature of connective tissue.
Fluorescence	Fluorescence is a luminescence that is mostly found as an optical phenomenon in cold bodies, in which the molecular absorption of a photon triggers the emission of a lower-energy photon with a longer wavelength. The energy difference between the absorbed and emitted photons ends up as molecular vibrations or heat.
Bleaching	Bleaching is a phenomenon where severely stressed corals turn white, frequently due to high water temperatures. This color change is mainly due to the corals expelling their zooxanthellae.
Population	Group of organisms of the same species occupying a certain area and sharing a common gene pool is referred to as population.
Cytoskeleton	Cytoskeleton refers to a meshwork of fine fibers in the cytoplasm of a eukaryotic cell; includes microfilaments, intermediate filaments, and microtubules.
Microscopy	Microscopy is any technique for producing visible images of structures or details too small to otherwise be seen by the human eye, using a microscope or other magnification tool.
Tight junction	Region between cells where adjacent plasma membrane proteins join to form an impermeable barrier is a tight junction.
Cell junction	A structure that connects tissue cells to one another is called cell junction.
Basal lamina	Thin mat of extracellular matrix that separates epithelial sheets, and many other types of cells such as muscle or fat cells, from connective tissue is called basal lamina.

Tissue	Group of similar cells which perform a common function is called tissue.
Solute	Substance that is dissolved in a solvent, forming a solution is referred to as a solute.
Ion channel	An ion channel is a pore-forming protein that helps establish the small voltage gradient that exists across the membrane of all living cells, by allowing the flow of ions down their electrochemical gradient. They are present in the membranes that surround all biological cells.
Hydrophobic force	Force exerted by the hydrogen-bonded network of water molecules that brings two nonpolar surfaces together by excluding water between them is a hydrophobic force.

Membrane transport protein	Membrane transport protein refers to membrane protein that mediates the passage of ions or molecules across a membrane. Examples are ion channels and carrier proteins.
Concentration gradient	Gradual change in chemical concentration from one point to another is called concentration gradient.
Active transport	Active transport is the mediated transport of biochemicals, and other atomic/molecular substances, across membranes. In this form of transport, molecules move against either an electrical or concentration gradient.
Plasma membrane	Membrane surrounding the cytoplasm that consists of a phospholipid bilayer with embedded proteins is referred to as plasma membrane.
Lipid bilayer	A lipid bilayer is a membrane or zone of a membrane composed of lipid molecules (usually phospholipids). The lipid bilayer is a critical component of all biological membranes, including cell membranes, and is a prerequisite for cell-based organisms.
Molecule	A molecule is the smallest particle of a pure chemical substance that still retains its chemical composition and properties.
Protein	A protein is a complex, high-molecular-weight organic compound that consists of amino acids joined by peptide bonds. They are essential to the structure and function of all living cells and viruses. Many are enzymes or subunits of enzymes.
Solute	Substance that is dissolved in a solvent, forming a solution is referred to as a solute.
Cell	The cell is the structural and functional unit of all living organisms, and is sometimes called the "building block of life."
Ion	Ion refers to an atom or molecule that has gained or lost one or more electrons, thus acquiring an electrical charge.
Passive transport	Passive transport is a means of moving biochemicals, and other atomic or molecular substances, across membranes. Passive transport is dependent on the permeability of the cell membrane, which, in turn, is dependent on the organization and characteristics of the membrane lipids and proteins.
Hydrophobic	Hydrophobic refers to being electrically neutral and nonpolar, and thus prefering other neutral and nonpolar solvents or molecular environments. Hydrophobic is often used interchangeably with "oily" or "lipophilic."
Plasma	In physics and chemistry, a plasma is an ionized gas, and is usually considered to be a distinct phase of matter. "Ionized" in this case means that at least one electron has been dissociated from a significant fraction of the molecules.
Phosphate group	The functional group $-OPO_3H_2$; the transfer of energy from one compound to another is often accomplished by the transfer of a phosphate group.
Metabolic waste	Metabolic waste is the substances left over from metabolic processes and cannot be used by other processes, and must therefore be excreted.
Hydrolysis	Hydrolysis is a chemical process in which a molecule is cleaved into two parts by the addition of a molecule of water.
Amino acid	An amino acid is any molecule that contains both amino and carboxylic acid functional groups. They are the basic structural building units of proteins. They form short polymer chains called peptides or polypeptides which in turn form structures called proteins.
Gradient	Gradient refers to a difference in concentration, pressure, or electrical charge between two regions.

Sugar	A sugar is the simplest molecule that can be identified as a carbohydrate. These include monosaccharides and disaccharides, trisaccharides and the oligosaccharides. The term "glyco-" indicates the presence of a sugar in an otherwise non-carbohydrate substance.
Macromolecule	A macromolecule is a molecule of high relative molecular mass, the structure of which essentially comprises the multiple repetition of units derived, actually or conceptually, from molecules of low relative molecular mass.
Bacteria	The domain that contains procaryotic cells with primarily diacyl glycerol diesters in their membranes and with bacterial rRNA. Bacteria also is a general term for organisms that are composed of procaryotic cells and are not multicellular.
Carrier protein	Protein molecule that combines with a substance and transports it through the plasma membrane is called a carrier protein.
Ion channel	An ion channel is a pore-forming protein that helps establish the small voltage gradient that exists across the membrane of all living cells, by allowing the flow of ions down their electrochemical gradient. They are present in the membranes that surround all biological cells.
Channel protein	Membrane transport protein that forms an aqueous pore in the membrane through which a specific solute, usually an ion, can pass is the channel protein.
Hydrophilic	A hydrophilic molecule or portion of a molecule is one that is typically charge-polarized and capable of hydrogen bonding, enabling it to dissolve more readily in water than in oil or other hydrophobic solvents.
Diffusion	Diffusion refers to the spontaneous movement of particles of any kind from where they are more concentrated to where they are less concentrated.
Nerve	A nerve is an enclosed, cable-like bundle of nerve fibers or axons, which includes the glia that ensheath the axons in myelin.
Cell membrane	A component of every biological cell, the selectively permeable cell membrane is a thin and structured bilayer of phospholipid and protein molecules that envelopes the cell. It separates a cell's interior from its surroundings and controls what moves in and out.
Organelle	In cell biology, an organelle is one of several structures with specialized functions, suspended in the cytoplasm of a eukaryotic cell.
Solubility	A solution at equilibrium that cannot hold any more solute is said to be saturated. The equilibrium of a solution is mainly dependent on temperature. The maximum equilibrium amount of solute which can normally dissolve per amount of solvent is the solubility of that solute in that solvent.
Nonpolar	Lacking any asymmetric accumulation of positive and negative charge. Nonpolar molecules are generally insoluble in water.
Glycerol	Glycerol is a three-carbon substance that forms the backbone of fatty acids in fats. When the body uses stored fat as a source of energy, glycerol and fatty acids are released into the bloodstream. The glycerol component can be converted to glucose by the liver and provides energy for cellular metabolism.
Glucose	Glucose, a simple monosaccharide sugar, is one of the most important carbohydrates and is used as a source of energy in animals and plants. Glucose is one of the main products of photosynthesis and starts respiration.
Ethanol	Ethanol is a flammable, colorless chemical compound, one of the alcohols that is most often found in alcoholic beverages. In common parlance, it is often referred to simply as alcohol. Its chemical formula is C_2H_5OH, also written as C_2H_6O.

Go to **Cram101.com** for the Practice Tests for this Chapter.

Dalton	A measure of mass for atoms and subatomic particles is a dalton.
Hydrocarbon	A chemical compound composed only of the elements carbon and hydrogen is called hydrocarbon.
Transport protein	A transport protein is a protein involved in facilitated diffusion. Changes in the conformation move the binding site to the opposite side of the protein.
Polypeptide	Polypeptide refers to polymer of many amino acids linked by peptide bonds.
Conformation	The three-dimensional shape of a molecule is its conformation. The conformation is particularly important in proteins.
Specificity	A medical diagnostic test for a certain disease, specificity is the proportion of true negatives of all the negative samples tested.
Substrate	A substrate is a molecule which is acted upon by an enzyme. Each enzyme recognizes only the specific substrate of the reaction it catalyzes. A surface in or on which an organism lives.
Enzyme	An enzyme is a protein that catalyzes, or speeds up, a chemical reaction. They are essential to sustain life because most chemical reactions in biological cells would occur too slowly, or would lead to different products, without them.
Facilitated diffusion	Facilitated diffusion is a process of diffusion, a form of passive transport, via which molecules diffuse across membranes, with the assistance of transport proteins.
Carbon dioxide	Carbon dioxide is an atmospheric gas comprized of one carbon and two oxygen atoms. A very widely known chemical compound, it is frequently called by its formula CO_2. In its solid state, it is commonly known as dry ice.
Oxygen	Oxygen is a chemical element in the periodic table. It has the symbol O and atomic number 8. Oxygen is the second most common element on Earth, composing around 46% of the mass of Earth's crust and 28% of the mass of Earth as a whole, and is the third most common element in the universe.
Cytosol	The cytosol is the internal fluid of the cell, and a large part of cell metabolism occurs here. Proteins within the cytosol play an important role in signal transduction pathways, glycolysis; also, they act as intracellular receptors and form part of the ribosomes, enabling further protein synthesis
Endoplasmic reticulum	The endoplasmic reticulum is an organelle found in all eukaryotic cells. It modifies proteins, makes macromolecules, and transfers substances throughout the cell.
Bacteriorhod-psin	Bacteriorhodopsin is the photosynthetic pigment used by archaea, most notably halobacteria. It acts as a proton pump, i.e. it captures light energy and uses it to move protons across the membrane out of the cell.
Skeletal muscle	Skeletal muscle is a type of striated muscle, attached to the skeleton. They are used to facilitate movement, by applying force to bones and joints; via contraction. They generally contract voluntarily (via nerve stimulation), although they can contract involuntarily.
Sarcoplasmic reticulum	Smooth endoplasmic reticulum of skeletal muscle cells specially adapted for calcium ion storage and release is called sarcoplasmic reticulum.
Calcium	Calcium is the chemical element in the periodic table that has the symbol Ca and atomic number 20. Calcium is a soft grey alkaline earth metal that is used as a reducing agent in the extraction of thorium, zirconium and uranium. Calcium is also the fifth most abundant element in the Earth's crust.
X-ray crystallography	Technique for determining the three-dimensional arrangement of atoms in a molecule based on the diffraction pattern of X-rays passing through a crystal of the molecule is x-ray crystallography.

Microscopy	Microscopy is any technique for producing visible images of structures or details too small to otherwise be seen by the human eye, using a microscope or other magnification tool.
Electron	The electron is a light fundamental subatomic particle that carries a negative electric charge. The electron is a spin-1/2 lepton, does not participate in strong interactions and has no substructure.
Muscle	Muscle is a contractile form of tissue. It is one of the four major tissue types, the other three being epithelium, connective tissue and nervous tissue. Muscle contraction is used to move parts of the body, as well as to move substances within the body.
Phosphorylation	Phosphorylation refers to reaction in which a phosphate group becomes covalently coupled to another molecule.
Rearrangement	A change in the usual order and arrangement of genetic material either within the chromosome complement or within a gene locus is rearrangement. Where the nature of the rearrangement has been determined, the type may be searched for directly under the following designations: reciprocal translocation, Robertsonian translocation, insertion, transposition, inversion, deletion, and duplication.
Activator	An activator, is a DNA-binding protein that regulates one or more genes by increasing the rate of transcription.
Domain	In biology, a domain is the top-level grouping of organisms in scientific classification.
Liver	The liver is an organ in vertebrates, including humans. It plays a major role in metabolism and has a number of functions in the body including drug detoxification, glycogen storage, and plasma protein synthesis. It also produces bile, which is important for digestion.
Glycolysis	Glycolysis refers to the multistep chemical breakdown of a molecule of glucose into two molecules of pyruvic acid; the first stage of cellular respiration in all organisms; occurs in the cytoplasmic fluid.
Voltage	A measure of the electrical difference that exists between two different points or objects is called voltage.
Membrane potential	Membrane potential is the electrical potential difference (voltage) across a cell's plasma membrane.
Animal cell	An animal cell is a form of eukaryotic cell which make up many tissues in animals. The animal cell is distinct from other eukaryotes, most notably those of plants, as they lack cell walls and chloroplasts, and they have smaller vacuoles.
Hydrolyze	Hydrolyze refers to break a chemical bond, as in a peptide linkage, with the insertion of the components of water, -H and -OH, at the cleaved ends of a chain. The digestion of proteins is hydrolysis.
ATPase	ATPase is a class of enzymes that catalyze the decomposition of adenosine triphosphate into adenosine diphosphate and a free phosphate ion. This dephosphorylation reaction releases energy, which the enzyme harnesses to drive other chemical reactions that would not otherwise occur. This process is widely used in all known forms of life.
Potential energy	Stored energy as a result of location or spatial arrangement is referred to as potential energy.
Toxin	Toxin refers to a microbial product or component that can injure another cell or organism at low concentrations. Often the term refers to a poisonous protein, but toxins may be lipids and other substances.
Linkage	Linkage refers to the patterns of assortment of genes that are located on the same chromosome. Important because if the genes are located relatively far apart, crossing over is

	more likely to occur between them than if they are close together.
Symport	A membrane transport process that carries two substances in the same direction across the membrane is a symport.
Phosphate	A phosphate is a polyatomic ion or radical consisting of one phosphorus atom and four oxygen. In the ionic form, it carries a -3 formal charge, and is denoted $PO_4{}^{3-}$.
Coupled transport	Membrane transport process in which the transfer of one molecule depends on the simultaneous or sequential transfer of a second molecule is called coupled transport.
Epithelial	Functions of epithelial cells include secretion, absorption, protection, transcellular transport, sensation detection, and selective permeability.
Epithelium	Epithelium is a tissue composed of a layer of cells. Epithelium can be found lining internal (e.g. endothelium, which lines the inside of blood vessels) or external (e.g. skin) free surfaces of the body. Functions include secretion, absorption and protection.
Osmotic pressure	Osmotic pressure is the pressure produced by a solution in a space that is enclosed by a differentially permeable membrane.
Tight junction	Region between cells where adjacent plasma membrane proteins join to form an impermeable barrier is a tight junction.
Microvillus	A microvillus is a small extension of the cell surface of absorptive and secretory epithelial cells, such as kidney and intestinal cells. These structures increase the surface area of cells by approximately 600 fold (human), thus facilitating absorption and secretion.
Swell	Swell refers to a wave with a flatter, rounded wave crest and trough. Swells are found away from the area where waves are generated by the wind .
Tissue	Group of similar cells which perform a common function is called tissue.
Inhibitor	An inhibitor is a type of effector (biology) that decreases or prevents the rate of a chemical reaction. They are often called negative catalysts.
Plant cell	A cell that is a structural and functional unit of a plant is a plant cell.
Cell wall	Cell wall refers to a protective layer external to the plasma membrane in plant cells, bacteria, fungi, and some protists; protects the cell and helps maintain its shape.
Osmosis	Osmosis is the diffusion of a solvent through a semipermeable membrane from a region of low solute concentration to a region of high solute concentration.
Vacuole	A vacuole is a large membrane-bound compartment within some eukaryotic cells where they serve a variety of different functions: capturing food materials or unwanted structural debris surrounding the cell, sequestering materials that might be toxic to the cell, maintaining fluid balance (called turgor) within the cell.
Turgor pressure	Turgor pressure is the pressure produced by a solution in a space that is enclosed by a differentially permeable membrane.
Gas exchange	In humans and other mammals, respiratory gas exchange or ventilation is carried out by mechanisms of the lungs. The actual gas exchange occurs in the alveoli.
Guard cell	A specialized epidermal cell in plants that regulates the size of a stoma, allowing gas exchange between the surrounding air and the photosynthetic cells in the leaf is called guard cell.
Stomata	A stomata is a tiny opening or pore, found mostly on the undersurface of a plant leaf, and used for gas exchange.
Leaf	In botany, a leaf is an above-ground plant organ specialized for photosynthesis. For this

purpose, a leaf is typically flat (laminar) and thin, to expose the chloroplast containing cells (chlorenchyma tissue) to light over a broad area, and to allow light to penetrate fully into the tissues.

Contractile vacuole	A fluid-filled vacuole in certain protists that takes up excess water from the cytoplasm, contracts, and expels the water outside the cell through a pore in the plasma membrane is a contractile vacuole.
Extracellular fluid	In some animals, including mammals, the extracellular fluid can be divided into 2 major subcompartments, interstitial fluid and blood plasma. The extracellular fluid can be further divided into 2 minor subcompartments, transcellular fluid and lymph.
Antiporter	Carrier protein that transports two different ions or small molecules across a membrane in opposite directions, either simultaneously or in sequence is referred to as antiporter.
Secretion	Secretion is the process of segregating, elaborating, and releasing chemicals from a cell, or a secreted chemical substance or amount of substance.
Micrograph	A micrograph is a photograph or similar image taken through a microscope or similar device to show a magnified image of an item.
Proton	Positive subatomic particle, located in the nucleus and having a weight of approximately one atomic mass unit is referred to as a proton.
Acid	An acid is a water-soluble, sour-tasting chemical compound that when dissolved in water, gives a solution with a pH of less than 7.
Central vacuole	A membrane-enclosed sac occupying most of the interior of a mature plant cell, having diverse roles in reproduction, growth, and development is called central vacuole.
Lysosome	Lysosome refers to a digestive organelle in eukaryotic cells; contains hydrolytic enzymes that digest the cell's food and wastes. They are found in both plant and animal cells, and are built in the Golgi apparatus.
Distribution	Distribution in pharmacology is a branch of pharmacokinetics describing reversible transfer of drug from one location to another within the body.
Vestibule	Vestibule refers to the cavity enclosed by the labia minora, it is the space into which the vagina and urethral opening empty.
Selectivity filter	That part of an ion channel structure that determines which ions it can transport is referred to as selectivity filter.
Carbonyl	A carbonyl group is a functional group composed of a carbon atom double-bonded to an oxygen atom. The term carbonyl can also refer to carbon monoxide as a ligand in an inorganic or organometallic complex.
Atom	An atom is the smallest possible particle of a chemical element that retains its chemical properties.
Side chain	In organic chemistry and biochemistry a side chain is a part of a molecule attached to a core structure. Often the side chain can vary for a given core. In biochemistry the peptide or protein side chains are the variable parts of amino acids extending from the peptide backbone.
Insect	An arthropod that usually has three body segments , three pairs of legs, and one or two pairs of wings is called an insect. They are the largest and (on land) most widely-distributed taxon within the phylum Arthropoda. They comprise the most diverse group of animals on the earth, with around 925,000 species described
Pulse	The rhythmic stretching of the arteries caused by the pressure of blood forced through the

arteries by contractions of the ventricles during systole is a pulse.

Nerve cell	A cell specialized to originate or transmit nerve impulses is referred to as nerve cell.
Patch-clamp recording	Patch-clamp recording refers to electrophysiological technique in which a tiny electrode tip is sealed onto a patch of cell membrane, thereby making it possible to record the flow of current through individual ion channels in the patch.
Microelectrode	An electrical wire so small that it can be used either to monitor the electrical activity of a single neuron or to stimulate activity within it is a microelectrode.
Yeast	Yeast refers to common term for several families of unicellular fungi. Includes species used for brewing beer and making bread, as well as pathogenic species.
Eye	An eye is an organ that detects light. Different kinds of light-sensitive organs are found in a variety of creatures.
Acetylcholine	The chemical compound acetylcholine was the first neurotransmitter to be identified. It is a chemical transmitter in both the peripheral nervous system (PNS) and central nervous system (CNS) in many organisms including humans.
Gene	Gene refers to a discrete unit of hereditary information consisting of a specific nucleotide sequence in DNA . Most of the genes of a eukaryote are located in its chromosomal DNA; a few are carried by the DNA of mitochondria and chloroplasts.
Acetylcholine receptor	An acetylcholine receptor is an integral membrane protein that responds to the binding of the neurotransmitter acetylcholine. They are ion channels, and, like other members of the "cys-loop" ligand-gated ion channel superfamily, are composed of five protein subunits arranged like staves around a barrel.
Ligand	Any molecule that binds to a specific receptor site on a protein or other molecule is called a ligand.
Acetyl	The acetyl radical contains a methyl group single-bonded to a carbonyl. The carbon of the carbonyl has an lone electron available, with which it forms a chemical bond to the remainder of the molecule.
Cation	A positively charged ion which has fewer electrons than protons is a cation.
Hair cell	The hair cell is a sensory cell of both the auditory system and the vestibular system in all vertebrates. In mammals, the auditory hair cells are located within the organ of Corti on a thin basilar membrane in the cochlea of the inner ear.
Organ of corti	The organ of Corti is the organ in the inner ear of mammals that contains the auditory sensory cells, the so-called hair cells. It is situated on the basilar membrane and protrudes into the scala media. It contains four rows of hair cells whose hair bundles stick out from its surface.
Protein domain	Protein domain refers to portion of a protein that has a tertiary structure of its own. Larger proteins are generally composed of several domains, each connected to the next by short flexible regions of polypeptide chain.
Inner ear	The Inner ear consists of the cochlea, where a wave is created by a difference in pressure between the scala vestibuli and the scala tympani. The cochlea has three fluid filled sections. The perilymph fluid in the canals differs from the endolymph fluid in the cochlear duct. The organ of Corti is the sensor of pressure variations.
Cochlea	The cochlea is a coiled, tapered tube containing the auditory branch of the mammalian inner ear. Its core component is the Organ of Corti, the sensory organ of hearing.
Stereocilia	Stereocilia are mechanosensing organelles of hair cells, which respond to fluid motion or

fluid pressure changes in numerous types of animals for numerous functions. As acoustic sensors in mammals, they are lined up in the Organ of Corti in the cochlea of the inner ear.

Threshold
Electrical potential level at which an action potential or nerve impulse is produced is called threshold.

Supporting cell
In the nervous system, a cell that protects, insulates, and reinforces a neuron is called a supporting cell. A cell that bears one or more carpagonial branches.

Basilar membrane
The basilar membrane within the cochlea of the inner ear separates two liquid filled tubes that run along the coil of the cochlea, the scala media and the scala tympani. This separation is the main function of the basilar membrane in the hearing organ of all land vertebrates.

Stereocilium
A large, rigid microvillus found in 'organ pipe' arrays on the apical surface of hair cells in the ear. A stereocilium contains a bundle of actin filaments, rather than microtubules, and is thus not a true cilium.

Filament
The stamen is the male organ of a flower. Each stamen generally has a stalk called the filament, and, on top of the filament, an anther. The filament is a long chain of proteins, such as those found in hair, muscle, or in flagella.

Brain
The part of the central nervous system involved in regulating and controlling body activity and interpreting information from the senses transmitted through the nervous system is referred to as the brain.

Potential difference
A difference in electrical charge on two sides of a membrane caused by an unequal distribution of ions is a potential difference.

Hydrogen ion
A single proton with a charge of + 1. The dissociation of a water molecule leads to the generation of a hydroxide ion and a hydrogen ion. The hydrogen ion is hydrated in aqueous solutions and is usually written as H_2O^+.

Anion
A negatively-charged ion, which has more electrons in its electron shell than it has protons in its nucleus, is known as an anion, for it is attracted to anodes; a positively-charged ion, which has fewer electrons than protons, is known as a cation, for it is attracted to cathodes.

Leaflet
A leaflet in botany is a part of a compound leaf. A leaflet may resemble a complete leaf, but it is not borne on a stem as a leaf is, but rather on a vein of the whole leaf. Compound leaves are common in many plant families.

Stalk
The stalk is the longish piece that supports the seed-carrying parts of a plant, or, more simply, the stem. A leaf's petiole; the slender stem that supports the blade of a leaf and attaches it to a larger stem of the plant.

Net movement
Net movement refers to movement in one direction minus the movement in the other.

Nernst equation
Quantitative expression that relates the equilibrium ratio of concentrations of an ion on either side of a permeable membrane to the voltage difference across the membrane is the nernst equation.

Central nervous system
The central nervous system comprized of the brain and spinal cord, represents the largest part of the nervous system. Together with the peripheral nervous system, it has a fundamental role in the control of behavior.

Spinal cord
The spinal cord is a part of the vertebrate nervous system that is enclosed in and protected by the vertebral column (it passes through the spinal canal). It consists of nerve cells. The spinal cord carries sensory signals and motor innervation to most of the skeletal muscles in the body.

Neuron	The neuron is a major class of cells in the nervous system. In vertebrates, they are found in the brain, the spinal cord and in the nerves and ganglia of the peripheral nervous system, and their primary role is to process and transmit neural information.
Organ	Organ refers to a structure consisting of several tissues adapted as a group to perform specific functions.
Gland	A gland is an organ in an animal's body that synthesizes a substance for release such as hormones, often into the bloodstream or into cavities inside the body or its outer surface.
Motor neuron	A nerve cell that conveys command signals from the central nervous system to effector cells, such as muscle cells or gland cells is a motor neuron.
Cell body	The part of a cell, such as a neuron, that houses the nucleus is the cell body.
Nucleus	In cell biology, the nucleus is found in all eukaryotic cells that contains most of the cell's genetic material. The nucleus has two primary functions: to control chemical reactions within the cytoplasm and to store information needed for cellular division.
Target cell	A cell that responds to a regulatory signal, such as a hormone is a target cell.
Antennae	Antennae are paired appendages connected to the front-most segments of arthropods. In crustaceans, they are biramous and present on the first two segments of the head, with the smaller pair known as antennules. In insects, olfactory receptors on the antennae bind to odor molecules, including pheromones.
Dendrite	A dendrite is a slender, typically branched projection of a neuron, which conducts the electrical stimulation received from other cells to and from the cell body or soma of the neuron from which it projects. This stimulation arrives through synapses, which are located at various points throughout the dendritic arbor.
Axon	An axon is a long slender projection of a nerve cell, or neuron, which conducts electrical impulses away from the neuron's cell body or soma. They are in effect the primary transmission lines of the nervous system, and as bundles they help make up nerves.
Action potential	An action potential is a wave of electrical discharge that travels along the membrane of a cell. They communicate fast internal messages between tissues making them an essential feature of animal life at the microscopic level.
Axon terminal	A swelling at the end of an axon that is designed to release a chemical substance onto another neuron, muscle cell, or gland cell is called the axon terminal.
Patch clamping	Patch clamping refers to a technique for isolating a tiny patch of membrane to allow the study of ion movement through a particular channel.
Stimulus	Stimulus in a nervous system, a factor that triggers sensory transduction.
Amplification	In molecular biology, amplification (polymerase chain reaction or PCR) is the method for creating multiple copies of DNA (or RNA) without using a living organism, such as E. coli or yeast.
Electrode	An electrode is a conductor used to make contact with a nonmetallic part of a circuit (e.g. a semiconductor, an electrolyte or a vacuum).
Depolarization	Depolarization is a decrease in the absolute value of a cell's membrane potential.
Depolarized	Depolarized refers to having lost the electrical difference existing between two points or objects.
Predator	A predator is an animal or other organism that hunts and kills other organisms for food in an act called predation.

Go to **Cram101.com** for the Practice Tests for this Chapter.

Mantle cavity	A mantle skirt is a double fold of mantle that encloses a water space. This space is called the mantle cavity, and it is a central feature of mollusk biology, containing the mollusk's gills, anus, osphradium, nephridiopores, and gonopores.
Siphon	The tube-like extension through which water flows in and out of the mantle cavity in bivalves and cephalopods, and in tunicates is called siphon.
Muscle contraction	A muscle contraction occurs when a muscle cell (called a muscle fiber) shortens. There are three general types: skeletal, heart, and smooth.
Nervous system	The nervous system of an animal coordinates the activity of the muscles, monitors the organs, constructs and processes input from the senses, and initiates actions.
Capillary	A capillary is the smallest of a body's blood vessels, measuring 5-10 micro meters. They connect arteries and veins, and most closely interact with tissues. Their walls are composed of a single layer of cells, the endothelium. This layer is so thin that molecules such as oxygen, water and lipids can pass through them by diffusion and enter the tissues.
Cytoplasm	Cytoplasm refers to everything inside a cell between the plasma membrane and the nucleus; consists of a semifluid medium and organelles.
Equilibrium potential	In a biological membrane, the reversal potential of a particular ion is the membrane voltage at which there is no net flow of ions from one side of the membrane to the other. For a single ion system ionly, the term reversal potential is synonymous with equilibrium potential.
Resting potential	The resting potential of a cell is the membrane potential that would be maintained if there were no action potentials, synaptic potentials, or other active changes in the membrane potential.
Sodium	Sodium is the chemical element in the periodic table that has the symbol Na (Natrium in Latin) and atomic number 11. Sodium is a soft, waxy, silvery reactive metal belonging to the alkali metals that is abundant in natural compounds (especially halite). It is highly reactive.
Synapse	A junction, or relay point, between two neurons, or between a neuron and an effector cell. Electrical and chemical signals are relayed from one cell to another at a synapse.
Postsynaptic cell	The cell whose membranes receive the neurotransmitter released at a synapse is a postsynaptic cell.
Neurotransmitter	A neurotransmitter is a chemical that is used to relay, amplify and modulate electrical signals between a neuron and another cell.
Synaptic cleft	A narrow gap separating the synaptic knob of a transmitting neuron from a receiving neuron or an effector cell is a synaptic cleft.
Synaptic vesicle	Small neurotransmitter-filled secretory vesicle formed at the axon terminals of nerve cells and whose contents are released into the synaptic cleft by exocytosis when an action potential reaches the axon terminal is called synaptic vesicle.
Fusion	Fusion refers to the combination of two atoms into a single atom as a result of a collision, usually accompanied by the release of energy.
Receptor	A receptor is a protein on the cell membrane or within the cytoplasm or cell nucleus that binds to a specific molecule (a ligand), such as a neurotransmitter, hormone, or other substance, and initiates the cellular response to the ligand. Receptor, in immunology, the region of an antibody which shows recognition of an antigen.
Nerve impulse	Action potential traveling along a neuron is a nerve impulse.

Go to **Cram101.com** for the Practice Tests for this Chapter.

Reuptake	Reuptake is the reabsorption of a neurotransmitter by the molecular transporter of a pre-synaptic neuron after it has performed its function of transmitting a neural impulse.
Postsynaptic membrane	The area of plasma membrane of a postsynaptic cell, either a muscle fiber or a neuron, that is within the synapse and has areas especially adapted for receiving neurotransmitters is a postsynaptic membrane.
Neuromuscular junction	A neuromuscular junction is the junction of the axon terminal of a motoneuron with the motor end plate, the highly-excitable region of muscle fiber plasma membrane responsible for initiation of action potentials across the muscle's surface.
Strychnine	Strychnine is a very toxic, colorless crystalline alkaloid used as a pesticide, particularly for killing small vertebrates such as rodents.
Paralysis	Paralysis is the complete loss of muscle function for one or more muscle groups. Paralysis may be localized, or generalized, or it may follow a certain pattern.
Curare	Curare is a drug that once entered into the bloodstream and reaches the muscles it blocks the receptors on the muscles, paralyzing the muscles.
Inhibitory neurotransmitter	Neurotransmitter that opens transmitter-gated Cl- or K+ channels in the postsynaptic membrane of a nerve or muscle cell and thus tends to inhibit the generation of an action potential is an inhibitory neurotransmitter.
Glutamate	Glutamate is one of the 20 standard amino acids used by all organisms in their proteins. It is critical for proper cell function, but it is not an essential nutrient in humans because it can be manufactured from other compounds.
Threshold potential	The threshold potential is the membrane potential to which a membrane must be depolarized to initiate an action potential.
Glycine	Glycine (Gly, G) is a nonpolar amino acid. It is the simplest of the 20 standard (proteinogenic) amino acids: its side chain is a hydrogen atom. Because there is a second hydrogen atom at the α carbon, glycine is not optically active.
Barbiturate	A Barbiturate is a drug that act as central nervous system (CNS) depressants, and by virtue of this they produce a wide spectrum of effects, from mild sedation to anesthesia. Some are also used as anticonvulsants.
Tranquilizer	A sedative, or tranquilizer, is a drug that depresses the central nervous system (CNS), which causes calmness, relaxation, reduction of anxiety, sleepiness, slowed breathing, slurred speech, staggering gait, poor judgment, and slow, uncertain reflexes.
Serotonin	Serotonin is a monoamine neurotransmitter synthesized in serotonergic neurons in the central nervous system and enterochromaffin cells in the gastrointestinal tract. It is believed to play an important part of the biochemistry of depression, migraine, bipolar disorder and anxiety.
Psychoactive drug	A psychoactive drug or psychotropic substance is a chemical that alters brain function, resulting in temporary changes in perception, mood, consciousness, or behavior. Such drugs are often used for recreational and spiritual purposes, as well as in medicine, especially for treating neurological and psychological illnesses.
Population	Group of organisms of the same species occupying a certain area and sharing a common gene pool is referred to as population.
Antibody	An antibody is a protein used by the immune system to identify and neutralize foreign objects like bacteria and viruses. Each antibody recognizes a specific antigen unique to its target.
Nonpolar molecule	A molecule whose electric charge is evenly balanced from one end of the molecule to the other is called nonpolar molecule.

Polar molecule	Molecule that displays an uneven distribution of electrons over its structure, for example, water is a polar molecule.
Metabolite	The term metabolite is usually restricted to small molecules. They are the intermediates and products of metabolism. A primary metabolite is directly involved in the normal growth, development, and reproduction. A secondary metabolite is not directly involved in those processes, but usually has important ecological function.
Vesicle	In cell biology, a vesicle is a relatively small and enclosed compartment, separated from the cytosol by at least one lipid bilayer.
Endosome	Membrane-bounded organelle in animal cells that carries materials newly ingested by endocytosis and passes many of them on to lysosomes for degradation is referred to as endosome.
Mutation	Mutation refers to a change in the nucleotide sequence of DNA; the ultimate source of genetic diversity.

Go to **Cram101.com** for the Practice Tests for this Chapter.

Molecule	A molecule is the smallest particle of a pure chemical substance that still retains its chemical composition and properties.
Sugar	A sugar is the simplest molecule that can be identified as a carbohydrate. These include monosaccharides and disaccharides, trisaccharides and the oligosaccharides. The term "glyco-" indicates the presence of a sugar in an otherwise non-carbohydrate substance.
Photosynthesis	Photosynthesis is a biochemical process in which plants, algae, and some bacteria harness the energy of light to produce food. Ultimately, nearly all living things depend on energy produced from photosynthesis for their nourishment, making it vital to life on Earth.
Starch	Biochemically, starch is a combination of two polymeric carbohydrates (polysaccharides) called amylose and amylopectin.
Bacteria	The domain that contains procaryotic cells with primarily diacyl glycerol diesters in their membranes and with bacterial rRNA. Bacteria also is a general term for organisms that are composed of procaryotic cells and are not multicellular.
Activation energy	The activation energy is the threshold energy, or the energy that must be overcome in order for a chemical reaction to occur. Activation energy may otherwise be denoted as the minimum energy necessary for a specific chemical reaction to occur.
Free energy	The term thermodynamic free energy denotes the total amount of energy in a physical system which can be converted to do work.
Oxidation	Oxidation refers to the loss of electrons from a substance involved in a redox reaction; always accompanies reduction.
Enzyme	An enzyme is a protein that catalyzes, or speeds up, a chemical reaction. They are essential to sustain life because most chemical reactions in biological cells would occur too slowly, or would lead to different products, without them.
Cell	The cell is the structural and functional unit of all living organisms, and is sometimes called the "building block of life."
Animal cell	An animal cell is a form of eukaryotic cell which make up many tissues in animals. The animal cell is distinct from other eukaryotes, most notably those of plants, as they lack cell walls and chloroplasts, and they have smaller vacuoles.
Polysaccharide	Polymer made from sugar monomers is a polysaccharide. They are relatively complex carbohydrates.
Protein	A protein is a complex, high-molecular-weight organic compound that consists of amino acids joined by peptide bonds. They are essential to the structure and function of all living cells and viruses. Many are enzymes or subunits of enzymes.
Lipid	Lipid is one class of aliphatic hydrocarbon-containing organic compounds essential for the structure and function of living cells. They are characterized by being water-insoluble but soluble in nonpolar organic solvents.
Macromolecule	A macromolecule is a molecule of high relative molecular mass, the structure of which essentially comprises the multiple repetition of units derived, actually or conceptually, from molecules of low relative molecular mass.
Digestion	Digestion refers to the mechanical and chemical breakdown of food into molecules small enough for the body to absorb; the second main stage of food processing, following ingestion.
Cytosol	The cytosol is the internal fluid of the cell, and a large part of cell metabolism occurs here. Proteins within the cytosol play an important role in signal transduction pathways, glycolysis; also, they act as intracellular receptors and form part of the ribosomes, enabling further protein synthesis

Go to **Cram101.com** for the Practice Tests for this Chapter.

Glycolysis	Glycolysis refers to the multistep chemical breakdown of a molecule of glucose into two molecules of pyruvic acid; the first stage of cellular respiration in all organisms; occurs in the cytoplasmic fluid.
Catabolism	Catabolism is the part of metabolism that partitions molecules into smaller units. It is made up of degradative chemical reactions in the living cell. Large polymeric molecules are processed into their constituent monomeric units.
Pyruvate	Pyruvate is the ionized form of pyruvic acid. It is an important chemical compound in biochemistry. It is the output of the breakdown of glucose known as glycolysis, and (in aerobic respiration) the main input for the citric acid cycle via acetyl-CoA.
Glucose	Glucose, a simple monosaccharide sugar, is one of the most important carbohydrates and is used as a source of energy in animals and plants. Glucose is one of the main products of photosynthesis and starts respiration.
Activated carrier	Activated carrier is a small diffusible molecule in cells that stores easily exchangeable energy in the form of one or more energy-rich covalent bonds. Examples are ATP and NADPH.
Mitochondria	Mitochondria are organelles found in most eukaryotic cells, including those of plants, animals, fungi, and protists. Mitochondria are sometimes described as "cellular power plants", because their primary function is to convert organic materials into energy in the form of ATP.
Fatty acid	A fatty acid is a carboxylic acid (or organic acid), often with a long aliphatic tail (long chains), either saturated or unsaturated.
Acetyl	The acetyl radical contains a methyl group single-bonded to a carbonyl. The carbon of the carbonyl has an lone electron available, with which it forms a chemical bond to the remainder of the molecule.
Coenzyme A	Small molecule used in the enzymatic transfer of acyl groups in the cell is coenzyme A.
Cellular metabolism	The sum of all chemical changes that take place in a cell through which energy and basic components are provided for essential processes, including the synthesis of new molecules and the breakdown and removal of others is called cellular metabolism.
Plasma membrane	Membrane surrounding the cytoplasm that consists of a phospholipid bilayer with embedded proteins is referred to as plasma membrane.
Mitochondrion	Mitochondrion refers to an organelle in eukaryotic cells where cellular respiration occurs. Enclosed by two concentric membranes, it is where most of the cell's ATP is made.
Organelle	In cell biology, an organelle is one of several structures with specialized functions, suspended in the cytoplasm of a eukaryotic cell.
Lysosome	Lysosome refers to a digestive organelle in eukaryotic cells; contains hydrolytic enzymes that digest the cell's food and wastes. They are found in both plant and animal cells, and are built in the Golgi apparatus.
Acid	An acid is a water-soluble, sour-tasting chemical compound that when dissolved in water, gives a solution with a pH of less than 7.
Oxidative phosphorylation	Oxidative phosphorylation is a biochemical process in cells. It is the final metabolic pathway of cellular respiration, after glycolysis and the citric acid cycle.
Chemical energy	Chemical energy refers to energy stored in the chemical bonds of molecules; a form of potential energy.
Lysis	Lysis refers to the death of a cell by bursting, often by viral or osmotic mechanisms that compromise the integrity of the cellular membrane.

Go to **Cram101.com** for the Practice Tests for this Chapter.

Microorganism	A microorganism is an organism that is so small that it is microscopic (invisible to the naked eye). They are often illustrated using single-celled, or unicellular organisms; however, some unicellular protists are visible to the naked eye, and some multicellular species are microscopic.
Anaerobic	An anaerobic organism is any organism that does not require oxygen for growth.
Oxygen	Oxygen is a chemical element in the periodic table. It has the symbol O and atomic number 8. Oxygen is the second most common element on Earth, composing around 46% of the mass of Earth's crust and 28% of the mass of Earth as a whole, and is the third most common element in the universe.
Atmosphere	Earth's atmosphere is a layer of gases surrounding the planet Earth and retained by the Earth's gravity. It contains roughly 78% nitrogen and 21% oxygen, with trace amounts of other gases.
Carbon	Carbon is a chemical element in the periodic table that has the symbol C and atomic number 6. An abundant nonmetallic, tetravalent element, carbon has several allotropic forms.
Atom	An atom is the smallest possible particle of a chemical element that retains its chemical properties.
Electron	The electron is a light fundamental subatomic particle that carries a negative electric charge. The electron is a spin-1/2 lepton, does not participate in strong interactions and has no substructure.
Electron carrier	Electron carrier refers to a molecule that conveys electrons within a cell; one of several membrane molecules that make up electron transport chains.
Hexokinase	A hexokinase is an enzyme that phosphorylates a six-carbon sugar, a hexose, to a hexose phosphate. In most tissues and organisms, glucose is the most important substrate of hexokinases, and glucose 6-phosphate the most important product.
Phosphate	A phosphate is a polyatomic ion or radical consisting of one phosphorus atom and four oxygen. In the ionic form, it carries a -3 formal charge, and is denoted PO_4^{3-}.
Rearrangement	A change in the usual order and arrangement of genetic material either within the chromosome complement or within a gene locus is rearrangement. Where the nature of the rearrangement has been determined, the type may be searched for directly under the following designations: reciprocal translocation, Robertsonian translocation, insertion, transposition, inversion, deletion, and duplication.
Carbonyl	A carbonyl group is a functional group composed of a carbon atom double-bonded to an oxygen atom. The term carbonyl can also refer to carbon monoxide as a ligand in an inorganic or organometallic complex.
Hydroxyl group	The term hydroxyl group is used to describe the functional group -OH when it is a substituent in an organic compound.
Fructose	Fructose is a simple sugar (monosaccharide) found in many foods and one of the three most important blood sugars along with glucose and galactose.
Phosphate group	The functional group $-OPO_3H_2$; the transfer of energy from one compound to another is often accomplished by the transfer of a phosphate group.
Ester linkage	Ester linkage refers to a condensation reaction in which the carboxyl group of a fatty acid reacts with the hydroxyl group of an alcohol. Lipids are formed in this way.
Hydrolysis	Hydrolysis is a chemical process in which a molecule is cleaved into two parts by the addition of a molecule of water.

Go to **Cram101.com** for the Practice Tests for this Chapter.

Linkage	Linkage refers to the patterns of assortment of genes that are located on the same chromosome. Important because if the genes are located relatively far apart, crossing over is more likely to occur between them than if they are close together.
Phosphoenolp-ruvate	Phosphoenolpyruvate is an important chemical compound in biochemistry. It has a high energy phosphate bond, and is involved in glycolysis and gluconeogenesis. In plants, it is also involved in the biosynthesis of various aromatic compounds, and in carbon fixation.
Skeletal muscle	Skeletal muscle is a type of striated muscle, attached to the skeleton. They are used to facilitate movement, by applying force to bones and joints; via contraction. They generally contract voluntarily (via nerve stimulation), although they can contract involuntarily.
Tissue	Group of similar cells which perform a common function is called tissue.
Ethanol	Ethanol is a flammable, colorless chemical compound, one of the alcohols that is most often found in alcoholic beverages. In common parlance, it is often referred to simply as alcohol. Its chemical formula is C_2H_5OH, also written as C_2H_6O.
Muscle	Muscle is a contractile form of tissue. It is one of the four major tissue types, the other three being epithelium, connective tissue and nervous tissue. Muscle contraction is used to move parts of the body, as well as to move substances within the body.
Yeast	Yeast refers to common term for several families of unicellular fungi. Includes species used for brewing beer and making bread, as well as pathogenic species.
Fermentation	Fermentation is the anaerobic metabolic breakdown of a nutrient molecule, such as glucose, without net oxidation. Fermentation does not release all the available energy in a molecule; it merely allows glycolysis to continue by replenishing reduced coenzymes.
Biochemistry	Biochemistry studies how complex chemical reactions give rise to life. It is a hybrid branch of chemistry which specialises in the chemical processes in living organisms.
Carbon dioxide	Carbon dioxide is an atmospheric gas comprized of one carbon and two oxygen atoms. A very widely known chemical compound, it is frequently called by its formula CO_2. In its solid state, it is commonly known as dry ice.
Chemical reaction	Chemical reaction refers to a process leading to chemical changes in matter; involves the making and/or breaking of chemical bonds.
Aldehyde	An aldehyde is either a functional group consisting of a terminal carbonyl group or a compound containing a terminal carbonyl group.
Substrate	A substrate is a molecule which is acted upon by an enzyme. Each enzyme recognizes only the specific substrate of the reaction it catalyzes. A surface in or on which an organism lives.
Ion	Ion refers to an atom or molecule that has gained or lost one or more electrons, thus acquiring an electrical charge.
Coupled reaction	Coupled reaction refers to a pair of reactions, one exergonic and one endergonic, that are linked together such that the energy produced by the exergonic reaction provides the energy needed to drive the endergonic reaction.
Aerobic metabolism	Aerobic metabolism is rather more efficient than anaerobic metabolism. They share the initial pathway of glycolysis but aerobic metabolism continues with the Krebs cycle and oxidative phosphorylation. The post glycolytic reactions take place in the mitochondria in eukaryotic cells, and at the cell membrane in prokaryotic cells.
Dehydrogenase	An enzyme that catalyzes a chemical reaction during which one or more hydrogen atoms are removed from a molecule is dehydrogenase.
Carboxylic acid	An organic compound containing a carboxyl group is a carboxylic acid.

Go to **Cram101.com** for the Practice Tests for this Chapter.

Thioester bond	Thioester bond refers to high-energy bond formed by a condensation reaction between an acid group and a thiol group; seen, for example, in acetyl coa and in many enzyme-substrate complexes.
Covalent bond	A covalent bond is an intramolecular form of chemical bonding characterized by the sharing of one or more pairs of electrons between two elements, producing a mutual attraction that holds the resultant molecule together.
Hydrogen	Hydrogen is a chemical element in the periodic table that has the symbol H and atomic number 1. At standard temperature and pressure it is a colorless, odorless, nonmetallic, univalent, tasteless, highly flammable diatomic gas.
Proton	Positive subatomic particle, located in the nucleus and having a weight of approximately one atomic mass unit is referred to as a proton.
High-energy molecule	A molecule whose hydrolysis under standard conditions makes available a large amount of free energy ; a high-energy molecule readily decomposes and transfers groups such as phosphate to acceptors.
Hydrogen atom	A hydrogen atom is an atom of the element hydrogen. It is composed of a single negatively-charged electron, attending a positively-charged proton which is the nucleus of the hydrogen atom. The electron is bound to the proton by the Coulomb force.
Standard free-energy change	Free-energy change of two reacting molecules at standard temperature and pressure when all components are present at a concentration of 1 mole per liter is called standard free-energy change.
Polypeptide	Polypeptide refers to polymer of many amino acids linked by peptide bonds.
Mitochondrial matrix	Mitochondrial matrix refers to the fluid contained within the inner membrane of a mitochondrion.
Glycerol	Glycerol is a three-carbon substance that forms the backbone of fatty acids in fats. When the body uses stored fat as a source of energy, glycerol and fatty acids are released into the bloodstream. The glycerol component can be converted to glucose by the liver and provides energy for cellular metabolism.
Adipocyte	A adipocyte is a cell present in adipose tissue, specialized in storing energy as fat. There are two types of adipose tissue (white fat and brown fat).
Carboxyl	A carboxyl is the univalent radical -COOH; present in and characteristic of organic acids.
Acyl	An acyl group obtained from a carboxylic acid by the removal of the carboxylic hydroxyl group. Acyl groups thus have the general formula -COR, with a double bond between the carbon and oxygen atoms (forming a carbonyl group) and a single bond between the carbon and R; R denotes the group that occurs in the original carboxylic acid RCOOH.
Lactic acid	Lactic acid accumulates in skeletal muscles during extensive anaerobic exercise, causing temporary muscle pain. Lactic acid is quickly removed from muscles when they resume aerobic metabolism.
Krebs cycle	The Krebs cycle is a series of chemical reactions of central importance in all living cells that utilize oxygen as part of cellular respiration. In these aerobic organisms, the Krebs cycle is a metabolic pathway that forms part of the break down of carbohydrates, fats and proteins into carbon dioxide and water in order to generate energy.
Electron acceptor	Atom or molecule that takes up electrons readily, thereby gaining an electron and becoming reduced is referred to as electron acceptor.
Skeleton	In biology, the skeleton or skeletal system is the biological system providing physical support in living organisms.

Go to **Cram101.com** for the Practice Tests for this Chapter.

Cell metabolism	Cell metabolism is the process (or really the sum of many ongoing individual processes) by which living cells process nutrient molecules and maintain a living state.
Guanine	Guanine is one of the five main nucleobases found in nucleic acids. Guanine is a purine derivative, and in Watson-Crick base pairing forms three hydrogen bonds with cytosine. Guanine "stacks" vertically with the other nucleobases via aromatic interactions.
Catalysis	Catalysis is the acceleration of the reaction rate of a chemical reaction by means of a substance, called a catalyst, that is itself not consumed by the overall reaction.
Kidney	The kidney is a bean-shaped excretory organ in vertebrates. Part of the urinary system, the kidneys filter wastes (especially urea) from the blood and excrete them, along with water, as urine.
Liver	The liver is an organ in vertebrates, including humans. It plays a major role in metabolism and has a number of functions in the body including drug detoxification, glycogen storage, and plasma protein synthesis. It also produces bile, which is important for digestion.
Cellular respiration	Cellular respiration is the process in which the chemical bonds of energy-rich molecules such as glucose are converted into energy usable for life processes.
Metabolism	Metabolism is the biochemical modification of chemical compounds in living organisms and cells. This includes the biosynthesis of complex organic molecules (anabolism) and their breakdown (catabolism).
Metabolite	The term metabolite is usually restricted to small molecules. They are the intermediates and products of metabolism. A primary metabolite is directly involved in the normal growth, development, and reproduction. A secondary metabolite is not directly involved in those processes, but usually has important ecological function.
Competitive inhibitor	A substance that reduces the activity of an enzyme by binding to the enzyme's active site in place of the substrate is referred to as a competitive inhibitor; It's structure mimics that of the enzyme's substrate.
Respiration	Respiration is the process by which an organism obtains energy by reacting oxygen with glucose to give water, carbon dioxide and ATP (energy). Respiration takes place on a cellular level in the mitochondria of the cells and provide the cells with energy.
Glycogen	Glycogen refers to a complex, extensively branched polysaccharide of many glucose monomers; serves as an energy-storage molecule in liver and muscle cells.
Metabolic processes	The total of all chemical reactions within an organism are the metabolic processes.
Metabolic pathway	A metabolic pathway is a series of chemical reactions occurring within a cell, catalyzed by enzymes, to achieve in either the formation of a metabolic product to be used or stored by the cell, or the initiation of another metabolic pathway.
Mass spectrometry	Mass spectrometry is an analytical technique used to measure the mass-to-charge ratio (m/q) of ions. It is most generally used to find the composition of a physical sample by generating a mass spectrum representing the masses of sample components.
Radioactive	A term used to describe the property of releasing energy or particles from an unstable atom is called radioactive.
Reagent	When purchasing or preparing chemicals, reagent describes chemical substances of sufficient purity for use in chemical analysis, chemical reactions or physical testing.
Inner membrane	The inner membrane is a membrane (phospholipid bilayer) of an organelle that is within the outer membrane. The inner membrane is present within the mitochondria and the chloroplast of cells.

Go to **Cram101.com** for the Practice Tests for this Chapter.

Evolution	In biology, evolution is the process by which novel traits arise in populations and are passed on from generation to generation. Its action over large stretches of time explains the origin of new species and ultimately the vast diversity of the biological world.
Triacylglycerol	Triacylglycerol refers to molecule composed of three fatty acids esterified to glycerol. The main constituent of fat droplets in animal tissues and of vegetable oils.
Cytoplasm	Cytoplasm refers to everything inside a cell between the plasma membrane and the nucleus; consists of a semifluid medium and organelles.
Granule	A granule is a small grain. In describing cells, a granule may be any structure barely visible by light microscopy, but most often a secretory vesicle.
Adipose tissue	Adipose tissue is an anatomical term for loose connective tissue composed of adipocytes. Its main role is to store energy in the form of fat, although it also cushions and insulates the body. It has an important endocrine function in producing recently-discovered hormones such as leptin, resistin and TNFalpha.
Polymer	Polymer is a generic term used to describe a very long molecule consisting of structural units and repeating units connected by covalent chemical bonds.
Micrograph	A micrograph is a photograph or similar image taken through a microscope or similar device to show a magnified image of an item.
Chloroplast	A chloroplast is an organelle found in plant cells and eukaryotic algae which conduct photosynthesis. They are similar to mitochondria but are found only in plants. They are surrounded by a double membrane with an intermembrane space; they have their own DNA and are involved in energy metabolism;
Plant cell	A cell that is a structural and functional unit of a plant is a plant cell.
Thylakoid	Flattened sac within a granum whose membrane contains chlorophyll and where the light-dependent reactions of photosynthesis occur is referred to as a thylakoid.
Sunlight	Sunlight in the broad sense is the total spectrum of electromagnetic radiation given off by the Sun.
Embryo	Embryo refers to a developing stage of a multicellular organism. In humans, the stage in the development of offspring from the first division of the zygote until body structures begin to appear, about the ninth week of gestation.
Biosynthesis	Biosynthesis is a phenomenon where chemical compounds are produced from simpler reagents. Biosynthesis, unlike chemical synthesis, takes place within living organisms and is generally catalysed by enzymes. The process is vital part of metabolism.
Nut	A nut in botany is a simple dry fruit with one seed (rarely two) in which the ovary wall becomes very hard (stony or woody) at maturity, and where the seed remains unattached or unfused with the ovary wall.
Glycoprotein	A macromolecule consisting of one or more polypeptides linked to short chains of sugars is called glycoprotein.
Nucleotide	A nucleotide is a chemical compound that consists of a heterocyclic base, a sugar, and one or more phosphate groups. In the most common nucleotides the base is a derivative of purine or pyrimidine, and the sugar is pentose - deoxyribose or ribose. They are the structural units of RNA and DNA.
Amino acid	An amino acid is any molecule that contains both amino and carboxylic acid functional groups. They are the basic structural building units of proteins. They form short polymer chains called peptides or polypeptides which in turn form structures called proteins.

Go to **Cram101.com** for the Practice Tests for this Chapter.

Alanine	Alanine (Ala) also 2-aminopropanoic acid is a non-essential α-amino acid. It exists as two distinct enantiomers - L-alanine and D-alanine. L-alanine is one of the 20 amino acids most widely used in protein synthesis, second to leucine.
Serine	Serine, organic compound, one of the 20 amino acids commonly found in animal proteins. Only the L-stereoisomer appears in mammalian protein. It is not essential to the human diet, since it can be synthesized in the body from other metabolites, including glycine.
Matrix	In biology, matrix (plural: matrices) is the material between animal or plant cells, the material (or tissue) in which more specialized structures are embedded, and a specific part of the mitochondrion that is the site of oxidation of organic molecules.
Phosphorylation	Phosphorylation refers to reaction in which a phosphate group becomes covalently coupled to another molecule.
Carbonyl group	In an organic molecule, a functional group consisting of a carbon atom linked by a double bond to an oxygen atom is the carbonyl group.
Mole	The atomic weight of a substance, expressed in grams. One mole is defined as the mass of 6.0222 3 1023 atoms.
Isotope	An isotope is a form of an element whose nuclei have the same atomic number - the number of protons in the nucleus - but different mass numbers because they contain different numbers of neutrons.
Carboxyl group	In an organic molecule, a functional group consisting of an oxygen atom doublebonded to a carbon atom that is also bonded to a hydroxyl group is referred to as a carboxyl group.

Go to **Cram101.com** for the Practice Tests for this Chapter.

Chloroplast	A chloroplast is an organelle found in plant cells and eukaryotic algae which conduct photosynthesis. They are similar to mitochondria but are found only in plants. They are surrounded by a double membrane with an intermembrane space; they have their own DNA and are involved in energy metabolism;
Evolution	In biology, evolution is the process by which novel traits arise in populations and are passed on from generation to generation. Its action over large stretches of time explains the origin of new species and ultimately the vast diversity of the biological world.
Cell	The cell is the structural and functional unit of all living organisms, and is sometimes called the "building block of life."
Fermentation	Fermentation is the anaerobic metabolic breakdown of a nutrient molecule, such as glucose, without net oxidation. Fermentation does not release all the available energy in a molecule; it merely allows glycolysis to continue by replenishing reduced coenzymes.
Molecule	A molecule is the smallest particle of a pure chemical substance that still retains its chemical composition and properties.
Chemical energy	Chemical energy refers to energy stored in the chemical bonds of molecules; a form of potential energy.
Oxidation	Oxidation refers to the loss of electrons from a substance involved in a redox reaction; always accompanies reduction.
Cytosol	The cytosol is the internal fluid of the cell, and a large part of cell metabolism occurs here. Proteins within the cytosol play an important role in signal transduction pathways, glycolysis; also, they act as intracellular receptors and form part of the ribosomes, enabling further protein synthesis
Mitochondria	Mitochondria are organelles found in most eukaryotic cells, including those of plants, animals, fungi, and protists. Mitochondria are sometimes described as "cellular power plants", because their primary function is to convert organic materials into energy in the form of ATP.
Cell biology	The biological discipline involving the study of cells and their functions is called cell biology. This includes their physiological properties such as their structure and the organelles they contain, their environment and interactions, their life cycle, division and function (physiology) and eventual death.
Protein	A protein is a complex, high-molecular-weight organic compound that consists of amino acids joined by peptide bonds. They are essential to the structure and function of all living cells and viruses. Many are enzymes or subunits of enzymes.
Chemiosmotic hypothesis	Chemiosmotic hypothesis refers to the hypothesis that a proton gradient and an electrochemical gradient are generated by electron transport and then used to drive ATP synthesis by oxidative phosphorylation.
Chemiosmotic coupling	Mechanism in which a gradient of hydrogen ions across a membrane is used to drive an energy-requiring process, such as ATP production or the rotation of bacterial flagella is referred to as chemiosmotic coupling.
Proton gradient	The proton gradient can be used as an intermediate energy storage for heat production and flagellar rotation. Additionally, it is an interconvertible form of energy in active transport, electron potential generation, NADPH synthesis, and ATP synthesis/hydrolysis.
ATP synthase	Enzyme complex in the inner membrane of a mitochondrion and the thylakoid membrane of a chloroplast that catalyzes the formation of ATP from ADP and inorganic phosphate during oxidative phosphorylation and photosynthesis, respectively is referred to as ATP synthase.

Go to **Cram101.com** for the Practice Tests for this Chapter.

Phosphate	A phosphate is a polyatomic ion or radical consisting of one phosphorus atom and four oxygen. In the ionic form, it carries a -3 formal charge, and is denoted $PO_4{}^{3-}$.
Electron	The electron is a light fundamental subatomic particle that carries a negative electric charge. The electron is a spin-1/2 lepton, does not participate in strong interactions and has no substructure.
Linkage	Linkage refers to the patterns of assortment of genes that are located on the same chromosome. Important because if the genes are located relatively far apart, crossing over is more likely to occur between them than if they are close together.
Proton	Positive subatomic particle, located in the nucleus and having a weight of approximately one atomic mass unit is referred to as a proton.
Enzyme	An enzyme is a protein that catalyzes, or speeds up, a chemical reaction. They are essential to sustain life because most chemical reactions in biological cells would occur too slowly, or would lead to different products, without them.
Bacteria	The domain that contains procaryotic cells with primarily diacyl glycerol diesters in their membranes and with bacterial rRNA. Bacteria also is a general term for organisms that are composed of procaryotic cells and are not multicellular.
Chemiosmosis	Chemiosmosis refers to the production of ATP using the energy of hydrogen-ion gradients across membranes to phosphorylate ADP; powers most ATP synthesis in cells.
Sunlight	Sunlight in the broad sense is the total spectrum of electromagnetic radiation given off by the Sun.
Versatile	The anther can be attached to the filament in two ways, versatile is when it is attached at its center to the filament; pollen is then released through pores (poricidal dehiscence).
Gradient	Gradient refers to a difference in concentration, pressure, or electrical charge between two regions.
Oxidative phosphorylation	Oxidative phosphorylation is a biochemical process in cells. It is the final metabolic pathway of cellular respiration, after glycolysis and the citric acid cycle.
Microorganism	A microorganism is an organism that is so small that it is microscopic (invisible to the naked eye). They are often illustrated using single-celled, or unicellular organisms; however, some unicellular protists are visible to the naked eye, and some multicellular species are microscopic.
Organelle	In cell biology, an organelle is one of several structures with specialized functions, suspended in the cytoplasm of a eukaryotic cell.
Free energy	The term thermodynamic free energy denotes the total amount of energy in a physical system which can be converted to do work.
Glycolysis	Glycolysis refers to the multistep chemical breakdown of a molecule of glucose into two molecules of pyruvic acid; the first stage of cellular respiration in all organisms; occurs in the cytoplasmic fluid.
Pyruvate	Pyruvate is the ionized form of pyruvic acid. It is an important chemical compound in biochemistry. It is the output of the breakdown of glucose known as glycolysis, and (in aerobic respiration) the main input for the citric acid cycle via acetyl-CoA.
Glucose	Glucose, a simple monosaccharide sugar, is one of the most important carbohydrates and is used as a source of energy in animals and plants. Glucose is one of the main products of photosynthesis and starts respiration.
Metabolism	Metabolism is the biochemical modification of chemical compounds in living organisms and

	cells. This includes the biosynthesis of complex organic molecules (anabolism) and their breakdown (catabolism).
Sugar	A sugar is the simplest molecule that can be identified as a carbohydrate. These include monosaccharides and disaccharides, trisaccharides and the oligosaccharides. The term "glyco-" indicates the presence of a sugar in an otherwise non-carbohydrate substance.
Outer membrane	The outer membrane refers to the outside membrane of an organelle which surrounds the rest of the organelle components. Both the chloroplast and the mitochondria have an outer membrane.
Inner membrane	The inner membrane is a membrane (phospholipid bilayer) of an organelle that is within the outer membrane. The inner membrane is present within the mitochondria and the chloroplast of cells.
Mitochondrion	Mitochondrion refers to an organelle in eukaryotic cells where cellular respiration occurs. Enclosed by two concentric membranes, it is where most of the cell's ATP is made.
Flagellum	A flagellum is a whip-like organelle that many unicellular organisms, and some multicellular ones, use to move about.
Muscle	Muscle is a contractile form of tissue. It is one of the four major tissue types, the other three being epithelium, connective tissue and nervous tissue. Muscle contraction is used to move parts of the body, as well as to move substances within the body.
Sperm	Sperm refers to the male sex cell with three distinct parts at maturity: head, middle piece, and tail.
Cardiac muscle	Cardiac muscle is a type of striated muscle found within the heart. Its function is to "pump" blood through the circulatory system. Unlike skeletal muscle, which contracts in response to nerve stimulation, and like smooth muscle, cardiac muscle is myogenic, meaning that it stimulates its own contraction without a requisite electrical impulse.
Hydrolysis	Hydrolysis is a chemical process in which a molecule is cleaved into two parts by the addition of a molecule of water.
Myofibril	Myofibril is a cylindrical organelle, found within muscle cells. They are bundles of filaments that run from one end of the cell to the other and are attached to the cell surface membrane at each end.
Skeletal muscle	Skeletal muscle is a type of striated muscle, attached to the skeleton. They are used to facilitate movement, by applying force to bones and joints; via contraction. They generally contract voluntarily (via nerve stimulation), although they can contract involuntarily.
Membrane transport protein	Membrane transport protein refers to membrane protein that mediates the passage of ions or molecules across a membrane. Examples are ion channels and carrier proteins.
Ion	Ion refers to an atom or molecule that has gained or lost one or more electrons, thus acquiring an electrical charge.
Mitochondrial matrix	Mitochondrial matrix refers to the fluid contained within the inner membrane of a mitochondrion.
Matrix	In biology, matrix (plural: matrices) is the material between animal or plant cells, the material (or tissue) in which more specialized structures are embedded, and a specific part of the mitochondrion that is the site of oxidation of organic molecules.
Transport protein	A transport protein is a protein involved in facilitated diffusion. Changes in the conformation move the binding site to the opposite side of the protein.
Fatty acid	A fatty acid is a carboxylic acid (or organic acid), often with a long aliphatic tail (long

Go to **Cram101.com** for the Practice Tests for this Chapter.

chains), either saturated or unsaturated.

Lipid	Lipid is one class of aliphatic hydrocarbon-containing organic compounds essential for the structure and function of living cells. They are characterized by being water-insoluble but soluble in nonpolar organic solvents.
Liver	The liver is an organ in vertebrates, including humans. It plays a major role in metabolism and has a number of functions in the body including drug detoxification, glycogen storage, and plasma protein synthesis. It also produces bile, which is important for digestion.
Intermembrane space	The intermembrane space is the region between the inner membrane and the outer membrane of a mitochondrion or a chloroplast. The main function of the intermembrane space is nucleotide phosphorylation.
Mitochondrial DNA	Mitochondrial DNA is DNA not located in the nucleus of the cell but in the mitochondria, parts of the cell that generate fuel in the form of adenosine triphosphate, which drives the varied machinery of the cell. Unlike most of the cell, the function of which is defined by the nuclear DNA, the mitochondria have their own DNA and are assumed to have evolved separately.
Ribosome	A ribosome is an organelle composed of rRNA and ribosomal proteins. It translates mRNA into a polypeptide chain (e.g., a protein). It can be thought of as a factory that builds a protein from a set of genetic instructions.
Genome	The genome of an organism is the whole hereditary information of an organism that is encoded in the DNA (or, for some viruses, RNA). This includes both the genes and the non-coding sequences. The genome of an organism is a complete DNA sequence of one set of chromosomes.
Gene	Gene refers to a discrete unit of hereditary information consisting of a specific nucleotide sequence in DNA . Most of the genes of a eukaryote are located in its chromosomal DNA; a few are carried by the DNA of mitochondria and chloroplasts.
Metabolite	The term metabolite is usually restricted to small molecules. They are the intermediates and products of metabolism. A primary metabolite is directly involved in the normal growth, development, and reproduction. A secondary metabolite is not directly involved in those processes, but usually has important ecological function.
Dalton	A measure of mass for atoms and subatomic particles is a dalton.
Porin	A porin is a transmembrane protein that is large enough to facilitate passive diffusion. They are prevalent in the outer membrane of the mitochondria and Gram-negative bacteria.
Acid	An acid is a water-soluble, sour-tasting chemical compound that when dissolved in water, gives a solution with a pH of less than 7.
Hydrogen atom	A hydrogen atom is an atom of the element hydrogen. It is composed of a single negatively-charged electron, attending a positively-charged proton which is the nucleus of the hydrogen atom. The electron is bound to the proton by the Coulomb force.
Oxygen	Oxygen is a chemical element in the periodic table. It has the symbol O and atomic number 8. Oxygen is the second most common element on Earth, composing around 46% of the mass of Earth's crust and 28% of the mass of Earth as a whole, and is the third most common element in the universe.
Acetyl	The acetyl radical contains a methyl group single-bonded to a carbonyl. The carbon of the carbonyl has an lone electron available, with which it forms a chemical bond to the remainder of the molecule.
Oxidative metabolism	A collective term for metabolic reactions requiring oxygen is referred to as oxidative metabolism.

Go to **Cram101.com** for the Practice Tests for this Chapter.

Activated carrier	Activated carrier is a small diffusible molecule in cells that stores easily exchangeable energy in the form of one or more energy-rich covalent bonds. Examples are ATP and NADPH.
Aerobic metabolism	Aerobic metabolism is rather more efficient than anaerobic metabolism. They share the initial pathway of glycolysis but aerobic metabolism continues with the Krebs cycle and oxidative phosphorylation. The post glycolytic reactions take place in the mitochondria in eukaryotic cells, and at the cell membrane in prokaryotic cells.
Phosphate group	The functional group -OPO_3H_2; the transfer of energy from one compound to another is often accomplished by the transfer of a phosphate group.
Respiratory chain	Electron-transport chain in the inner mitochondrial membrane that receives high-energy electrons derived from the citric acid cycle and generates the proton gradient across the membrane that is used to power ATP synthesis is a respiratory chain.
Phosphorylation	Phosphorylation refers to reaction in which a phosphate group becomes covalently coupled to another molecule.
Lipid bilayer	A lipid bilayer is a membrane or zone of a membrane composed of lipid molecules (usually phospholipids). The lipid bilayer is a critical component of all biological membranes, including cell membranes, and is a prerequisite for cell-based organisms.
Vesicle	In cell biology, a vesicle is a relatively small and enclosed compartment, separated from the cytosol by at least one lipid bilayer.
Bioenergetics	The study of how organisms manage their energy resources is called bioenergetics.
Proton-motive force	Driving force that moves protons across a membrane as a result of an electrochemical proton gradient is the proton-motive force.
Brown fat	Brown fat refers to fat tissue in mammals that is specialized to produce heat. It has many mitochondria and capillaries, and a protein that uncouples oxidative phosphorylation.
Bacteriorhod-psin	Bacteriorhodopsin is the photosynthetic pigment used by archaea, most notably halobacteria. It acts as a proton pump, i.e. it captures light energy and uses it to move protons across the membrane out of the cell.
Substrate	A substrate is a molecule which is acted upon by an enzyme. Each enzyme recognizes only the specific substrate of the reaction it catalyzes. A surface in or on which an organism lives.
Purple membrane	Purple membrane refers to an area of the plasma membrane of Halobacterium that contains bacteriorhodopsin and is active in photosynthetic light energy trapping.
ATPase	ATPase is a class of enzymes that catalyze the decomposition of adenosine triphosphate into adenosine diphosphate and a free phosphate ion. This dephosphorylation reaction releases energy, which the enzyme harnesses to drive other chemical reactions that would not otherwise occur. This process is widely used in all known forms of life.
Cytochrome c	Cytochrome c is a small heme protein found loosely associated with the inner membrane of the mitochondrion. It is a soluble protein, unlike other cytochromes, and is an essential component of the electron transfer chain.
Transmembrane protein	Membrane protein that extends through the lipid bilayer, with part of its mass on either side of the membrane is referred to as a transmembrane protein.
Cytochrome oxidase complex	Cytochrome oxidase complex refers to third of the three electron-driven proton pumps in the respiratory chain. It accepts electrons from cytochrome c and generates water using molecular oxygen as an electron acceptor.
Cytochrome b-cl complex	Cytochrome b-cl complex refers to second of the three electron-driven proton pumps in the respiratory chain. It accepts electrons from ubiquinone.

Dehydrogenase	An enzyme that catalyzes a chemical reaction during which one or more hydrogen atoms are removed from a molecule is dehydrogenase.
Chemical group	A set of covalently linked atoms, such as a hydroxyl group or an amino group, the chemical behavior of which is well characterized is referred to as a chemical group.
Cytochrome	Cytochrome refers to colored, heme-containing protein that transfers electrons during cellular respiration and photosynthesis.
Chemical reaction	Chemical reaction refers to a process leading to chemical changes in matter; involves the making and/or breaking of chemical bonds.
Potential energy	Stored energy as a result of location or spatial arrangement is referred to as potential energy.
Electrolyte	An electrolyte is a substance that dissociates into free ions when dissolved (or molten), to produce an electrically conductive medium. Because they generally consist of ions in solution, they are also known as ionic solutions.
Electrode	An electrode is a conductor used to make contact with a nonmetallic part of a circuit (e.g. a semiconductor, an electrolyte or a vacuum).
Manganese	Manganese is a chemical element in the periodic table that has the symbol Mn and atomic number 25.
Carbon	Carbon is a chemical element in the periodic table that has the symbol C and atomic number 6. An abundant nonmetallic, tetravalent element, carbon has several allotropic forms.
Zinc	Zinc is a chemical element in the periodic table that has the symbol Zn and atomic number 30.
Atom	An atom is the smallest possible particle of a chemical element that retains its chemical properties.
Plasma	In physics and chemistry, a plasma is an ionized gas, and is usually considered to be a distinct phase of matter. "Ionized" in this case means that at least one electron has been dissociated from a significant fraction of the molecules.
Algae	The algae consist of several different groups of living organisms that capture light energy through photosynthesis, converting inorganic substances into simple sugars with the captured energy.
Micrograph	A micrograph is a photograph or similar image taken through a microscope or similar device to show a magnified image of an item.
Plant cell	A cell that is a structural and functional unit of a plant is a plant cell.
Stalk	The stalk is the longish piece that supports the seed-carrying parts of a plant, or, more simply, the stem. A leaf's petiole; the slender stem that supports the blade of a leaf and attaches it to a larger stem of the plant.
Chemical bond	Chemical bond refers to an attraction between two atoms resulting from a sharing of outer-shell electrons or the presence of opposite charges on the atoms. The bonded atoms gain complete outer electron shells.
Conformation	The three-dimensional shape of a molecule is its conformation. The conformation is particularly important in proteins.
X-ray crystallography	Technique for determining the three-dimensional arrangement of atoms in a molecule based on the diffraction pattern of X-rays passing through a crystal of the molecule is x-ray crystallography.
Coupled	Membrane transport process in which the transfer of one molecule depends on the simultaneous

transport	or sequential transfer of a second molecule is called coupled transport.
Carrier protein	Protein molecule that combines with a substance and transports it through the plasma membrane is called a carrier protein.
Nucleotide	A nucleotide is a chemical compound that consists of a heterocyclic base, a sugar, and one or more phosphate groups. In the most common nucleotides the base is a derivative of purine or pyrimidine, and the sugar is pentose - deoxyribose or ribose. They are the structural units of RNA and DNA.
Co-transport	Membrane transport process in which the transfer of one molecule depends on the simultaneous or sequential transfer of a second molecule is called co-transport.
Voltage	A measure of the electrical difference that exists between two different points or objects is called voltage.
Protein synthesis	The process whereby the tRNA utilizes the mRNA as a guide to arrange the amino acids in their proper sequence according to the genetic information in the chemical code of DNA is referred to as protein synthesis.
Electron carrier	Electron carrier refers to a molecule that conveys electrons within a cell; one of several membrane molecules that make up electron transport chains.
Redox potential	Redox potential is the tendency of a chemical species to acquire electrons and thereby be reduced. Each species has its own intrinsic reduction potential; the more positive the potential, the greater the species' affinity for electrons and tendency to be reduced.
Oxidation-reduction reactions	Electron-transport reactions in which the molecules losing electrons become oxidized and those gaining electrons become reduced are called oxidation-reduction reactions.
Redox reaction	Redox reaction refers to a chemical reaction in which electrons are lost from one substance and added to another. Oxidation and reduction always occur together.
Hydrogen	Hydrogen is a chemical element in the periodic table that has the symbol H and atomic number 1. At standard temperature and pressure it is a colorless, odorless, nonmetallic, univalent, tasteless, highly flammable diatomic gas.
Standard free-energy change	Free-energy change of two reacting molecules at standard temperature and pressure when all components are present at a concentration of 1 mole per liter is called standard free-energy change.
Reactant	A reactant is any substance initially present in a chemical reaction. These reactants react with each other to form the products of a chemical reaction. In a chemical equation, the reactants are the elements or compounds on the left hand side of the reaction equation.
Hydrophobic	Hydrophobic refers to being electrically neutral and nonpolar, and thus prefering other neutral and nonpolar solvents or molecular environments. Hydrophobic is often used interchangeably with "oily" or "lipophilic."
Quinone	Small, lipid soluble, mobile electron carrier molecule found in the respiratory and photosynthetic electron-transport chains is referred to as a quinone.
Iron	Iron is essential to all organisms, except for a few bacteria. It is mostly stably incorporated in the inside of metalloproteins, because in exposed or in free form it causes production of free radicals that are generally toxic to cells.
Sulfur	Sulfur is the chemical element in the periodic table that has the symbol S and atomic number 16. It is an abundant, tasteless, odorless, multivalent non-metal. Sulfur, in its native form, is a yellow crystaline solid. In nature, it can be found as the pure element or as sulfide and sulfate minerals.

Go to **Cram101.com** for the Practice Tests for this Chapter.

Flavin	Flavin is a tricyclic heteronuclear organic ring whose biochemical source is the vitamin riboflavin.
Heme	A or heme is a metal-containing cofactor that consists of an iron atom contained in the center of a large heterocyclic organic ring called a porphyrin. Although porphyrins do not necessarily contain iron, a substantial fraction of porphyrin-containing metalloproteins do in fact have heme as their prosthetic subunit. It is made a matter of common knowledge, because of its vitality as a part of hemoglobin, vital in the human body's red blood cells.
Active site	The active site of an enzyme is the binding site where catalysis occurs. The structure and chemical properties of the active site allow the recognition and binding of the substrate.
Side chain	In organic chemistry and biochemistry a side chain is a part of a molecule attached to a core structure. Often the side chain can vary for a given core. In biochemistry the peptide or protein side chains are the variable parts of amino acids extending from the peptide backbone.
Hemoglobin	Hemoglobin is the iron-containing oxygen-transport metalloprotein in the red cells of the blood in mammals and other animals. Hemoglobin transports oxygen from the lungs to the rest of the body, such as to the muscles, where it releases the oxygen load.
Diffraction	Diffraction is the bending and spreading of waves when they meet an obstruction. It can occur with any type of wave, including sound waves, water waves, and electromagnetic waves such as light and radio waves.
Cytoplasm	Cytoplasm refers to everything inside a cell between the plasma membrane and the nucleus; consists of a semifluid medium and organelles.
Copper	Copper is a chemical element in the periodic table that has the symbol Cu (L.: Cuprum) and atomic number 29. It is a ductile metal with excellent electrical conductivity, and finds extensive use as a building material, as an electrical conductor, and as a component of various alloys.
Electron acceptor	Atom or molecule that takes up electrons readily, thereby gaining an electron and becoming reduced is referred to as electron acceptor.
Protein subunit	A protein subunit is a single protein molecule that assembles (or "coassembles") with other protein molecules to form a multimeric or oligomeric protein. Many naturally-occurring proteins and enzymes are multimeric.
Mammal	Homeothermic vertebrate characterized especially by the presence of hair and mammary glands is a mammal.
Monomer	In chemistry, a monomer is a small molecule that may become chemically bonded to other monomers to form a polymer.
Dimer	A dimer refers to a molecule composed of two similar subunits or monomers linked together. It is a special case of a polymer.
Exit site	The location on a ribosome to which an empty tRNA moves from the P site before it finally leaves the ribosome during protein synthesis is referred to as the exit site.
Carbohydrate	Carbohydrate is a chemical compound that contains oxygen, hydrogen, and carbon atoms. They consist of monosaccharide sugars of varying chain lengths and that have the general chemical formula $C_n(H_2O)_n$ or are derivatives of such.
Respiration	Respiration is the process by which an organism obtains energy by reacting oxygen with glucose to give water, carbon dioxide and ATP (energy). Respiration takes place on a cellular level in the mitochondria of the cells and provide the cells with energy.
Bond energy	Strength of the chemical linkage between two atoms, measured by the energy in kilocalories or

Go to **Cram101.com** for the Practice Tests for this Chapter.

	kilojoules needed to break it is called bond energy.
Coupled reaction	Coupled reaction refers to a pair of reactions, one cxergonic and one endergonic, that are linked together such that the energy produced by the exergonic reaction provides the energy needed to drive the endergonic reaction.
Proton pump	An active transport mechanism in cell membranes that consumes ATP to force hydrogen ions out of a cell and, in the process, generates a membrane potential is referred to as proton pump.
Organic compound	An organic compound is any member of a large class of chemical compounds whose molecules contain carbon, with the exception of carbides, carbonates, carbon oxides and gases containing carbon.
Photosynthesis	Photosynthesis is a biochemical process in which plants, algae, and some bacteria harness the energy of light to produce food. Ultimately, nearly all living things depend on energy produced from photosynthesis for their nourishment, making it vital to life on Earth.
Carbon dioxide	Carbon dioxide is an atmospheric gas comprized of one carbon and two oxygen atoms. A very widely known chemical compound, it is frequently called by its formula CO_2. In its solid state, it is commonly known as dry ice.
Cyanobacteria	Cyanobacteria are a phylum of bacteria that obtain their energy through photosynthesis. They are often referred to as blue-green algae, even though it is now known that they are not directly related to any of the other algal groups, which are all eukaryotes.
Atmosphere	Earth's atmosphere is a layer of gases surrounding the planet Earth and retained by the Earth's gravity. It contains roughly 78% nitrogen and 21% oxygen, with trace amounts of other gases.
Animal cell	An animal cell is a form of eukaryotic cell which make up many tissues in animals. The animal cell is distinct from other eukaryotes, most notably those of plants, as they lack cell walls and chloroplasts, and they have smaller vacuoles.
Lagoon	A lagoon is a body of comparatively shallow salt water separated from the deeper sea by a shallow or exposed sandbank, coral reef, or similar feature. Thus, the enclosed body of water behind a barrier reef or barrier islands or enclosed by an atoll reef is called a lagoon.
Fossil	A preserved remnant or impression of an organism that lived in the past is referred to as fossil.
Cell wall	Cell wall refers to a protective layer external to the plasma membrane in plant cells, bacteria, fungi, and some protists; protects the cell and helps maintain its shape.
Nucleus	In cell biology, the nucleus is found in all eukaryotic cells that contains most of the cell's genetic material. The nucleus has two primary functions: to control chemical reactions within the cytoplasm and to store information needed for cellular division.
Vacuole	A vacuole is a large membrane-bound compartment within some eukaryotic cells where they serve a variety of different functions: capturing food materials or unwanted structural debris surrounding the cell, sequestering materials that might be toxic to the cell, maintaining fluid balance (called turgor) within the cell.
Leaf	In botany, a leaf is an above-ground plant organ specialized for photosynthesis. For this purpose, a leaf is typically flat (laminar) and thin, to expose the chloroplast containing cells (chlorenchyma tissue) to light over a broad area, and to allow light to penetrate fully into the tissues.
Granule	A granule is a small grain. In describing cells, a granule may be any structure barely visible by light microscopy, but most often a secretory vesicle.
Stroma	A thick fluid enclosed by the inner membrane of a chloroplast. Sugars are made in the stroma

	by the enzymes of the Calvin cycle. Also refers to the connective supportive framework of a biological cell, tissue, or organ.
Starch	Biochemically, starch is a combination of two polymeric carbohydrates (polysaccharides) called amylose and amylopectin.
Thylakoid	Flattened sac within a granum whose membrane contains chlorophyll and where the light-dependent reactions of photosynthesis occur is referred to as a thylakoid.
Grana	Areas of the chloroplast membrane where chlorophyll molecules are concentrated are grana. They are stacks of thylakoids found in the discoid chloroplasts of land plants and some green algae.
Bacterium	Most bacterium are microscopic and unicellular, with a relatively simple cell structure lacking a cell nucleus, and organelles such as mitochondria and chloroplasts. They are the most abundant of all organisms. They are ubiquitous in soil, water, and as symbionts of other organisms.
Photosynthetic electron-transfer	Light-driven reactions in photosynthesis in which electrons move along the electron-transport chain in the thylakoid membrane, generating ATP and NADPH is referred to as photosynthetic electron-transfer.
Light reactions	The first of two stages in photosynthesis, the steps in which solar energy is absorbed and converted to chemical energy in the form of ATP and NADPH. The light reactions power the sugar-producing Calvin cycle but produce no sugar themselves.
Chlorophyll	Chlorophyll is a green photosynthetic pigment found in plants, algae, and cyanobacteria. In plant photosynthesis incoming light is absorbed by chlorophyll and other accessory pigments in the antenna complexes of photosystem I and photosystem II.
Epidermis	Epidermis is the outermost layer of the skin. It forms the waterproof, protective wrap over the body's surface and is made up of stratified squamous epithelium with an underlying basement membrane. It contains no blood vessels, and is nourished by diffusion from the dermis. In plants, the outermost layer of cells covering the leaves and young parts of a plant is the epidermis.
Pigment	Pigment is any material resulting in color in plant or animal cells which is the result of selective absorption.
Granum	Granum refers to a stack of hollow disks formed of thylakoid membrane in a chloroplast. They are the sites where light energy is trapped by chlorophyll and converted to chemical energy during the light reactions of photosynthesis.
Fixation	Fixation in population genetics occurs when the frequency of a gene reaches 1. Fixation in biochemistry, histology, cell biology and pathology refers to the technique of preserving a specimen for microscopic study, making it intact and stable, but dead.
Sucrose	A disaccharide composed of glucose and fructose is called sucrose.
Amino acid	An amino acid is any molecule that contains both amino and carboxylic acid functional groups. They are the basic structural building units of proteins. They form short polymer chains called peptides or polypeptides which in turn form structures called proteins.
Tissue	Group of similar cells which perform a common function is called tissue.
Carbon fixation	Carbon fixation refers to the incorporation of carbon from atmospheric CO_2 into the carbon in organic compounds.
Double bond	Double bond refers to a type of covalent bond in which two atoms share two pairs of electrons; symbolized by a pair of lines between the bonded atoms. An example is in ethylene (between the carbon atoms). It usually consists of one sigma bond and one pi bond.

Photosystem	Cluster of light-absorbing pigment molecules within thylakoid membranes is a photosystem.
Porphyrin	A porphyrin is a heterocyclic macrocycle made from 4 pyrrole subunits linked on opposite sides (á position) through 4 methine bridges (=CH-).
Magnesium	Magnesium is the chemical element in the periodic table that has the symbol Mg and atomic number 12 and an atomic mass of 24.31.
Reaction center	A photosynthetic reaction center is a protein which is the site of the light reactions of photosynthesis. The reaction center contains pigments such as chlorophyll and phaeophytin. These absorb light, promoting an electron to a higher energy level within the pigment.
Photosystem II	A photosystem is the site of the light reactions, found in the thylakoids. Photosystem II ultimately shuffles electrons to a quinone terminal electron acceptor.
Photosystem I	A photosystem is the site of the light reactions, found in the thylakoids. Photosystem I uses ferredoxin-like iron-sulfur cluster proteins as terminal electron acceptors
Water-splitting	A process in photosystem II of photosynthesis whereby water molecules are split with the release of oxygen is called water-splitting.
Electron donor	An electron donor is a chemical entity that donates electrons to another compound. It is a reducing agent that, by virtue of its donating electrons, is itself oxidized in the process.
Electron transport chain	The electron transport chain is any series of protein complexes and lipid-soluble messengers that convert the reductive potential of energized electrons into a cross-membrane proton gradient.
Ribulose	A 5-carbon sugar molecule used in photosynthesis is ribulose.
Ribulose bisphosphate	Five-carbon compound that combines with and fixes carbon dioxide during the Calvin cycle and is later regenerated by the same cycle is ribulose bisphosphate.
Rubisco	RUBISCO is the common name of ribulose-1,5-bisphosphate carboxylase/oxygenase, an enzyme that is used in the Calvin cycle to catalyze the first major step of carbon fixation. RUBISCO catalyzes either the carboxylation or oxygenation of ribulose-1,5-bisphosphate (also known as RuBP) with carbon dioxide or oxygen.
Metabolic pathway	A metabolic pathway is a series of chemical reactions occurring within a cell, catalyzed by enzymes, to achieve in either the formation of a metabolic product to be used or stored by the cell, or the initiation of another metabolic pathway.
Radioisotope	Radioisotope refers to a radioactive isotope of an element. Examples are carbon-14 and hydrogen-3, or tritium.
Biochemistry	Biochemistry studies how complex chemical reactions give rise to life. It is a hybrid branch of chemistry which specialises in the chemical processes in living organisms.
Disaccharide	A disaccharide is a sugar (a carbohydrate) composed of two monosaccharides. The two monosaccharides are bonded via a condensation reaction.
Vascular bundle	A vascular bundle is a part of the transport system in vascular plants. The transport itself happens in vascular tissue, which exists in two forms: xylem and phloem. Both these tissues are present in a vascular bundle, which in addition will include supporting and protective tissues.
Blood	Blood is a circulating tissue composed of fluid plasma and cells. The main function of blood is to supply nutrients (oxygen, glucose) and constitutional elements to tissues and to remove waste products.
Glycogen	Glycogen refers to a complex, extensively branched polysaccharide of many glucose monomers; serves as an energy-storage molecule in liver and muscle cells.

317

Polymer	Polymer is a generic term used to describe a very long molecule consisting of structural units and repeating units connected by covalent chemical bonds.
Cell nucleus	The cell nucleus is found in all eukaryotic cells that contains most of the cell's genetic material. They have two primary functions: to control chemical reactions within the cytoplasm and to store information needed for cellular division.
Mitochondrial genome	The mitochondrial genome is the genetic material of the mitochondria. The mitochondria are organelles that reproduce themselves semi-autonomously within eukaryotic cells.
Habitat	Habitat refers to a place where an organism lives; an environmental situation in which an organism lives.
Microbe	A microbe is an organism that is so small that it is microscopic (invisible to the naked eye). Microorganisms are often illustrated using single-celled, or unicellular organisms; however, some unicellular protists are visible to the naked eye, and some multicellular species are microscopic.
Fission	A means of asexual reproduction whereby a parent separates into two or more genetically identical individuals of about equal size is referred to as fission.
Fusion	Fusion refers to the combination of two atoms into a single atom as a result of a collision, usually accompanied by the release of energy.
Excretion	Excretion is the biological process by which an organism chemically separates waste products from its body. The waste products are then usually expelled from the body by elimination.
Plasma membrane	Membrane surrounding the cytoplasm that consists of a phospholipid bilayer with embedded proteins is referred to as plasma membrane.
Anaerobic bacteria	Anaerobic bacteria refers to bacteria that do not need oxygen.
Cellular respiration	Cellular respiration is the process in which the chemical bonds of energy-rich molecules such as glucose are converted into energy usable for life processes.
Multicellular	Multicellular organisms are those organisms consisting of more than one cell, and having differentiated cells that perform specialized functions. Most life that can be seen with the naked eye is multicellular, as are all animals (i.e. members of the kingdom Animalia) and plants (i.e. members of the kingdom Plantae).
Aerobic respiration	Aerobic respiration requires oxygen in order to generate energy. It is the preferred method of pyruvate breakdown from glycolysis and requires that pyruvate enter the mitochondrion to be fully oxidised by the Krebs cycle.
Hydrothermal vent	A hydrothermal vent is a fissure in a planet's surface from which geothermally heated water issues. Hydrothermal vents are commonly found in places that are also volcanically active, where hot magma is relatively near the planet's surface.
Deep ocean	The deep ocean is the lowest layer in an ocean, existing below the thermocline. The deep ocean is not well mixed, consists of horizontal layers of equal density, and is often as cold as -1 to 4 degrees Celsius. Ninety percent of the total volume of Earth's oceans is found in the deep ocean.
Archaea	The Archaea are a major division of living organisms. Although there is still uncertainty in the exact phylogeny of the groups, Archaea, Eukaryotes and Bacteria are the fundamental classifications in what is called the three-domain system.
Nitrogen	A colorless and tasteless and mostly inert diatomic non-metal gas that is an essential constituent of proteins is nitrogen.

Go to **Cram101.com** for the Practice Tests for this Chapter.

Nitrogen fixation	Nitrogen fixation is the process by which nitrogen is taken from its relatively inert molecular form (N_2) in the atmosphere and converted into nitrogen compounds useful for other chemical processes.
Ammonia	Ammonia is a compound of nitrogen and hydrogen with the formula NH_3. At standard temperature and pressure ammonia is a gas. It is toxic and corrosive to some materials, and has a characteristic pungent odor.
Carbon monoxide	Carbon monoxide refers to a highly poisonous gas, the molecules of which consist of a carbon atom with one oxygen attached. Not to be confused with nonpoisonous carbon dioxide, a natural gas in the atmosphere.
Methyl	In chemistry, a methyl group is a hydrophobic alkyl functional group derived from methane (CH_4). It has the formula $-CH_3$ and is very often abbreviated -Me.
Biosynthesis	Biosynthesis is a phenomenon where chemical compounds are produced from simpler reagents. Biosynthesis, unlike chemical synthesis, takes place within living organisms and is generally catalysed by enzymes. The process is vital part of metabolism.
Active transport	Active transport is the mediated transport of biochemicals, and other atomic/molecular substances, across membranes. In this form of transport, molecules move against either an electrical or concentration gradient.

Go to **Cram101.com** for the Practice Tests for this Chapter.

Chemical reaction	Chemical reaction refers to a process leading to chemical changes in matter; involves the making and/or breaking of chemical bonds.
Cell	The cell is the structural and functional unit of all living organisms, and is sometimes called the "building block of life."
Peptide bond	A peptide bond is a chemical bond formed between two molecules when the carboxyl group of one molecule reacts with the amino group of the other molecule, releasing a molecule of water.
Hydrolyze	Hydrolyze refers to break a chemical bond, as in a peptide linkage, with the insertion of the components of water, -H and -OH, at the cleaved ends of a chain. The digestion of proteins is hydrolysis.
Glucose	Glucose, a simple monosaccharide sugar, is one of the most important carbohydrates and is used as a source of energy in animals and plants. Glucose is one of the main products of photosynthesis and starts respiration.
Enzyme	An enzyme is a protein that catalyzes, or speeds up, a chemical reaction. They are essential to sustain life because most chemical reactions in biological cells would occur too slowly, or would lead to different products, without them.
Protein	A protein is a complex, high-molecular-weight organic compound that consists of amino acids joined by peptide bonds. They are essential to the structure and function of all living cells and viruses. Many are enzymes or subunits of enzymes.
Metabolic processes	The total of all chemical reactions within an organism are the metabolic processes.
Cytosol	The cytosol is the internal fluid of the cell, and a large part of cell metabolism occurs here. Proteins within the cytosol play an important role in signal transduction pathways, glycolysis; also, they act as intracellular receptors and form part of the ribosomes, enabling further protein synthesis
Vesicle	In cell biology, a vesicle is a relatively small and enclosed compartment, separated from the cytosol by at least one lipid bilayer.
Endocytosis	Endocytosis is a process where cells absorb material (molecules or other cells) from outside by engulfing it with their cell membranes.
Exocytosis	Exocytosis is the process by which a cell is able to release large biomolecules through its membrane. While in protozoa the exocytosis may serve the function of wasting unnecessary products, in multicellular organisms exocytosis serves signalling or regulatory function.
Receptor-mediated endocytosis	Receptor-mediated endocytosis refers to the movement of specific molecules into a cell by the inward budding of membranous vesicles. The vesicles contain proteins with receptor sites specific to the molecules being taken in.
Intracellular digestion	Intracellular digestion refers to a form of digestion in which food is taken into cells by phagocytosis. It is found in sponges and most protozoa and coelenterates.
Endoplasmic reticulum	The endoplasmic reticulum is an organelle found in all eukaryotic cells. It modifies proteins, makes macromolecules, and transfers substances throughout the cell.
Vesicular transport	Transport of proteins from one cellular compartment to another by means of membrane-bounded intermediaries such as vesicles or organelle fragments is called vesicular transport.
Secretory protein	In eukaryotes, a secretory protein is a protein synthesized on rough endoplasmic reticulum and destined for export. Nearly all proteins secreted from cells are glycosylated. In prokaryotes, a secreted protein may be synthesized on ribosomes associated with the plasma membrane or exported post translation.

Golgi apparatus	Golgi apparatus refers to an organelle in eukaryotic cells consisting of stacks of membranous sacs that modify, store, and ship products of the endoplasmic reticulum.
Plasma membrane	Membrane surrounding the cytoplasm that consists of a phospholipid bilayer with embedded proteins is referred to as plasma membrane.
Lipid bilayer	A lipid bilayer is a membrane or zone of a membrane composed of lipid molecules (usually phospholipids). The lipid bilayer is a critical component of all biological membranes, including cell membranes, and is a prerequisite for cell-based organisms.
Macromolecule	A macromolecule is a molecule of high relative molecular mass, the structure of which essentially comprises the multiple repetition of units derived, actually or conceptually, from molecules of low relative molecular mass.
Mitochondria	Mitochondria are organelles found in most eukaryotic cells, including those of plants, animals, fungi, and protists. Mitochondria are sometimes described as "cellular power plants", because their primary function is to convert organic materials into energy in the form of ATP.
Nuclear pore	Opening in the nuclear envelope which permits the passage of proteins into the nucleus and ribosomal subunits out of the nucleus is a nuclear pore.
Chloroplast	A chloroplast is an organelle found in plant cells and eukaryotic algae which conduct photosynthesis. They are similar to mitochondria but are found only in plants. They are surrounded by a double membrane with an intermembrane space; they have their own DNA and are involved in energy metabolism;
Animal cell	An animal cell is a form of eukaryotic cell which make up many tissues in animals. The animal cell is distinct from other eukaryotes, most notably those of plants, as they lack cell walls and chloroplasts, and they have smaller vacuoles.
Pinocytosis	Process by which vesicle formation brings macromolecules into the cell is called pinocytosis.
Specificity	A medical diagnostic test for a certain disease, specificity is the proportion of true negatives of all the negative samples tested.
Organelle	In cell biology, an organelle is one of several structures with specialized functions, suspended in the cytoplasm of a eukaryotic cell.
Lysosome	Lysosome refers to a digestive organelle in eukaryotic cells; contains hydrolytic enzymes that digest the cell's food and wastes. They are found in both plant and animal cells, and are built in the Golgi apparatus.
Endosome	Membrane-bounded organelle in animal cells that carries materials newly ingested by endocytosis and passes many of them on to lysosomes for degradation is referred to as endosome.
Er lumen	The space enclosed by the membrane of the endoplasmic reticulum is the er lumen.
Budding	A means of asexual reproduction whereby a new individual developed from an outgrowth of a parent splits off and lives independently is referred to as budding.
Nucleus	In cell biology, the nucleus is found in all eukaryotic cells that contains most of the cell's genetic material. The nucleus has two primary functions: to control chemical reactions within the cytoplasm and to store information needed for cellular division.
Nuclear envelope	The nuclear envelope refers to the double membrane of the nucleus that encloses genetic material in eukaryotic cells. It separates the contents of the nucleus (DNA in particular) from the cytosol.
Nuclear membrane	The double layered structure surrounding the nucleus that separates the nucleoplasm from the

Go to **Cram101.com** for the Practice Tests for this Chapter.

cytoplasm is referred to as nuclear membrane.

Rough endoplasmic reticulum	Rough endoplasmic reticulum manufactures and transports proteins destined for membranes and secretion. It is called "rough" because ribosomes present on the cytosolic side of the membrane give it a rough appearance.
Ribosome	A ribosome is an organelle composed of rRNA and ribosomal proteins. It translates mRNA into a polypeptide chain (e.g., a protein). It can be thought of as a factory that builds a protein from a set of genetic instructions.
Glycogen	Glycogen refers to a complex, extensively branched polysaccharide of many glucose monomers; serves as an energy-storage molecule in liver and muscle cells.
Granule	A granule is a small grain. In describing cells, a granule may be any structure barely visible by light microscopy, but most often a secretory vesicle.
Molecule	A molecule is the smallest particle of a pure chemical substance that still retains its chemical composition and properties.
Adrenal	In mammals, the adrenal glands are the triangle-shaped endocrine glands that sit atop the kidneys. They are chiefly responsible for regulating the stress response through the synthesis of corticosteroids and catecholamines, including cortisol and adrenaline.
Alcohol	Alcohol is a general term, applied to any organic compound in which a hydroxyl group (-OH) is bound to a carbon atom, which in turn is bound to other hydrogen and/or carbon atoms. The general formula for a simple acyclic alcohol is $C_nH_{2n+1}OH$.
Liver	The liver is an organ in vertebrates, including humans. It plays a major role in metabolism and has a number of functions in the body including drug detoxification, glycogen storage, and plasma protein synthesis. It also produces bile, which is important for digestion.
Gland	A gland is an organ in an animal's body that synthesizes a substance for release such as hormones, often into the bloodstream or into cavities inside the body or its outer surface.
Peroxisome	Enzyme-filled vesicle in which fatty acids and amino acids are metabolized to hydrogen peroxide that is broken down to harmless products is called peroxisome.
Filament	The stamen is the male organ of a flower. Each stamen generally has a stalk called the filament, and, on top of the filament, an anther. The filament is a long chain of proteins, such as those found in hair, muscle, or in flagella.
Selectively permeable membrane	A selectively permeable membrane is a membrane which will allow certain molecules or ions to pass through it by diffusion (sometimes "facilitated diffusion"). The rate of passage depends on the pressure, concentration and temperature
Light microscope	An optical instrument with lenses that refract visible light to magnify images and project them into a viewer's eye or onto photographic film is referred to as light microscope.
Microorganism	A microorganism is an organism that is so small that it is microscopic (invisible to the naked eye). They are often illustrated using single-celled, or unicellular organisms; however, some unicellular protists are visible to the naked eye, and some multicellular species are microscopic.
Bacteria	The domain that contains procaryotic cells with primarily diacyl glycerol diesters in their membranes and with bacterial rRNA. Bacteria also is a general term for organisms that are composed of procaryotic cells and are not multicellular.
Lipid	Lipid is one class of aliphatic hydrocarbon-containing organic compounds essential for the structure and function of living cells. They are characterized by being water-insoluble but soluble in nonpolar organic solvents.

Bacterium	Most bacterium are microscopic and unicellular, with a relatively simple cell structure lacking a cell nucleus, and organelles such as mitochondria and chloroplasts. They are the most abundant of all organisms. They are ubiquitous in soil, water, and as symbionts of other organisms.
Evolution	In biology, evolution is the process by which novel traits arise in populations and are passed on from generation to generation. Its action over large stretches of time explains the origin of new species and ultimately the vast diversity of the biological world.
Endomembrane system	The endomembrane system is the system of internal membranes within eukaryotic cells that divide the cell into functional and structural compartments, or organelles.
Invagination	Invagination means to fold inward or to sheath.
Plasma	In physics and chemistry, a plasma is an ionized gas, and is usually considered to be a distinct phase of matter. "Ionized" in this case means that at least one electron has been dissociated from a significant fraction of the molecules.
Membrane protein	A membrane protein is a protein molecule that is attached to, or associated with the membrane of a cell or an organelle. Membrane proteins can be classified into two groups, based on their attachment to the membrane.
Anaerobic	An anaerobic organism is any organism that does not require oxygen for growth.
Cell division	Cell division is the process by which a cell (called the parent cell) divides into two cells (called daughter cells). Cell division is usually a small segment of a larger cell cycle. In meiosis, however, a cell is permanently transformed and cannot divide again.
Daughter cell	A cell formed by cell division of a parent cell is a daughter cell.
Amino acid	An amino acid is any molecule that contains both amino and carboxylic acid functional groups. They are the basic structural building units of proteins. They form short polymer chains called peptides or polypeptides which in turn form structures called proteins.
Sorting signal	Amino acid sequence that directs the delivery of a protein to a specific location outside the cytosol is called a sorting signal.
Protein translocator	Membrane-bound protein that mediates the transport of another protein across an organelle membrane is referred to as protein translocator.
Diffusion	Diffusion refers to the spontaneous movement of particles of any kind from where they are more concentrated to where they are less concentrated.
Snake	A snake also known as ophidians, are cold blooded legless reptiles closely related to lizards, which share the order Squamata.
Recombinant DNA	Recombinant DNA is an artificial DNA sequence resulting from the combining of two other DNA sequences in a plasmid.
Hydrophobic	Hydrophobic refers to being electrically neutral and nonpolar, and thus prefering other neutral and nonpolar solvents or molecular environments. Hydrophobic is often used interchangeably with "oily" or "lipophilic."
N-terminus	The N-terminus refers to the extremity of a protein or polypeptide terminated by an amino acid with a free amine group ($-NH_2$).
C-terminus	The C-terminus of a protein or polypeptide is the extremity of the amino acid chain terminated by a free carboxyl group (-COOH).
Lamina	A structurally complete leaf of an angiosperm consists of a petiole (leaf stem), a lamina (leaf blade), and stipules (small processes located to either side of the base of the petiole).

Go to **Cram101.com** for the Practice Tests for this Chapter.

Protein subunit	A protein subunit is a single protein molecule that assembles (or "coassembles") with other protein molecules to form a multimeric or oligomeric protein. Many naturally-occurring proteins and enzymes are multimeric.
Micrograph	A micrograph is a photograph or similar image taken through a microscope or similar device to show a magnified image of an item.
Electron	The electron is a light fundamental subatomic particle that carries a negative electric charge. The electron is a spin-1/2 lepton, does not participate in strong interactions and has no substructure.
Receptor	A receptor is a protein on the cell membrane or within the cytoplasm or cell nucleus that binds to a specific molecule (a ligand), such as a neurotransmitter, hormone, or other substance, and initiates the cellular response to the ligand. Receptor, in immunology, the region of an antibody which shows recognition of an antigen.
Diaphragm	The diaphragm is a shelf of muscle extending across the bottom of the ribcage. It is critically important in respiration: in order to draw air into the lungs, the diaphragm contracts, thus enlarging the thoracic cavity and reducing intra-thoracic pressure.
Nuclear transport	Gated transport mechanisms by which proteins or RNA are moved across the nuclear membrane is referred to as nuclear transport.
Transport protein	A transport protein is a protein involved in facilitated diffusion. Changes in the conformation move the binding site to the opposite side of the protein.
Conformation	The three-dimensional shape of a molecule is its conformation. The conformation is particularly important in proteins.
Outer membrane	The outer membrane refers to the outside membrane of an organelle which surrounds the rest of the organelle components. Both the chloroplast and the mitochondria have an outer membrane.
Thylakoid	Flattened sac within a granum whose membrane contains chlorophyll and where the light-dependent reactions of photosynthesis occur is referred to as a thylakoid.
Transmembrane protein	Membrane protein that extends through the lipid bilayer, with part of its mass on either side of the membrane is referred to as a transmembrane protein.
Inner membrane	The inner membrane is a membrane (phospholipid bilayer) of an organelle that is within the outer membrane. The inner membrane is present within the mitochondria and the chloroplast of cells.
Insertion	At DNA level, an insertion means the insertion of a few base pairs into a genetic sequence. This can often happen in microsatellite regions due to the DNA polymerase slipping.
Phospholipid	Phospholipid is a class of lipids formed from four components: fatty acids, a negatively-charged phosphate group, an alcohol and a backbone. Phospholipids with a glycerol backbone are known as glycerophospholipids or phosphoglycerides.
Mitochondrion	Mitochondrion refers to an organelle in eukaryotic cells where cellular respiration occurs. Enclosed by two concentric membranes, it is where most of the cell's ATP is made.
Secretion	Secretion is the process of segregating, elaborating, and releasing chemicals from a cell, or a secreted chemical substance or amount of substance.
Fusion	Fusion refers to the combination of two atoms into a single atom as a result of a collision, usually accompanied by the release of energy.
Signal peptidase	Signal peptidase refers to enzyme that removes a terminal signal sequence from a protein once the sorting process is complete.
Chaperone	Protein that helps other proteins avoid misfolding pathways that produce inactive or

Go to **Cram101.com** for the Practice Tests for this Chapter.

aggregated polypeptides is called a chaperone.

Fluorescence	Fluorescence is a luminescence that is mostly found as an optical phenomenon in cold bodies, in which the molecular absorption of a photon triggers the emission of a lower-energy photon with a longer wavelength. The energy difference between the absorbed and emitted photons ends up as molecular vibrations or heat.
Plant cell	A cell that is a structural and functional unit of a plant is a plant cell.
Pancreas	The pancreas is a retroperitoneal organ that serves two functions: exocrine - it produces pancreatic juice containing digestive enzymes, and endocrine - it produces several important hormones, namely insulin.
Polypeptide	Polypeptide refers to polymer of many amino acids linked by peptide bonds.
Membrane-bound ribosome	Membrane-bound ribosome refers to ribosome attached to the cytosolic face of the endoplasmic reticulum. The site of synthesis of proteins that enter the endoplasmic reticulum.
Free ribosome	Free ribosome occur in all cells, and also in mitochondria and chloroplasts of eukaryotic cells. Free ribosome usually produce proteins used in the cytosol or organelle in which they occur. As the name implies, they are free in solution and not bound to anything within the cell.
Protein synthesis	The process whereby the tRNA utilizes the mRNA as a guide to arrange the amino acids in their proper sequence according to the genetic information in the chemical code of DNA is referred to as protein synthesis.
Translocation	A chromosomal mutation in which a portion of one chromosome breaks off and becomes attached to another chromosome is referred to as translocation.
Signal peptide	A stretch of amino acids on a polypeptide that targets the protein to a specific destination in a eukaryotic cell is referred to as signal peptide.
Polyribosome	String of ribosomes simultaneously translating regions of the same mRNA strand during protein synthesis is referred to as a polyribosome.
Signal-recognition particle	Ribonucleoprotein particle that binds an ER signal sequence on a partially synthesized polypeptide chain and directs the polypeptide and its attached ribosome to the endoplasmic reticulum is a signal-recognition particle.
Peptide	Peptide is the family of molecules formed from the linking, in a defined order, of various amino acids. The link between one amino acid residue and the next is an amide bond, and is sometimes referred to as a peptide bond.
Protein structure	A protein structure are amino acid chains, made up from 20 different L-α-amino acids, also referred to as residues, that fold into unique three-dimensional structures.
Disulfide bond	A disulfide bond (SS-bond), also called a disulfide bridge, is a strong covalent bond between two sulfhydryl (-SH) groups. This bond is very important to the folding, structure, and function of proteins.
Carbohydrate	Carbohydrate is a chemical compound that contains oxygen, hydrogen, and carbon atoms. They consist of monosaccharide sugars of varying chain lengths and that have the general chemical formula $C_n(H_2O)_n$ or are derivatives of such.
Side chain	In organic chemistry and biochemistry a side chain is a part of a molecule attached to a core structure. Often the side chain can vary for a given core. In biochemistry the peptide or protein side chains are the variable parts of amino acids extending from the peptide backbone.
Biosynthesis	Biosynthesis is a phenomenon where chemical compounds are produced from simpler reagents.

	Biosynthesis, unlike chemical synthesis, takes place within living organisms and is generally catalysed by enzymes. The process is vital part of metabolism.
Coated vesicle	Coated vesicle refers to small membrane-bounded organelle with a cage of proteins on its cytosolic surface. It is formed by the pinching off of a coated region of membrane. Some coats are made of clathrin, whereas others are made from other proteins.
Clathrin	Clathrin is a protein that is the major constituent of the 'coat' of the clathrin coated pits and coated vesicles formed during endocytosis of materials at the surface of cells.
Dynamin	Cytosolic GTPase that binds to the neck of a clathrin-coated vesicle in the process of budding from the membrane, and which is involved in completing vesicle formation is referred to as dynamin.
Skin	Skin is an organ of the integumentary system composed of a layer of tissues that protect underlying muscles and organs.
Adaptin	Protein that binds clathrin to the membrane surface in clathrin-coated vesicles is called adaptin.
Molecular marker	A segment of DNA found at a specific site in a genome that has variants which can be recognized and followed is called a molecular marker.
Oxidation	Oxidation refers to the loss of electrons from a substance involved in a redox reaction; always accompanies reduction.
Cysteine	Cysteine is a naturally occurring hydrophobic amino acid which has a thiol group and is found in most proteins, though only in small quantities.
Oligosaccharide	An oligosaccharide is a saccharide polymer containing a small number (typically three to six) of component sugars, also known as simple sugars. They are generally found either O- or N-linked to compatible amino acid side chains in proteins or to lipid moieties.
Glycoprotein	A macromolecule consisting of one or more polypeptides linked to short chains of sugars is called glycoprotein.
Residue	A residue refers to a portion of a larger molecule, a specific monomer of a polysaccharide, protein or nucleic acid.
Sugar	A sugar is the simplest molecule that can be identified as a carbohydrate. These include monosaccharides and disaccharides, trisaccharides and the oligosaccharides. The term "glyco-" indicates the presence of a sugar in an otherwise non-carbohydrate substance.
Active site	The active site of an enzyme is the binding site where catalysis occurs. The structure and chemical properties of the active site allow the recognition and binding of the substrate.
Transferase	In biochemistry, a transferase is an enzyme that catalyzes the transfer of a functional group from one molecule (called the donor) to another (called the acceptor).
Asparagine	Asparagine is one of the 20 most common natural amino acids on Earth. It has carboxamide as the side chain's functional group. It is considered a non-essential amino acid.
Linkage	Linkage refers to the patterns of assortment of genes that are located on the same chromosome. Important because if the genes are located relatively far apart, crossing over is more likely to occur between them than if they are close together.
N-linked oligosaccharide	Chain of sugars attached to a protein through the NH_2 group of the side chain of an asparagine residue is called n-linked oligosaccharide.
Mannose	Mannose is a sugar monomer of the hexose series of carbohydrates. Mannose enters the carbohydrate metabolism stream by phosphorylation and conversion to fructose-6-phosphate.

Multimeric protein	In structural biology, a protein subunit or subunit protein is a single protein molecule that assembles (or "coassembles") with other protein molecules to form a multimeric protein or oligomeric protein.
Antibody	An antibody is a protein used by the immune system to identify and neutralize foreign objects like bacteria and viruses. Each antibody recognizes a specific antigen unique to its target.
Cystic fibrosis	Cystic fibrosis refers to a genetic disease that occurs in people with two copies of a certain recessive allele; characterized by an excessive secretion of mucus and consequent vulnerability to infection; fatal if untreated.
Mutation	Mutation refers to a change in the nucleotide sequence of DNA; the ultimate source of genetic diversity.
Mutant	A mutant (also known to early geneticists as a "monster") is an individual, organism, or new genetic character arising or resulting from an instance of mutation, which is a sudden structural change within the DNA of a gene or chromosome of an organism resulting in the creation of a new character or trait not found in the parental type.
Cell nucleus	The cell nucleus is found in all eukaryotic cells that contains most of the cell's genetic material. They have two primary functions: to control chemical reactions within the cytoplasm and to store information needed for cellular division.
Cell center	Cell center is the centrally located organelle of animal cells that is the primary microtubule-organizing center and is duplicated to form the spindle poles during mitosis. In most animal cells it contains a pair of centrioles.
Centrosome	Centrosome refers to material in the cytoplasm of a eukaryotic cell that gives rise to microtubules; important in mitosis and meiosis; also called microtubule-organizing center.
Golgi	Golgi discovered a method of staining nervous tissue which would stain a limited number of cells at random, in their entirety. This enabled him to view the paths of nerve cells in the brain for the first time. He called his discovery the black reaction. It is now known universally as the Golgi stain.
Cis	A double bond in which the greater radical on both ends is on the same side of the bond is called a cis.
Trans face	Trans face refers to face of a Golgi stack at which material leaves the organelle for the cell surface or another cell compartment. It is adjacent to the trans Golgi network.
Cis face	Cis face refers to face of a Golgi stack at which material enters the organelle. It is adjacent to the cis Golgi network.
Cisterna	Flattened membrane-bounded compartment, as found in the endoplasmic reticulum or Golgi apparatus is called a cisterna.
Fibroblast	A fibroblast is a cell that makes the structural fibers and ground substance of connective tissue.
Complex oligosaccharide	Complex oligosaccharide refers to a chain of sugars attached to a glycoprotein that is generated by trimming of the original oligosaccharide attached in the endoplasmic reticulum and subsequent addition of further sugars.
Protease	Protease refers to an enzyme that breaks peptide bonds between amino acids of proteins.
Digestion	Digestion refers to the mechanical and chemical breakdown of food into molecules small enough for the body to absorb; the second main stage of food processing, following ingestion.
Migration	Migration occurs when living things move from one biome to another. In most cases organisms migrate to avoid local shortages of food, usually caused by winter. Animals may also migrate

Go to **Cram101.com** for the Practice Tests for this Chapter.

to a certain location to breed, as is the case with some fish.

Radioactive	A term used to describe the property of releasing energy or particles from an unstable atom is called radioactive.
Translation	Translation is the second process of protein biosynthesis. In translation, messenger RNA is decoded to produce a specific polypeptide according to the rules specified by the genetic code.
In vitro	In vitro is an experimental technique where the experiment is performed in a test tube, or generally outside a living organism or cell.
Yeast	Yeast refers to common term for several families of unicellular fungi. Includes species used for brewing beer and making bread, as well as pathogenic species.
Gene	Gene refers to a discrete unit of hereditary information consisting of a specific nucleotide sequence in DNA . Most of the genes of a eukaryote are located in its chromosomal DNA; a few are carried by the DNA of mitochondria and chloroplasts.
Microscope	A microscope is an instrument for viewing objects that are too small to be seen by the naked or unaided eye.
Temperature-sensitive mutant	Organism or cell carrying a genetically altered protein that performs normally at one temperature but is abnormal at another temperature is called temperature-sensitive mutant.
Fusion protein	A fusion protein is a protein created through genetic engineering from two or more proteins/peptides. This is achieved by creating a fusion gene: removing the stop codon from the DNA sequence of the first protein, then appending the DNA sequence of the second protein in frame. That DNA sequence will then be expressed by a cell as a single protein.
Virus	Obligate intracellular parasite of living cells consisting of an outer capsid and an inner core of nucleic acid is referred to as virus. The term virus usually refers to those particles that infect eukaryotes whilst the term bacteriophage or phage is used to describe those infecting prokaryotes.
Viral	Viral phenomena are objects or patterns able to replicate themselves or convert other objects into copies of themselves when these objects are exposed to them.
Exit site	The location on a ribosome to which an empty tRNA moves from the P site before it finally leaves the ribosome during protein synthesis is referred to as the exit site.
Extracellular matrix	Extracellular matrix is any material part of a tissue that is not part of any cell. Extracellular matrix is the defining feature of connective tissue.
Extracellular fluid	In some animals, including mammals, the extracellular fluid can be divided into 2 major subcompartments, interstitial fluid and blood plasma. The extracellular fluid can be further divided into 2 minor subcompartments, transcellular fluid and lymph.
Default pathway	Constitutive secretory pathway that automatically delivers material from the Golgi apparatus to the plasma membrane if no other sorting signals are present is a default pathway.
Secretory vesicle	Secretory vesicle is a membrane-bounded organelle in which molecules destined for secretion are stored prior to release. Sometimes called secretory granule because darkly staining contents make the organelle visible as a small solid object.
Hormone	A hormone is a chemical messenger from one cell to another. All multicellular organisms produce hormones. The best known hormones are those produced by endocrine glands of vertebrate animals, but hormones are produced by nearly every organ system and tissue type in a human or animal body. Hormone molecules are secreted directly into the bloodstream, they move by circulation or diffusion to their target cells, which may be nearby cells in the same

tissue or cells of a distant organ of the body.

Mucus	Mucus is a slippery secretion of the lining of various membranes in the body (mucous membranes). Mucus aids in the protection of the lungs by trapping foreign particles that enter the nose during normal breathing. Additionally, it prevents tissues from drying out.
Insulin	Insulin is a polypeptide hormone that regulates carbohydrate metabolism. Apart from being the primary effector in carbohydrate homeostasis, it also has a substantial effect on small vessel muscle tone, controls storage and release of fat (triglycerides) and cellular uptake of both amino acids and some electrolytes.
Blood	Blood is a circulating tissue composed of fluid plasma and cells. The main function of blood is to supply nutrients (oxygen, glucose) and constitutional elements to tissues and to remove waste products.
Metabolite	The term metabolite is usually restricted to small molecules. They are the intermediates and products of metabolism. A primary metabolite is directly involved in the normal growth, development, and reproduction. A secondary metabolite is not directly involved in those processes, but usually has important ecological function.
Phagocytosis	Phagocytosis is a form of endocytosis where large particles are enveloped by the cell membrane of a (usually larger) cell and internalized to form a phagosome, or "food vacuole."
Phagosome	Phagosome refers to large intracellular membrane-bounded vesicle that is formed as a result of phagocytosis. Contains ingested extracellular material.
Protozoa	Protozoa are single-celled eukaryotes (organisms with nuclei) that show some characteristics usually associated with animals, most notably mobility and heterotrophy. They are often grouped in the kingdom Protista together with the plant-like algae.
Multicellular	Multicellular organisms are those organisms consisting of more than one cell, and having differentiated cells that perform specialized functions. Most life that can be seen with the naked eye is multicellular, as are all animals (i.e. members of the kingdom Animalia) and plants (i.e. members of the kingdom Plantae).
Neutrophil	Neutrophil refers to phagocytic white blood cell that can engulf bacteria and viruses in infected tissue; part of the body's nonspecific defense system.
Pseudopod	Pseudopod is a temporary projection of a eukaryotic cell. Cells having this faculty are generally referred to as amoeboids.
Macrophage	Macrophage is a cell found in tissues that are responsible for phagocytosis of pathogens, dead cells and cellular debris. They are part of the innate immune system. Their main role is the removal of pathogens and necrotic debris.
Tissue	Group of similar cells which perform a common function is called tissue.
Mycobacterium	Mycobacterium is the a genus of actinobacteria, given its own family, the Mycobacteriaceae. It includes many pathogens known to cause serious diseases in mammals, including tuberculosis and leprosy.
Tuberculosis	Tuberculosis is an infection caused by the bacterium Mycobacterium tuberculosis, which most commonly affects the lungs but can also affect the central nervous system, lymphatic system, circulatory system, genitourinary system, bones and joints.
Cholesterol	Cholesterol is a steroid, a lipid, and an alcohol, found in the cell membranes of all body tissues, and transported in the blood plasma of all animals. It is an important component of the membranes of cells, providing stability; it makes the membrane's fluidity stable over a bigger temperature interval.
Low-density	Low-density lipoprotein refers to a class and range of lipoprotein particles, varying in

lipoprotein	their size (18-25 nm in diameter) and contents, which carry cholesterol in the blood and around the body, for use by cells. It is the final stage of VLDL (very low-density lipoprotein) which is produced by the liver.
Acid	An acid is a water-soluble, sour-tasting chemical compound that when dissolved in water, gives a solution with a pH of less than 7.
Hydrolytic enzyme	A hydrolytic enzyme breaks down proteins, carbohydrates, and fat molecules into their simplest units. The hydrolysis of polymers by hydrolytic enzymes results in free monomers.
Receptor protein	Protein located in the plasma membrane or within the cell that binds to a substance that alters some metabolic aspect of the cell is referred to as receptor protein. It will only link up with a substance that has a certain shape that allows it to bind to the receptor.
Heart attack	A heart attack, is a serious, sudden heart condition usually characterized by varying degrees of chest pain or discomfort, weakness, sweating, nausea, vomiting, and arrhythmias, sometimes causing loss of consciousness. It occurs when the blood supply to a part of the heart is interrupted, causing death and scarring of the local heart tissue.
Influenza	Influenza or flu refers to an acute viral infection of the respiratory tract, occurring in isolated cases, epidemics, and pandemics. Influenza is caused by three strains of influenza virus, labeled types A, B, and C, based on the antigens of their protein coats.
Electron microscope	The electron microscope is a microscope that can magnify very small details with high resolving power due to the use of electrons as the source of illumination, magnifying at levels up to 500,000 times.
Proton	Positive subatomic particle, located in the nucleus and having a weight of approximately one atomic mass unit is referred to as a proton.
Transcytosis	Transport of macromolecules across a cell, which consists of the endocytosis of a macromolecule at one side of a monolayer and its exocytosis at the other side is transcytosis.
Domain	In biology, a domain is the top-level grouping of organisms in scientific classification.
Ligand	Any molecule that binds to a specific receptor site on a protein or other molecule is called a ligand.
Nucleotide	A nucleotide is a chemical compound that consists of a heterocyclic base, a sugar, and one or more phosphate groups. In the most common nucleotides the base is a derivative of purine or pyrimidine, and the sugar is pentose - deoxyribose or ribose. They are the structural units of RNA and DNA.
ATPase	ATPase is a class of enzymes that catalyze the decomposition of adenosine triphosphate into adenosine diphosphate and a free phosphate ion. This dephosphorylation reaction releases energy, which the enzyme harnesses to drive other chemical reactions that would not otherwise occur. This process is widely used in all known forms of life.
Hydrolase	Hydrolase is a general term for any enzyme that catalyzes a hydrolysis reaction, the chemical breakdown of polymers into smaller molecules through the addition of water molecules.
Nuclease	Enzyme that cleaves phosphodiester bonds in nucleic acids is referred to as nuclease.
Acid hydrolase	An acid hydrolase (lysosomal acid lipase) is an enzyme that works best at acidic pHs. It is commonly located in lysozomes, which have an acidic milieu.
Hemoglobin	Hemoglobin is the iron-containing oxygen-transport metalloprotein in the red cells of the blood in mammals and other animals. Hemoglobin transports oxygen from the lungs to the rest of the body, such as to the muscles, where it releases the oxygen load.

Go to Cram101.com for the Practice Tests for this Chapter.

Iron	Iron is essential to all organisms, except for a few bacteria. It is mostly stably incorporated in the inside of metalloproteins, because in exposed or in free form it causes production of free radicals that are generally toxic to cells.
Ion	Ion refers to an atom or molecule that has gained or lost one or more electrons, thus acquiring an electrical charge.
Autophagy	Autophagy is a process of organelle degradation that takes place inside the cell. It is executed by lysosomes and is part of everyday normal cell growth and development. Its main purpose is to maintain a balance between biogenesis of cell structures, and their degradation and turnover.
Nuclear localization signal	Signal sequences or signal patches found in proteins destined for the nucleus and which enable their selective transport into the nucleus from the cytosol through the nuclear pore complexes is called nuclear localization signal.
Active transport	Active transport is the mediated transport of biochemicals, and other atomic/molecular substances, across membranes. In this form of transport, molecules move against either an electrical or concentration gradient.
Cell membrane	A component of every biological cell, the selectively permeable cell membrane is a thin and structured bilayer of phospholipid and protein molecules that envelopes the cell. It separates a cell's interior from its surroundings and controls what moves in and out.
Ammonia	Ammonia is a compound of nitrogen and hydrogen with the formula NH_3. At standard temperature and pressure ammonia is a gas. It is toxic and corrosive to some materials, and has a characteristic pungent odor.
Urine	Concentrated filtrate produced by the kidneys and excreted via the bladder is called urine.
Drosophila	Drosophila is part of the phylum Arthropoda, a phylum of segmented animals with paired, jointed appendages and a hard exoskeleton made of chitin. They have an open circulatory system with a dorsal heart, with hemocoel occupying most of the body cavity, and a reduced coelom.
Synapse	A junction, or relay point, between two neurons, or between a neuron and an effector cell. Electrical and chemical signals are relayed from one cell to another at a synapse.
Mitosis	Mitosis is the process by which a cell separates its duplicated genome into two identical halves. It is generally followed immediately by cytokinesis which divides the cytoplasm and cell membrane.
Pineal gland	The pineal gland is a small endocrine gland in the brain. It is located near the center of the brain, between the two hemispheres, tucked in a groove where the two rounded thalamic bodies join.
Photoreceptor cells	Photoreceptor cells are found in the retina of the eye and are responsible for transducing, or converting, light into nerve signals that can be ultimately transmitted to the brain via the optic nerve. In vertebrates, there are two types of photoreceptor cells called rods and cones.
Neurotransmitter	A neurotransmitter is a chemical that is used to relay, amplify and modulate electrical signals between a neuron and another cell.
Nerve cell	A cell specialized to originate or transmit nerve impulses is referred to as nerve cell.
Retina	The retina is a thin layer of cells at the back of the eyeball of vertebrates and some cephalopods; it is the part of the eye which converts light into nervous signals.
Brain	The part of the central nervous system involved in regulating and controlling body activity and interpreting information from the senses transmitted through the nervous system is

referred to as the brain.

Multicellular	Multicellular organisms are those organisms consisting of more than one cell, and having differentiated cells that perform specialized functions. Most life that can be seen with the naked eye is multicellular, as are all animals (i.e. members of the kingdom Animalia) and plants (i.e. members of the kingdom Plantae).
Cell	The cell is the structural and functional unit of all living organisms, and is sometimes called the "building block of life."
Bacterium	Most bacterium are microscopic and unicellular, with a relatively simple cell structure lacking a cell nucleus, and organelles such as mitochondria and chloroplasts. They are the most abundant of all organisms. They are ubiquitous in soil, water, and as symbionts of other organisms.
Predator	A predator is an animal or other organism that hunts and kills other organisms for food in an act called predation.
Protein	A protein is a complex, high-molecular-weight organic compound that consists of amino acids joined by peptide bonds. They are essential to the structure and function of all living cells and viruses. Many are enzymes or subunits of enzymes.
Yeast	Yeast refers to common term for several families of unicellular fungi. Includes species used for brewing beer and making bread, as well as pathogenic species.
Cell cycle	An orderly sequence of events that extends from the time a eukaryotic cell divides to form two daughter cells to the time those daughter cells divide again is called cell cycle.
Physiology	The study of the function of cells, tissues, and organs is referred to as physiology.
Embryo	Embryo refers to a developing stage of a multicellular organism. In humans, the stage in the development of offspring from the first division of the zygote until body structures begin to appear, about the ninth week of gestation.
Animal cell	An animal cell is a form of eukaryotic cell which make up many tissues in animals. The animal cell is distinct from other eukaryotes, most notably those of plants, as they lack cell walls and chloroplasts, and they have smaller vacuoles.
Plant cell	A cell that is a structural and functional unit of a plant is a plant cell.
Target cell	A cell that responds to a regulatory signal, such as a hormone is a target cell.
Molecule	A molecule is the smallest particle of a pure chemical substance that still retains its chemical composition and properties.
Signal molecule	Extracellular or intracellular molecule that cues the response of a cell to the behavior of other cells or objects in the environment is called signal molecule.
Receptor protein	Protein located in the plasma membrane or within the cell that binds to a substance that alters some metabolic aspect of the cell is referred to as receptor protein. It will only link up with a substance that has a certain shape that allows it to bind to the receptor.
Signal transduction	Signal transduction is any process by which a cell converts one kind of signal or stimulus into another. Processes referred to as signal transduction often involve a sequence of biochemical reactions inside the cell, which are carried out by enzymes and linked through second messengers.
Endocrine gland	An endocrine gland is one of a set of internal organs involved in the secretion of hormones into the blood. These glands are known as ductless, which means they do not have tubes inside them.
Endocrine cell	Endocrine cell refers to specialized animal cell that secretes a hormone into the blood. Usually part of a gland, such as the thyroid or pituitary gland.

Go to **Cram101.com** for the Practice Tests for this Chapter.

Nucleotide	A nucleotide is a chemical compound that consists of a heterocyclic base, a sugar, and one or more phosphate groups. In the most common nucleotides the base is a derivative of purine or pyrimidine, and the sugar is pentose - deoxyribose or ribose. They are the structural units of RNA and DNA.
Fatty acid	A fatty acid is a carboxylic acid (or organic acid), often with a long aliphatic tail (long chains), either saturated or unsaturated.
Amino acid	An amino acid is any molecule that contains both amino and carboxylic acid functional groups. They are the basic structural building units of proteins. They form short polymer chains called peptides or polypeptides which in turn form structures called proteins.
Pancreas	The pancreas is a retroperitoneal organ that serves two functions: exocrine - it produces pancreatic juice containing digestive enzymes, and endocrine - it produces several important hormones, namely insulin.
Hormone	A hormone is a chemical messenger from one cell to another. All multicellular organisms produce hormones. The best known hormones are those produced by endocrine glands of vertebrate animals, but hormones are produced by nearly every organ system and tissue type in a human or animal body. Hormone molecules are secreted directly into the bloodstream, they move by circulation or diffusion to their target cells, which may be nearby cells in the same tissue or cells of a distant organ of the body.
Insulin	Insulin is a polypeptide hormone that regulates carbohydrate metabolism. Apart from being the primary effector in carbohydrate homeostasis, it also has a substantial effect on small vessel muscle tone, controls storage and release of fat (triglycerides) and cellular uptake of both amino acids and some electrolytes.
Glucose	Glucose, a simple monosaccharide sugar, is one of the most important carbohydrates and is used as a source of energy in animals and plants. Glucose is one of the main products of photosynthesis and starts respiration.
Peptide	Peptide is the family of molecules formed from the linking, in a defined order, of various amino acids. The link between one amino acid residue and the next is an amide bond, and is sometimes referred to as a peptide bond.
Steroid	A steroid is a lipid characterized by a carbon skeleton with four fused rings. Different steroids vary in the functional groups attached to these rings. Hundreds of distinct steroids have been identified in plants and animals. Their most important role in most living systems is as hormones.
Style	The style is a stalk connecting the stigma with the ovary below containing the transmitting tract, which facilitates the movement of the male gamete to the ovule.
Paracrine signaling	Paracrine signaling is a form of signalling in which the target cell is close to the signal releasing cell, and the signal chemical is broken down too quickly to be carried to other parts of the body.
Neuron	The neuron is a major class of cells in the nervous system. In vertebrates, they are found in the brain, the spinal cord and in the nerves and ganglia of the peripheral nervous system, and their primary role is to process and transmit neural information.
Spinal cord	The spinal cord is a part of the vertebrate nervous system that is enclosed in and protected by the vertebral column (it passes through the spinal canal). It consists of nerve cells. The spinal cord carries sensory signals and motor innervation to most of the skeletal muscles in the body.
Axon	An axon is a long slender projection of a nerve cell, or neuron, which conducts electrical impulses away from the neuron's cell body or soma. They are in effect the primary

Go to **Cram101.com** for the Practice Tests for this Chapter.

transmission lines of the nervous system, and as bundles they help make up nerves.

Nerve cell	A cell specialized to originate or transmit nerve impulses is referred to as nerve cell.
Neurotransmitter	A neurotransmitter is a chemical that is used to relay, amplify and modulate electrical signals between a neuron and another cell.
Axon terminal	A swelling at the end of an axon that is designed to release a chemical substance onto another neuron, muscle cell, or gland cell is called the axon terminal.
Pulse	The rhythmic stretching of the arteries caused by the pressure of blood forced through the arteries by contractions of the ventricles during systole is a pulse.
Nerve	A nerve is an enclosed, cable-like bundle of nerve fibers or axons, which includes the glia that ensheath the axons in myelin.
Contact-dependent signaling	Contact-dependent signaling refers to cell-cell communication in which the signal molecule remains bound to the signaling cell and only influences cells that physically contact it.
Plasma membrane	Membrane surrounding the cytoplasm that consists of a phospholipid bilayer with embedded proteins is referred to as plasma membrane.
Receptor	A receptor is a protein on the cell membrane or within the cytoplasm or cell nucleus that binds to a specific molecule (a ligand), such as a neurotransmitter, hormone, or other substance, and initiates the cellular response to the ligand. Receptor, in immunology, the region of an antibody which shows recognition of an antigen.
Tissue	Group of similar cells which perform a common function is called tissue.
Cell body	The part of a cell, such as a neuron, that houses the nucleus is the cell body.
Synapse	A junction, or relay point, between two neurons, or between a neuron and an effector cell. Electrical and chemical signals are relayed from one cell to another at a synapse.
Extracellular fluid	In some animals, including mammals, the extracellular fluid can be divided into 2 major subcompartments, interstitial fluid and blood plasma. The extracellular fluid can be further divided into 2 minor subcompartments, transcellular fluid and lymph.
Nervous system	The nervous system of an animal coordinates the activity of the muscles, monitors the organs, constructs and processes input from the senses, and initiates actions.
Epithelial	Functions of epithelial cells include secretion, absorption, protection, transcellular transport, sensation detection, and selective permeability.
Transmembrane protein	Membrane protein that extends through the lipid bilayer, with part of its mass on either side of the membrane is referred to as a transmembrane protein.
Mutant	A mutant (also known to early geneticists as a "monster") is an individual, organism, or new genetic character arising or resulting from an instance of mutation, which is a sudden structural change within the DNA of a gene or chromosome of an organism resulting in the creation of a new character or trait not found in the parental type.
Acetylcholine	The chemical compound acetylcholine was the first neurotransmitter to be identified. It is a chemical transmitter in both the peripheral nervous system (PNS) and central nervous system (CNS) in many organisms including humans.
Salivary gland	The salivary gland produces saliva, which keeps the mouth and other parts of the digestive system moist. It also helps break down carbohydrates and lubricates the passage of food down from the oro-pharynx to the esophagus to the stomach.
Muscle	Muscle is a contractile form of tissue. It is one of the four major tissue types, the other

353

	three being epithelium, connective tissue and nervous tissue. Muscle contraction is used to move parts of the body, as well as to move substances within the body.
Skeletal muscle	Skeletal muscle is a type of striated muscle, attached to the skeleton. They are used to facilitate movement, by applying force to bones and joints; via contraction. They generally contract voluntarily (via nerve stimulation), although they can contract involuntarily.
Transduction	In physiology, transduction is transportation of a stimuli to the nervous system. In genetics, transduction is the transfer of viral, bacterial, or both bacterial and viral DNA from one cell to another via bacteriophage.
Intracellular signaling protein	The intracellular signaling protein relays a signal as part of an intracellular signaling pathway. It may either activate the next protein in the pathway or generate a small intracellular mediator.
Rhodopsin	Rhodopsin is expressed in vertebrate photoreceptor cells. It is a pigment of the retina that is responsible for both the formation of the photoreceptor cells and the first events in the perception of light. Rhodopsins belong to the class of G-protein coupled receptors. It is the chemical that allows night-vision, and is extremely sensitive to light.
Cytoskeleton	Cytoskeleton refers to a meshwork of fine fibers in the cytoplasm of a eukaryotic cell; includes microfilaments, intermediate filaments, and microtubules.
Enzyme	An enzyme is a protein that catalyzes, or speeds up, a chemical reaction. They are essential to sustain life because most chemical reactions in biological cells would occur too slowly, or would lead to different products, without them.
Gene	Gene refers to a discrete unit of hereditary information consisting of a specific nucleotide sequence in DNA . Most of the genes of a eukaryote are located in its chromosomal DNA; a few are carried by the DNA of mitochondria and chloroplasts.
Hydrolyze	Hydrolyze refers to break a chemical bond, as in a peptide linkage, with the insertion of the components of water, -H and -OH, at the cleaved ends of a chain. The digestion of proteins is hydrolysis.
Cytosol	The cytosol is the internal fluid of the cell, and a large part of cell metabolism occurs here. Proteins within the cytosol play an important role in signal transduction pathways, glycolysis; also, they act as intracellular receptors and form part of the ribosomes, enabling further protein synthesis
Nitric oxide	Nitric oxide refers to gaseous signal molecule in both animals and plants. In animals it regulates smooth muscle contraction, for example; in plants it is involved in responses to injury or infection.
Hydrophilic	A hydrophilic molecule or portion of a molecule is one that is typically charge-polarized and capable of hydrogen bonding, enabling it to dissolve more readily in water than in oil or other hydrophobic solvents.
Hydrophobic	Hydrophobic refers to being electrically neutral and nonpolar, and thus prefering other neutral and nonpolar solvents or molecular environments. Hydrophobic is often used interchangeably with "oily" or "lipophilic."
Nucleus	In cell biology, the nucleus is found in all eukaryotic cells that contains most of the cell's genetic material. The nucleus has two primary functions: to control chemical reactions within the cytoplasm and to store information needed for cellular division.
Arginine	Arginine is an α-amino acid. The L-form is one of the 20 most common natural amino acids. In mammals, arginine is classified as a semiessential or conditionally essential amino acid, depending on the developmental stage and health status of the individual.

Go to **Cram101.com** for the Practice Tests for this Chapter.

Half-life	The half-life of a quantity subject to exponential decay is the time required for the quantity to fall to half of its initial value.
Nitrate	Nitrate refers to a salt of nitric acid; a compound containing the radical NO_3; biologically, the final form of nitrogen from the oxidation of organic nitrogen compounds.
Oxygen	Oxygen is a chemical element in the periodic table. It has the symbol O and atomic number 8. Oxygen is the second most common element on Earth, composing around 46% of the mass of Earth's crust and 28% of the mass of Earth as a whole, and is the third most common element in the universe.
Endothelial cell	The endothelial cell controls the passage of materials — and the transit of white blood cells — into and out of the bloodstream. In some organs, there are highly differentiated cells to perform specialized 'filtering' functions.
Blood vessel	A blood vessel is a part of the circulatory system and function to transport blood throughout the body. The most important types, arteries and veins, are so termed because they carry blood away from or towards the heart, respectively.
Penis	The penis is the male reproductive organ and for mammals additionally serves as the external male organ of urination.
Impotence	Erectile dysfunction, also known as impotence, is a sexual dysfunction characterized by the inability to develop or maintain an erection of the penis for satisfactory sexual intercourse regardless of the capability of ejaculation.
Smooth muscle	Smooth muscle is a type of non-striated muscle, found within the "walls" of hollow organs; such as blood vessels, the bladder, the uterus, and the gastrointestinal tract. Smooth muscle is used to move matter within the body, via contraction; it generally operates "involuntarily", without nerve stimulation.
Diffusion	Diffusion refers to the spontaneous movement of particles of any kind from where they are more concentrated to where they are less concentrated.
Thyroid hormones	The thyroid hormones, thyroxine (T4) and triiodothyronine (T3), are tyrosine-based hormones produced by the thyroid gland. An important component in the synthesis is iodine. They act on the body to increase the basal metabolic rate, affect protein synthesis and increase the body's sensitivity to catecholamines.
Steroid hormone	A lipid made from cholesterol that activates the transcription of specific genes in target cells is referred to as steroid hormone.
Testosterone	Testosterone is a steroid hormone from the androgen group. Testosterone is secreted in the testes of men and the ovaries of women. It is the principal male sex hormone and the "original" anabolic steroid. In both males and females, it plays key roles in health and well-being.
Estradiol	Estradiol is a sex hormone. Labelled the "female" hormone but also present in males it represents the major estrogen in humans. Critical for sexual functioning estradiol also supports bone growth.
Thyroxine	The thyroid hormone thyroxine is a tyrosine-based hormone produced by the thyroid gland. An important component in the synthesis is iodine. It acts on the body to increase the basal metabolic rate, affect protein synthesis and increase the body's sensitivity to catecholamines.
Cortisol	Cortisol is a corticosteroid hormone that is involved in the response to stress; it increases blood pressure and blood sugar levels and suppresses the immune system.
Gene regulatory	General name for any protein that binds to a specific DNA sequence to alter the expression of

Go to **Cram101.com** for the Practice Tests for this Chapter.

protein	a gene is referred to as gene regulatory protein.
Sex hormone	A hormone that controls the timing of reproduction and sexual characteristics in vertebrates is the sex hormone.
Genitalia	The Latin term genitalia is used to describe the sex organs, and in the English language this term and genital area are most often used to describe the externally visible sex organs or external genitalia: in males the penis and scrotum, in females the vulva.
Puberty	A time in the life of a developing individual characterized by the increasing production of sex hormones, which cause it to reach sexual maturity is called puberty.
Brain	The part of the central nervous system involved in regulating and controlling body activity and interpreting information from the senses transmitted through the nervous system is referred to as the brain.
Fetus	Fetus refers to a developing human from the ninth week of gestation until birth; has all the major structures of an adult.
Nuclear pore	Opening in the nuclear envelope which permits the passage of proteins into the nucleus and ribosomal subunits out of the nucleus is a nuclear pore.
Regulatory sequence	Regulatory sequence refers to dNA sequence to which a gene regulatory protein binds to control the rate of assembly of the transcirptional complex at the promoter.
Transcription	Transcription is the process through which a DNA sequence is enzymatically copied by an RNA polymerase to produce a complementary RNA. Or, in other words, the transfer of genetic information from DNA into RNA.
Human growth hormone	Human growth hormone is a polypeptide hormone synthesized and secreted by the anterior pituitary gland which stimulates growth and cell reproduction in humans and other vertebrate animals.
Recombinant DNA	Recombinant DNA is an artificial DNA sequence resulting from the combining of two other DNA sequences in a plasmid.
Domain	In biology, a domain is the top-level grouping of organisms in scientific classification.
X-Ray	X-Ray refers to diagnostic test in which an image is created using low doses of radiation.
G protein	G protein, short for guanine nucleotide binding proteins, are a family of proteins involved in second messenger cascades. They are so called because of their signaling mechanism, which uses the exchange of guanosine diphosphate (GDP) for guanosine triphosphate (GTP) as a molecular "switch" to allow or inhibit biochemical reactions inside the cell.
Ion channel	An ion channel is a pore-forming protein that helps establish the small voltage gradient that exists across the membrane of all living cells, by allowing the flow of ions down their electrochemical gradient. They are present in the membranes that surround all biological cells.
Enzyme activity	Enzyme activity is the catalytic effect exerted by an enzyme.
Tranquilizer	A sedative, or tranquilizer, is a drug that depresses the central nervous system (CNS), which causes calmness, relaxation, reduction of anxiety, sleepiness, slowed breathing, slurred speech, staggering gait, poor judgment, and slow, uncertain reflexes.
Heroin	Heroin is widely and illegally used as a powerful and addictive drug producing intense euphoria, which often disappears with increasing tolerance. Heroin is a semi-synthetic opioid. It is the 3,6-diacetyl derivative of morphine and is synthesized from it by acetylation.
Amplification	In molecular biology, amplification (polymerase chain reaction or PCR) is the method for

359

creating multiple copies of DNA (or RNA) without using a living organism, such as E. coli or yeast.

Membrane potential	Membrane potential is the electrical potential difference (voltage) across a cell's plasma membrane.
Conformation	The three-dimensional shape of a molecule is its conformation. The conformation is particularly important in proteins.
Ion	Ion refers to an atom or molecule that has gained or lost one or more electrons, thus acquiring an electrical charge.
G-protein	G-protein, short for guanine nucleotide binding proteins, are a family of proteins involved in second messenger cascades. They are so called because of their signaling mechanism, which uses the exchange of guanosine diphosphate (GDP) for guanosine triphosphate (GTP) as a molecular "switch" to allow or inhibit biochemical reactions inside the cell.
Transducer	Transducer refers to a device that converts signals from one form to another. A sensory receptor is a transducer that converts environmental stimuli, such as heat, light, or vibration, into electrical signals recognized by the nervous system.
Phosphate group	The functional group $-OPO_3H_2$; the transfer of energy from one compound to another is often accomplished by the transfer of a phosphate group.
Phosphate	A phosphate is a polyatomic ion or radical consisting of one phosphorus atom and four oxygen. In the ionic form, it carries a -3 formal charge, and is denoted $PO_4{}^{3-}$.
G-protein linked receptor	A signal receptor protein in the plasma membrane that responds to the binding signal molecule by activating a G protein is referred to as g-protein linked receptor.
Protein phosphatase	Protein phosphatase refers to an enzyme that removes phosphate groups from proteins, often functioning to reverse the effect of a protein kinase.
Phosphorylation	Phosphorylation refers to reaction in which a phosphate group becomes covalently coupled to another molecule.
Protein kinase	Enzyme that transfers the terminal phosphate group of ATP to a specific amino acid of a target protein is protein kinase.
Hydrolysis	Hydrolysis is a chemical process in which a molecule is cleaved into two parts by the addition of a molecule of water.
Ligand	Any molecule that binds to a specific receptor site on a protein or other molecule is called a ligand.
Transmembrane receptor	A transmembrane receptor is an integral membrane protein, which resides and operates typically within a cell's plasma membrane, but also in the membranes of some subcellular compartments and organelles. Binding to a signalling molecule or sometimes to a pair of such molecules on one side of the membrane, they initiate a response on the other side.
Lipid bilayer	A lipid bilayer is a membrane or zone of a membrane composed of lipid molecules (usually phospholipids). The lipid bilayer is a critical component of all biological membranes, including cell membranes, and is a prerequisite for cell-based organisms.
Photoreceptor	A photoreceptor is a specialized type of neuron that is capable of phototransduction. More specifically, the photoreceptor sends signals to other neurons by a change in its membrane potential when it absorbs photons.
Polypeptide	Polypeptide refers to polymer of many amino acids linked by peptide bonds.
Vertebrate	Vertebrate is a subphylum of chordates, specifically, those with backbones or spinal columns. They started to evolve about 530 million years ago during the Cambrian explosion, which is

	part of the Cambrian period.
Eye	An eye is an organ that detects light. Different kinds of light-sensitive organs are found in a variety of creatures.
Downstream	Downstream refers to a relative position in DNA or RNA. Relative to the position on the strand, downstream is the region towards the 3' end of the strand.
Protein subunit	A protein subunit is a single protein molecule that assembles (or "coassembles") with other protein molecules to form a multimeric or oligomeric protein. Many naturally-occurring proteins and enzymes are multimeric.
GTPase	Enzyme activity that converts GTP to GDP Also the common name used for monomeric GTP-binding proteins is GTPase.
Intestine	The intestine is the portion of the alimentary canal extending from the stomach to the anus and, in humans and mammals, consists of two segments, the small intestine and the large intestine. The intestine is the part of the body responsible for extracting nutrition from food.
Cholera	Cholera is a water-borne disease caused by the bacterium Vibrio cholerae, which are typically ingested by drinking contaminated water, or by eating improperly cooked fish, especially shellfish.
Toxin	Toxin refers to a microbial product or component that can injure another cell or organism at low concentrations. Often the term refers to a poisonous protein, but toxins may be lipids and other substances.
Pertussis	An acute, highly contagious infection of the respiratory tract, most frequently affecting young children, usually caused by Bordetella pertussis or B. parapertussis. Consists of peculiar paroxysms of coughing, ending in a prolonged crowing or whooping respiration.
Mutation	Mutation refers to a change in the nucleotide sequence of DNA; the ultimate source of genetic diversity.
Adenylyl cyclase	Adenylyl cyclase is a lyase, an enzyme that catalyzes the conversion of ATP to 3',5'-cyclic AMP (cAMP) and pyrophosphate. cAMP is an important molecule in eukaryotic signal transduction, a so-called second messenger.
Bacteria	The domain that contains procaryotic cells with primarily diacyl glycerol diesters in their membranes and with bacterial rRNA. Bacteria also is a general term for organisms that are composed of procaryotic cells and are not multicellular.
Dissociation	Dissociation is a general process in which complexes, molecules, or salts separate or split into smaller molecules, ions, or radicals, usually in a reversible manner.
Fiber	Fiber is a class of materials that are continuous filaments or are in discrete elongated pieces, similar to lengths of thread. They are of great importance in the biology of both plants and animals, for holding tissues together.
Inositol	Inositol, or cis-1,2,3,5-trans-4,6-cyclohexanehexol, is a cyclic polyalcohol that plays an important role as a second messenger in a cell, in the form of inositol phosphates. It is found in many foods, namely cereals with high bran content.
Second messenger	An intermediary compound that couples extracellular signals to intracellular processes and also amplifies a hormonal signal is referred to as second messenger.
Stimulant	A stimulant is a drug which increases the activity of the sympathetic nervous system and produces a sense of euphoria or awakeness.
Sugar	A sugar is the simplest molecule that can be identified as a carbohydrate. These include

Go to **Cram101.com** for the Practice Tests for this Chapter.

monosaccharides and disaccharides, trisaccharides and the oligosaccharides. The term "glyco-" indicates the presence of a sugar in an otherwise non-carbohydrate substance.

Fluorescence	Fluorescence is a luminescence that is mostly found as an optical phenomenon in cold bodies, in which the molecular absorption of a photon triggers the emission of a lower-energy photon with a longer wavelength. The energy difference between the absorbed and emitted photons ends up as molecular vibrations or heat.
Serotonin	Serotonin is a monoamine neurotransmitter synthesized in serotonergic neurons in the central nervous system and enterochromaffin cells in the gastrointestinal tract. It is believed to play an important part of the biochemistry of depression, migraine, bipolar disorder and anxiety.
Organelle	In cell biology, an organelle is one of several structures with specialized functions, suspended in the cytoplasm of a eukaryotic cell.
Adrenergic receptor	An adrenergic receptor is a class of G-protein coupled receptors that is the target of catecholamines. They specifically bind their endogenous ligands, the catecholamines adrenaline and noradrenaline (also called epinephrine and norepinephrine) and are activated by these.
Adrenaline	Adrenaline is a hormone released by chromaffin cells and by some neurons in response to stress. Produces 'fight or flight' responses, including increased heart rate and blood sugar levels.
Adrenal	In mammals, the adrenal glands are the triangle-shaped endocrine glands that sit atop the kidneys. They are chiefly responsible for regulating the stress response through the synthesis of corticosteroids and catecholamines, including cortisol and adrenaline.
Gland	A gland is an organ in an animal's body that synthesizes a substance for release such as hormones, often into the bloodstream or into cavities inside the body or its outer surface.
Glycogen	Glycogen refers to a complex, extensively branched polysaccharide of many glucose monomers; serves as an energy-storage molecule in liver and muscle cells.
Gene expression	Gene expression is the process by which a gene's information is converted into the structures and functions of a cell. Gene expression is a multi-step process that begins with transcription, post transcriptional modification and translation, followed by folding, post-translational modification and targeting.
Metabolism	Metabolism is the biochemical modification of chemical compounds in living organisms and cells. This includes the biosynthesis of complex organic molecules (anabolism) and their breakdown (catabolism).
Peptide hormone	Type of hormone that is a protein, a peptide, or is derived from an amino acid that is secreted into the blood stream and has endocrine functions in living animals is a peptide hormone.
Somatostatin	Somatostatin is hormone secreted not only by cells of the hypothalamus but also by so called delta cells of stomach, intestine and pancreas. It binds to somatostatin receptors. All actions of the hormone are inhibitory.
Hypothalamus	Located below the thalamus, the hypothalamus links the nervous system to the endocrine system by synthesizing and secreting neurohormones often called releasing hormones because they function by stimulating the secretion of hormones from the anterior pituitary gland.
Secretion	Secretion is the process of segregating, elaborating, and releasing chemicals from a cell, or a secreted chemical substance or amount of substance.
Phospholipid	Phospholipid is a class of lipids formed from four components: fatty acids, a negatively-

Go to **Cram101.com** for the Practice Tests for this Chapter.

charged phosphate group, an alcohol and a backbone. Phospholipids with a glycerol backbone are known as glycerophospholipids or phosphoglycerides.

DNA transcription	DNA transcription is the process through which a DNA sequence is enzymatically copied by an RNA polymerase to produce a complementary RNA. In the case of protein-encoding DNA, transcription is the beginning of the process that ultimately leads to the translation of the genetic code into a functional peptide or protein.
Lipid	Lipid is one class of aliphatic hydrocarbon-containing organic compounds essential for the structure and function of living cells. They are characterized by being water-insoluble but soluble in nonpolar organic solvents.
Endoplasmic reticulum	The endoplasmic reticulum is an organelle found in all eukaryotic cells. It modifies proteins, makes macromolecules, and transfers substances throughout the cell.
Sperm	Sperm refers to the male sex cell with three distinct parts at maturity: head, middle piece, and tail.
Egg	An egg is the zygote, resulting from fertilization of the ovum. It nourishes and protects the embryo.
Calmodulin	Calmodulin refers to ubiquitous calcium-binding protein whose binding to other proteins is governed by changes in intracellular $Ca2+$ concentration. Its binding modifies the activity of many target enzymes and membrane transport proteins.
Protozoa	Protozoa are single-celled eukaryotes (organisms with nuclei) that show some characteristics usually associated with animals, most notably mobility and heterotrophy. They are often grouped in the kingdom Protista together with the plant-like algae.
Helix	A helix is a twisted shape like a spring, screw or a spiral staircase. They are important in biology, as DNA and many proteins have spiral substructures, known a alpha helix.
Retina	The retina is a thin layer of cells at the back of the eyeball of vertebrates and some cephalopods; it is the part of the eye which converts light into nervous signals.
Opsin	Opsin is a group of light-sensitive, 7 pass transmembrane protein/pigment found in photoreceptor cells.
Vesicle	In cell biology, a vesicle is a relatively small and enclosed compartment, separated from the cytosol by at least one lipid bilayer.
Retinal	Retinal is fundamental in the transduction of light into visual signals in the photoreceptor level of the retina.
Rod cell	Rod cell refers to photoreceptor cells in the retina of the eye that can function in less intense light than can the other type of photoreceptor, cone cells. Since they are more light-sensitive, they are responsible for night vision. There are about 100 million of them in the human retina.
Photoreceptor cells	Photoreceptor cells are found in the retina of the eye and are responsible for transducing, or converting, light into nerve signals that can be ultimately transmitted to the brain via the optic nerve. In vertebrates, there are two types of photoreceptor cells called rods and cones.
Cone	Cone refers to a reproductive structure of gymnosperms that produces pollen in males or eggs in females.
Sunlight	Sunlight in the broad sense is the total spectrum of electromagnetic radiation given off by the Sun.
Negative	Negative feedback refers to a control mechanism in which a chemical reaction, metabolic

feedback	pathway, or hormonesecreting gland is inhibited by the products of the reaction, pathway, or gland.
Adaptation	A biological adaptation is an anatomical structure, physiological process or behavioral trait of an organism that has evolved over a period of time by the process of natural selection such that it increases the expected long-term reproductive success of the organism.
Migration	Migration occurs when living things move from one biome to another. In most cases organisms migrate to avoid local shortages of food, usually caused by winter. Animals may also migrate to a certain location to breed, as is the case with some fish.
Cancer	Cancer is a class of diseases or disorders characterized by uncontrolled division of cells and the ability of these cells to invade other tissues, either by direct growth into adjacent tissue through invasion or by implantation into distant sites by metastasis.
Side chain	In organic chemistry and biochemistry a side chain is a part of a molecule attached to a core structure. Often the side chain can vary for a given core. In biochemistry the peptide or protein side chains are the variable parts of amino acids extending from the peptide backbone.
Tyrosine	Tyrosine is one of the 20 amino acids that are used by cells to synthesize proteins. It plays a key role in signal transduction, since it can be tagged (phosphorylated) with a phosphate group by protein kinases to alter the functionality and activity of certain enzymes.
Tyrosine kinase	An enzyme that catalyzes the transfer of phosphate groups from ATP to the amino acid tyrosine on a substrate protein is called tyrosine kinase.
Dimer	A dimer refers to a molecule composed of two similar subunits or monomers linked together. It is a special case of a polymer.
Phosphatase	A phosphatase is an enzyme that hydrolyses phosphoric acid monoesters into a phosphate ion and a molecule with a free hydroxyl group.
Endocytosis	Endocytosis is a process where cells absorb material (molecules or other cells) from outside by engulfing it with their cell membranes.
Digestion	Digestion refers to the mechanical and chemical breakdown of food into molecules small enough for the body to absorb; the second main stage of food processing, following ingestion.
Lysosome	Lysosome refers to a digestive organelle in eukaryotic cells; contains hydrolytic enzymes that digest the cell's food and wastes. They are found in both plant and animal cells, and are built in the Golgi apparatus.
Threonine	Nutritionally, in humans, threonine is an essential amino acid. Threonine contains two chiral centers, so there are four possible stereoisomers of threonine, or two possible diastereomers of L-threonine.
Serine	Serine, organic compound, one of the 20 amino acids commonly found in animal proteins. Only the L-stereoisomer appears in mammalian protein. It is not essential to the human diet, since it can be synthesized in the body from other metabolites, including glycine.
Cell division	Cell division is the process by which a cell (called the parent cell) divides into two cells (called daughter cells). Cell division is usually a small segment of a larger cell cycle. In meiosis, however, a cell is permanently transformed and cannot divide again.
Growth factor	Growth factor is a protein that acts as a signaling molecule between cells (like cytokines and hormones) that attaches to specific receptors on the surface of a target cell and promotes differentiation and maturation of these cells.
Adaptor protein	An adaptor protein is a protein which is accessory to main proteins in a signal transduction pathway. These proteins tend to lack any intrinsic enzymatic activity themselves but instead

mediate specific protein-protein interactions that drive the formation of protein complexes.

RAS protein	Ras protein refers to very important molecular switches for a wide variety of signal pathways that control such processes as cytoskeletal integrity, proliferation, cell adhesion, apoptosis, and cell migration.
Antibody	An antibody is a protein used by the immune system to identify and neutralize foreign objects like bacteria and viruses. Each antibody recognizes a specific antigen unique to its target.
Radioactive	A term used to describe the property of releasing energy or particles from an unstable atom is called radioactive.
Substrate	A substrate is a molecule which is acted upon by an enzyme. Each enzyme recognizes only the specific substrate of the reaction it catalyzes. A surface in or on which an organism lives.
Dominant negative	Dominant negative refers to mechanism of dominance in which some alleles of genes encode subunits of multimers that block the activity of the subunits produced by wild-type alleles.
Mutagen	A chemical or physical agent that interacts with DNA and causes a mutation is referred to as mutagen.
Fruit	A fruit is the ripened ovary—together with seeds—of a flowering plant. In many species, the fruit incorporates the ripened ovary and surrounding tissues.
Alanine	Alanine (Ala) also 2-aminopropanoic acid is a non-essential α-amino acid. It exists as two distinct enantiomers - L-alanine and D-alanine. L-alanine is one of the 20 amino acids most widely used in protein synthesis, second to leucine.
Genetic screen	A genetic screen is a procedure or test to identify and select individuals which possess a phenotype of interest. A genetic screen for new genes is often referred to as forward genetics as opposed to reverse genetics that is the term used for identifying mutant alleles in genes that are already known.
Insertion	At DNA level, an insertion means the insertion of a few base pairs into a genetic sequence. This can often happen in microsatellite regions due to the DNA polymerase slipping.
Upstream	Upstream refers to movement opposite the direction RNA follows when moving along a gene.
Cytokine	A cytokine is a soluble proteinaceous substance produced by a wide variety of haemopoietic and non-haemopoietic cell types, and is critical to the functioning of both innate and adaptive immune responses.
Cytokine Receptor	Type of cell-surface receptor whose ligands are cytokines such as interferons, growth hormone and prolactin, and which acts through the Jak-STAT pathway is a cytokine receptor.
Activator	An activator, is a DNA-binding protein that regulates one or more genes by increasing the rate of transcription.
Sequencing	Determining the order of nucleotides in a DNA or RNA molecule or the order of amino acids in a protein is sequencing.
Genome	The genome of an organism is the whole hereditary information of an organism that is encoded in the DNA (or, for some viruses, RNA). This includes both the genes and the non-coding sequences. The genome of an organism is a complete DNA sequence of one set of chromosomes.
Germination	The resumption of growth and development by a spore or seed is called germination. It is the process in botany where growth emerges from a resting stage.
Ethylene	Ethylene functions as a hormone in plants. It stimulates Ethylene (or IUPAC name ethene) is the simplest alkene hydrocarbon, consisting of four hydrogen atoms and two carbon atoms connected by a double bond.

Histidine	Histidine is one of the 20 most common natural amino acids present in proteins. In the nutritional sense, in humans, histidine is considered an essential amino acid, but mostly only in children.
Blood	Blood is a circulating tissue composed of fluid plasma and cells. The main function of blood is to supply nutrients (oxygen, glucose) and constitutional elements to tissues and to remove waste products.
Apoptosis	In biology, apoptosis is one of the main types of programmed cell death (PCD). As such, it is a process of deliberate life relinquishment by an unwanted cell in a multicellular organism.
Membrane protein	A membrane protein is a protein molecule that is attached to, or associated with the membrane of a cell or an organelle. Membrane proteins can be classified into two groups, based on their attachment to the membrane.
Sarcoplasmic reticulum	Smooth endoplasmic reticulum of skeletal muscle cells specially adapted for calcium ion storage and release is called sarcoplasmic reticulum.

Go to **Cram101.com** for the Practice Tests for this Chapter.
And, **NEVER** highlight a book again!

Cytoskeleton	Cytoskeleton refers to a meshwork of fine fibers in the cytoplasm of a eukaryotic cell; includes microfilaments, intermediate filaments, and microtubules.
Animal cell	An animal cell is a form of eukaryotic cell which make up many tissues in animals. The animal cell is distinct from other eukaryotes, most notably those of plants, as they lack cell walls and chloroplasts, and they have smaller vacuoles.
Cell wall	Cell wall refers to a protective layer external to the plasma membrane in plant cells, bacteria, fungi, and some protists; protects the cell and helps maintain its shape.
Cytoplasm	Cytoplasm refers to everything inside a cell between the plasma membrane and the nucleus; consists of a semifluid medium and organelles.
Filament	The stamen is the male organ of a flower. Each stamen generally has a stalk called the filament, and, on top of the filament, an anther. The filament is a long chain of proteins, such as those found in hair, muscle, or in flagella.
Protein	A protein is a complex, high-molecular-weight organic compound that consists of amino acids joined by peptide bonds. They are essential to the structure and function of all living cells and viruses. Many are enzymes or subunits of enzymes.
Cell	The cell is the structural and functional unit of all living organisms, and is sometimes called the "building block of life."
Skeleton	In biology, the skeleton or skeletal system is the biological system providing physical support in living organisms.
Muscle	Muscle is a contractile form of tissue. It is one of the four major tissue types, the other three being epithelium, connective tissue and nervous tissue. Muscle contraction is used to move parts of the body, as well as to move substances within the body.
Embryo	Embryo refers to a developing stage of a multicellular organism. In humans, the stage in the development of offspring from the first division of the zygote until body structures begin to appear, about the ninth week of gestation.
Sperm	Sperm refers to the male sex cell with three distinct parts at maturity: head, middle piece, and tail.
Egg	An egg is the zygote, resulting from fertilization of the ovum. It nourishes and protects the embryo.
Cell division	Cell division is the process by which a cell (called the parent cell) divides into two cells (called daughter cells). Cell division is usually a small segment of a larger cell cycle. In meiosis, however, a cell is permanently transformed and cannot divide again.
Daughter cell	A cell formed by cell division of a parent cell is a daughter cell.
Segregation	The separation of homologous chromosomes during mitosis and meiosis. Known as Mendel's theory of Segregation.
Chromosome	A chromosome is, minimally, a very long, continuous piece of DNA, which contains many genes, regulatory elements and other intervening nucleotide sequences.
Organelle	In cell biology, an organelle is one of several structures with specialized functions, suspended in the cytoplasm of a eukaryotic cell.
Mitosis	Mitosis is the process by which a cell separates its duplicated genome into two identical halves. It is generally followed immediately by cytokinesis which divides the cytoplasm and cell membrane.
Bacteria	The domain that contains procaryotic cells with primarily diacyl glycerol diesters in their membranes and with bacterial rRNA. Bacteria also is a general term for organisms that are

Go to **Cram101.com** for the Practice Tests for this Chapter.

composed of procaryotic cells and are not multicellular.

Intermediate filament	Intermediate filament refers to an intermediate-sized protein fiber that is one of the three main kinds of fibers making up the cytoskeleton of eukaryotic cells; ropelike, made of fibrous proteins.
Actin filament	An actin filament is a helical protein filament formed by the polymerization of globular actin molecules. They provide mechanical support for the cell, determine the cell shape, enable cell movements; and participate in certain cell junctions.
Microtubule	Microtubule is a protein structure found within cells, one of the components of the cytoskeleton. They have diameter of ~ 24 nm and varying length from several micrometers to possible millimeters in axons of nerve cells. They serve as structural components within cells and are involved in many cellular processes including mitosis, cytokinesis, and vesicular transport.
Protein subunit	A protein subunit is a single protein molecule that assembles (or "coassembles") with other protein molecules to form a multimeric or oligomeric protein. Many naturally-occurring proteins and enzymes are multimeric.
Tubulin	The protein subunit of microtubules is referred to as tubulin.
Actin	Actin is a globular protein that polymerizes helically forming filaments, which like the other two components of the cellular cytoskeleton form a three-dimensional network inside an eukaryotic cell. They provide mechanical support for the cell, determine the cell shape, enable cell movements .
Fibroblast	A fibroblast is a cell that makes the structural fibers and ground substance of connective tissue.
Skin	Skin is an organ of the integumentary system composed of a layer of tissues that protect underlying muscles and organs.
Smooth muscle	Smooth muscle is a type of non-striated muscle, found within the "walls" of hollow organs; such as blood vessels, the bladder, the uterus, and the gastrointestinal tract. Smooth muscle is used to move matter within the body, via contraction; it generally operates "involuntarily", without nerve stimulation.
Myosin	Myosin is a large family of motor proteins found in eukaryotic tissues. They are responsible for actin-based motility.
Epithelial	Functions of epithelial cells include secretion, absorption, protection, transcellular transport, sensation detection, and selective permeability.
Heterogeneous	A heterogeneous compound, mixture, or other such object is one that consists of many different items, which are often not easily sorted or separated, though they are clearly distinct.
Fiber	Fiber is a class of materials that are continuous filaments or are in discrete elongated pieces, similar to lengths of thread. They are of great importance in the biology of both plants and animals, for holding tissues together.
Inner nuclear membrane	Inner nuclear membrane refers to the innermost of the two nuclear membranes. It contains binding sites for chromatin and the nuclear lamina on its internal face.
Nuclear lamina	Nuclear lamina refers to fibrous meshwork of proteins on the inner surface of the inner nuclear membrane. It is made up of a network of intermediate filaments formed from nuclear lamins.
Microtubule-organizing	Region in a cell, such as a centrosome or a basal body, from which microtubules grow is called a microtubule-organizing center.

Go to **Cram101.com** for the Practice Tests for this Chapter.

center	
Centrosome	Centrosome refers to material in the cytoplasm of a eukaryotic cell that gives rise to microtubules; important in mitosis and meiosis; also called microtubule-organizing center.
Microfilament	Microfilament refers to the thinnest of the three main kinds of protein fibers making up the cytoskeleton of a eukaryotic cell; a solid, helical rod composed of the globular protein actin.
Helical	A helix is a twisted shape like a spring, screw or a spiral staircase. Helices are important in biology, as DNA is helical and many proteins have helical substructures, known as alpha helices.
Polymer	Polymer is a generic term used to describe a very long molecule consisting of structural units and repeating units connected by covalent chemical bonds.
Plasma membrane	Membrane surrounding the cytoplasm that consists of a phospholipid bilayer with embedded proteins is referred to as plasma membrane.
Cortex	In anatomy and zoology the cortex is the outermost or superficial layer of an organ or the outer portion of the stem or root of a plant.
Micrograph	A micrograph is a photograph or similar image taken through a microscope or similar device to show a magnified image of an item.
Nuclear envelope	The nuclear envelope refers to the double membrane of the nucleus that encloses genetic material in eukaryotic cells. It separates the contents of the nucleus (DNA in particular) from the cytosol.
Desmosome	A strong cell-tocell junction that attaches adjacent cells to one another is referred to as desmosome.
Nucleus	In cell biology, the nucleus is found in all eukaryotic cells that contains most of the cell's genetic material. The nucleus has two primary functions: to control chemical reactions within the cytoplasm and to store information needed for cellular division.
Epithelium	Epithelium is a tissue composed of a layer of cells. Epithelium can be found lining internal (e.g. endothelium, which lines the inside of blood vessels) or external (e.g. skin) free surfaces of the body. Functions include secretion, absorption and protection.
Electron	The electron is a light fundamental subatomic particle that carries a negative electric charge. The electron is a spin-1/2 lepton, does not participate in strong interactions and has no substructure.
Domain	In biology, a domain is the top-level grouping of organisms in scientific classification.
Coiled-coil	Especially stable rodlike structure in proteins which is formed by two of these a helices coiled around each other is a coiled-coil.
Amino acid	An amino acid is any molecule that contains both amino and carboxylic acid functional groups. They are the basic structural building units of proteins. They form short polymer chains called peptides or polypeptides which in turn form structures called proteins.
Tetramer	A tetramer is a protein with four subunits. There are homo-tetramers (all subunits are identical) such as glutathione S-transferase, dimers of hetero-dimers such as haemoglobin (a dimer of an alpha/beta dimer), and hetero-tetramers, where each subunit is different.
Dimer	A dimer refers to a molecule composed of two similar subunits or monomers linked together. It is a special case of a polymer.
Monomer	In chemistry, a monomer is a small molecule that may become chemically bonded to other monomers to form a polymer.

Go to **Cram101.com** for the Practice Tests for this Chapter.

Element	A chemical element, often called simply element, is a chemical substance that cannot be divided or changed into other chemical substances by any ordinary chemical technique. An element is a class of substances that contain the same number of protons in all its atoms.
Matrix	In biology, matrix (plural: matrices) is the material between animal or plant cells, the material (or tissue) in which more specialized structures are embedded, and a specific part of the mitochondrion that is the site of oxidation of organic molecules.
Carbon	Carbon is a chemical element in the periodic table that has the symbol C and atomic number 6. An abundant nonmetallic, tetravalent element, carbon has several allotropic forms.
Connective-tissue cell	Connective-tissue cell refers to any of the various cell types found in connective tissue, e.g. Fibroblasts, cartilage cells, bone cells, fat cells and smooth muscle cells.
Nuclear membrane	The double layered structure surrounding the nucleus that separates the nucleoplasm from the cytoplasm is referred to as nuclear membrane.
Supporting cell	In the nervous system, a cell that protects, insulates, and reinforces a neuron is called a supporting cell. A cell that bears one or more carpagonial branches.
Nervous system	The nervous system of an animal coordinates the activity of the muscles, monitors the organs, constructs and processes input from the senses, and initiates actions.
Polymerization	Polymerization is a process of reacting monomer molecules together in a chemical reaction to form linear chains or a three-dimensional network of polymer chains.
Nuclear lamin	Protein subunit of the intermediate filaments of the nuclear lamina is nuclear lamin.
Neurofilament	Neurofilament refers to a family of intermediate filaments that are found in high concentrations along the axons of vertebrate neurons.
Nerve cell	A cell specialized to originate or transmit nerve impulses is referred to as nerve cell.
Keratin	Keratin is a family of fibrous structural proteins; tough and insoluble, they form the hard but nonmineralized structures found in reptiles, birds and mammals.
Epidermis	Epidermis is the outermost layer of the skin. It forms the waterproof, protective wrap over the body's surface and is made up of stratified squamous epithelium with an underlying basement membrane. It contains no blood vessels, and is nourished by diffusion from the dermis. In plants, the outermost layer of cells covering the leaves and young parts of a plant is the epidermis.
Mutation	Mutation refers to a change in the nucleotide sequence of DNA; the ultimate source of genetic diversity.
Gene	Gene refers to a discrete unit of hereditary information consisting of a specific nucleotide sequence in DNA . Most of the genes of a eukaryote are located in its chromosomal DNA; a few are carried by the DNA of mitochondria and chloroplasts.
Muscular dystrophy	The muscular dystrophy is a group of genetic and hereditary muscle diseases; characterized by progressive skeletal muscle weakness, defects in muscle proteins, and the death of muscle cells and tissue. In some forms of muscular dystrophy, cardiac and smooth muscles are affected.
Tissue	Group of similar cells which perform a common function is called tissue.
Lamin	Lamin refers to paired chromosome in meiosis in immature amphibian eggs, in which the chromatin forms large stiff loops extending out from the linear axis of the chromosome.
Nerve	A nerve is an enclosed, cable-like bundle of nerve fibers or axons, which includes the glia that ensheath the axons in myelin.

Go to **Cram101.com** for the Practice Tests for this Chapter.

Linkage	Linkage refers to the patterns of assortment of genes that are located on the same chromosome. Important because if the genes are located relatively far apart, crossing over is more likely to occur between them than if they are close together.
Escherichia coli	Escherichia coli is one of the main species of bacteria that live in the lower intestines of warm-blooded animals, including birds and mammals. They are necessary for the proper digestion of food and are part of the intestinal flora. Its presence in groundwater is a common indicator of fecal contamination.
Digestive tract	The digestive tract is the system of organs within multicellular animals which takes in food, digests it to extract energy and nutrients, and expels the remaining waste.
Spinal cord	The spinal cord is a part of the vertebrate nervous system that is enclosed in and protected by the vertebral column (it passes through the spinal canal). It consists of nerve cells. The spinal cord carries sensory signals and motor innervation to most of the skeletal muscles in the body.
Amoeba	Amoeba is a genus of protozoa that moves by means of temporary projections called pseudopods, and is well-known as a representative unicellular organism. Amoeba itself is found in freshwater, typically on decaying vegetation from streams, but is not especially common in nature.
Chromatin	Chromatin refers to the combination of DNA and proteins that constitute chromosomes; often used to refer to the diffuse, very extended form taken by the chromosomes when a eukaryotic cell is not dividing.
Oocyte	An oocyte is a female gametocyte. Such that an oocyte is large and essentially stationary. The oocyte becomes functional when a lala (male gametocyte) attaches to it, thus allowing the meiosis of the secondary oocyte to occur.
Lamina	A structurally complete leaf of an angiosperm consists of a petiole (leaf stem), a lamina (leaf blade), and stipules (small processes located to either side of the base of the petiole).
Mitotic spindle	Mitotic spindle refers to a spindle-shaped structure formed of microtubules and associated proteins that is involved in the movement of chromosomes during mitosis and meiosis.
Flagellum	A flagellum is a whip-like organelle that many unicellular organisms, and some multicellular ones, use to move about.
Cilium	A cilium is an organelle projecting from a eukaryotic cell. They are extensions of the plasma membrane containing doublets of parallel microtubules.
Motor protein	Protein that uses energy derived from nucleoside triphosphate hydrolysis to propel itself along a protein filament or another polymeric molecule is called motor protein.
Globular protein	Globular protein refers to any protein with an approximately rounded shape. Such proteins are contrasted with highly elongated, fibrous proteins such as collagen.
Molecule	A molecule is the smallest particle of a pure chemical substance that still retains its chemical composition and properties.
Minus end	The end of a microtubule or actin filament at which the addition of monomers occurs least readily; the 'slow-growing' end of the microtubule or actin filament is called the minus end.
Plus end	The end of a microtubule or actin filament at which addition of monomers occurs most readily; the 'fast-growing' end of a microtubule or actin filament. The plus end of an actin filament is also known as the barbed end.
In vitro	In vitro is an experimental technique where the experiment is performed in a test tube, or generally outside a living organism or cell.

Go to **Cram101.com** for the Practice Tests for this Chapter.

Basal body	A basal body is an organelle formed from a centriole, a short cylindrical array of microtubules. It is found at the base of a eukaryotic cell cilium or flagellum and serves as a nucleation site for the growth of the axoneme microtubules.
Polarity	In cell biology, polarity refers to cells not being point-symmetrical in their spatial organization. In horticulture, polarity refers to the condition in which cuttings grow shoots at the distil end and roots at the proximal end.
Electron microscope	The electron microscope is a microscope that can magnify very small details with high resolving power due to the use of electrons as the source of illumination, magnifying at levels up to 500,000 times.
Cell nucleus	The cell nucleus is found in all eukaryotic cells that contains most of the cell's genetic material. They have two primary functions: to control chemical reactions within the cytoplasm and to store information needed for cellular division.
Nucleation	Nucleation is the onset of a phase transition in a small but stable region.
Centriole	A centriole is a barrel shaped microtubule structure found in most animal cells, and cells of fungi and algae though not frequently in plants. The walls of each centriole are usually composed of nine triplet microtubules.
Plant cell	A cell that is a structural and functional unit of a plant is a plant cell.
Hydrolyze	Hydrolyze refers to break a chemical bond, as in a peptide linkage, with the insertion of the components of water, -H and -OH, at the cleaved ends of a chain. The digestion of proteins is hydrolysis.
Stem	Stem refers to that part of a plant's shoot system that supports the leaves and reproductive structures.
Conformation	The three-dimensional shape of a molecule is its conformation. The conformation is particularly important in proteins.
Cytosol	The cytosol is the internal fluid of the cell, and a large part of cell metabolism occurs here. Proteins within the cytosol play an important role in signal transduction pathways, glycolysis; also, they act as intracellular receptors and form part of the ribosomes, enabling further protein synthesis
Competent	Description of a state of cells able to take up DNA from the medium is called competent.
Cancer cell	A cell that divides and reproduces abnormally and has the potential to spread throughout the body, crowding out normal cells and tissue is referred to as a cancer cell.
Colchicine	Colchicine is a highly poisonous alkaloid, originally extracted from plants of the genus Colchicum. Originally used to treat rheumatic complaints and especially gout, it was also prescribed for its cathartic and emetic effects. Its present use is mainly in the treatment of gout.
Cell cortex	Cell cortex refers to specialized layer of cytoplasm on the inner face of the plasma membrane. It functions as a mechanical support of the plasma membrane. In animal cells it is an actin-rich layer responsible for movements of the cell surface.
Golgi apparatus	Golgi apparatus refers to an organelle in eukaryotic cells consisting of stacks of membranous sacs that modify, store, and ship products of the endoplasmic reticulum.
Secretion	Secretion is the process of segregating, elaborating, and releasing chemicals from a cell, or a secreted chemical substance or amount of substance.
Axon	An axon is a long slender projection of a nerve cell, or neuron, which conducts electrical impulses away from the neuron's cell body or soma. They are in effect the primary

transmission lines of the nervous system, and as bundles they help make up nerves.

Axon terminal	A swelling at the end of an axon that is designed to release a chemical substance onto another neuron, muscle cell, or gland cell is called the axon terminal.
Membrane protein	A membrane protein is a protein molecule that is attached to, or associated with the membrane of a cell or an organelle. Membrane proteins can be classified into two groups, based on their attachment to the membrane.
Cell body	The part of a cell, such as a neuron, that houses the nucleus is the cell body.
Diffusion	Diffusion refers to the spontaneous movement of particles of any kind from where they are more concentrated to where they are less concentrated.
Microtubule-associated protein	Microtubule-associated protein refers to any protein that binds to microtubules and modifies their properties. Many different kinds have been found, including structural proteins, such as MAP-2, and motor proteins, such as dynein.
Distribution	Distribution in pharmacology is a branch of pharmacokinetics describing reversible transfer of drug from one location to another within the body.
Light microscope	An optical instrument with lenses that refract visible light to magnify images and project them into a viewer's eye or onto photographic film is referred to as light microscope.
Mitochondria	Mitochondria are organelles found in most eukaryotic cells, including those of plants, animals, fungi, and protists. Mitochondria are sometimes described as "cellular power plants", because their primary function is to convert organic materials into energy in the form of ATP.
Vesicle	In cell biology, a vesicle is a relatively small and enclosed compartment, separated from the cytosol by at least one lipid bilayer.
Kinesin	Kinesin is a class of motor protein dimer found in biological cells. A kinesin attaches to microtubules, and moves along the tubule in order to transport cellular cargo, such as vesicles.
Dynein	Member of a family of large motor proteins that undergo ATP-dependent movement along microtubules. In cilia, dynein forms the side arms in the axoneme that cause adjacent microtubule doublets to slide past one another.
Enzyme	An enzyme is a protein that catalyzes, or speeds up, a chemical reaction. They are essential to sustain life because most chemical reactions in biological cells would occur too slowly, or would lead to different products, without them.
ATPase	ATPase is a class of enzymes that catalyze the decomposition of adenosine triphosphate into adenosine diphosphate and a free phosphate ion. This dephosphorylation reaction releases energy, which the enzyme harnesses to drive other chemical reactions that would not otherwise occur. This process is widely used in all known forms of life.
Heavy chain	The larger of the two types of polypeptide in an immunoglobulin molecule is referred to as heavy chain.
Polypeptide	Polypeptide refers to polymer of many amino acids linked by peptide bonds.
Inhibitor	An inhibitor is a type of effector (biology) that decreases or prevents the rate of a chemical reaction. They are often called negative catalysts.
Substrate	A substrate is a molecule which is acted upon by an enzyme. Each enzyme recognizes only the specific substrate of the reaction it catalyzes. A surface in or on which an organism lives.
Active transport	Active transport is the mediated transport of biochemicals, and other atomic/molecular substances, across membranes. In this form of transport, molecules move against either an

Go to **Cram101.com** for the Practice Tests for this Chapter.

	electrical or concentration gradient.
Cell membrane	A component of every biological cell, the selectively permeable cell membrane is a thin and structured bilayer of phospholipid and protein molecules that envelopes the cell. It separates a cell's interior from its surroundings and controls what moves in and out.
Ion	Ion refers to an atom or molecule that has gained or lost one or more electrons, thus acquiring an electrical charge.
Microscopy	Microscopy is any technique for producing visible images of structures or details too small to otherwise be seen by the human eye, using a microscope or other magnification tool.
Axoplasm	Axoplasm is the cytoplasm within the axon of a neuron. Neural processes (axons and dendrites) contain about 99.6% of the cell's cytoplasm, and 99.7% of that is in the axons.
Microscope	A microscope is an instrument for viewing objects that are too small to be seen by the naked or unaided eye.
Motility	Motility is the ability to move spontaneously and independently. The term can apply to single cells, or to multicellular organisms.
Buffer	A chemical substance that resists changes in pH by accepting H^+ ions from or donating H^+ ions to solutions is called a buffer.
Translocation	A chromosomal mutation in which a portion of one chromosome breaks off and becomes attached to another chromosome is referred to as translocation.
Active site	The active site of an enzyme is the binding site where catalysis occurs. The structure and chemical properties of the active site allow the recognition and binding of the substrate.
Silica	Silica is a mineral similar to glass that is the major component of the cell wall, shell, or skeleton of many marine organisms.
Optical tweezer	Optical tweezer refers to the use of a focused laser beam to drag and isolate a specific microorganism from a complex microbial mixture oral candidiasis.
Hydrolysis	Hydrolysis is a chemical process in which a molecule is cleaved into two parts by the addition of a molecule of water.
Endoplasmic reticulum	The endoplasmic reticulum is an organelle found in all eukaryotic cells. It modifies proteins, makes macromolecules, and transfers substances throughout the cell.
Cell center	Cell center is the centrally located organelle of animal cells that is the primary microtubule-organizing center and is duplicated to form the spindle poles during mitosis. In most animal cells it contains a pair of centrioles.
Receptor protein	Protein located in the plasma membrane or within the cell that binds to a substance that alters some metabolic aspect of the cell is referred to as receptor protein. It will only link up with a substance that has a certain shape that allows it to bind to the receptor.
Cilia	Numerous short, hairlike structures projecting from the cell surface that enable locomotion are cilia.
Respiratory tract	In humans the respiratory tract is the part of the anatomy that has to do with the process of respiration or breathing.
Organ	Organ refers to a structure consisting of several tissues adapted as a group to perform specific functions.
Flagella	Flagella are whip-like organelle that many unicellular organisms, and some multicellular ones, use to move about.
Protozoa	Protozoa are single-celled eukaryotes (organisms with nuclei) that show some characteristics

Go to **Cram101.com** for the Practice Tests for this Chapter.

usually associated with animals, most notably mobility and heterotrophy. They are often grouped in the kingdom Protista together with the plant-like algae.

Mucus	Mucus is a slippery secretion of the lining of various membranes in the body (mucous membranes). Mucus aids in the protection of the lungs by trapping foreign particles that enter the nose during normal breathing. Additionally, it prevents tissues from drying out.
Stroke	A stroke or cerebrovascular accident (CVA) occurs when the blood supply to a part of the brain is suddenly interrupted.
Tunicate	One of a group of invertebrate chordates in the subphylum of saclike filter feeders with input and output siphons is referred to as a tunicate.
Plasma	In physics and chemistry, a plasma is an ionized gas, and is usually considered to be a distinct phase of matter. "Ionized" in this case means that at least one electron has been dissociated from a significant fraction of the molecules.
Phagocytosis	Phagocytosis is a form of endocytosis where large particles are enveloped by the cell membrane of a (usually larger) cell and internalized to form a phagosome, or "food vacuole."
Actin-binding protein	Actin-binding protein refers to protein that associates with either actin monomers or actin filaments in cells and modifies their properties. Examples include myosin, a-actinin, and profilin.
Contractile ring	Ring containing actin and myosin that forms under the surface of animal cells undergoing cell division and contracts to pinch the two daughter cells apart is a contractile ring.
Lamellipodia	The lamellipodia are cytoskeletal actin projections on the mobile edge of the cell. It is essentially a two-dimensional actin mesh that pulls the cell across a substrate. Within the lamellipodia are ribs of actin called microspikes, which, when they spread beyond the lamellipodium frontier, are called filopodia.
Filopodia	The filopodia are slender cytoplasmic projections, similar to lamellipodia, which extend from the leading edge of migrating cells.
Helix	A helix is a twisted shape like a spring, screw or a spiral staircase. They are important in biology, as DNA and many proteins have spiral substructures, known a alpha helix.
Nucleoside	Molecule composed of a purine or pyrimidine base covalently linked to a ribose or deoxyribose sugar is a nucleoside.
Nucleotide	A nucleotide is a chemical compound that consists of a heterocyclic base, a sugar, and one or more phosphate groups. In the most common nucleotides the base is a derivative of purine or pyrimidine, and the sugar is pentose - deoxyribose or ribose. They are the structural units of RNA and DNA.
Sponge	An invertebrates that consist of a complex aggregation of cells, including collar cells, and has a skeleton of fibers and/or spicules is a sponge. They are primitive, sessile, mostly marine, waterdwelling filter feeders that pump water through their matrix to filter out particulates of food matter.
Toxin	Toxin refers to a microbial product or component that can injure another cell or organism at low concentrations. Often the term refers to a poisonous protein, but toxins may be lipids and other substances.
Dynamic equilibrium	The condition in which molecules are equally dispersed, therefore movement is equal in all directions is dynamic equilibrium.
Spectrin	Spectrin is a cytoskeletal protein that lines the intracellular side of the plasma membrane of many cell types in pentagonal or hexagonal arrangements, forming a scaffolding and playing an important role in maintenance of plasma membrane integrity and cytoskeletal structure

Go to **Cram101.com** for the Practice Tests for this Chapter.

Ankyrin	Protein mainly responsible for attaching the spectrin cytoskeleton to the red blood cell plasma membrane is called ankyrin.
Vertebrate	Vertebrate is a subphylum of chordates, specifically, those with backbones or spinal columns. They started to evolve about 530 million years ago during the Cambrian explosion, which is part of the Cambrian period.
Neutrophil	Neutrophil refers to phagocytic white blood cell that can engulf bacteria and viruses in infected tissue; part of the body's nonspecific defense system.
Blood	Blood is a circulating tissue composed of fluid plasma and cells. The main function of blood is to supply nutrients (oxygen, glucose) and constitutional elements to tissues and to remove waste products.
Growth factor	Growth factor is a protein that acts as a signaling molecule between cells (like cytokines and hormones) that attaches to specific receptors on the surface of a target cell and promotes differentiation and maturation of these cells.
Growth cone	Migrating motile tip of a growing nerve cell axon or dendrite is called growth cone. It is a actin-supported extension of a developing axon seeking its synaptic target.
Substratum	Substratum is the underlying layer, or base to which a lichen is fixed.
Transmembrane protein	Membrane protein that extends through the lipid bilayer, with part of its mass on either side of the membrane is referred to as a transmembrane protein.
Extracellular matrix	Extracellular matrix is any material part of a tissue that is not part of any cell. Extracellular matrix is the defining feature of connective tissue.
Integrin	An integrin is an integral membrane protein in the plasma membrane of cells. It plays a role in the attachment of a cell to the extracellular matrix (ECM) and in signal transduction from the ECM to the cell.
Filopodium	Thin, spike-like protrusion with an actin filament core, generated on the leading edge of a crawling animal cell is referred to as filopodium.
Staining	Staining is a biochemical technique of adding a class-specific (DNA, proteins, lipids, carbohydrates) dye to a substrate to qualify or quantify the presence of a specific compound. They are frequently used to highlight structures in tissues for viewing, often with the aid of different microscopes.
Fixation	Fixation in population genetics occurs when the frequency of a gene reaches 1.Fixation in biochemistry, histology, cell biology and pathology refers to the technique of preserving a specimen for microscopic study, making it intact and stable, but dead.
Skeletal muscle	Skeletal muscle is a type of striated muscle, attached to the skeleton. They are used to facilitate movement, by applying force to bones and joints; via contraction. They generally contract voluntarily (via nerve stimulation), although they can contract involuntarily.
Rearrangement	A change in the usual order and arrangement of genetic material either within the chromosome complement or within a gene locus is rearrangement. Where the nature of the rearrangement has been determined, the type may be searched for directly under the following designations: reciprocal translocation, Robertsonian translocation, insertion, transposition, inversion, deletion, and duplication.
Muscle fiber	Cell with myofibrils containing actin and myosin filaments arranged within sarcomeres is a muscle fiber.
Muscle contraction	A muscle contraction occurs when a muscle cell (called a muscle fiber) shortens. There are three general types: skeletal, heart, and smooth.

Cardiac muscle	Cardiac muscle is a type of striated muscle found within the heart. Its function is to "pump" blood through the circulatory system. Unlike skeletal muscle, which contracts in response to nerve stimulation, and like smooth muscle, cardiac muscle is myogenic, meaning that it stimulates its own contraction without a requisite electrical impulse.
Peristalsis	Peristalsis is the process of involuntary wave-like successive muscular contractions by which food is moved through the digestive tract. The large, hollow organs of the digestive system contains muscles that enable their walls to move.
Myofibril	Myofibril is a cylindrical organelle, found within muscle cells. They are bundles of filaments that run from one end of the cell to the other and are attached to the cell surface membrane at each end.
Sarcomere	A sarcomere is the basic unit of a cross striated muscle's myofibril. They are multi-protein complexes composed of three different filament systems. A sarcomere is defined as the segment between two neighboring Z-lines (or Z-discs).
Thick filament	In the sarcomere, a bundle of myosin that interacts with thin filaments, producing muscle contraction is a thick filament.
Sarcoplasmic reticulum	Smooth endoplasmic reticulum of skeletal muscle cells specially adapted for calcium ion storage and release is called sarcoplasmic reticulum.
Tropomyosin	Protein that blocks muscle contraction until calcium ions are present is referred to as tropomyosin.
Troponin	A molecule found in thin filaments of muscle that helps regulate when muscle cells contract is referred to as troponin.
Rigor mortis	Rigor mortis is a recognizable sign of death that is caused by a chemical change in the muscles, causing the limbs of the corpse to become stiff and difficult to move or manipulate.
Phosphate	A phosphate is a polyatomic ion or radical consisting of one phosphorus atom and four oxygen. In the ionic form, it carries a -3 formal charge, and is denoted PO_4^{3-}.
Phosphorylation	Phosphorylation refers to reaction in which a phosphate group becomes covalently coupled to another molecule.
Intestine	The intestine is the portion of the alimentary canal extending from the stomach to the anus and, in humans and mammals, consists of two segments, the small intestine and the large intestine. The intestine is the part of the body responsible for extracting nutrition from food.
Stomach	The stomach is an organ in the alimentary canal used to digest food. It's primary function is not the absorption of nutrients from digested food; rather, the main job of the stomach is to break down large food molecules into smaller ones, so that they can be absorbed into the blood more easily.
Uterus	The uterus is the major female reproductive organ of most mammals. One end, the cervix, opens into the vagina; the other is connected on both sides to the fallopian tubes. The main function is to accept a fertilized ovum which becomes implanted into the endometrium, and derives nourishment from blood vessels which develop exclusively for this purpose.
T tubule	A T tubule is a deep invagination of the plasma membrane found in skeletal and cardiac muscle cells. These invaginations allow depolarization of the membrane to quickly penetrate to the interior of the cell.
Thin filament	Thin filament in the sarcomere, a protein strand that interacts with thick filaments, producing muscle contraction; composed primarily of actin, with accessory proteins.

Go to **Cram101.com** for the Practice Tests for this Chapter.

Homologous	Homologous refers to describes organs or molecules that are similar because of their common evolutionary origin. Specifically it describes similarities in protein or nucleic acid sequence.
Alkaloid	Alkaloid refers to small but chemically complex nitrogen-containing metabolite produced by plants as a defense against herbivores. Examples include caffeine, morphine, and colchicine.
Bark	Bark is the outermost layer of stems and roots of woody plants such as trees. It overlays the wood and consists of three layers, the cork, the phloem, and the vascular cambium.
Migration	Migration occurs when living things move from one biome to another. In most cases organisms migrate to avoid local shortages of food, usually caused by winter. Animals may also migrate to a certain location to breed, as is the case with some fish.
Calcium	Calcium is the chemical element in the periodic table that has the symbol Ca and atomic number 20. Calcium is a soft grey alkaline earth metal that is used as a reducing agent in the extraction of thorium, zirconium and uranium. Calcium is also the fifth most abundant element in the Earth's crust.
Cell biology	The biological discipline involving the study of cells and their functions is called cell biology. This includes their physiological properties such as their structure and the organelles they contain, their environment and interactions, their life cycle, division and function (physiology) and eventual death.
Cell cycle	An orderly sequence of events that extends from the time a eukaryotic cell divides to form two daughter cells to the time those daughter cells divide again is called cell cycle.

Cell	The cell is the structural and functional unit of all living organisms, and is sometimes called the "building block of life."
Multicellular	Multicellular organisms are those organisms consisting of more than one cell, and having differentiated cells that perform specialized functions. Most life that can be seen with the naked eye is multicellular, as are all animals (i.e. members of the kingdom Animalia) and plants (i.e. members of the kingdom Plantae).
Unicellular	Unicellular organisms carry out all the functions of life. Unicellular species are those whose members consist of a single cell throughout their life cycle. This latter qualification is significant since most multicellular organisms consist of a single cell at the beginning of their life cycles.
Bacterium	Most bacterium are microscopic and unicellular, with a relatively simple cell structure lacking a cell nucleus, and organelles such as mitochondria and chloroplasts. They are the most abundant of all organisms. They are ubiquitous in soil, water, and as symbionts of other organisms.
Mammal	Homeothermic vertebrate characterized especially by the presence of hair and mammary glands is a mammal.
Cell cycle	An orderly sequence of events that extends from the time a eukaryotic cell divides to form two daughter cells to the time those daughter cells divide again is called cell cycle.
Daughter cell	A cell formed by cell division of a parent cell is a daughter cell.
Macromolecule	A macromolecule is a molecule of high relative molecular mass, the structure of which essentially comprises the multiple repetition of units derived, actually or conceptually, from molecules of low relative molecular mass.
Chromosome	A chromosome is, minimally, a very long, continuous piece of DNA, which contains many genes, regulatory elements and other intervening nucleotide sequences.
Organelle	In cell biology, an organelle is one of several structures with specialized functions, suspended in the cytoplasm of a eukaryotic cell.
Genome	The genome of an organism is the whole hereditary information of an organism that is encoded in the DNA (or, for some viruses, RNA). This includes both the genes and the non-coding sequences. The genome of an organism is a complete DNA sequence of one set of chromosomes.
Cell-cycle control system	Cell-cycle control system refers to network of regulatory proteins that governs progression of a eucaryotic cell through the cell cycle.
Protein	A protein is a complex, high-molecular-weight organic compound that consists of amino acids joined by peptide bonds. They are essential to the structure and function of all living cells and viruses. Many are enzymes or subunits of enzymes.
DNA replication	DNA replication is the process of copying a double-stranded DNA strand in a cell, prior to cell division. The two resulting double strands are identical (if the replication went well), and each of them consists of one original and one newly synthesized strand.
Phosphorylation	Phosphorylation refers to reaction in which a phosphate group becomes covalently coupled to another molecule.
Survival factor	Survival factor refers to extracellular signal required for a cell to survive; in its absence the cell will undergo apoptosis and die.
Protein kinase	Enzyme that transfers the terminal phosphate group of ATP to a specific amino acid of a target protein is protein kinase.
Cell division	Cell division is the process by which a cell (called the parent cell) divides into two cells

(called daughter cells). Cell division is usually a small segment of a larger cell cycle. In meiosis, however, a cell is permanently transformed and cannot divide again.

Growth factor	Growth factor is a protein that acts as a signaling molecule between cells (like cytokines and hormones) that attaches to specific receptors on the surface of a target cell and promotes differentiation and maturation of these cells.
Animal cell	An animal cell is a form of eukaryotic cell which make up many tissues in animals. The animal cell is distinct from other eukaryotes, most notably those of plants, as they lack cell walls and chloroplasts, and they have smaller vacuoles.
Apoptosis	In biology, apoptosis is one of the main types of programmed cell death (PCD). As such, it is a process of deliberate life relinquishment by an unwanted cell in a multicellular organism.
Mitogen	A mitogen is a chemical, usually some form of a protein that encourages a cell to commence cell division, triggering mitosis.
Cyclin	Cyclin refers to protein that periodically rises and falls in concentration in step with the eucaryotic cell cycle. They activate crucial protein kinases and thereby help control progression from one stage of the cell cycle to the next.
Duplicated chromosome	Duplicated chromosome refers to a eukaryotic chromosome following DNA replication; consists of two sister chromatids joined at the centromeres.
Segregation	The separation of homologous chromosomes during mitosis and meiosis. Known as Mendel's theory of Segregation.
Tissue	Group of similar cells which perform a common function is called tissue.
Cancer	Cancer is a class of diseases or disorders characterized by uncontrolled division of cells and the ability of these cells to invade other tissues, either by direct growth into adjacent tissue through invasion or by implantation into distant sites by metastasis.
Cytokinesis	The division of the cytoplasm to form two separate daughter cells. Cytokinesis usually occurs during telophase of mitosis, and the two processes make up the mitotic phase of the cell cycle.
Microscope	A microscope is an instrument for viewing objects that are too small to be seen by the naked or unaided eye.
Nucleus	In cell biology, the nucleus is found in all eukaryotic cells that contains most of the cell's genetic material. The nucleus has two primary functions: to control chemical reactions within the cytoplasm and to store information needed for cellular division.
Mitosis	Mitosis is the process by which a cell separates its duplicated genome into two identical halves. It is generally followed immediately by cytokinesis which divides the cytoplasm and cell membrane.
M phase	Mitosis and cytokinesis together is defined as the mitotic M phase of the cell cycle, the division of the mother cell into two daughter cells, each the genetic equivalent of the parent cell.
Interphase	The period in the eukaryotic cell cycle when the cell is not actually dividing is referred to as interphase. During interphase, the cell obtains nutrients, and duplicates its chromosomes.
S phase	Stage of the cell cycle during which chromosome replication occurs is called S phase.
Gap phase	Gap phase refers to the stage of interphase when proteins, carbohydrates, and lipids are synthesized in preparation for impending mitosis.
G2 phase	Stage of the cell cycle from the completion of chromosome replication until the onset of cell division is called g2 phase.

Gene	Gene refers to a discrete unit of hereditary information consisting of a specific nucleotide sequence in DNA . Most of the genes of a eukaryote are located in its chromosomal DNA; a few are carried by the DNA of mitochondria and chloroplasts.
Population	Group of organisms of the same species occupying a certain area and sharing a common gene pool is referred to as population.
Fluorescence	Fluorescence is a luminescence that is mostly found as an optical phenomenon in cold bodies, in which the molecular absorption of a photon triggers the emission of a lower-energy photon with a longer wavelength. The energy difference between the absorbed and emitted photons ends up as molecular vibrations or heat.
Cytoplasm	Cytoplasm refers to everything inside a cell between the plasma membrane and the nucleus; consists of a semifluid medium and organelles.
Fertilization	Fertilization is fusion of gametes to form a new organism. In animals, the process involves a sperm fusing with an ovum, which eventually leads to the development of an embryo.
Cleavage	Cleavage refers to cytokinesis in animal cells and in some protists, characterized by pinching in of the plasma membrane.
Embryo	Embryo refers to a developing stage of a multicellular organism. In humans, the stage in the development of offspring from the first division of the zygote until body structures begin to appear, about the ninth week of gestation.
Egg	An egg is the zygote, resulting from fertilization of the ovum. It nourishes and protects the embryo.
Chromosome condensation	Process by which a chromosome becomes packed up into a more compact structure prior to M phase of the cell cycle is chromosome condensation.
Mitotic spindle	Mitotic spindle refers to a spindle-shaped structure formed of microtubules and associated proteins that is involved in the movement of chromosomes during mitosis and meiosis.
Phosphate group	The functional group $-OPO_3H_2$; the transfer of energy from one compound to another is often accomplished by the transfer of a phosphate group.
Side chain	In organic chemistry and biochemistry a side chain is a part of a molecule attached to a core structure. Often the side chain can vary for a given core. In biochemistry the peptide or protein side chains are the variable parts of amino acids extending from the peptide backbone.
Amino acid	An amino acid is any molecule that contains both amino and carboxylic acid functional groups. They are the basic structural building units of proteins. They form short polymer chains called peptides or polypeptides which in turn form structures called proteins.
Enzyme	An enzyme is a protein that catalyzes, or speeds up, a chemical reaction. They are essential to sustain life because most chemical reactions in biological cells would occur too slowly, or would lead to different products, without them.
Protein phosphatase	Protein phosphatase refers to an enzyme that removes phosphate groups from proteins, often functioning to reverse the effect of a protein kinase.
M-cyclin	Type of cyclin found in all eucaryotic cells that promotes the events of mitosis is called M-cyclin.
Ubiquitin	Ubiquitin is a small protein that occurs in all eukaryotic cells. Its main function is to mark other proteins for destruction, known as proteolysis. Several ubiquitin molecules attach to the condemned protein, and it then moves to a proteasome, a barrel-shaped structure where the proteolysis occurs.

Anaphase	Anaphase is the stage of meiosis or mitosis when chromosomes separate in a eukaryotic cell. Each chromatid moves to opposite poles of the cell, the opposite ends of the mitotic spindle, near the microtubule organizing centers.
Ubiquitination	Ubiquitination refers to the process particular to eukaryotes whereby a protein is post-translationally modified by covalent attachment of a small protein.
Black box	Black box is technical jargon for a device or system or object when it is viewed primarily in terms of its input and output characteristics
Transcription	Transcription is the process through which a DNA sequence is enzymatically copied by an RNA polymerase to produce a complementary RNA. Or, in other words, the transfer of genetic information from DNA into RNA.
Ovary	In the flowering plants, an ovary is a part of the female reproductive organ of the flower or gynoecium.
Oocyte	An oocyte is a female gametocyte. Such that an oocyte is large and essentially stationary. The oocyte becomes functional when a lala (male gametocyte) attaches to it, thus allowing the meiosis of the secondary oocyte to occur.
Yeast	Yeast refers to common term for several families of unicellular fungi. Includes species used for brewing beer and making bread, as well as pathogenic species.
Mutant	A mutant (also known to early geneticists as a "monster") is an individual, organism, or new genetic character arising or resulting from an instance of mutation, which is a sudden structural change within the DNA of a gene or chromosome of an organism resulting in the creation of a new character or trait not found in the parental type.
Evolution	In biology, evolution is the process by which novel traits arise in populations and are passed on from generation to generation. Its action over large stretches of time explains the origin of new species and ultimately the vast diversity of the biological world.
Divergent evolution	A basic evolutionary pattern in which individual speciation events cause many branches in the evolution of a group of organisms is divergent evolution.
Molecule	A molecule is the smallest particle of a pure chemical substance that still retains its chemical composition and properties.
Phosphatase	A phosphatase is an enzyme that hydrolyses phosphoric acid monoesters into a phosphate ion and a molecule with a free hydroxyl group.
Phosphate	A phosphate is a polyatomic ion or radical consisting of one phosphorus atom and four oxygen. In the ionic form, it carries a -3 formal charge, and is denoted PO_4^{3-}.
Cytoskeleton	Cytoskeleton refers to a meshwork of fine fibers in the cytoplasm of a eukaryotic cell; includes microfilaments, intermediate filaments, and microtubules.
Microtubule	Microtubule is a protein structure found within cells, one of the components of the cytoskeleton. They have diameter of ~ 24 nm and varying length from several micrometers to possible millimeters in axons of nerve cells. They serve as structural components within cells and are involved in many cellular processes including mitosis, cytokinesis, and vesicular transport.
Nucleotide	A nucleotide is a chemical compound that consists of a heterocyclic base, a sugar, and one or more phosphate groups. In the most common nucleotides the base is a derivative of purine or pyrimidine, and the sugar is pentose - deoxyribose or ribose. They are the structural units of RNA and DNA.
Mutation	Mutation refers to a change in the nucleotide sequence of DNA; the ultimate source of genetic diversity.

Cation	A positively charged ion which has fewer electrons than protons is a cation.
Replication origin	Location on a DNA molecule at which DNA replication is initiated is referred to as the replication origin.
Inhibitor	An inhibitor is a type of effector (biology) that decreases or prevents the rate of a chemical reaction. They are often called negative catalysts.
Gene regulatory protein	General name for any protein that binds to a specific DNA sequence to alter the expression of a gene is referred to as gene regulatory protein.
Epithelial	Functions of epithelial cells include secretion, absorption, protection, transcellular transport, sensation detection, and selective permeability.
Liver	The liver is an organ in vertebrates, including humans. It plays a major role in metabolism and has a number of functions in the body including drug detoxification, glycogen storage, and plasma protein synthesis. It also produces bile, which is important for digestion.
Vertebrate nervous system	The vertebrate nervous system is often divided into a central nervous system (CNS) and the peripheral nervous system (PNS). The CNS consists of the brain and spinal cord. The PNS consists of all other nerves and neurons that do not lie within the CNS.
Nerve cell	A cell specialized to originate or transmit nerve impulses is referred to as nerve cell.
Bone marrow	Bone marrow is the tissue comprising the center of large bones. It is the place where new blood cells are produced. Bone marrow contains two types of stem cells: hemopoietic (which can produce blood cells) and stromal (which can produce fat, cartilage and bone).
Intestine	The intestine is the portion of the alimentary canal extending from the stomach to the anus and, in humans and mammals, consists of two segments, the small intestine and the large intestine. The intestine is the part of the body responsible for extracting nutrition from food.
Metamorphosis	Metamorphosis is a process in biology by which an individual physically develops after birth or hatching, and involves significant change in form as well as growth and differentiation.
Tadpole	A tadpole is a larval frog, toad, salamander, newt, or caecilian. In this stage it breathes by means of external or internal gills, is at first lacking legs, and has a finlike tail with which it swims as most fish do, by lateral undulation.
Hormone	A hormone is a chemical messenger from one cell to another. All multicellular organisms produce hormones. The best known hormones are those produced by endocrine glands of vertebrate animals, but hormones are produced by nearly every organ system and tissue type in a human or animal body. Hormone molecules are secreted directly into the bloodstream, they move by circulation or diffusion to their target cells, which may be nearby cells in the same tissue or cells of a distant organ of the body.
Thyroid	The thyroid is one of the larger endocrine glands in the body. It is located in the neck and produces hormones, principally thyroxine and triiodothyronine, that regulate the rate of metabolism and affect the growth and rate of function of many other systems in the body.
Blood	Blood is a circulating tissue composed of fluid plasma and cells. The main function of blood is to supply nutrients (oxygen, glucose) and constitutional elements to tissues and to remove waste products.
Tissue culture	Process of growing tissue artificially in usually a liquid medium in laboratory glassware is referred to as tissue culture.
Necrosis	Necrosis is the name given to unprogrammed death of cells/living tissue. There are many causes of necrosis including injury, infection, cancer, infarction, and inflammation. Necrosis is caused by special enzymes that are released by lysosomes.

Electron	The electron is a light fundamental subatomic particle that carries a negative electric charge. The electron is a spin-1/2 lepton, does not participate in strong interactions and has no substructure.
Vacuole	A vacuole is a large membrane-bound compartment within some eukaryotic cells where they serve a variety of different functions: capturing food materials or unwanted structural debris surrounding the cell, sequestering materials that might be toxic to the cell, maintaining fluid balance (called turgor) within the cell.
Swell	Swell refers to a wave with a flatter, rounded wave crest and trough. Swells are found away from the area where waves are generated by the wind .
Nuclear envelope	The nuclear envelope refers to the double membrane of the nucleus that encloses genetic material in eukaryotic cells. It separates the contents of the nucleus (DNA in particular) from the cytosol.
Protease	Protease refers to an enzyme that breaks peptide bonds between amino acids of proteins.
Caspase	Any of a family of intracellular proteases that are involved in initiating the cellular events of apoptosis is referred to as caspase.
Nuclear lamin	Protein subunit of the intermediate filaments of the nuclear lamina is nuclear lamin.
Nuclear lamina	Nuclear lamina refers to fibrous meshwork of proteins on the inner surface of the inner nuclear membrane. It is made up of a network of intermediate filaments formed from nuclear lamins.
Lamin	Lamin refers to paired chromosome in meiosis in immature amphibian eggs, in which the chromatin forms large stiff loops extending out from the linear axis of the chromosome.
All-or-none	All-or-none indicates a situation in which there are two possibilities (a binary choice set), one of which is 100% and one of which is 0%. It is a phrase commonly used to describe action potentials of neurons, which, if they fire at all, propagate from the beginning to the end of the axonal process.
Intermembrane space	The intermembrane space is the region between the inner membrane and the outer membrane of a mitochondrion or a chloroplast. The main function of the intermembrane space is nucleotide phosphorylation.
Cytochrome c	Cytochrome c is a small heme protein found loosely associated with the inner membrane of the mitochondrion. It is a soluble protein, unlike other cytochromes, and is an essential component of the electron transfer chain.
Cytochrome	Cytochrome refers to colored, heme-containing protein that transfers electrons during cellular respiration and photosynthesis.
Cytosol	The cytosol is the internal fluid of the cell, and a large part of cell metabolism occurs here. Proteins within the cytosol play an important role in signal transduction pathways, glycolysis; also, they act as intracellular receptors and form part of the ribosomes, enabling further protein synthesis
Adaptor protein	An adaptor protein is a protein which is accessory to main proteins in a signal transduction pathway. These proteins tend to lack any intrinsic enzymatic activity themselves but instead mediate specific protein-protein interactions that drive the formation of protein complexes.
Mitochondria	Mitochondria are organelles found in most eukaryotic cells, including those of plants, animals, fungi, and protists. Mitochondria are sometimes described as "cellular power plants", because their primary function is to convert organic materials into energy in the form of ATP.
Organ	Organ refers to a structure consisting of several tissues adapted as a group to perform

	specific functions.
Bacteria	The domain that contains procaryotic cells with primarily diacyl glycerol diesters in their membranes and with bacterial rRNA. Bacteria also is a general term for organisms that are composed of procaryotic cells and are not multicellular.
Extracellular matrix	Extracellular matrix is any material part of a tissue that is not part of any cell. Extracellular matrix is the defining feature of connective tissue.
Signal molecule	Extracellular or intracellular molecule that cues the response of a cell to the behavior of other cells or objects in the environment is called signal molecule.
Receptor	A receptor is a protein on the cell membrane or within the cytoplasm or cell nucleus that binds to a specific molecule (a ligand), such as a neurotransmitter, hormone, or other substance, and initiates the cellular response to the ligand. Receptor, in immunology, the region of an antibody which shows recognition of an antigen.
Retinoblastoma	Retinoblastoma is a cancer of the retina. Development of this tumor is initiated by mutations that inactivate both copies of the RB1-gene, which codes for the Rb-1 protein. It occurs mostly in children before the age 5 years and accounts for about 3% of the cancers occurring in children younger than 15 years.
Tumor	An abnormal mass of cells that forms within otherwise normal tissue is a tumor. This growth can be either malignant or benign
Eye	An eye is an organ that detects light. Different kinds of light-sensitive organs are found in a variety of creatures.
Vertebrate	Vertebrate is a subphylum of chordates, specifically, those with backbones or spinal columns. They started to evolve about 530 million years ago during the Cambrian explosion, which is part of the Cambrian period.
Serum	Serum is the same as blood plasma except that clotting factors (such as fibrin) have been removed. Blood plasma contains fibrinogen.
Micrograph	A micrograph is a photograph or similar image taken through a microscope or similar device to show a magnified image of an item.
Hepatocyte	Hepatocyte cells make up 60-80% of the cytoplasmic mass of the liver. They are involved in protein synthesis, protein storage and transformation of carbohydrates, synthesis of cholesterol, bile salts and phospholipids, and detoxification, modification and excretion of exogenous and endogenous substances.
Nervous system	The nervous system of an animal coordinates the activity of the muscles, monitors the organs, constructs and processes input from the senses, and initiates actions.
Target cell	A cell that responds to a regulatory signal, such as a hormone is a target cell.
Neuron	The neuron is a major class of cells in the nervous system. In vertebrates, they are found in the brain, the spinal cord and in the nerves and ganglia of the peripheral nervous system, and their primary role is to process and transmit neural information.
Lymphocyte	A lymphocyte is a type of white blood cell involved in the human body's immune system. There are two broad categories, namely T cells and B cells.
Nerve	A nerve is an enclosed, cable-like bundle of nerve fibers or axons, which includes the glia that ensheath the axons in myelin.
Skeletal muscle	Skeletal muscle is a type of striated muscle, attached to the skeleton. They are used to facilitate movement, by applying force to bones and joints; via contraction. They generally contract voluntarily (via nerve stimulation), although they can contract involuntarily.

Myoblast	Myoblast is a type of stem cell that exists in muscles. Skeletal muscle cells are called muscle fibers and are made when myoblasts fuse together; muscle fibers therefore have multiple nuclei.
Muscle	Muscle is a contractile form of tissue. It is one of the four major tissue types, the other three being epithelium, connective tissue and nervous tissue. Muscle contraction is used to move parts of the body, as well as to move substances within the body.
Cancer cell	A cell that divides and reproduces abnormally and has the potential to spread throughout the body, crowding out normal cells and tissue is referred to as a cancer cell.
Proteolysis	Degradation of a protein by cellular enzymes called proteases or by intramolecular digestion at one or more of its peptide bonds is referred to as proteolysis.
Protein synthesis	The process whereby the tRNA utilizes the mRNA as a guide to arrange the amino acids in their proper sequence according to the genetic information in the chemical code of DNA is referred to as protein synthesis.
Ionizing radiation	Ionizing radiation is a type of particle radiation in which an individual particle carries enough energy to ionize an atom or molecule. If the individual particles do not carry this amount of energy, it is essentially impossible for even a large flood of particles to cause ionization.
Radioactive	A term used to describe the property of releasing energy or particles from an unstable atom is called radioactive.

Cell	The cell is the structural and functional unit of all living organisms, and is sometimes called the "building block of life."
Cell division	Cell division is the process by which a cell (called the parent cell) divides into two cells (called daughter cells). Cell division is usually a small segment of a larger cell cycle. In meiosis, however, a cell is permanently transformed and cannot divide again.
Multicellular	Multicellular organisms are those organisms consisting of more than one cell, and having differentiated cells that perform specialized functions. Most life that can be seen with the naked eye is multicellular, as are all animals (i.e. members of the kingdom Animalia) and plants (i.e. members of the kingdom Plantae).
Unicellular	Unicellular organisms carry out all the functions of life. Unicellular species are those whose members consist of a single cell throughout their life cycle. This latter qualification is significant since most multicellular organisms consist of a single cell at the beginning of their life cycles.
Bacteria	The domain that contains procaryotic cells with primarily diacyl glycerol diesters in their membranes and with bacterial rRNA. Bacteria also is a general term for organisms that are composed of procaryotic cells and are not multicellular.
Yeast	Yeast refers to common term for several families of unicellular fungi. Includes species used for brewing beer and making bread, as well as pathogenic species.
Egg	An egg is the zygote, resulting from fertilization of the ovum. It nourishes and protects the embryo.
Daughter cell	A cell formed by cell division of a parent cell is a daughter cell.
Cell cycle	An orderly sequence of events that extends from the time a eukaryotic cell divides to form two daughter cells to the time those daughter cells divide again is called cell cycle.
M phase	Mitosis and cytokinesis together is defined as the mitotic M phase of the cell cycle, the division of the mother cell into two daughter cells, each the genetic equivalent of the parent cell.
Cell-cycle control system	Cell-cycle control system refers to network of regulatory proteins that governs progression of a eucaryotic cell through the cell cycle.
Interphase	The period in the eukaryotic cell cycle when the cell is not actually dividing is referred to as interphase. During interphase, the cell obtains nutrients, and duplicates its chromosomes.
Gap phase	Gap phase refers to the stage of interphase when proteins, carbohydrates, and lipids are synthesized in preparation for impending mitosis.
S phase	Stage of the cell cycle during which chromosome replication occurs is called S phase.
Cyclin-dependent kinase	Cyclin-dependent kinase refers to protein kinase that has to be complexed with a cyclin protein in order to act. Different complexes trigger different steps in the cell-division cycle by phosphorylating specific target proteins.
Protein	A protein is a complex, high-molecular-weight organic compound that consists of amino acids joined by peptide bonds. They are essential to the structure and function of all living cells and viruses. Many are enzymes or subunits of enzymes.
Daughter chromosomes	Separated chromatids become daughter chromosomes during anaphase of mitosis and anaphase II of meiosis.
Nuclear envelope	The nuclear envelope refers to the double membrane of the nucleus that encloses genetic material in eukaryotic cells. It separates the contents of the nucleus (DNA in particular) from the cytosol.

Go to **Cram101.com** for the Practice Tests for this Chapter.

Contractile ring	Ring containing actin and myosin that forms under the surface of animal cells undergoing cell division and contracts to pinch the two daughter cells apart is a contractile ring.
Mitotic spindle	Mitotic spindle refers to a spindle-shaped structure formed of microtubules and associated proteins that is involved in the movement of chromosomes during mitosis and meiosis.
Prometaphase	Prometaphase refers to the stage of mitosis just after the breakdown of the nuclear envelope, when the chromosomes connect to the spindle apparatus and begin to move toward the metaphase plate.
Cytoskeleton	Cytoskeleton refers to a meshwork of fine fibers in the cytoplasm of a eukaryotic cell; includes microfilaments, intermediate filaments, and microtubules.
Cytokinesis	The division of the cytoplasm to form two separate daughter cells. Cytokinesis usually occurs during telophase of mitosis, and the two processes make up the mitotic phase of the cell cycle.
Animal cell	An animal cell is a form of eukaryotic cell which make up many tissues in animals. The animal cell is distinct from other eukaryotes, most notably those of plants, as they lack cell walls and chloroplasts, and they have smaller vacuoles.
Microtubule	Microtubule is a protein structure found within cells, one of the components of the cytoskeleton. They have diameter of ~ 24 nm and varying length from several micrometers to possible millimeters in axons of nerve cells. They serve as structural components within cells and are involved in many cellular processes including mitosis, cytokinesis, and vesicular transport.
Segregation	The separation of homologous chromosomes during mitosis and meiosis. Known as Mendel's theory of Segregation.
Plant cell	A cell that is a structural and functional unit of a plant is a plant cell.
Centrosome	Centrosome refers to material in the cytoplasm of a eukaryotic cell that gives rise to microtubules; important in mitosis and meiosis; also called microtubule-organizing center.
Chromosome	A chromosome is, minimally, a very long, continuous piece of DNA, which contains many genes, regulatory elements and other intervening nucleotide sequences.
Cell wall	Cell wall refers to a protective layer external to the plasma membrane in plant cells, bacteria, fungi, and some protists; protects the cell and helps maintain its shape.
Organelle	In cell biology, an organelle is one of several structures with specialized functions, suspended in the cytoplasm of a eukaryotic cell.
Metaphase	The second stage of mitosis. During metaphase, all the cell's duplicated chromosomes are lined up at an imaginary plane equidistant between the poles of the mitotic spindle.
Telophase	Telophase is a stage in either meiosis or mitosis in a eukaryotic cell reversing the effects of prophase and prometaphase events, when the nucleus is dissolved and the chromatin in the cell is condensed into chromosomes.
Prophase	Prophase is a stage of mitosis in which chromatin, condenses into a highly ordered structure called a chromosome. This process, called chromatin condenzation, is mediated by condensin.
Anaphase	Anaphase is the stage of meiosis or mitosis when chromosomes separate in a eukaryotic cell. Each chromatid moves to opposite poles of the cell, the opposite ends of the mitotic spindle, near the microtubule organizing centers.
Cleavage	Cleavage refers to cytokinesis in animal cells and in some protists, characterized by pinching in of the plasma membrane.
Mitosis	Mitosis is the process by which a cell separates its duplicated genome into two identical

Go to **Cram101.com** for the Practice Tests for this Chapter.

	halves. It is generally followed immediately by cytokinesis which divides the cytoplasm and cell membrane.
Myosin	Myosin is a large family of motor proteins found in eukaryotic tissues. They are responsible for actin-based motility.
Genome	The genome of an organism is the whole hereditary information of an organism that is encoded in the DNA (or, for some viruses, RNA). This includes both the genes and the non-coding sequences. The genome of an organism is a complete DNA sequence of one set of chromosomes.
Gamete	A gamete is a specialized germ cell that unites with another gamete during fertilization in organisms that reproduce sexually. They are haploid cells; that is, they contain one complete set of chromosomes. When they unite they form a zygote—a cell having two complete sets of chromosomes and therefore diploid.
Actin	Actin is a globular protein that polymerizes helically forming filaments, which like the other two components of the cellular cytoskeleton form a three-dimensional network inside an eukaryotic cell. They provide mechanical support for the cell, determine the cell shape, enable cell movements .
Duplicated chromosome	Duplicated chromosome refers to a eukaryotic chromosome following DNA replication; consists of two sister chromatids joined at the centromeres.
Cytoplasm	Cytoplasm refers to everything inside a cell between the plasma membrane and the nucleus; consists of a semifluid medium and organelles.
Sister chromatid	One of two genetically identical chromosomal units that are the result of DNA replication and are attached to each other at the centromere is called sister chromatid.
Cohesin	Cohesin is the protein responsible for binding the sister chromatids during mitosis. Its hydrolysis by separase triggers anaphase
Chromosome condensation	Process by which a chromosome becomes packed up into a more compact structure prior to M phase of the cell cycle is chromosome condensation.
Molecule	A molecule is the smallest particle of a pure chemical substance that still retains its chemical composition and properties.
Centromere	The centromere is a region of a eukaryotic chromosome where the kinetochore is assembled; the site where spindle fibers of the mitotic spindle attach to the chromosome during mitosis. It is also the site of the primary constriction visible in microscopy images of chromosomes. Finally, it is the site at which a chromatid and its identical sister attach together during the process of cell reproduction.
Filament	The stamen is the male organ of a flower. Each stamen generally has a stalk called the filament, and, on top of the filament, an anther. The filament is a long chain of proteins, such as those found in hair, muscle, or in flagella.
Centriole	A centriole is a barrel shaped microtubule structure found in most animal cells, and cells of fungi and algae though not frequently in plants. The walls of each centriole are usually composed of nine triplet microtubules.
Matrix	In biology, matrix (plural: matrices) is the material between animal or plant cells, the material (or tissue) in which more specialized structures are embedded, and a specific part of the mitochondrion that is the site of oxidation of organic molecules.
Duplication	Duplication refers to repetition of part of a chromosome resulting from fusion with a fragment from a homologous chromosome; can result from an error in meiosis or from mutagenesis.
Microtubule-	Region in a cell, such as a centrosome or a basal body, from which microtubules grow is

organizing center	called a microtubule-organizing center.
Nucleus	In cell biology, the nucleus is found in all eukaryotic cells that contains most of the cell's genetic material. The nucleus has two primary functions: to control chemical reactions within the cytoplasm and to store information needed for cellular division.
Centrosome cycle	Centrosome cycle refers to duplication of the centrosome and separation of the two new centrosomes, which provides two centrosomes to form the poles of the mitotic spindle.
Chromatid	Chromatid refers to one of two component parts of a chromosome formed by replication and attached at the centromere.
Minus end	The end of a microtubule or actin filament at which the addition of monomers occurs least readily; the 'slow-growing' end of the microtubule or actin filament is called the minus end.
Plus end	The end of a microtubule or actin filament at which addition of monomers occurs most readily; the 'fast-growing' end of a microtubule or actin filament. The plus end of an actin filament is also known as the barbed end.
Polymerization	Polymerization is a process of reacting monomer molecules together in a chemical reaction to form linear chains or a three-dimensional network of polymer chains.
Cytosol	The cytosol is the internal fluid of the cell, and a large part of cell metabolism occurs here. Proteins within the cytosol play an important role in signal transduction pathways, glycolysis; also, they act as intracellular receptors and form part of the ribosomes, enabling further protein synthesis
Kinetochore	The kinetochore is the protein structure in eukaryotes which assembles on the centromere and links the chromosome to microtubule polymers from the mitotic spindle during mitosis.
Astral microtubule	In the mitotic spindle, any of the microtubules radiating from the aster which are not attached to a kinetochore of a chromosome is called an astral microtubule.
Cleavage furrow	Cleavage furrow refers to the first sign of cytokinesis during cell division in an animal cell; a shallow groove in the cell surface near the old metaphase plate.
Motor protein	Protein that uses energy derived from nucleoside triphosphate hydrolysis to propel itself along a protein filament or another polymeric molecule is called motor protein.
Fluorescence	Fluorescence is a luminescence that is mostly found as an optical phenomenon in cold bodies, in which the molecular absorption of a photon triggers the emission of a lower-energy photon with a longer wavelength. The energy difference between the absorbed and emitted photons ends up as molecular vibrations or heat.
Embryo	Embryo refers to a developing stage of a multicellular organism. In humans, the stage in the development of offspring from the first division of the zygote until body structures begin to appear, about the ninth week of gestation.
Insect	An arthropod that usually has three body segments , three pairs of legs, and one or two pairs of wings is called an insect. They are the largest and (on land) most widely-distributed taxon within the phylum Arthropoda. They comprise the most diverse group of animals on the earth, with around 925,000 species described
Micrograph	A micrograph is a photograph or similar image taken through a microscope or similar device to show a magnified image of an item.
Fertilization	Fertilization is fusion of gametes to form a new organism. In animals, the process involves a sperm fusing with an ovum, which eventually leads to the development of an embryo.
Sperm	Sperm refers to the male sex cell with three distinct parts at maturity: head, middle piece,

	and tail.
Vesicle	In cell biology, a vesicle is a relatively small and enclosed compartment, separated from the cytosol by at least one lipid bilayer.
DNA sequence	A DNA sequence is a succession of letters representing the primary structure of a real or hypothetical DNA molecule or strand, The possible letters are A, C, G, and T, representing the four nucleotide subunits of a DNA strand (adenine, cytosine, guanine, thymine).
Microscopy	Microscopy is any technique for producing visible images of structures or details too small to otherwise be seen by the human eye, using a microscope or other magnification tool.
Recombinant DNA	Recombinant DNA is an artificial DNA sequence resulting from the combining of two other DNA sequences in a plasmid.
Tubulin	The protein subunit of microtubules is referred to as tubulin.
Catastrophe	An unpredictable event that has a strong effect on a population is referred to as a catastrophe.
Kinesin	Kinesin is a class of motor protein dimer found in biological cells. A kinesin attaches to microtubules, and moves along the tubule in order to transport cellular cargo, such as vesicles.
Antibody	An antibody is a protein used by the immune system to identify and neutralize foreign objects like bacteria and viruses. Each antibody recognizes a specific antigen unique to its target.
Metaphase plate	Metaphase plate refers to a disc formed during metaphase in which all of a cell's chromosomes lie in a single plane at right angles to the spindle fibers.
Species	Group of similarly constructed organisms capable of interbreeding and producing fertile offspring is a species.
Colchicine	Colchicine is a highly poisonous alkaloid, originally extracted from plants of the genus Colchicum. Originally used to treat rheumatic complaints and especially gout, it was also prescribed for its cathartic and emetic effects. Its present use is mainly in the treatment of gout.
Ubiquitination	Ubiquitination refers to the process particular to eukaryotes whereby a protein is post-translationally modified by covalent attachment of a small protein.
Enzyme	An enzyme is a protein that catalyzes, or speeds up, a chemical reaction. They are essential to sustain life because most chemical reactions in biological cells would occur too slowly, or would lead to different products, without them.
Cell cortex	Cell cortex refers to specialized layer of cytoplasm on the inner face of the plasma membrane. It functions as a mechanical support of the plasma membrane. In animal cells it is an actin-rich layer responsible for movements of the cell surface.
Elongation	Elongation refers to a phase of DNA replication, transcription, or translation that successively adds nucleotides or amino acids to a growing macromolecule.
Hydrolysis	Hydrolysis is a chemical process in which a molecule is cleaved into two parts by the addition of a molecule of water.
Dynein	Member of a family of large motor proteins that undergo ATP-dependent movement along microtubules. In cilia, dynein forms the side arms in the axoneme that cause adjacent microtubule doublets to slide past one another.
Daughter nuclei	Two nuclei formed by mitosis are referred to as daughter nuclei.
Transcription	Transcription is the process through which a DNA sequence is enzymatically copied by an RNA

Go to **Cram101.com** for the Practice Tests for this Chapter.

polymerase to produce a complementary RNA. Or, in other words, the transfer of genetic information from DNA into RNA.

Gene	Gene refers to a discrete unit of hereditary information consisting of a specific nucleotide sequence in DNA . Most of the genes of a eukaryote are located in its chromosomal DNA; a few are carried by the DNA of mitochondria and chloroplasts.
Complement	Complement is a group of proteins of the complement system, found in blood serum which act in concert with antibodies to achieve the destruction of non-self particles such as foreign blood cells or bacteria.
Nuclear pore	Opening in the nuclear envelope which permits the passage of proteins into the nucleus and ribosomal subunits out of the nucleus is a nuclear pore.
Fusion	Fusion refers to the combination of two atoms into a single atom as a result of a collision, usually accompanied by the release of energy.
Lamin	Lamin refers to paired chromosome in meiosis in immature amphibian eggs, in which the chromatin forms large stiff loops extending out from the linear axis of the chromosome.
Phosphorylation	Phosphorylation refers to reaction in which a phosphate group becomes covalently coupled to another molecule.
Nuclear lamina	Nuclear lamina refers to fibrous meshwork of proteins on the inner surface of the inner nuclear membrane. It is made up of a network of intermediate filaments formed from nuclear lamins.
Mitochondria	Mitochondria are organelles found in most eukaryotic cells, including those of plants, animals, fungi, and protists. Mitochondria are sometimes described as "cellular power plants", because their primary function is to convert organic materials into energy in the form of ATP.
Chloroplast	A chloroplast is an organelle found in plant cells and eukaryotic algae which conduct photosynthesis. They are similar to mitochondria but are found only in plants. They are surrounded by a double membrane with an intermembrane space; they have their own DNA and are involved in energy metabolism;
Nuclear membrane	The double layered structure surrounding the nucleus that separates the nucleoplasm from the cytoplasm is referred to as nuclear membrane.
Golgi apparatus	Golgi apparatus refers to an organelle in eukaryotic cells consisting of stacks of membranous sacs that modify, store, and ship products of the endoplasmic reticulum.
Plasma membrane	Membrane surrounding the cytoplasm that consists of a phospholipid bilayer with embedded proteins is referred to as plasma membrane.
Electron	The electron is a light fundamental subatomic particle that carries a negative electric charge. The electron is a spin-1/2 lepton, does not participate in strong interactions and has no substructure.
Actin filament	An actin filament is a helical protein filament formed by the polymerization of globular actin molecules. They provide mechanical support for the cell, determine the cell shape, enable cell movements; and participate in certain cell junctions.
Fibroblast	A fibroblast is a cell that makes the structural fibers and ground substance of connective tissue.
Muscle	Muscle is a contractile form of tissue. It is one of the four major tissue types, the other three being epithelium, connective tissue and nervous tissue. Muscle contraction is used to move parts of the body, as well as to move substances within the body.

Substratum	Substratum is the underlying layer, or base to which a lichen is fixed.
Membrane protein	A membrane protein is a protein molecule that is attached to, or associated with the membrane of a cell or an organelle. Membrane proteins can be classified into two groups, based on their attachment to the membrane.
Integrin	An integrin is an integral membrane protein in the plasma membrane of cells. It plays a role in the attachment of a cell to the extracellular matrix (ECM) and in signal transduction from the ECM to the cell.
Plasma	In physics and chemistry, a plasma is an ionized gas, and is usually considered to be a distinct phase of matter. "Ionized" in this case means that at least one electron has been dissociated from a significant fraction of the molecules.
Extracellular matrix	Extracellular matrix is any material part of a tissue that is not part of any cell. Extracellular matrix is the defining feature of connective tissue.
Tissue	Group of similar cells which perform a common function is called tissue.
Phragmoplast	Phragmoplast refers to structure made of microtubules and actin filaments that forms in the prospective plane of division of a plant cell and guides formation of the cell plate.
Cellulose	A large polysaccharide composed of many glucose monomers linked into cable-like fibrils that provide structural support in plant cell walls is referred to as cellulose.
Reproduction	Biological reproduction is the biological process by which new individual organisms are produced. Reproduction is a fundamental feature of all known life; each individual organism exists as the result of reproduction by an antecedent.
Diploid	Diploid cells have two copies (homologs) of each chromosome (both sex- and non-sex determining chromosomes), usually one from the mother and one from the father. Most somatic cells (body cells) of complex organisms are diploid.
Sexual reproduction	The propagation of organisms involving the union of gametes from two parents is sexual reproduction.
Meiosis	In biology, meiosis is the process that transforms one diploid cell into four haploid cells in eukaryotes in order to redistribute the diploid's cell's genome. Meiosis forms the basis of sexual reproduction and can only occur in eukaryotes.
Golgi	Golgi discovered a method of staining nervous tissue which would stain a limited number of cells at random, in their entirety. This enabled him to view the paths of nerve cells in the brain for the first time. He called his discovery the black reaction. It is now known universally as the Golgi stain.
Endoplasmic reticulum	The endoplasmic reticulum is an organelle found in all eukaryotic cells. It modifies proteins, makes macromolecules, and transfers substances throughout the cell.
Distribution	Distribution in pharmacology is a branch of pharmacokinetics describing reversible transfer of drug from one location to another within the body.

Genetics	Genetics is the science of genes, heredity, and the variation of organisms.
Meiosis	In biology, meiosis is the process that transforms one diploid cell into four haploid cells in eukaryotes in order to redistribute the diploid's cell's genome. Meiosis forms the basis of sexual reproduction and can only occur in eukaryotes.
Species	Group of similarly constructed organisms capable of interbreeding and producing fertile offspring is a species.
Heritable	Heritable refers to able to be inherited; in biology usually refers to genetically determined traits.
Heredity	The transmission of characteristics from parent to offspring is heredity.
Fertilization	Fertilization is fusion of gametes to form a new organism. In animals, the process involves a sperm fusing with an ovum, which eventually leads to the development of an embryo.
Chromosome	A chromosome is, minimally, a very long, continuous piece of DNA, which contains many genes, regulatory elements and other intervening nucleotide sequences.
Cell	The cell is the structural and functional unit of all living organisms, and is sometimes called the "building block of life."
Uniparental inheritance	Uniparental inheritance refers to transmission of genes via one parent. Most species transmit mtdna and cpdna through the mother.
Ovarian follicle	Ovarian follicle is the roughly spherical cell aggregation in the ovary containing an ovum and from which the egg is released during ovulation.
Embryo	Embryo refers to a developing stage of a multicellular organism. In humans, the stage in the development of offspring from the first division of the zygote until body structures begin to appear, about the ninth week of gestation.
Microscope	A microscope is an instrument for viewing objects that are too small to be seen by the naked or unaided eye.
Sperm	Sperm refers to the male sex cell with three distinct parts at maturity: head, middle piece, and tail.
Lens	The lens or crystalline lens is a transparent, biconvex structure in the eye that, along with the cornea, helps to refract light to focus on the retina. Its function is thus similar to a man-made optical lens.
Trait	In biology, a trait or character is a genetically inherited feature of an organism: Eye color is a character; brown eyes and blue eyes is a trait.
Charles Darwin	Charles Darwin was a British naturalist who achieved lasting fame as originator of the theory of evolution through natural selection.
Egg	An egg is the zygote, resulting from fertilization of the ovum. It nourishes and protects the embryo.
Gamete	A gamete is a specialized germ cell that unites with another gamete during fertilization in organisms that reproduce sexually. They are haploid cells; that is, they contain one complete set of chromosomes. When they unite they form a zygote—a cell having two complete sets of chromosomes and therefore diploid.
Cell division	Cell division is the process by which a cell (called the parent cell) divides into two cells (called daughter cells). Cell division is usually a small segment of a larger cell cycle. In meiosis, however, a cell is permanently transformed and cannot divide again.
Multicellular	Multicellular organisms are those organisms consisting of more than one cell, and having

differentiated cells that perform specialized functions. Most life that can be seen with the naked eye is multicellular, as are all animals (i.e. members of the kingdom Animalia) and plants (i.e. members of the kingdom Plantae).

Bacteria	The domain that contains procaryotic cells with primarily diacyl glycerol diesters in their membranes and with bacterial rRNA. Bacteria also is a general term for organisms that are composed of procaryotic cells and are not multicellular.
Animal kingdom	Animal kingdom is one of the main divisions or life-waves of entities on earth, separated from the human kingdom by its lack of the emanated or evolved self-conscious mind
Bacterium	Most bacterium are microscopic and unicellular, with a relatively simple cell structure lacking a cell nucleus, and organelles such as mitochondria and chloroplasts. They are the most abundant of all organisms. They are ubiquitous in soil, water, and as symbionts of other organisms.
Sexual reproduction	The propagation of organisms involving the union of gametes from two parents is sexual reproduction.
Genome	The genome of an organism is the whole hereditary information of an organism that is encoded in the DNA (or, for some viruses, RNA). This includes both the genes and the non-coding sequences. The genome of an organism is a complete DNA sequence of one set of chromosomes.
Haploid cell	A cell with half the normal compliment of chromosomes, typically a germ cell is a haploid cell.
Diploid	Diploid cells have two copies (homologs) of each chromosome (both sex- and non-sex determining chromosomes), usually one from the mother and one from the father. Most somatic cells (body cells) of complex organisms are diploid.
Sex chromosome	The X or Y chromosome in human beings that determines the sex of an individual. Females have two X chromosomes in diploid cells; males have an X and aY chromosome. The sex chromosome comprises the 23rd chromosome pair in a karyotype.
Gene pool	The gene pool of a species or a population is the complete set of unique alleles that would be found by inspecting the genetic material of every living member of that species or population.
Gene	Gene refers to a discrete unit of hereditary information consisting of a specific nucleotide sequence in DNA . Most of the genes of a eukaryote are located in its chromosomal DNA; a few are carried by the DNA of mitochondria and chloroplasts.
Germ cell	A germ cell is a kind of cell that is part of the germline, and is involved in the reproduction of organisms. There are different kinds, which include gametogonia, gametocytes, and gametes.
Haploid	Haploid cells bear one copy of each chromosome.
Zygote	Diploid cell formed by the union of sperm and egg is referred to as zygote.
Somatic cell	A somatic cell is generally taken to mean any cell forming the body of an organism.
Fusion	Fusion refers to the combination of two atoms into a single atom as a result of a collision, usually accompanied by the release of energy.
Reproduction	Biological reproduction is the biological process by which new individual organisms are produced. Reproduction is a fundamental feature of all known life; each individual organism exists as the result of reproduction by an antecedent.
Population	Group of organisms of the same species occupying a certain area and sharing a common gene pool is referred to as population.

Mutation	Mutation refers to a change in the nucleotide sequence of DNA; the ultimate source of genetic diversity.
Natural selection	Natural selection is the process by which biological individuals that are endowed with favorable or deleterious traits end up reproducing more or less than other individuals that do not possess such traits.
Heterozygous	Heterozygous means that the organism carries a different version of that gene on each of the two corresponding chromosomes.
Roundworm	A member of the phylum Nematoda is called roundworm. They are one of the most common phyla of animals, with over 20,000 different described species.
DNA replication	DNA replication is the process of copying a double-stranded DNA strand in a cell, prior to cell division. The two resulting double strands are identical (if the replication went well), and each of them consists of one original and one newly synthesized strand.
S phase	Stage of the cell cycle during which chromosome replication occurs is called S phase.
Ovaries	Ovaries are egg-producing reproductive organs found in female organisms.
Testes	The testes are the male generative glands in animals. Male mammals have two testes, which are often contained within an extension of the abdomen called the scrotum.
Homologs	Genes or regulatory DNA sequences that are similar in different species because of descent from a common ancestral sequence are homologs.
Daughter cell	A cell formed by cell division of a parent cell is a daughter cell.
Mitosis	Mitosis is the process by which a cell separates its duplicated genome into two identical halves. It is generally followed immediately by cytokinesis which divides the cytoplasm and cell membrane.
Homologous chromosome	Homologous chromosome refers to similarly constructed chromosomes with the same shape and that contain genes for the same traits.
Sister chromatid	One of two genetically identical chromosomal units that are the result of DNA replication and are attached to each other at the centromere is called sister chromatid.
Metaphase plate	Metaphase plate refers to a disc formed during metaphase in which all of a cell's chromosomes lie in a single plane at right angles to the spindle fibers.
Cytokinesis	The division of the cytoplasm to form two separate daughter cells. Cytokinesis usually occurs during telophase of mitosis, and the two processes make up the mitotic phase of the cell cycle.
Metaphase	The second stage of mitosis. During metaphase, all the cell's duplicated chromosomes are lined up at an imaginary plane equidistant between the poles of the mitotic spindle.
Prophase	Prophase is a stage of mitosis in which chromatin, condenses into a highly ordered structure called a chromosome. This process, called chromatin condenzation, is mediated by condensin.
Anaphase	Anaphase is the stage of meiosis or mitosis when chromosomes separate in a eukaryotic cell. Each chromatid moves to opposite poles of the cell, the opposite ends of the mitotic spindle, near the microtubule organizing centers.
Division I of meiosis	In division I of meiosis the cell's genetic material, which is normally in a loosely arranged pile known as chromatin, condenses into visible threadlike structures. Along the thread, centromeres are visible as small beads of tightly coiled chromatin.
Homologous	Homologous refers to describes organs or molecules that are similar because of their common evolutionary origin. Specifically it describes similarities in protein or nucleic acid

sequence.

Allele	An allele is any one of a number of viable DNA codings of the same gene (sometimes the term refers to a non-gene sequence) occupying a given locus (position) on a chromosome.
Complementary DNA	Complementary DNA is DNA synthesized from a mature mRNA template. It is often used to clone eukaryotic genes in prokaryotes.
Base pair	Two nucleotides on opposite complementary DNA or RNA strands that are connected via hydrogen bonds are called a base pair.
Duplicated chromosome	Duplicated chromosome refers to a eukaryotic chromosome following DNA replication; consists of two sister chromatids joined at the centromeres.
Chromatid	Chromatid refers to one of two component parts of a chromosome formed by replication and attached at the centromere.
Bivalent	Two or more atoms bound together as a single unit and forming part of a molecule is called bivalent.
Recombination	Genetic recombination is the transmission-genetic process by which the combinations of alleles observed at different loci in two parental individuals become shuffled in offspring individuals.
Genetic recombination	Genetic recombination refers to the production, by crossing over and/or independent assortment of chromosomes during meiosis, of offspring with allele combinations different from those in the parents.
Crossing-over	Exchange of corresponding segments of genetic material between nonsister chromatids of homologous chromosomes during synapsis of meiosis I is called crossing-over.
Double helix	Double helix refers to the form of native DNA, referring to its two adjacent polynucleotide strands wound into a spiral shape.
Synaptonemal complex	The synaptonemal complex is a protein structure that forms between two homologous chromosomes during meiosis and that is thought to mediate chromosome pairing, synapsis, and recombination.
Protein	A protein is a complex, high-molecular-weight organic compound that consists of amino acids joined by peptide bonds. They are essential to the structure and function of all living cells and viruses. Many are enzymes or subunits of enzymes.
Chiasmata	Observable regions in which nonsister chromatids exchange genetic material during chromosomal crossover during meiosis is chiasmata.
Cohesin	Cohesin is the protein responsible for binding the sister chromatids during mitosis. Its hydrolysis by separase triggers anaphase
Micrograph	A micrograph is a photograph or similar image taken through a microscope or similar device to show a magnified image of an item.
Kinetochore	The kinetochore is the protein structure in eukaryotes which assembles on the centromere and links the chromosome to microtubule polymers from the mitotic spindle during mitosis.
Microtubule	Microtubule is a protein structure found within cells, one of the components of the cytoskeleton. They have diameter of ~ 24 nm and varying length from several micrometers to possible millimeters in axons of nerve cells. They serve as structural components within cells and are involved in many cellular processes including mitosis, cytokinesis, and vesicular transport.
Segregation	The separation of homologous chromosomes during mitosis and meiosis. Known as Mendel's theory of Segregation.

Chiasma	Chiasma refers to the microscopically visible site where crossing over has occurred between chromatids of homologous chromosomes during prophase I of meiosis.
Centromere	The centromere is a region of a eukaryotic chromosome where the kinetochore is assembled; the site where spindle fibers of the mitotic spindle attach to the chromosome during mitosis. It is also the site of the primary constriction visible in microscopy images of chromosomes. Finally, it is the site at which a chromatid and its identical sister attach together during the process of cell reproduction.
Daughter nuclei	Two nuclei formed by mitosis are referred to as daughter nuclei.
Interphase	The period in the eukaryotic cell cycle when the cell is not actually dividing is referred to as interphase. During interphase, the cell obtains nutrients, and duplicates its chromosomes.
Division II of meiosis	Division II of meiosis we see in this prophase the disappearance of the nucleoli and the nuclear envelope again as well as the shortening and thickening of the chromatids. Centrioles move to the polar regions and are arranged by spindle fibres.
Reassortment	Reassortment is the exchange of DNA between viruses inside a host cell. Two or more viruses of different strains (but usually the same species) infect a single cell and pool their genetic material creating numerous genetically diverse progeny viruses.
Independent assortment	Independent assortment is a term in genetics for the independent segregation and assortment of chromosomes during sexual reproduction. Independent assortment occurs during meiosis in eukaryotic organisms.
Crossing over	An essential element of meiosis occurring during prophase when nonsister chromatids exchange portions of DNA strands is called crossing over.
DNA sequence	A DNA sequence is a succession of letters representing the primary structure of a real or hypothetical DNA molecule or strand, The possible letters are A, C, G, and T, representing the four nucleotide subunits of a DNA strand (adenine, cytosine, guanine, thymine).
Distribution	Distribution in pharmacology is a branch of pharmacokinetics describing reversible transfer of drug from one location to another within the body.
Nondisjunction	Nondisjunction refers to an accident of meiosis or mitosis in which a pair of homologous chromosomes or a pair of sister chromatids fail to separate at anaphase.
Down syndrome	Down syndrome refers to a human genetic disorder resulting from the presence of an extra chromosome 21; characterized by heart and respiratory defects and varying degrees of mental retardation.
Oocyte	An oocyte is a female gametocyte. Such that an oocyte is large and essentially stationary. The oocyte becomes functional when a lala (male gametocyte) attaches to it, thus allowing the meiosis of the secondary oocyte to occur.
Miscarriage	Miscarriage or spontaneous abortion is the natural or accidental termination of a pregnancy at a stage where the embryo or the fetus is incapable of surviving, generally defined at a gestation of prior to 20 weeks.
Abortion	An abortion is the termination of a pregnancy associated with the death of an embryo or a fetus.
Oviduct	In oviparous animals (those that lay eggs), the passage from the ovaries to the outside of the body is known as the oviduct. The eggs travel along the oviduct.
Coitus	Sexual intercourse, specifically coitus, is the human form of copulation.
Molecule	A molecule is the smallest particle of a pure chemical substance that still retains its chemical composition and properties.

Go to **Cram101.com** for the Practice Tests for this Chapter.

Go to **Cram101.com** for the Practice Tests for this Chapter.
And, **NEVER** highlight a book again!

Zona pellucida	The zona pellucida is a glycoprotein matrix surrounding the plasma membrane of an oocyte. This structure binds spermatozoa, and is required to initiate the acrosome reaction.
Plasma membrane	Membrane surrounding the cytoplasm that consists of a phospholipid bilayer with embedded proteins is referred to as plasma membrane.
Cytoplasm	Cytoplasm refers to everything inside a cell between the plasma membrane and the nucleus; consists of a semifluid medium and organelles.
Ion	Ion refers to an atom or molecule that has gained or lost one or more electrons, thus acquiring an electrical charge.
Nucleus	In cell biology, the nucleus is found in all eukaryotic cells that contains most of the cell's genetic material. The nucleus has two primary functions: to control chemical reactions within the cytoplasm and to store information needed for cellular division.
Embryogenesis	Embryogenesis is the process by which the embryo is formed and develops. It starts with the fertilization of the ovum, which is then called a zygote.
Biology	Biology is the branch of science dealing with the study of life. It is concerned with the characteristics, classification, and behaviors of organisms, how species come into existence, and the interactions they have with each other and with the environment.
Mendel	Mendel is often called the "father of genetics" for his study of the inheritance of traits in pea plants. Mendel showed that there was particulate inheritance of traits according to his laws of inheritance.
Gallstone	A gallstone is a crystalline body formed within the body by accretion or concretion of normal or abnormal bile components. They can occur anywhere within the biliary tree, including the gallbladder and the common bile duct.
Eye	An eye is an organ that detects light. Different kinds of light-sensitive organs are found in a variety of creatures.
Fruit	A fruit is the ripened ovary—together with seeds—of a flowering plant. In many species, the fruit incorporates the ripened ovary and surrounding tissues.
Receptor protein	Protein located in the plasma membrane or within the cell that binds to a substance that alters some metabolic aspect of the cell is referred to as receptor protein. It will only link up with a substance that has a certain shape that allows it to bind to the receptor.
Amino acid	An amino acid is any molecule that contains both amino and carboxylic acid functional groups. They are the basic structural building units of proteins. They form short polymer chains called peptides or polypeptides which in turn form structures called proteins.
Receptor	A receptor is a protein on the cell membrane or within the cytoplasm or cell nucleus that binds to a specific molecule (a ligand), such as a neurotransmitter, hormone, or other substance, and initiates the cellular response to the ligand. Receptor, in immunology, the region of an antibody which shows recognition of an antigen.
Flower	A flower is the reproductive structure of a flowering plant. The flower structure contains the plant's reproductive organs, and its function is to produce seeds through sexual reproduction.
Pollen	The male gametophyte in gymnosperms and angiosperms is referred to as pollen.
Skin	Skin is an organ of the integumentary system composed of a layer of tissues that protect underlying muscles and organs.
True-breeding	True-breeding refers to organisms for which sexual reproduction produces offspring with inherited trait identical to those of the parents. The organisms are homozygous for the

Go to **Cram101.com** for the Practice Tests for this Chapter.

characteristic under consideration.

F1 generation	In Mendelian genetics, F1 generation refers to the first filial generation. Filial generations, with their etymologic root in the Latin word filius, are defined as the resultant successive generations of progeny in a breeding experiment from a controlled cross between two parents.
Phenotype	The phenotype of an individual organism is either its total physical appearance and constitution or a specific manifestation of a trait, such as size or eye color, that varies between individuals. It is determined to some extent by genotype.
Genotype	The genotype is the specific genetic makeup (the specific genome) of an individual, usually in the form of DNA. It codes for the phenotype of that individual.
Homozygous	When an organism is referred to as being homozygous for a specific gene, it means that it carries two identical copies of that gene for a given trait on the two corresponding chromosomes.
Hybrid	Hybrid refers to the offspring of parents of two different species or of two different varieties of one species; the offspring of two parents that differ in one or more inherited traits; an individual that is heterozygous for one or more pair of genes.
Dominant allele	Dominant allele refers to an allele that exerts its phenotypic effect in the heterozygote.
Dominance	Dominance is the state of having high social status relative to other individuals, who react submissively to dominant individuals.
Law of segregation	When haploid gametes are formed by a diploid organism, the two alleles that control a trait separate from one another into different gametes, retaining their individuality, we have the law of segregation.
Pollen grain	Pollen grain in seed plants, the sperm-producing microgametophyte.
Albinism	Albinism is a lack of pigmentation in the eyes, skin and hair. It is an inherited condition resulting from the combination of recessive alleles passed from both parents of an individual.
Pigment	Pigment is any material resulting in color in plant or animal cells which is the result of selective absorption.
Melanin	Broadly, melanin is any of the polyacetylene, polyaniline, and polypyrrole "blacks" or their mixed copolymers. The most common form of biological melanin is a polymer of either or both of two monomer molecules: indolequinone, and dihydroxyindole carboxylic acid.
Retina	The retina is a thin layer of cells at the back of the eyeball of vertebrates and some cephalopods; it is the part of the eye which converts light into nervous signals.
Enzyme	An enzyme is a protein that catalyzes, or speeds up, a chemical reaction. They are essential to sustain life because most chemical reactions in biological cells would occur too slowly, or would lead to different products, without them.
Blood vessel	A blood vessel is a part of the circulatory system and function to transport blood throughout the body. The most important types, arteries and veins, are so termed because they carry blood away from or towards the heart, respectively.
Hemoglobin	Hemoglobin is the iron-containing oxygen-transport metalloprotein in the red cells of the blood in mammals and other animals. Hemoglobin transports oxygen from the lungs to the rest of the body, such as to the muscles, where it releases the oxygen load.
Pupil	Pupil refers to the opening in the iris that admits light into the interior of the vertebrate eye. Muscles in the iris regulate its size.

Go to **Cram101.com** for the Practice Tests for this Chapter.

Recessive allele	Recessive allele causes a phenotype (visible or detectable characteristic) that is only seen in a homozygous genotype (an organism that has two copies of the same allele). Every person has two copies of every gene, one from mother and one from father. If a genetic trait is recessive, a person only needs to inherit two copies of the gene for the trait to be expressed.
F2 generation	F2 generation is the second filial generation, produced by selfing or intercrossing the F1 generation. F2 generation stands for second filial.
Pedigree	A record of one's ancestors, offspring, siblings, and their offspring that may be used to determine the pattern of certain genes or disease inheritance within a family is a pedigree.
Monohybrid cross	A monohybrid cross, in genetics, is the mating between two heterozygous individuals. Generally, dominant characteristics are represented with a capital letter, A, and recessive characteristics are represented by a lower case letter, a.
Dihybrid cross	A dihybrid cross is a cross in which two dihybrids are mated to test for dominant genes and recessive genes in two separate characteristics.
Phenotypic ratio	The ratio of phenotypic classes expected in the progeny of a particular cross is referred to as phenotypic ratio.
Law of independent assortment	The most important principle of Mendel's law of independent assortment is that the emergence of one trait will not affect the emergence of another.
Self-fertilization	Self-fertilization occurs in hermaphroditic organisms where the two gametes fused in fertilization come from the same individual. This is common in plants and certain protozoans.
Cross-fertilization	Cross-fertilization refers to the union of sperm and egg from two individuals of the same species.
Cystic fibrosis	Cystic fibrosis refers to a genetic disease that occurs in people with two copies of a certain recessive allele; characterized by an excessive secretion of mucus and consequent vulnerability to infection; fatal if untreated.
Genetic map	A genetic map is a chromosome map of a species or experimental population that shows the position of its known genes and/or markers relative to each other, rather than as specific physical points on each chromosome.
Cloning	Cloning is the process of creating an identical copy of an original.
Starch	Biochemically, starch is a combination of two polymeric carbohydrates (polysaccharides) called amylose and amylopectin.
Sugar	A sugar is the simplest molecule that can be identified as a carbohydrate. These include monosaccharides and disaccharides, trisaccharides and the oligosaccharides. The term "glyco-" indicates the presence of a sugar in an otherwise non-carbohydrate substance.
Mutant	A mutant (also known to early geneticists as a "monster") is an individual, organism, or new genetic character arising or resulting from an instance of mutation, which is a sudden structural change within the DNA of a gene or chromosome of an organism resulting in the creation of a new character or trait not found in the parental type.
Drosophila	Drosophila is part of the phylum Arthropoda, a phylum of segmented animals with paired, jointed appendages and a hard exoskeleton made of chitin. They have an open circulatory system with a dorsal heart, with hemocoel occupying most of the body cavity, and a reduced coelom.
Polymorphism	The presence in a population of more than one allele of a gene at a frequency greater than that of newly arising mutations is referred to as polymorphism.

Go to **Cram101.com** for the Practice Tests for this Chapter.

Human genome	The human genome is the genome of Homo sapiens. It is made up of 23 chromosome pairs with a total of about 3 billion DNA base pairs.
Linkage map	A map of a chromosome showing the relative positions of genes is referred to as linkage map.
Nucleotide	A nucleotide is a chemical compound that consists of a heterocyclic base, a sugar, and one or more phosphate groups. In the most common nucleotides the base is a derivative of purine or pyrimidine, and the sugar is pentose - deoxyribose or ribose. They are the structural units of RNA and DNA.
Single-nucleotide polymorphism	A Single-Nucleotide Polymorphism is a DNA sequence variation, occurring when a single nucleotide: adenine (A), thymine (T), cytosine (C) or guanine (G) - in the genome is altered.
Membrane transport protein	Membrane transport protein refers to membrane protein that mediates the passage of ions or molecules across a membrane. Examples are ion channels and carrier proteins.
Highly conserved	Highly conserved refers to genes or proteins whose sequences are very similar in different species.
Wild-type allele	The non-mutant form of a gene, encoding the normal genetic function is a wild-type allele. Generally, but not always a dominant allele.
Heterozygote	Heterozygote refers to a diploid or polypoid individual carrying two different alleles of a gene on its two homologous chromosomes.
Cancer	Cancer is a class of diseases or disorders characterized by uncontrolled division of cells and the ability of these cells to invade other tissues, either by direct growth into adjacent tissue through invasion or by implantation into distant sites by metastasis.
Gene mutation	Mutation (point or larger change) that results from changes within the structure of a gene is gene mutation.
Sickle-cell anemia	Sickle-cell anemia refers to a disease caused by a point mutation. This malfunction produces sickle-shaped red blood cells. Sickle-cell anemia is the name of a specific form of sickle cell disease in which there is homozygosity for the mutation that causes Hgb S.
Conditional mutation	Conditional mutation is a mutation that has wild-type phenotype under certain environmental conditions and a mutant phenotype under certain selective conditions. A conditional mutation may also be lethal.
Polypeptide	Polypeptide refers to polymer of many amino acids linked by peptide bonds.
Oxygen	Oxygen is a chemical element in the periodic table. It has the symbol O and atomic number 8. Oxygen is the second most common element on Earth, composing around 46% of the mass of Earth's crust and 28% of the mass of Earth as a whole, and is the third most common element in the universe.
Blood	Blood is a circulating tissue composed of fluid plasma and cells. The main function of blood is to supply nutrients (oxygen, glucose) and constitutional elements to tissues and to remove waste products.
Lungs	Lungs are the essential organs of respiration in air-breathing vertebrates. Their principal function is to transport oxygen from the atmosphere into the bloodstream, and to excrete carbon dioxide from the bloodstream into the atmosphere.
Permissive condition	Permissive condition refers to an environmental condition under which a conditional mutation shows the wild-type phenotype.
Complementation	Process in which heterozygosity for chromosomes bearing mutant recessive alleles for two

different genes produces a normal phenotype is complementation.

Anemia	Anemia is a deficiency of red blood cells and/or hemoglobin. This results in a reduced ability of blood to transfer oxygen to the tissues, and this causes hypoxia; since all human cells depend on oxygen for survival, varying degrees of anemia can have a wide range of clinical consequences.
Malaria	Malaria refers to potentially fatal human disease caused by the protozoan parasite Plasmodium, which is transmitted by the bite of an infected mosquito.
Biochemistry	Biochemistry studies how complex chemical reactions give rise to life. It is a hybrid branch of chemistry which specialises in the chemical processes in living organisms.
Cell biology	The biological discipline involving the study of cells and their functions is called cell biology. This includes their physiological properties such as their structure and the organelles they contain, their environment and interactions, their life cycle, division and function (physiology) and eventual death.
Physiology	The study of the function of cells, tissues, and organs is referred to as physiology.
Genetic screen	A genetic screen is a procedure or test to identify and select individuals which possess a phenotype of interest. A genetic screen for new genes is often referred to as forward genetics as opposed to reverse genetics that is the term used for identifying mutant alleles in genes that are already known.
Mutagen	A chemical or physical agent that interacts with DNA and causes a mutation is referred to as mutagen.
Gene function	Gene function refers to generally, to govern the synthesis of a polypeptide; in Mendelian terms, a gene's specific contribution to phenotype.
Model organism	A model organism is a species that is extensively studied to understand particular biological phenomena, with the expectation that discoveries made in the organism model will provide insight into the workings of other organisms.
Yeast	Yeast refers to common term for several families of unicellular fungi. Includes species used for brewing beer and making bread, as well as pathogenic species.
Temperature-sensitive mutant	Organism or cell carrying a genetically altered protein that performs normally at one temperature but is abnormal at another temperature is called temperature-sensitive mutant.
Cell cycle	An orderly sequence of events that extends from the time a eukaryotic cell divides to form two daughter cells to the time those daughter cells divide again is called cell cycle.
Replica plating	Replica plating refers to a technique for isolating mutants from a population by plating cells from each colony growing on a nonselective agar medium onto plates with selective media or environmental conditions, such as the lack of a nutrient or the presence of an antibiotic or a phage; the location of mutants on the original plate can be determined from growth patterns on the replica plates.
Petri dish	Petri dish refers to a shallow dish consisting of two round, overlapping halves that is used to grow microorganisms on solid culture medium; the top is larger than the bottom of the dish to prevent contamination of the culture.
Complement	Complement is a group of proteins of the complement system, found in blood serum which act in concert with antibodies to achieve the destruction of non-self particles such as foreign blood cells or bacteria.
Galactose	Galactose is a type of sugar found in dairy products, in sugar beets and other gums and mucilages. It is also synthesized by the body, where it forms part of glycolipids and

Go to **Cram101.com** for the Practice Tests for this Chapter.

	glycoproteins in several tissues.
Flagellum	A flagellum is a whip-like organelle that many unicellular organisms, and some multicellular ones, use to move about.
Haplotype	A haplotype is the genetic constitution of an individual chromosome.
Identical twins	Identical twins occur when a single egg is fertilized to form one zygote (monozygotic) but the zygote then divides into two separate embryos. The two embryos develop into foetuses sharing the same womb. Monozygotic twins are genetically identical unless there has been a mutation in development, and they are almost always the same gender.
Genetic marker	A genetic marker is a specific piece of DNA with a known position on the genome. It is a genetic technique to follow a certain disease or gene. It is known that pieces of DNA that lie near each other, tend to be inherited to the next organism together.
Neutral variation	Genetic variation that provides no apparent selective advantage for some individuals over others is referred to as neutral variation.
Polygenic trait	A trait affected by many genes, and no single gene has an over-riding influence is a polygenic trait.
Blood pressure	Blood pressure is the pressure exerted by the blood on the walls of the blood vessels.
Asthma	Asthma is a disease of the human respiratory system in which the airways narrow, often in response to a "trigger" such as exposure to an allergen, cold air, exercise, or emotional stress.
Nutrition	Nutrition refers to collectively, the processes involved in taking in, assimilating, and utilizing nutrients.
Fraternal twins	Fraternal twins usually occur when two fertilized eggs are implanted in the uterine wall at the same time. The two eggs form two zygotes, and these twins are therefore also known as dizygotic. Dizygotic twins are no more similar genetically than any siblings.
Discrete trait	Inherited trait that clearly exhibits an either/or status is referred to as a discrete trait.
Insulin	Insulin is a polypeptide hormone that regulates carbohydrate metabolism. Apart from being the primary effector in carbohydrate homeostasis, it also has a substantial effect on small vessel muscle tone, controls storage and release of fat (triglycerides) and cellular uptake of both amino acids and some electrolytes.
Thomas Hunt Morgan	Thomas Hunt Morgan (September 25, 1866 – December 4, 1945) was an American geneticist and embryologist. In his famous Fly Room at Columbia University Morgan was able to demonstrate that genes are carried on chromosomes and are the mechanical basis of heredity.
Coral	Group of cnidarians having a calcium carbonate skeleton that participate in the formation of reefs is coral.

Multicellular	Multicellular organisms are those organisms consisting of more than one cell, and having differentiated cells that perform specialized functions. Most life that can be seen with the naked eye is multicellular, as are all animals (i.e. members of the kingdom Animalia) and plants (i.e. members of the kingdom Plantae).
Cancer cell	A cell that divides and reproduces abnormally and has the potential to spread throughout the body, crowding out normal cells and tissue is referred to as a cancer cell.
Tissue	Group of similar cells which perform a common function is called tissue.
Cell	The cell is the structural and functional unit of all living organisms, and is sometimes called the "building block of life."
Extracellular matrix	Extracellular matrix is any material part of a tissue that is not part of any cell. Extracellular matrix is the defining feature of connective tissue.
Blood vessel	A blood vessel is a part of the circulatory system and function to transport blood throughout the body. The most important types, arteries and veins, are so termed because they carry blood away from or towards the heart, respectively.
Nerve	A nerve is an enclosed, cable-like bundle of nerve fibers or axons, which includes the glia that ensheath the axons in myelin.
Mutant	A mutant (also known to early geneticists as a "monster") is an individual, organism, or new genetic character arising or resulting from an instance of mutation, which is a sudden structural change within the DNA of a gene or chromosome of an organism resulting in the creation of a new character or trait not found in the parental type.
Cancer	Cancer is a class of diseases or disorders characterized by uncontrolled division of cells and the ability of these cells to invade other tissues, either by direct growth into adjacent tissue through invasion or by implantation into distant sites by metastasis.
Natural selection	Natural selection is the process by which biological individuals that are endowed with favorable or deleterious traits end up reproducing more or less than other individuals that do not possess such traits.
Molecular biology	Molecular biology overlaps with other areas of biology and chemistry, particularly genetics and biochemistry. Molecular biology chiefly concerns itself with understanding the interactions between the various systems of a cell, including the interrelationship of DNA, RNA and protein synthesis and learning how these interactions are regulated.
DNA repair	Collective name for those biochemical processes that correct accidental changes in the DNA is referred to as dna repair.
Cell biology	The biological discipline involving the study of cells and their functions is called cell biology. This includes their physiological properties such as their structure and the organelles they contain, their environment and interactions, their life cycle, division and function (physiology) and eventual death.
Fruit	A fruit is the ripened ovary—together with seeds—of a flowering plant. In many species, the fruit incorporates the ripened ovary and surrounding tissues.
Nuclear transplantation	A technique in which the nucleus of one cell is placed into another cell that already has a nucleus or in which the nucleus has been previously destroyed is a nuclear transplantation.
Differentiated cell	Differentiated cell refers to a mature cell specialized for a specific function and do not maintain the ability to generate other kinds of cells, or revert back to a less specialized cell; in plants, a differentiated cell normally does not divide.
Therapeutic cloning	The cloning of human cells by nuclear transplantation for therapeutic purposes, such as the replacement of body cells that have been irreversibly damaged by disease or injury is

referred to as therapeutic cloning.

Colorectal cancer	Colorectal cancer includes cancerous growths in the colon, rectum and appendix. It is the third most common form of cancer and the second leading cause of death among cancers in the Western world.
Connective tissue	Connective tissue is any type of biological tissue with an extensive extracellular matrix and often serves to support, bind together, and protect organs.
Tight junction	Region between cells where adjacent plasma membrane proteins join to form an impermeable barrier is a tight junction.
Polysaccharide	Polymer made from sugar monomers is a polysaccharide. They are relatively complex carbohydrates.
Epidemiology	Epidemiology is the scientific study of factors affecting the health and illness of individuals and populations, and serves as the foundation and logic of interventions made in the interest of public health and preventive medicine.
Gap junction	A gap junction is a junction between certain animal/plant cell-types that allows different molecules and ions to pass freely between cells. The junction connects the cytoplasm of cells.
Basal lamina	Thin mat of extracellular matrix that separates epithelial sheets, and many other types of cells such as muscle or fat cells, from connective tissue is called basal lamina.
Cytoskeleton	Cytoskeleton refers to a meshwork of fine fibers in the cytoplasm of a eukaryotic cell; includes microfilaments, intermediate filaments, and microtubules.
Plant cell	A cell that is a structural and functional unit of a plant is a plant cell.
Epithelial	Functions of epithelial cells include secretion, absorption, protection, transcellular transport, sensation detection, and selective permeability.
Epithelium	Epithelium is a tissue composed of a layer of cells. Epithelium can be found lining internal (e.g. endothelium, which lines the inside of blood vessels) or external (e.g. skin) free surfaces of the body. Functions include secretion, absorption and protection.
Cellulose	A large polysaccharide composed of many glucose monomers linked into cable-like fibrils that provide structural support in plant cell walls is referred to as cellulose.
Stem cell	A stem cell is a primal undifferentiated cell which retains the ability to differentiate into other cell types. This ability allows them to act as a repair system for the body, replenishing other cells as long as the organism is alive.
Molecule	A molecule is the smallest particle of a pure chemical substance that still retains its chemical composition and properties.
Mutation	Mutation refers to a change in the nucleotide sequence of DNA; the ultimate source of genetic diversity.
Integrin	An integrin is an integral membrane protein in the plasma membrane of cells. It plays a role in the attachment of a cell to the extracellular matrix (ECM) and in signal transduction from the ECM to the cell.
Collagen	Collagen is the main protein of connective tissue in animals and the most abundant protein in mammals, making up about 1/4 of the total. It is one of the long, fibrous structural proteins whose functions are quite different from those of globular proteins such as enzymes.
Protein	A protein is a complex, high-molecular-weight organic compound that consists of amino acids joined by peptide bonds. They are essential to the structure and function of all living cells and viruses. Many are enzymes or subunits of enzymes.

Matrix	In biology, matrix (plural: matrices) is the material between animal or plant cells, the material (or tissue) in which more specialized structures are embedded, and a specific part of the mitochondrion that is the site of oxidation of organic molecules.
Fiber	Fiber is a class of materials that are continuous filaments or are in discrete elongated pieces, similar to lengths of thread. They are of great importance in the biology of both plants and animals, for holding tissues together.
Tumor	An abnormal mass of cells that forms within otherwise normal tissue is a tumor. This growth can be either malignant or benign
Gene	Gene refers to a discrete unit of hereditary information consisting of a specific nucleotide sequence in DNA . Most of the genes of a eukaryote are located in its chromosomal DNA; a few are carried by the DNA of mitochondria and chloroplasts.
Ion	Ion refers to an atom or molecule that has gained or lost one or more electrons, thus acquiring an electrical charge.
Leaf	In botany, a leaf is an above-ground plant organ specialized for photosynthesis. For this purpose, a leaf is typically flat (laminar) and thin, to expose the chloroplast containing cells (chlorenchyma tissue) to light over a broad area, and to allow light to penetrate fully into the tissues.
Cell wall	Cell wall refers to a protective layer external to the plasma membrane in plant cells, bacteria, fungi, and some protists; protects the cell and helps maintain its shape.
Epidermis	Epidermis is the outermost layer of the skin. It forms the waterproof, protective wrap over the body's surface and is made up of stratified squamous epithelium with an underlying basement membrane. It contains no blood vessels, and is nourished by diffusion from the dermis. In plants, the outermost layer of cells covering the leaves and young parts of a plant is the epidermis.
Tendon	A tendon or sinew is a tough band of fibrous connective tissue that connects muscle to bone. They are similar to ligaments except that ligaments join one bone to another.
Muscle	Muscle is a contractile form of tissue. It is one of the four major tissue types, the other three being epithelium, connective tissue and nervous tissue. Muscle contraction is used to move parts of the body, as well as to move substances within the body.
Swell	Swell refers to a wave with a flatter, rounded wave crest and trough. Swells are found away from the area where waves are generated by the wind .
Intermediate filament	Intermediate filament refers to an intermediate-sized protein fiber that is one of the three main kinds of fibers making up the cytoskeleton of eukaryotic cells; ropelike, made of fibrous proteins.
Animal cell	An animal cell is a form of eukaryotic cell which make up many tissues in animals. The animal cell is distinct from other eukaryotes, most notably those of plants, as they lack cell walls and chloroplasts, and they have smaller vacuoles.
Intestine	The intestine is the portion of the alimentary canal extending from the stomach to the anus and, in humans and mammals, consists of two segments, the small intestine and the large intestine. The intestine is the part of the body responsible for extracting nutrition from food.
Mammal	Homeothermic vertebrate characterized especially by the presence of hair and mammary glands is a mammal.
Stem	Stem refers to that part of a plant's shoot system that supports the leaves and reproductive structures.

Go to **Cram101.com** for the Practice Tests for this Chapter.

Micrograph	A micrograph is a photograph or similar image taken through a microscope or similar device to show a magnified image of an item.
Electron	The electron is a light fundamental subatomic particle that carries a negative electric charge. The electron is a spin-1/2 lepton, does not participate in strong interactions and has no substructure.
Root	In vascular plants, the root is that organ of a plant body that typically lies below the surface of the soil. However, this is not always the case, since a root can also be aerial (that is, growing above the ground) or aerating (that is, growing up above the ground or especially above water).
Gas exchange	In humans and other mammals, respiratory gas exchange or ventilation is carried out by mechanisms of the lungs. The actual gas exchange occurs in the alveoli.
Vascular tissue	Plant tissue consisting of cells joined into tubes that transport water and nutrients throughout the plant body is referred to as vascular tissue.
Vascular	In botany vascular refers to tissues that contain vessels for transporting liquids. In anatomy and physiology, vascular means related to blood vessels, which are part of the Circulatory system.
Phloem	In vascular plants, phloem is the living tissue that carries organic nutrients, particularly sucrose, to all parts of the plant where needed. In trees, the phloem is underneath and difficult to distinguish from bark,
Xylem	The nonliving portion of a plant's vascular system that provides support and conveys water and inorganic nutrients from the roots to the rest of the plant. Xylem is made up of vessel elements and/or tracheids, water-conducting cells.
Ground tissue	Tissue that constitutes most of the body of a plant is ground tissue.
Root apical meristem	Undifferentiated, embryonic tissue located at the apex of the stem is root apical meristem.
Organ	Organ refers to a structure consisting of several tissues adapted as a group to perform specific functions.
Shoot	In botany, the shoot is one of two primary sections of a plant; the other is the root. The shoot refers to what is generally the upper portion of a plant, and consists of stems, leaves, flowers, and fruits. It is derived from the embryonic epicotyl, the portion of the embryo above the point of attachment to the seed leaves (cotyledons).
Sclerenchyma	Sclerenchyma cells are the principal supporting cells in plant tissues that have ceased elongation. Two groups of sclerenchyma cells exist: fibres and sclereids. Their walls consist of cellulose and/or lignin.
Collenchyma	Plant tissue composed of cells with unevenly thickened walls is a collenchyma. They provide structural support, particularly in growing shoots and leaves.
Parenchyma	The parenchyma are the functional parts of an organ in the body (i.e. the nephrons of the kidney, the alveoli of the lungs). In plants parenchyma cells are thin-walled cells of the ground tissue that make up the bulk of most nonwoody structures, although sometimes their cell walls can be lignified.
Mesophyll	Mesophyll refers to the green tissue in the interior of a leaf; a leaf's ground tissue system, the main site of photosynthesis.
Regeneration	Regeneration is the ability to restore lost or damaged tissues, organs or limbs. It is a common feature in invertebrates, but far more limited in most vertebrates.

Go to **Cram101.com** for the Practice Tests for this Chapter.

Collenchyma cell	In plants, a cell with a thick primary wall and no secondary wall, functioning mainly in supporting growing parts is referred to as a collenchyma cell.
Vascular bundle	A vascular bundle is a part of the transport system in vascular plants. The transport itself happens in vascular tissue, which exists in two forms: xylem and phloem. Both these tissues are present in a vascular bundle, which in addition will include supporting and protective tissues.
Chloroplast	A chloroplast is an organelle found in plant cells and eukaryotic algae which conduct photosynthesis. They are similar to mitochondria but are found only in plants. They are surrounded by a double membrane with an intermembrane space; they have their own DNA and are involved in energy metabolism;
Meristem	Meristem is a type of embryonic tissue in plants consisting of unspecialized, youthful cells called meristematic cells and found in areas of the plant where growth is or will take place - the roots and shoots.
Nucleus	In cell biology, the nucleus is found in all eukaryotic cells that contains most of the cell's genetic material. The nucleus has two primary functions: to control chemical reactions within the cytoplasm and to store information needed for cellular division.
Seed coat	Protective covering for the seed, formed by the hardening of the ovule wall is a seed coat.
Transfer cell	A modified parenchyma cell that transports solutes from its cytoplasm into its cell wall, thus moving the solutes from the symplast into the apoplast is called transfer cell.
Plasma membrane	Membrane surrounding the cytoplasm that consists of a phospholipid bilayer with embedded proteins is referred to as plasma membrane.
Solute	Substance that is dissolved in a solvent, forming a solution is referred to as a solute.
Endodermis	Endodermis is the bottom layer of skin. In plants, it is a thin layer of parenchyma found in roots, just outside the vascular cylinder. It regulates the flow of water.
Pericycle	Found in the stele of plants, the pericycle is a cylinder of cells that lies just inside the endodermis. It conducts water and nutrients inward to the vascular tissue. In dicots, it is also has the capacity to produce lateral roots.
Trichome	A trichome is a fine outgrowth or appendage on plants and protists. These are of diverse of structure and function. Examples are hairs, glandular hairs, scales, and papillae.
Vein	Vein in animals, is a vessel that returns blood to the heart. In plants, a vascular bundle in a leaf, composed of xylem and phloem.
Absorption	Absorption is a physical or chemical phenomenon or a process in which atoms, molecules, or ions enter some bulk phase - gas, liquid or solid material. In nutrition, amino acids are broken down through digestion, which begins in the stomach.
Secretion	Secretion is the process of segregating, elaborating, and releasing chemicals from a cell, or a secreted chemical substance or amount of substance.
Stomata	A stomata is a tiny opening or pore, found mostly on the undersurface of a plant leaf, and used for gas exchange.
Cuticle	Cuticle in animals, a tough, nonliving outer layer of the skin. In plants, a waxy coating on the surface of stems and leaves that helps retain water.
Element	A chemical element, often called simply element, is a chemical substance that cannot be divided or changed into other chemical substances by any ordinary chemical technique. An element is a class of substances that contain the same number of protons in all its atoms.
Sieve tube	In phloem, a single strand of sievetube elements that transports sugar solutions is called

	sieve tube.
Sieve-tube element	Member that joins with others in the phloem tissue of plants as a means of transport for nutrient sap is referred to as sieve-tube element.
Companion cell	A cell adjacent to a sieve-tube element in phloem, involved in the control and nutrition of the sieve-tube element is called companion cell. It is a typical plant cell, except the companion cell, usually has a larger number of ribosomes and mitochondria.
Sieve plate	Perforated wall area in a sieve-tube element through which strands connecting sieve-tube protoplasts pass is a sieve plate.
Cytoplasm	Cytoplasm refers to everything inside a cell between the plasma membrane and the nucleus; consists of a semifluid medium and organelles.
Root hair	Root hair refers to an outgrowth of an epidermal cell on a root, which increases the root's absorptive surface area.
Vessel element	Vessel element refers to a short, open-ended, water-conducting and supportive cell in plants. They make up the water-conducting, supportive tubes in xylem.
Middle lamella	A thin layer of sticky polysaccharides, such as pectin, and other carbohydrates that separates and holds together the primary cell walls of adjacent plant cells is called middle lamella.
Plasma	In physics and chemistry, a plasma is an ionized gas, and is usually considered to be a distinct phase of matter. "Ionized" in this case means that at least one electron has been dissociated from a significant fraction of the molecules.
Turgor pressure	Turgor pressure is the pressure produced by a solution in a space that is enclosed by a differentially permeable membrane.
Macromolecule	A macromolecule is a molecule of high relative molecular mass, the structure of which essentially comprises the multiple repetition of units derived, actually or conceptually, from molecules of low relative molecular mass.
Structural protein	A protein that is important for holding cells and organisms together, such as the proteins that make up the cell membrane, muscles, tendons, and blood is a structural protein.
Lignin	Lignin is a chemical compound that is most commonly derived from wood and is an integral part of the cell walls of plants, especially in tracheids, xylem fibres and sclereids. It is the second most abundant organic compound on earth after cellulose. Lignin makes up about one-quarter to one-third of the dry mass of wood.
Polymer	Polymer is a generic term used to describe a very long molecule consisting of structural units and repeating units connected by covalent chemical bonds.
Enzyme	An enzyme is a protein that catalyzes, or speeds up, a chemical reaction. They are essential to sustain life because most chemical reactions in biological cells would occur too slowly, or would lead to different products, without them.
Microtubule	Microtubule is a protein structure found within cells, one of the components of the cytoskeleton. They have diameter of ~ 24 nm and varying length from several micrometers to possible millimeters in axons of nerve cells. They serve as structural components within cells and are involved in many cellular processes including mitosis, cytokinesis, and vesicular transport.
Seedling	Seedling refers to a young plant that has grown from a seed. The most common example of germination is the sprouting of a seedling from a seed of a flowering plant or gymnosperm.
Horizon	Horizon refers to levels within a soil profile that differ structurally and chemically.

Go to **Cram101.com** for the Practice Tests for this Chapter.

Generally divided into A, B, C, E, and 0 horizons.

Microscopy	Microscopy is any technique for producing visible images of structures or details too small to otherwise be seen by the human eye, using a microscope or other magnification tool.
Integral membrane protein	An Integral Membrane Protein is a protein molecule that in most cases spans the biological membrane with which it is associated or which, in any case, is sufficiently embedded in the membrane to remain with it during the initial steps of biochemical purification.
Elongation	Elongation refers to a phase of DNA replication, transcription, or translation that successively adds nucleotides or amino acids to a growing macromolecule.
Collagen fibril	Collagen fibril refers to extracellular structure formed by self-assembly of secreted fibrillar collagen subunits. An abundant constituent of the extracellular matrix in many animal tissues.
Phosphate	A phosphate is a polyatomic ion or radical consisting of one phosphorus atom and four oxygen. In the ionic form, it carries a -3 formal charge, and is denoted PO_4^{3-}.
Calcium	Calcium is the chemical element in the periodic table that has the symbol Ca and atomic number 20. Calcium is a soft grey alkaline earth metal that is used as a reducing agent in the extraction of thorium, zirconium and uranium. Calcium is also the fifth most abundant element in the Earth's crust.
Crystal	Crystal is a solid in which the constituent atoms, molecules, or ions are packed in a regularly ordered, repeating pattern extending in all three spatial dimensions.
Skin	Skin is an organ of the integumentary system composed of a layer of tissues that protect underlying muscles and organs.
Collagen fiber	White fiber in the matrix of connective tissue, giving flexibility and strength is called collagen fiber.
Polypeptide	Polypeptide refers to polymer of many amino acids linked by peptide bonds.
Helical	A helix is a twisted shape like a spring, screw or a spiral staircase. Helices are important in biology, as DNA is helical and many proteins have helical substructures, known as alpha helices.
Exocytosis	Exocytosis is the process by which a cell is able to release large biomolecules through its membrane. While in protozoa the exocytosis may serve the function of wasting unnecessary products, in multicellular organisms exocytosis serves signalling or regulatory function.
Domain	In biology, a domain is the top-level grouping of organisms in scientific classification.
Cartilage	Cartilage is a type of dense connective tissue. Cartilage is composed of cells called chondrocytes which are dispersed in a firm gel-like ground substance, called the matrix. Cartilage is avascular (contains no blood vessels) and nutrients are diffused through the matrix.
Arthritis	Arthritis is a group of conditions that affect the health of the bone joints in the body. One in three adult Americans suffer from some form of arthritis and the disease affects about twice as many women as men.
Protease	Protease refers to an enzyme that breaks peptide bonds between amino acids of proteins.
Joint	A joint (articulation) is the location at which two bones make contact (articulate). They are constructed to both allow movement and provide mechanical support.
Connective-tissue cell	Connective-tissue cell refers to any of the various cell types found in connective tissue, e.g. Fibroblasts, cartilage cells, bone cells, fat cells and smooth muscle cells.

Go to **Cram101.com** for the Practice Tests for this Chapter.

Fibroblast	A fibroblast is a cell that makes the structural fibers and ground substance of connective tissue.
Cornea	The cornea is the transparent front part of the eye that covers the iris, pupil, and anterior chamber and provides most of an eye's optical power.
Tadpole	A tadpole is a larval frog, toad, salamander, newt, or caecilian. In this stage it breathes by means of external or internal gills, is at first lacking legs, and has a finlike tail with which it swims as most fish do, by lateral undulation.
Explant	An explant is any portion taken from a plant that will be used to initiate a culture. It can be a portion of the shoot or of the leaves or even just some cells.
Receptor protein	Protein located in the plasma membrane or within the cell that binds to a substance that alters some metabolic aspect of the cell is referred to as receptor protein. It will only link up with a substance that has a certain shape that allows it to bind to the receptor.
Fibronectin	Fibronectin is a high molecular weight glycoprotein containing about 5% carbohydrate that bind to receptor proteins spanning the cell membrane called integrins. In addition to integrins, they also bind extracellular matrix components such as collagen, fibrin and heparin.
Linkage	Linkage refers to the patterns of assortment of genes that are located on the same chromosome. Important because if the genes are located relatively far apart, crossing over is more likely to occur between them than if they are close together.
Actin filament	An actin filament is a helical protein filament formed by the polymerization of globular actin molecules. They provide mechanical support for the cell, determine the cell shape, enable cell movements; and participate in certain cell junctions.
Lipid bilayer	A lipid bilayer is a membrane or zone of a membrane composed of lipid molecules (usually phospholipids). The lipid bilayer is a critical component of all biological membranes, including cell membranes, and is a prerequisite for cell-based organisms.
Protein kinase	Enzyme that transfers the terminal phosphate group of ATP to a specific amino acid of a target protein is protein kinase.
Molecular weight	The molecular mass of a substance, called molecular weight and abbreviated as MW, is the mass of one molecule of that substance, relative to the unified atomic mass unit u (equal to 1/12 the mass of one atom of carbon-12).
Eye	An eye is an organ that detects light. Different kinds of light-sensitive organs are found in a variety of creatures.
Conformation	The three-dimensional shape of a molecule is its conformation. The conformation is particularly important in proteins.
Hydrophilic	A hydrophilic molecule or portion of a molecule is one that is typically charge-polarized and capable of hydrogen bonding, enabling it to dissolve more readily in water than in oil or other hydrophobic solvents.
Glycosaminog-ycan	Glycosaminoglycan is a long unbranched polysaccharide, made up of repeating disaccharides that may be sulphated (e.g. glucuronic acid, iduronic acid, galactose, galactosamine, glucosamine).
Disaccharide	A disaccharide is a sugar (a carbohydrate) composed of two monosaccharides. The two monosaccharides are bonded via a condensation reaction.
Hyaluronan	Hyaluronan is a glycosaminoglycan distributed widely throughout connective, epithelial, and neural tissues. It is one of the chief components of the extracellular matrix, contributes significantly to cell proliferation and migration, and may also be involved in the

Go to **Cram101.com** for the Practice Tests for this Chapter.

Go to **Cram101.com** for the Practice Tests for this Chapter.
And, **NEVER** highlight a book again!

progression of some malignant tumors.

Monomer	In chemistry, a monomer is a small molecule that may become chemically bonded to other monomers to form a polymer.
Sugar	A sugar is the simplest molecule that can be identified as a carbohydrate. These include monosaccharides and disaccharides, trisaccharides and the oligosaccharides. The term "glyco-" indicates the presence of a sugar in an otherwise non-carbohydrate substance.
Cation	A positively charged ion which has fewer electrons than protons is a cation.
Proteoglycan	Molecule consisting of one or more glycosaminoglycan chains attached to a core protein is referred to as proteoglycan.
Cell differentiation	Cell differentiation is a concept from developmental biology describing the process by which cells acquire a "type". The morphology of a cell may change dramatically during differentiation, but the genetic material remains the same, with few exceptions.
Vertebrate	Vertebrate is a subphylum of chordates, specifically, those with backbones or spinal columns. They started to evolve about 530 million years ago during the Cambrian explosion, which is part of the Cambrian period.
Squamous	Squamous cells are basically types of cells which can be identified histologically by the fact that they look flattened and thin under a microscope. They are one of the cell types which comprise an epithelium.
Columnar	Columnar refers to the column shape of one type of epithelial cell which often line ducts or glands within the body. It tapers towards one end, like the shaft of a column.
Evolution	In biology, evolution is the process by which novel traits arise in populations and are passed on from generation to generation. Its action over large stretches of time explains the origin of new species and ultimately the vast diversity of the biological world.
Microorganism	A microorganism is an organism that is so small that it is microscopic (invisible to the naked eye). They are often illustrated using single-celled, or unicellular organisms; however, some unicellular protists are visible to the naked eye, and some multicellular species are microscopic.
Receptor	A receptor is a protein on the cell membrane or within the cytoplasm or cell nucleus that binds to a specific molecule (a ligand), such as a neurotransmitter, hormone, or other substance, and initiates the cellular response to the ligand. Receptor, in immunology, the region of an antibody which shows recognition of an antigen.
Goblet cell	A goblet cell is a glandular simple columnar epithelial cell that is specifically designed to secrete mucus.
Mucus	Mucus is a slippery secretion of the lining of various membranes in the body (mucous membranes). Mucus aids in the protection of the lungs by trapping foreign particles that enter the nose during normal breathing. Additionally, it prevents tissues from drying out.
Membrane transport protein	Membrane transport protein refers to membrane protein that mediates the passage of ions or molecules across a membrane. Examples are ion channels and carrier proteins.
Secretory vesicle	Secretory vesicle is a membrane-bounded organelle in which molecules destined for secretion are stored prior to release. Sometimes called secretory granule because darkly staining contents make the organelle visible as a small solid object.
Golgi apparatus	Golgi apparatus refers to an organelle in eukaryotic cells consisting of stacks of membranous sacs that modify, store, and ship products of the endoplasmic reticulum.

Go to **Cram101.com** for the Practice Tests for this Chapter.

Embryo	Embryo refers to a developing stage of a multicellular organism. In humans, the stage in the development of offspring from the first division of the zygote until body structures begin to appear, about the ninth week of gestation.
Laminin	Laminin is a family of heterotrimeric glycoproteins found in the basal lamina underlying epithelia. Their binding to type IV collagen contributes to the self-assembly of the basal lamina from components secreted by cells, and their recognition by growth cone integrins is important to the function of the basal lamina.
Lamina	A structurally complete leaf of an angiosperm consists of a petiole (leaf stem), a lamina (leaf blade), and stipules (small processes located to either side of the base of the petiole).
Anatomy	Anatomy is the branch of biology that deals with the structure and organization of living things. It can be divided into animal anatomy (zootomy) and plant anatomy (phytonomy).
Cell junction	A structure that connects tissue cells to one another is called cell junction.
Membrane protein	A membrane protein is a protein molecule that is attached to, or associated with the membrane of a cell or an organelle. Membrane proteins can be classified into two groups, based on their attachment to the membrane.
Adherens junction	Adherens junction refers to cell junction in which the cytoplasmic face of the plasma membrane is attached to actin filaments.
Hemidesmosome	A hemidesmosome is a very small stud- or rivet-like structures on the inner basal surface of keratinocytes in the epidermis of skin. They are similar in form to desmosomes.
Desmosome	A strong cell-tocell junction that attaches adjacent cells to one another is referred to as desmosome.
Diffusion	Diffusion refers to the spontaneous movement of particles of any kind from where they are more concentrated to where they are less concentrated.
Leaflet	A leaflet in botany is a part of a compound leaf. A leaflet may resemble a complete leaf, but it is not borne on a stem as a leaf is, but rather on a vein of the whole leaf. Compound leaves are common in many plant families.
Filament	The stamen is the male organ of a flower. Each stamen generally has a stalk called the filament, and, on top of the filament, an anther. The filament is a long chain of proteins, such as those found in hair, muscle, or in flagella.
Adhesion	The molecular attraction exerted between the surfaces of unlike bodies in contact, as water molecules to the walls of the narrow tubes that occur in plants is referred to as adhesion.
Cadherin	Cadherin is a class of proteins which are expressed on the surface of cells. They play important roles in cell adhesion whereby they ensure cells within tissues are bound together.
Keratin	Keratin is a family of fibrous structural proteins; tough and insoluble, they form the hard but nonmineralized structures found in reptiles, birds and mammals.
Actin	Actin is a globular protein that polymerizes helically forming filaments, which like the other two components of the cellular cytoskeleton form a three-dimensional network inside an eukaryotic cell. They provide mechanical support for the cell, determine the cell shape, enable cell movements .
Cell membrane	A component of every biological cell, the selectively permeable cell membrane is a thin and structured bilayer of phospholipid and protein molecules that envelopes the cell. It separates a cell's interior from its surroundings and controls what moves in and out.
Microvillus	A microvillus is a small extension of the cell surface of absorptive and secretory epithelial

468

cells, such as kidney and intestinal cells. These structures increase the surface area of cells by approximately 600 fold (human), thus facilitating absorption and secretion.

Vesicle	In cell biology, a vesicle is a relatively small and enclosed compartment, separated from the cytosol by at least one lipid bilayer.
Neural tube	The neural tube is the embryonal structure that gives rise to the brain and spinal cord. The neural tube is derived from a thickened area of ectoderm, the neural plate. The process of formation of the neural tube is called neurulation.
Eye cup	Eye cup refers to the simplest type of photoreceptor, a cluster of photoreceptor cells shaded by a cuplike cluster of pigmented cells; detects light intensity and direction.
Retina	The retina is a thin layer of cells at the back of the eyeball of vertebrates and some cephalopods; it is the part of the eye which converts light into nervous signals.
Lens	The lens or crystalline lens is a transparent, biconvex structure in the eye that, along with the cornea, helps to refract light to focus on the retina. Its function is thus similar to a man-made optical lens.
Electron microscope	The electron microscope is a microscope that can magnify very small details with high resolving power due to the use of electrons as the source of illumination, magnifying at levels up to 500,000 times.
Protein subunit	A protein subunit is a single protein molecule that assembles (or "coassembles") with other protein molecules to form a multimeric or oligomeric protein. Many naturally-occurring proteins and enzymes are multimeric.
Connexon	Connexon refers to water-filled pore in the plasma membrane formed by a ring of six protein subunits. Part of a gap junction: connexons from two adjoining cells join to form a continuous channel between the two cells.
Neurotransmitter	A neurotransmitter is a chemical that is used to relay, amplify and modulate electrical signals between a neuron and another cell.
Photoreceptor	A photoreceptor is a specialized type of neuron that is capable of phototransduction. More specifically, the photoreceptor sends signals to other neurons by a change in its membrane potential when it absorbs photons.
Dopamine	Dopamine is a chemical naturally produced in the body. In the brain, dopamine functions as a neurotransmitter, activating dopamine receptors. Dopamine is also a neurohormone released by the hypothalamus. Its main function as a hormone is to inhibit the release of prolactin from the anterior lobe of the pituitary.
Neuron	The neuron is a major class of cells in the nervous system. In vertebrates, they are found in the brain, the spinal cord and in the nerves and ganglia of the peripheral nervous system, and their primary role is to process and transmit neural information.
Cone	Cone refers to a reproductive structure of gymnosperms that produces pollen in males or eggs in females.
Ion channel	An ion channel is a pore-forming protein that helps establish the small voltage gradient that exists across the membrane of all living cells, by allowing the flow of ions down their electrochemical gradient. They are present in the membranes that surround all biological cells.
Plasmodesma	The connecting strands of protoplasm between the cytoplasm of adjacent cells which forms canals through the cell walls is plasmodesma. It may contain a desmotubule which links the endoplasmic reticulum of the adjacent cells.
Endoplasmic	The endoplasmic reticulum is an organelle found in all eukaryotic cells. It modifies

reticulum	proteins, makes macromolecules, and transfers substances throughout the cell.
Smooth endoplasmic reticulum	Smooth endoplasmic reticulum refers to endoplasmic reticulum without ribosomes. It has functions in several metabolic processes, including synthesis of lipids, metabolism of carbohydrates, and detoxification of drugs and poisons.
Genome	The genome of an organism is the whole hereditary information of an organism that is encoded in the DNA (or, for some viruses, RNA). This includes both the genes and the non-coding sequences. The genome of an organism is a complete DNA sequence of one set of chromosomes.
Clone	A group of genetically identical cells or organisms derived by asexual reproduction from a single parent is called a clone.
Egg	An egg is the zygote, resulting from fertilization of the ovum. It nourishes and protects the embryo.
Sea urchin	A sea urchin is a spiny sea creature of the class Echinoidea found in oceans all over the world. Their shell, which biologists call the test, is globular in shape, and covered with spines.
Nucleotide	A nucleotide is a chemical compound that consists of a heterocyclic base, a sugar, and one or more phosphate groups. In the most common nucleotides the base is a derivative of purine or pyrimidine, and the sugar is pentose - deoxyribose or ribose. They are the structural units of RNA and DNA.
Host	Host is an organism that harbors a parasite, mutual partner, or commensal partner; or a cell infected by a virus.
Macrophage	Macrophage is a cell found in tissues that are responsible for phagocytosis of pathogens, dead cells and cellular debris. They are part of the innate immune system. Their main role is the removal of pathogens and necrotic debris.
Lymphocyte	A lymphocyte is a type of white blood cell involved in the human body's immune system. There are two broad categories, namely T cells and B cells.
Blood	Blood is a circulating tissue composed of fluid plasma and cells. The main function of blood is to supply nutrients (oxygen, glucose) and constitutional elements to tissues and to remove waste products.
Endothelial cell	The endothelial cell controls the passage of materials — and the transit of white blood cells — into and out of the bloodstream. In some organs, there are highly differentiated cells to perform specialized 'filtering' functions.
Schwann cell	The Schwann cell is a variety of neuroglia that mainly provide myelin insulation to axons in the peripheral nervous system of jawed vertebrates. The vertebrate nervous system relies on this myelin sheath for insulation and as a method of decreasing membrane capacitance in the axon.
Bone marrow	Bone marrow is the tissue comprising the center of large bones. It is the place where new blood cells are produced. Bone marrow contains two types of stem cells: hemopoietic (which can produce blood cells) and stromal (which can produce fat, cartilage and bone).
Nerve cell	A cell specialized to originate or transmit nerve impulses is referred to as nerve cell.
Gland	A gland is an organ in an animal's body that synthesizes a substance for release such as hormones, often into the bloodstream or into cavities inside the body or its outer surface.
Axon	An axon is a long slender projection of a nerve cell, or neuron, which conducts electrical impulses away from the neuron's cell body or soma. They are in effect the primary transmission lines of the nervous system, and as bundles they help make up nerves.

Go to **Cram101.com** for the Practice Tests for this Chapter.

Go to **Cram101.com** for the Practice Tests for this Chapter.
And, **NEVER** highlight a book again!

Gene expression	Gene expression is the process by which a gene's information is converted into the structures and functions of a cell. Gene expression is a multi-step process that begins with transcription, post transcriptional modification and translation, followed by folding, post-translational modification and targeting.
Cell division	Cell division is the process by which a cell (called the parent cell) divides into two cells (called daughter cells). Cell division is usually a small segment of a larger cell cycle. In meiosis, however, a cell is permanently transformed and cannot divide again.
Loose connective tissue	Loose connective tissue is the most common type of connective tissue in vertebrates. It holds organs in place and attaches epithelial tissue to other underlying tissues. It also surrounds the blood vessels and nerves.
Langerhans cell	A Langerhans cell is an immature dendritic cell containing large granules called Birbeck granules. On infection of an area of skin, they will take up and process microbial antigens before travelling to the T-cell areas in the cortex of the draining lymph node and maturing to become fully-functional antigen-presenting cells.
Dendritic cell	The dendritic cell is an immune cell and forms part of the mammal immune system. Once activated, they migrate to the lymphoid tissues where they interact with T cells and B cells to initiate and shape the immune response.
Keratinocyte	The keratinocyte is the major cell type of the epidermis, making up about 90% of epidermal cells. They are shed and replaced continuously from the stratum corneum.
Melanocyte	Melanocyte cells are located in the bottom layer of the skin's epidermis. With a process called melanogenesis, they produce melanin, a pigment in the skin, eyes, and hair.
Hypodermis	The hypodermis, also called the hypoderm, is the lowermost layer of the integumentary system in vertebrates. It is derived from the mesoderm, but unlike the dermis, it is not derived from the dermatome region of the mesoderm. In arthropods, the hypodermis is an epidermal layer of cells that secretes the chitinous cuticle. The term also refers to a layer of cells lying immediately below the epidermis of plants.
Pigment	Pigment is any material resulting in color in plant or animal cells which is the result of selective absorption.
Dermis	The dermis is the layer of skin beneath the epidermis that consists of connective tissue and cushions the body from stress and strain.
Elastic fiber	Elastic fiber is a bundles of proteins (elastin) found in connective tissue and produced by fibroblasts and smooth muscle cells in arteries.
Osteoclast	An osteoclast is a multinucleated cell that degrades and reabsorbs bone. They are involved in the natural turnover of bone tissue along with osteoblasts.
Ionizing radiation	Ionizing radiation is a type of particle radiation in which an individual particle carries enough energy to ionize an atom or molecule. If the individual particles do not carry this amount of energy, it is essentially impossible for even a large flood of particles to cause ionization.
Radiation	The emission of electromagnetic waves by all objects warmer than absolute zero is referred to as radiation.
Small intestine	The small intestine is the part of the gastrointestinal tract between the stomach and the large intestine (colon). In humans over 5 years old it is about 7m long. It is divided into three structural parts: duodenum, jejunum and ileum.
Transit time	Transit time refers to the average time that a substance or energy remains in the biological realm or any compartment of a system; ratio of biomass to productivity.

Go to **Cram101.com** for the Practice Tests for this Chapter.
And, **NEVER** highlight a book again!

Migration	Migration occurs when living things move from one biome to another. In most cases organisms migrate to avoid local shortages of food, usually caused by winter. Animals may also migrate to a certain location to breed, as is the case with some fish.
Villus	Villus refers to a fingerlike projection of the inner surface of the small intestine. A fingerlike projection of the chorion of the mammalian placenta. Large numbers of villus increase the surface areas of these organs.
Hemopoiesis	Hemopoiesis is the formation of blood cellular components. This can occur in myeloid tissue, which is found in the bone marrow and lymphatic tissue, such as lymph nodes or the spleen.
Oxygen	Oxygen is a chemical element in the periodic table. It has the symbol O and atomic number 8. Oxygen is the second most common element on Earth, composing around 46% of the mass of Earth's crust and 28% of the mass of Earth as a whole, and is the third most common element in the universe.
Cytotoxic	Cytotoxic refers to being toxic to cells. Examples of toxic agents are a chemical substance or an immune cell.
Leukemia	Leukemia refers to a type of cancer of the bloodforming tissues, characterized by an excessive production of white blood cells and an abnormally high number of them in the blood; cancer of the bone marrow cells that produce leukocytes.
Paneth cell	Paneth cell refers to the granular cell located at the base of glands in the small intestine; it produces the enzyme lysozyme.
Hormone	A hormone is a chemical messenger from one cell to another. All multicellular organisms produce hormones. The best known hormones are those produced by endocrine glands of vertebrate animals, but hormones are produced by nearly every organ system and tissue type in a human or animal body. Hormone molecules are secreted directly into the bloodstream, they move by circulation or diffusion to their target cells, which may be nearby cells in the same tissue or cells of a distant organ of the body.
Germ cell	A germ cell is a kind of cell that is part of the germline, and is involved in the reproduction of organisms. There are different kinds, which include gametogonia, gametocytes, and gametes.
Muscular dystrophy	The muscular dystrophy is a group of genetic and hereditary muscle diseases; characterized by progressive skeletal muscle weakness, defects in muscle proteins, and the death of muscle cells and tissue. In some forms of muscular dystrophy, cardiac and smooth muscles are affected.
Skeletal muscle	Skeletal muscle is a type of striated muscle, attached to the skeleton. They are used to facilitate movement, by applying force to bones and joints; via contraction. They generally contract voluntarily (via nerve stimulation), although they can contract involuntarily.
Degenerate	Property of the genetic code in which several different codons can specify the same amino acid is called degenerate.
Signal molecule	Extracellular or intracellular molecule that cues the response of a cell to the behavior of other cells or objects in the environment is called signal molecule.
Cell lineage	The ancestry of a cell is called cell lineage. A pedigree of cells related through asexual division.
Recapitulation	"Successive stage in the development of an individual represents one of the adult forms that appeared in its evolutionary history." Haeckel formulated his theory as such: "Ontogeny recapitulates phylogeny". This notion later became simply known as recapitulation.
Blastocyst	A mammalian embryo made up of a hollow ball of cells that results from cleavage and that

Go to **Cram101.com** for the Practice Tests for this Chapter.

implants in the mother's endometrium is called blastocyst.

Growth factor	Growth factor is a protein that acts as a signaling molecule between cells (like cytokines and hormones) that attaches to specific receptors on the surface of a target cell and promotes differentiation and maturation of these cells.
Cloning	Cloning is the process of creating an identical copy of an original.
Reproductive cloning	Using a somatic cell from a multicellular organism to make one or more genetically identical individuals is referred to as reproductive cloning.
Haploid	Haploid cells bear one copy of each chromosome.
Diploid	Diploid cells have two copies (homologs) of each chromosome (both sex- and non-sex determining chromosomes), usually one from the mother and one from the father. Most somatic cells (body cells) of complex organisms are diploid.
Gamete	A gamete is a specialized germ cell that unites with another gamete during fertilization in organisms that reproduce sexually. They are haploid cells; that is, they contain one complete set of chromosomes. When they unite they form a zygote—a cell having two complete sets of chromosomes and therefore diploid.
Hybrid	Hybrid refers to the offspring of parents of two different species or of two different varieties of one species; the offspring of two parents that differ in one or more inherited traits; an individual that is heterozygous for one or more pair of genes.
Uterus	The uterus is the major female reproductive organ of most mammals. One end, the cervix, opens into the vagina; the other is connected on both sides to the fallopian tubes. The main function is to accept a fertilized ovum which becomes implanted into the endometrium, and derives nourishment from blood vessels which develop exclusively for this purpose.
Mitochondria	Mitochondria are organelles found in most eukaryotic cells, including those of plants, animals, fungi, and protists. Mitochondria are sometimes described as "cellular power plants", because their primary function is to convert organic materials into energy in the form of ATP.
Malnutrition	Malnutrition is a general term for the medical condition caused by an improper or insufficient. An individual will experience mulnutrition if the appropriate amount, kind or quality of nutrients comprising a healthy diet are not consumed for an extended period of time.
Malignant	In medicine, malignant is a clinical term that is used to describe a clinical course that progresses rapidly to death. It is typically applied to neoplasms that show aggressive behavior characterized by local invasion or distant metastasis.
Primary tumor	Primary tumor is the nomenclature used when the tumor has originated in the same organ, and has not metastasized to it.
Population	Group of organisms of the same species occupying a certain area and sharing a common gene pool is referred to as population.
Metastasis	The spread of cancer cells beyond their original site are called metastasis.
Colony	Colony refers to a cluster or assemblage of microorganisms growing on the surface of an agar culture medium. A colony also refers to several individual organisms of the same species living closely together, usually for mutual benefit, such as stronger defences, the ability to attack bigger prey, etc.
Colon	The colon is the part of the intestine from the cecum to the rectum. Its primary purpose is to extract water from feces.

Liver	The liver is an organ in vertebrates, including humans. It plays a major role in metabolism and has a number of functions in the body including drug detoxification, glycogen storage, and plasma protein synthesis. It also produces bile, which is important for digestion.
Virus	Obligate intracellular parasite of living cells consisting of an outer capsid and an inner core of nucleic acid is referred to as virus. The term virus usually refers to those particles that infect eukaryotes whilst the term bacteriophage or phage is used to describe those infecting prokaryotes.
Infectious disease	In medicine, infectious disease or communicable disease is disease caused by a biological agent such as by a virus, bacterium or parasite. This is contrasted to physical causes, such as burns or chemical ones such as through intoxication.
Bladder	A hollow muscular storage organ for storing urine is a bladder.
Death rate	Death rate refers is the number of deaths per 1000 people during a specified interval and typically reported an an annual basis.
Biology	Biology is the branch of science dealing with the study of life. It is concerned with the characteristics, classification, and behaviors of organisms, how species come into existence, and the interactions they have with each other and with the environment.
Germ-line mutation	Germ-line mutation refers to a mutation in a cell from which gametes are derived; the mutation can be passed on to offspring .
Somatic mutation	Somatic mutation refers to a mutation that occurs in any cell other than a germline cell and is thus non-heritable.
Spontaneous mutation	Spontaneous mutation is a mutation occurring in the absence of mutagens, usually due to errors in the normal functioning of cellular enzymes.
Mutagen	A chemical or physical agent that interacts with DNA and causes a mutation is referred to as mutagen.
Translocation	A chromosomal mutation in which a portion of one chromosome breaks off and becomes attached to another chromosome is referred to as translocation.
Chromosome	A chromosome is, minimally, a very long, continuous piece of DNA, which contains many genes, regulatory elements and other intervening nucleotide sequences.
Karyotype	A karyotype is the complete set of all chromosomes of a cell of any living organism. The chromosomes are arranged and displayed (often on a photo) in a standard format: in pairs, ordered by size.
Staining	Staining is a biochemical technique of adding a class-specific (DNA, proteins, lipids, carbohydrates) dye to a substrate to qualify or quantify the presence of a specific compound. They are frequently used to highlight structures in tissues for viewing, often with the aid of different microscopes.
Rearrangement	A change in the usual order and arrangement of genetic material either within the chromosome complement or within a gene locus is rearrangement. Where the nature of the rearrangement has been determined, the type may be searched for directly under the following designations: reciprocal translocation, Robertsonian translocation, insertion, transposition, inversion, deletion, and duplication.
Mutation rate	Mutation rate refers to the rate at which observable changes occur in a DNA sequence.
Lymph	Lymph originates as blood plasma lost from the circulatory system, which leaks out into the surrounding tissues. The lymphatic system collects this fluid by diffusion into lymph capillaries, and returns it to the circulatory system.

Apoptosis	In biology, apoptosis is one of the main types of programmed cell death (PCD). As such, it is a process of deliberate life relinquishment by an unwanted cell in a multicellular organism.
Daughter cell	A cell formed by cell division of a parent cell is a daughter cell.
Tumor suppressor gene	A tumor suppressor gene is a gene that reduces the probability that a cell in a multicellular organism will turn into a tumor cell. A mutation or deletion of such a gene will increase the probability of the formation of a tumor. In that way, a tumor suppressor gene is similar to an oncogene.
Tumor-suppressor gene	A gene whose product inhibits cell division, thereby preventing uncontrolled cell growth is referred to as tumor-suppressor gene.
Proto-oncogene	Normal gene that can become an oncogene through mutation or increased expression is referred to as proto-oncogene.
Protooncogene	A protooncogene is a normal gene that can become an oncogene, either after mutation or increased expression.
Oncogene	An oncogene is a modified gene that increases the malignancy of a tumor cell. Some oncogenes, usually involved in early stages of cancer development, increase the chance that a normal cell develops into a tumor cell, possibly resulting in cancer.
Allele	An allele is any one of a number of viable DNA codings of the same gene (sometimes the term refers to a non-gene sequence) occupying a given locus (position) on a chromosome.
Rectum	The rectum is the final straight portion of the large intestine in some mammals, and the gut in others, terminating in the anus.
Polyp	Small, abnormal growth that arises from the epithelial lining is referred to as polyp. In zoology, a polyp is one of two forms of individuals found in many species of cnidarians. They are approximately cylindrical, elongated on the axis of the body.
Polyposis	Polyposis refers to condition of having many polyps in an organ or structure.
Deletion	Deletion refers to the loss of one or more nucleotides from a gene by mutation; the loss of a fragment of a chromosome.
Phenotype	The phenotype of an individual organism is either its total physical appearance and constitution or a specific manifestation of a trait, such as size or eye color, that varies between individuals. It is determined to some extent by genotype.
Drosophila	Drosophila is part of the phylum Arthropoda, a phylum of segmented animals with paired, jointed appendages and a hard exoskeleton made of chitin. They have an open circulatory system with a dorsal heart, with hemocoel occupying most of the body cavity, and a reduced coelom.
Gene family	Set of closely related genes with slightly different functions that most likely arose from a succession of gene duplication events is a gene family.
Genetics	Genetics is the science of genes, heredity, and the variation of organisms.
Gene regulatory protein	General name for any protein that binds to a specific DNA sequence to alter the expression of a gene is referred to as gene regulatory protein.
Transcription	Transcription is the process through which a DNA sequence is enzymatically copied by an RNA polymerase to produce a complementary RNA. Or, in other words, the transfer of genetic information from DNA into RNA.
Antibody	An antibody is a protein used by the immune system to identify and neutralize foreign objects like bacteria and viruses. Each antibody recognizes a specific antigen unique to its target.

Amino acid	An amino acid is any molecule that contains both amino and carboxylic acid functional groups. They are the basic structural building units of proteins. They form short polymer chains called peptides or polypeptides which in turn form structures called proteins.
Cell adhesion	The study of cell adhesion is part of cell biology. Cells are often not found in isolation, rather they tend to stick to other cells or non-cellular components of their environment.
X-Ray	X-Ray refers to diagnostic test in which an image is created using low doses of radiation.
Parasite	A parasite is an organism that spends a significant portion of its life in or on the living tissue of a host organism and which causes harm to the host without immediately killing it. They also commonly show highly specialized adaptations allowing them to exploit host resources.
Chemotherapy	Treatment for cancer in which drugs are administered to disrupt cell division of the cancer cells is chemotherapy.
Toxin	Toxin refers to a microbial product or component that can injure another cell or organism at low concentrations. Often the term refers to a poisonous protein, but toxins may be lipids and other substances.
Remission	Disappearance of the signs of a disease is called remission.
Doubling time	Doubling time refers to number of years it takes for a population to double in size. Also the amount of time it takes for a cell to divide, or for a population of cells (such as a tumor) to double in size. As cells divide more rapidly, the doubling time becomes shorter.
Chromosome translocation	In genetics, a chromosome translocation is the interchange of parts between nonhomologous chromosomes. It is detected on cytogenetics or a karyotype of affected cells. There are two main types, reciprocal and Robertsonian.
Tyrosine kinase	An enzyme that catalyzes the transfer of phosphate groups from ATP to the amino acid tyrosine on a substrate protein is called tyrosine kinase.
Phosphate group	The functional group $-OPO_3H_2$; the transfer of energy from one compound to another is often accomplished by the transfer of a phosphate group.
Tyrosine	Tyrosine is one of the 20 amino acids that are used by cells to synthesize proteins. It plays a key role in signal transduction, since it can be tagged (phosphorylated) with a phosphate group by protein kinases to alter the functionality and activity of certain enzymes.
X-ray crystallography	Technique for determining the three-dimensional arrangement of atoms in a molecule based on the diffraction pattern of X-rays passing through a crystal of the molecule is x-ray crystallography.
Somatic cell	A somatic cell is generally taken to mean any cell forming the body of an organism.
Telomerase	An enzyme critical to the successful replication of telomeres at chromosome ends is called telomerase.
P53 gene	P53 gene refers to the 'guardian angel of the genome,' p53 is expressed when a cell's DNA is damaged. Its product, p53 protein, functions as a transcription factor for several genes.
Metabolite	The term metabolite is usually restricted to small molecules. They are the intermediates and products of metabolism. A primary metabolite is directly involved in the normal growth, development, and reproduction. A secondary metabolite is not directly involved in those processes, but usually has important ecological function.
Gelatin	Gelatin is a translucent brittle solid substance, colorless or slightly yellow, nearly tasteless and odorless, which is created by prolonged boiling of animal skin, connective tissue or bones. It has many uses in food, medicine, and manufacturing. Substances that

Go to **Cram101.com** for the Practice Tests for this Chapter.

contain or resemble gelatin are called gelatinous.

Carcinogen

Carcinogen refers to a cancer-causing agent, either high-energy radiation or a chemical.

Sex hormone

A hormone that controls the timing of reproduction and sexual characteristics in vertebrates is the sex hormone.

Estrogen

Estrogen is a steroid that functions as the primary female sex hormone. While present in both men and women, they are found in women in significantly higher quantities.

Prostate

The prostate is a gland that is part of male mammalian sex organs. Its main function is to secrete and store a clear, slightly basic fluid that is part of semen. The prostate differs considerably between species anatomically, chemically and physiologically.

Androgen

Androgen is the generic term for any natural or synthetic compound, usually a steroid hormone, that stimulates or controls the development and maintenance of masculine characteristics in vertebrates by binding to androgen receptors.

Go to **Cram101.com** for the Practice Tests for this Chapter.

Printed in the United Kingdom
by Lightning Source UK Ltd.
125286UK00001B/5-6/A